Socialism, Capitalism, Transformation

LESZEK BALCEROWICZ

Socialism, Capitalism, Transformation

CENTRAL EUROPEAN UNIVERSITY PRESS

BUDAPEST • LONDON • NEW YORK

First published in 1995 by Central European University Press
1051 Budapest, Nádor utca 9

Distributed by
Oxford University Press, Walton Street, Oxford OX2 6DP
Oxford New York Athens Auckland Bangkok Bombay Toronto
Calcutta Cape Town Dar es Salaam Delhi Florence Hong Kong
Istanbul Karachi Kuala Lumpur Madras Madrid Melbourne
Mexico City Nairobi Paris Singapore Taipei Tokyo Toronto
and associated companies in Berlin Ibadan
Distributed in the United States
by Oxford University Press Inc., New York

Several chapters in this book are revised versions of papers which appeared elsewhere under the same title. The author is grateful to the following publishers for kind permission to reproduce them in this volume:

'Problems with the Definition of Socialism in Today's World' appeared under the same title in Ota Šik (ed.), *Socialism Today? The Changing Meaning of Socialism*, Macmillan, Basingstoke and London, 1991, pp. 65–74.
'On the "Socialist Market Economy"' appeared under the same title in *Acta Oeconomica*, Budapest, Vol. 40, Nos. 3–4 (1989), pp. 184–8.
'The "Socialist Calculation Debate" and Reform Discussions in Socialist Countries' appeared under the same title in J.M. Kovács and M. Tardos (eds), *Reform and Transformation in Eastern Europe: Soviet-Type Economies on the Threshold of Change*, Routledge, London, 1992, pp. 5–18.
'On the "Reformability" of the Soviet-Type Economic System' appeared under the same title in K. Dopfer and K-F. Raible (eds), *The Evolution of Economic Systems*, Macmillan, Basingstoke and London, 1990, pp. 193–201.
'The Soviet-Type Economic System, Reformed Systems and Innovativeness' appeared under the same title in *Communist Economies*, vol. 2, no. 1, 1990, pp. 3–23.
'Understanding Postcommunist Traditions' appeared under the same title in *Journal of Democracy*, vol. 5, no. 4, October 1994, pp. 75–89, The Johns Hopkins University Press.
'Economic Transition in Central and Eastern Europe: Comparisons and Lessons' appeared under the same title in *The Australian Economic Review*, 1st Quarter 1994, pp. 47–59.
'Macropolicies in Transition to a Market Economy: A Three-Year Perspective' was written jointly with Alan Gelb of the Transition Economics Division of the World Bank. It first appeared in *Proceedings of the World Bank Annual Conference on Development Economics 1994* (Washington, DC: The World Bank, 1995), pp. 21–44. It is reproduced here by permission. The views and interpretations expressed do not necessarily represent the views of the World Bank or its member countries and should not be attributed to the World Bank or its affiliated organizations.
'Common Fallacies in the Debate on the Economic Transition in Central and Eastern Europe' appeared under the same title as a European Bank for Reconstruction and Development Working Paper (no. 11, October 1993).
'Polish Economic Reform, 1981–1988: An Overview' appeared under the same title in *Economic Reforms in the European Centrally Planned Economies* (United Nations Economic Commission for Europe, Economic Studies No. 1), United Nations, New York, 1989, pp. 42–50.
'Transition to the Market Economy: The Polish Case, 1989–93' appeared under the title 'Poland' in John Williamson (ed.), *The Political Economy of Policy Reform*, Institute for International Economics, Washington, DC, January 1994, pp. 153–77.

British Library Cataloguing in Publication Data
A CIP catalogue record for this book is available from the British Library

ISBN 1 85866 025 4 Hardback
ISBN 1 85866 026 2 Paperback

Library of Congress Cataloging in Publication Data
A CIP catalog record for this book is available from the Library of Congress

Typeset by Mayhew Typesetting, Rhayader, Powys
Printed and bound in Great Britain by Biddles of Guildford and King's Lynn

Contents

1. Introduction: Institutions, Human Nature and Behaviour   1

Part I: Socialism versus Capitalism

2. Problems with the Definition of Socialism in Today's World   19
3. On the 'Socialist Market Economy'   28
4. The 'Socialist Calculation Debate' and Reform Discussions in Socialist Countries   35
5. On the Reformability of the Soviet-Type Economic Systems   51
6. The Soviet-Type Economic System, Reformed Systems and Innovativeness   59
7. Towards an Analysis of Ownership   84
8. Political and Economic Regimes: Problems of Compatibility and Performance   124

Part II: From Socialism to Capitalism

9. Understanding Post-Communist Transitions   145
10. Economic Transition in Central and Eastern Europe: Comparisons and Lessons   166
11. Various Roads to a Private Market Economy   186
12. Macropolicies in Transition to a Market Economy: A Three-Year Perspective (*with Alan Gelb*)   202
13. Common Fallacies in the Debate on the Economic Transition in Central and Eastern Europe   232

Part III: Polish Economic Reform: 1989–93

14. Polish Economic Reform, 1981–88: An Overview   273

15. The Political Economy of Economic Reform: Poland,
    1989–92   290
16. Transition to the Market Economy: The Polish Case,
    1989–93   313
17. Conclusion: Personal Reflections on Poland   340

Index   371

1

Introduction: Institutions, Human Nature and Behaviour

Four Questions

This book deals with human behaviour and its outcomes under stable and changing institutional conditions. It belongs to a growing body of research which takes institutions as the central variable and tries to explain this change or their impact. Property rights theory, transactions costs economics, agency theory, comparative economic systems, public choice theory, institutional economics, political economy of economic reforms, economic theory of history – these are examples of the relatively recent revival of interest in institutional factors. These theoretical strands take up the development problems which were discussed long ago by great social thinkers, such as Adam Smith, John Stewart Mill, Karl Marx, Max Weber; and, closer to our times, Joseph Schumpeter, Ludwig von Mises and Freidrich A. von Hayek.

These problems were pushed into the background by the expansion of conventional neoclassical economics. This brought to economics a much needed rigour in reasoning from assumed premises, but at the cost of practical relevance. Mainstream economics was built upon assumptions (such as profit maximization by firms) which themselves needed explanation and reflected only certain institutional frameworks. It did not have a consistent set of premises regarding the nature or dispositions of the human beings whose behaviour it attempted to explain or to predict. The behaviour of people as consumers and as producers was assumed to be motivated by self-centred (and usually narrowly pecuniary) reasons, while in explaining or postulating the policies of the state some other motivation was implicitly or explicitly assumed for public officials.

Limits to individuals' capacity to absorb information were not usually considered. Herbert Simon, with his concept of 'bounded rationality', remained a great outsider for many years (Simon 1957).

However, mainstream economics has been changing. Institutionally-based theories, such as I listed above, entered centre-stage. And the most important macroeconomic problems, e.g. persistent unemployment or inflation, were increasingly explained by institutional factors such as the power of insiders within enterprises, staggered contracts, or the role of central banks. The theory of economic growth started to have references to its institutional determinants (for example – market distortions, tax systems, financial systems, political stability) which underline the conventional proximate variables such as the rate of savings and investment and total factor productivity.

However, much more work is needed to integrate the various institutionally-based theories and to elucidate the role of institutions as both dependent and independent variables. I believe that such work should focus on four problems: (1) elaborating a clear and methodologically sound analytical framework to study institutions and human behaviour; (2) a compatibility problem: which institutional arrangements can co-exist, which are necessarily linked to other arrangements, and which are fundamentally incompatible? For example, can democracy be combined with socialism? (3) a performance problem: what are the outcomes of different institutional arrangements and what is the role of these factors as compared to that of the non-institutional determinants? (4) institutional dynamics: what forces govern institutional change at various levels?

There is a definite logical order in approaching these four issues. A clear conceptual framework is obviously required to tackle the other problems. Too many debates in social sciences arise from conceptual confusion, and economics should pay attention not only to mathematics but also to formal logic, i.e. how to deal with concepts and how to reason with words. For example, one cannot begin to distinguish the intra-systemic from inter-systemic changes without clear definitions of various institutional systems.

The performance issue is in a certain sense contingent upon the compatibility question: there is little point in debating the performance of a set of institutional arrangements which cannot co-exist. Also, in analysing the impact of a given arrangement, one should consider the possibility that it is unavoidably linked to another institutional structure. These necessary links may be called 'functional necessities' (see Chapter 5). Therefore, the full impact of the first arrangement would include the consequences of the second one.

Alternative institutional systems, identified by certain institutional invariants, may differ in the scope of these functional necessities; this has a direct implication for the institutional dynamics. To make a transition from a system which is very rigidly built, i.e. contains many functional necessities, a massive change is needed to reach the 'critical mass'. The compatibility problem is related to the issue of institutional dynamics in another way, too. Internal consistencies within some sets of institutional arrangements may lead to their transformation into more lasting institutional systems. For example, an economic system dominated by socialist enterprises into which freedom of private entrepreneurship were introduced would tend to evolve into a capitalist system (see Chapter 7).

However, the problem of institutional change cannot be wholly reduced to the incompatibilities between the institutional arrangements existing in a given country. Socialist politico-economic systems, though very consistently built, collapsed. So there are other forces of change, including poor performance, which breeds social discontent with a given regime – here is the link between the performance and the dynamics issue. But again this link – poor performance leading to social discontent leading to regime change – is far from automatic. We have witnessed enough long-lasting and economically disastrous regimes, based on fear, isolation and indoctrination to refute such a claim. Growing social discontent due to the poor performance of a regime may be perhaps the necessary condition but is far from a sufficient condition for a massive institutional change. Other forces include the mass perception of new opportunities, related to a vision of an alternative regime. This was the role of religious or quasi-religious doctrines, such as Marxism, which had the power to arouse powerful emotions – hatred or hope – and to give a simple, but not necessarily true, interpretation of reality. Mass media, the mass producers of perceptions, should be included in analyses of institutional change, especially in the second half of the twentieth century, in the age of television. Positive examples of changes in other countries, conveyed partly by the media, constitute another factor which influences the perception of policy makers and the public at large. The adoption of such foreign models brings about cultural diffusion. The wave of market-oriented reforms in the 1990s to some extent belongs in this category.

Other external factors include foreign occupations, if the occupier introduces his own country's institutional arrangements. This explains changes in institutional regimes after the Second World War in West Germany and Japan, and – with very different results – in Eastern

Europe. Finally, in explaining massive institutional change, one should not forget the role of chance factors – unintended consequences permeate history.

There is also the role of particular individuals, whose appearance in a position of leadership is at least partly a chance factor. This factor interacts with long-term forces in bringing about institutional break-throughs. Such individuals may also play a decisive role in the short period of 'extraordinary politics' which then follows (see Chapter 9). During this period, a special mass psychology prevails, and the institutional constraints are still malleable, so there is much more scope than normal for the operation of a personality factor, i.e. for shaping a completely new institutional regime. Massive institutional change results, therefore, from the interplay between long-term forces related to a former regime in a given country, external influences and chance factors.

The Analytical Framework

This section focuses on the analytical framework which I find appropriate for the study of institutions and human behaviour, and which I have used throughout this book. An analytical framework defines the central variables and clarifies the related methodological assumptions. 'Institutions' (institutional factors) are obviously the central concept. I define institutions as all the non-material and at least relatively enduring factors which are external to the respective individuals and are capable of influencing their behaviour. 'Institutions', therefore, cover neither physical objects nor the biological and psychological features (dispositions or human nature) of individuals. The first exclusion is rather obvious, the second is perhaps more controversial but is analytically very important: only by defining institutions and human nature as separate, although interacting factors, can we clearly explain how changes (differences) in institutional factors lead to changes (differences) in human behaviour and its outcomes. And without the clear assumptions on human nature, the structure and change of institutions cannot be explained.

The institutions of a given country can be divided into three related categories (Balcerowicz 1989):

(1) The general legal framework and its constituent parts: the Constitution, property law, contract law, company law, electoral law, the penal code, etc. The legal norms on which all these laws are based

are a special type of social norm, i.e., those which are guaranteed by the threat of sanctions from other people. What distinguishes the legal norms is that the sanctions are executed by a special enforcement apparatus which has the monopoly of the use of force and, by definition, constitutes the core part of the state (Weber 1922). The legal framework results from the operation of the political system,[1] and massive changes in this framework mark the institutional breakthroughs we have discussed above.

(2) Institutional structures, also called formal organizations. Each structure may be understood as an internally connected set of roles. The respective structures may be identified by certain legally prescribed goals and, as in the case of physical persons, by their dates of birth. The types and the shares of existing organizations depend on their legal models, contained in the general legal framework. For example, depending on the ownership law, a country has either a capitalist or a socialist ownership structure (for more on this, see Chapter 7).

(3) Institutionally determined social mechanisms. They consist, by definition, of the actions or interactions of many people, and their type and properties depend on the general legal framework and on the institutional structures. Examples include democratic elections, which presuppose a wide range of civil and political liberties and – in large societies – the existence of 'intermediaries', that is, political parties. In the economic sphere, a centrally important mechanism is the market, which requires a large measure of economic freedom; and, if it is to function well, a developed infrastructure to operate and enforce the law. Markets have two kinds of participants: physical persons and organizations. It is the differences in the latter, especially in ownership types of enterprises, which strongly influence the scope and the properties of a market mechanism (see Chapter 7).

The totality of a country's institutions make up its institutional system. Based on certain conventional criteria, one can distinguish in it

---

[1] Different political regimes have different types of legal framework. A socialist state brought a peculiar structure to this framework. The constitutional norms which declared many individual liberties were, in fact, not binding on the state. This was a sort of empty law or facade not to be taken seriously in the analysis of the regime. However, there were regulations issued by the party, which did not formally enter the legal framework, but were in fact laws in the Weberian sense. To reconstruct the really binding legal framework, which mattered for human behaviour, one must, therefore, omit the empty law and add the 'party law'. In democratic capitalism, in contrast, the formal legal framework overlaps with the Weberian legal framework.

various subsystems, including the political and economic ones. One of the central questions, relating to the problem of institutional compatibility, is what type of political regime can co-exist with what type of economic regime (see Chapter 8).

Turning to the second central factor – human dispositions – I define them in psychological terms (Madsen 1968) as the lasting or relatively lasting features which human beings bring into various decision-making situations, including those which are shaped by institutions, such as the roles of an employee, manager, private owner, or public official. I consider it important to distinguish two different types of human dispositions: 'invariants' and 'variables'. The former is the traditional concept of human nature; the latter, by definition, may differ across countries and time. Both types have motivational and informational dispositions; the informational ones include the capacity to learn.

Before discussing the invariant and potentially variable dispositions, I need to make several comments. First, there is a problem in that 'dispositions' belong to individuals, who differ a great deal. In what sense, then, can one speak of 'invariant dispositions'? Obviously, not in the sense of identical features, but only in terms of what is common to, or dominant among, human beings. For example, people have different capacities for storing information, but each is limited in this respect, and there is a certain upper limit, established by psychology. Each society can be, in principle, described by the statistical distributions of the values of these individual limits and of the other dispositions of its members. The assumption of the invariants conceived in the above terms is crucial in explaining the processes based on mass actions or interactions, such as the operation of market mechanisms or of command planning. Inter-personal variability is, in turn, a necessary premise for explaining the role of the personality factor in social life. For, if people were identical, there would be no scope for this factor. One may try to link the personality factor to more systematic forces, i.e. the rules of selection of individuals to positions or leadership, rules which differ across various institutional systems. This is a worthwhile line of analysis, but one should remember the role of chance factors in the operation of such selection mechanisms and that the related indeterminacy of their results is large. Who, after all, predicted that a personality like Gorbachev would appear as leader of the Soviet party-state?

Also note that institutional systems differ in the type of institutional positions (types of activity) which individuals with some special characteristics may choose, and those differences are important for the use of societies' motivational and informational potential. For example, in each society there are some would-be innovators, but the scope they have for displaying their special talents depends on whether their country's ownership law allows private entrepreneurship. Each society contains some individuals who derive special satisfaction from pursuing some non-pecuniary objectives; the scope for the operation of these characteristics depends on the legal possibility of organizing non-profit institutions.

Second, one may question the distinction between the invariant and potentially variable dispositions, by pointing out that societies differ in psychological dimensions. So what, then, are these inter-societal invariants? I am referring here not only to the popular notion of different 'national characteristics', which may be questioned on methodological grounds, but also to the interdisciplinary work using anthropology and population genetics summarized by Claude Levi-Strauss (1983). He described human evolution as a two-stage process. In the first, 'pre-cultural' phase, true biologically determined universals emerged, such as manual dexterity, symbolic thinking, language. In the second stage, different cultures developed in isolated communities and some of their components, such as laws on marriage, hygiene, etc., interacted with the genetic factors in producing populations possibly displaying different distributions of certain types of human nature. However, this possibility does not undermine the case for assuming certain human invariants in the sense of what is common to or dominant among human beings. At least some of these invariants may be linked to the 'pre-cultural' stage. Furthermore, it is an open empirical question as to whether contemporary societies really differ because of the operation of these cultural and genetic forces. First, the past few centuries have brought about a great deal of homogenization of these cultural components which interact with genetic factors. Next, any potential differences may only be a matter of degree, but not of kind. For example, nobody would assume that contemporary societies display qualitatively different types of motivation. Finally, if societies nowadays differ in certain dimensions, then it is more likely to be due to differences in the content and scope of learning in successive generations; and this can be explained by the invariant capacities to learn interacting with the mechanisms of socialization (acquiring values and rules of behaviour) and of education. I will return to this in a while. But now let us turn to the issue of motivational dispositions.

By definition these dispositions shape an individual's preferential ordering of various courses of actions (options) he/she perceives in various decision-making situations, thanks to his informational disposition.[2] Motivational dispositions may be known, for example, as needs, aspirations, internal norms of behaviour, etc. Of these, needs seem to be the most fundamental in that they determine, for example, the range of behavioural norms an individual may acquire. One can envisage motivational dispositions as consisting of various layers. It is in the most fundamental layer and the dispositions which are its direct products that one has to look for motivational invariants. The other layers may express inter-cultural variability, which is nevertheless constrained by the fundamental motivational layer.

The totality of an individual's dispositions constitute his/her motivational potential, which determines what variables she/he perceives as motivators. A variable is a motivator if a change in its intensity is – to the person concerned – a reward or punishment in a psychological sense.[3,4] Expressed formally, motivators are the arguments in an individual's utility function. The expected differences in their values linked to the various options perceived in a given decision-making situation constitute positive or negative incentives.

The problem of motivational invariants includes the question of the relative importance of the self-centred versus the altruistic orientation. An altruistic orientation is present when a positive change in another person's motivator is perceived as a reward by a given individual (Karyłowski 1982). Expressed formally, motivators affecting other people are arguments in the utility function of a given individual in such a way that their improvement increases the value of this function and their decline reduces it (Collard 1978).

The other people could be an individual's relatives and friends or just strangers. One can speak of 'true altruism' when the other people in this definition are strangers, and of 'limited altruism' when they belong to his/her nearest circle. In both cases, altruism can be weak or strong, depending on the magnitude of sacrifices an individual is ready to make.

The issue of the relative strength of the self-centred versus altruistic orientation matters because each person is frequently faced with decision-making situations which involve moral dilemmas: he/she has

---

[2] Individuals' decisions and, therefore, their behaviour can be interpreted as resulting from their decision-making situations and their informational and motivational dispositions. Some situations are exogenous, i.e., independent of the actor. Other situations result from their previous decisions. For example, the situations a person faces in his/her professional activities largely result from the previous choice of a type of a job.

[3] Some motivators are of a binary nature, for example, preserving or losing a job; others are continuous, for example, pain or income.

[4] One of the central problems of psychology is to explain the internal process of motivation which produces these states (see Madsen 1968; Hebb 1971).

to choose between options which promise higher values of motivators to him/her, but lower values to other people, and options with the reverse motivational configurations. The assumption that people's dispositions are such that they tend to choose the first type of options, except when others belong to their inner emotional circle, has much stronger empirical backing than any alternative assumption on human motivational invariants (see Karyłowski 1982). Such an orientation can be called an enlarged self-interest.

Another issue regarding these invariants is what type of factors motivate the majority in every society: such motivators can be termed 'universal'. This question goes beyond the assumptions of conventional economics and gives the enlarged self-interest much fuller psychological content.

Psychologists agree that invariant motivational dispositions include primary needs, i.e. dispositions to feel pain, hunger, thirst, cold, sexual drive, boredom, and tiredness (Malewski 1975). Beyond that there is no widely accepted and integrated theory of human motivation. However, drawing on a number of theories (see Madsen 1968), one can point to two other types of powerful invariant dispositions: emotional or psychological needs and the tendency to maintain or increase self-esteem (for the latter, see Kozielecki 1987). It is also worth singling out – from among the primary needs – the need for sensory and intellectual stimulation, which, if not fulfilled, results in boredom (see Hebb 1971).

This disposition helps to distinguish two kinds of effort: one is self-rewarding and the other is not. The increases in the first type of effort demand much more pecuniary stimulation that those in the second. This has clear implications for behaviour in various kinds of jobs.

Self-esteem makes such factors as prestige or career prospects powerful motivators. Besides, it is a disposition which is at least partly related to two important theories of motivation. One of them is the theory of cognitive dissonance (see Festinger 1957; Aranson 1972); This dissonance is a perceived contradiction between a person's beliefs (including his self-image) and the incoming information or his behaviour. Since such an internal state is a punishment, the affected person tends to eliminate it by manipulating his/her beliefs, by selective reception of incoming information or by manipulating the content of this information. This theory is obviously relevant to the discussion of the issue of human informational invariants (see later). It can be fruitfully applied to the analysis of many economic problems.[5] Another theory is

---

[5] Akerlof & Dickens (1982), and Gilad *et al.* (1987) are some of the few economists who have done so.

that of achievement motivation, i.e., a tendency to value options perceived by the decision-maker to be moderately probable of ending in an outcome widely defined as 'successful' (McClelland 1961). This motivational disposition helps to explain the economic superiority of private ownership over alternative ownership forms (see Chapter 7).

The basic needs, the psychological needs, the need for sensory and intellectual stimulation, and self-esteem jointly generate the set of universal motivators which explain most of individuals' choices both in the economic and non-economic spheres. Some of these motivators may stem from more than one type of invariant disposition. For example, income, a motivator cherished by conventional economics, may matter not only because of its capacity to fulfil basic needs but also because it may serve as a measure of success (Röpke 1977). Besides income, other universal motivators include various kinds of expected effort, factors affecting cognitive dissonance, and variables influencing self-esteem.

The informational invariants of human beings are largely captured by Herbert Simon's notion of 'bounded rationality'. This concept was already implicit in the pre-war 'socialist calculation debate' in the writings of Brutzkus, von Mises and Hayek (see Chapter 4). In contrast, the proponents of various schemes of socialism, headed by Lange, were arguing within the framework of mainstream economic orthodoxy; this explains why they were – until recently – declared victors on 'theoretical' grounds. But it was a peculiar notion of a theory, which blinded its adherents to the rather obvious problems of the real world. The importance of realistic assumptions to human informational capabilities in the analysis of the impact of alternative institutional arrangements was demonstrated by the problems this theory encountered.[6]

Realistic assumptions would include limits to human memory, information processing and learning. They explain, among other things, the unavoidable existence of a hierarchical multi-level organizational structure under command socialism (see Chapter 5). Limits to the pace of learning, given differences in the required scope of learning, explain why different processes of institutional change have different maximum possible speeds, which in turn helps the understanding of such features of the post-socialist economic transition as its two-stage nature, or the tendency for tax evasion to increase temporarily (see Chapters 10 and 14).

---

[6] The proponents of the theoretical superiority of socialism also based their claims on usually implicit unrealistic assumptions about motivational dispositions, i.e., they either assumed complete altruism or total obedience to the socialist state. Oliver Williamson's (1975) 'opportunism' was thus not considered possible under socialism.

Another type of informational invariant, and one which is not captured by the notion of 'bounded rationality', is the tendency of individuals to engage in intra-personal distortion of incoming information, so as to reduce the cognitive dissonance. This tendency for self-manipulation includes attempts to block the sources of information in conflict with deeply held beliefs, or to distort the information. The extent to which individuals are allowed to engage in such intra-personal informational distortion may be linked to the nature of their institutional positions, and these positions to the nature of the whole institutional system. Strictly hierarchical systems devoid of open competition may be expected to be especially susceptible to such distortion. Hierarchies also produce a strong tendency for inter-personal distortion of information in the relationships between subordinates and their superiors.

Human dispositions may vary across countries and time. The special states of these variables may be called psycho-social peculiarities. This is a theoretical definition which should be distinguished from the empirical question of whether they exist, and how to establish their existence.[7] Such peculiarities may include internalized norms of behaviour towards other people, one's family or one's own future, due, for example, to certain religions, or to traditions passed down over generations. Such factors are often referred to as 'culture'. Another component is the stock of knowledge (human capital). There are two main questions concerning variable dispositions: (1) their role in explaining differences in performance by countries or regions of the same country; (2) their role in explaining or predicting transition from one institutional system to another.

Both problems are subject to much speculation, often in caricatured forms. For example, the poor economic performance of South Korea was sometimes explained by Confucianism, yet Confucianism is often cited as the main reason for that country's extraordinary economic success since the early 1960s. Also, certain countries are sometimes declared incapable of introducing successful economic reforms because of their special culture. To avoid such pseudo-theorizing one should, I think, follow a clear methodological rule: the existence of psycho-social peculiarities cannot *a priori* be ruled out. But their existence should be established empirically, and independently from specific behaviour. Otherwise one

---

[7] A given psycho-social peculiarity must be a feature of the relevant distribution of the values of a certain individual disposition in a given society, e.g. an especially high frequency of occurrence of high or low values; this high (low) level is usually understood as a special trait. Psychological investigations of the representative samples of various populations would be needed to test the existence of a given peculiarity. For an example of such research, see Shiller *et al.* (1991).

easily commits the fallacy of explaining specific behaviour by the specific dispositions which are deduced from that behaviour.

With respect to how to explain systematic differences in performance, I believe another rule should be followed. An explanation in terms of the interplay between different institutional factors and human invariants should have priority over the explanation in terms of some psycho-social peculiarities. In other words, only if the first explanation proves to be unsatisfactory (and the reference to other easily identifiable factors fails, too) is one justified in searching for an explanation in terms of some peculiarities. But, again, this is only justified if it is empirically possible to establish their existence.[8] And in analysing the impact of institutional variables, one must go beyond such conventional notions as 'capitalist economies', as they mask many differences in the institutional frameworks of these countries.

Throughout this book I try to explain differences in behaviour and performance in terms of the interplay between various institutional frameworks and invariant human dispositions. There is, however, one psycho-social variable which I included in this analysis of economic performance, especially with respect to an economy's innovativeness (see Chapter 6): the level and structure of human capital. There is a two-fold interaction between the type of the economic system and this capital. First, the type of economic system partly determines – via the expected returns to various lines of education – the structure of human capital, i.e. what sorts of skills are acquired in the educational institutions, and the content of the learning-by-doing acquired by graduates in the practice of their professions. Second, the type of economic system determines how the 'new' human capital, a product of the educational system, is to be used. Both issues have important implications for the transition from one economic regime to another. If the inherited general human capital is large but not adequately used under the previous regime, then an appropriate transition makes a rapid increase in the

---

[8] One of the few studies which meets this condition is the excellent work of Robert D. Putnam (1993) in which he shows that the differences in 'civic culture' between Southern and Northern Italy, which he links to the differences in their history, affected the operation of the regional governments, established in the early 1970s. However, this study is insufficient to establish a general case that certain psycho-social peculiarities are inescapably long-lasting so that they unavoidably and seriously differentiate behaviour under the same institutional framework. Much more extensive comparative research would be needed to establish such a case. Besides, even with respect to Italy, this study omits the possibility that the post-Second World War policy of massive public investment in Southern Italy might have perpetuated the inherited patron–client culture, which distinguishes it from Northern Italy, where such investments did not take place.

utilization of this potential possible, and also provides incentives to close up the gaps in its structure (for more on this, see Chapter 10).

This brings us to the second problem, i.e. how one should treat the issue of psycho-social variables in explaining or predicting inter-systemic transitions. First, one should realize that the assumption about human invariants prohibits a naive belief that a radical change of institutional regime may produce a completely 'new man', a dream of the early socialists. Human dispositions, therefore, should not be treated as epiphenomena of institutions.

I mentioned that the institutional breakthrough may produce a special state of mass psychology for a short time. However, this is not to say that radical institutional change produces special motivational dispositions; this extraordinary psychological atmosphere results from the interplay of certain invariant dispositions and a country's suddenly changed situation.

Second, what about the psycho-social inheritance of the former regime? One of its components, human capital, was already discussed. With regard to the others, there is a general rule which has already been mentioned: the recourse to psycho-social peculiarities is justified if they can be established empirically and independently from the specific behaviour one seeks to explain. This should prevent an easy use of the *homo sovieticus* hypothesis in explaining the post-socialist transition. This hypothesis is contradicted both by the very different transition paths in each of those countries which was exposed to socialism and by direct psychological research. The latter has shown that Soviet and American respondents were basically similar in their attitudes towards fairness, income equality, incentives, and their understanding of the functioning of markets (see Shiller *et al.* 1992). However, even if socialism had left some psycho-social peculiarities, there would still be a question of how one should consider them in structuring the transition away from socialism. And here psychology can be of help, once again. The theory of cognitive dissonance (Festinger 1957) tells us, among other things, that people are more likely to adapt internally to external changes if they are radical and, therefore, perceived as irreversible, than if they are small and thus regarded as easy to reverse (Balcerowicz 1989). This psychological argument strengthens the conclusions which one might have derived from studying 'the constructional logic' of command socialism (see Chapter 5).

It should be emphasized that the analytical framework presented here does not reduce theoretical institutional economics (or, more generally, the study of institutions) to psychology. It is an attempt to gain a better understanding of the structure, impact and change of

institutional arrangements and systems by using inputs from psychological theories, inputs which go beyond the traditional psychological
assumptions adopted in conventional economics. The propositions
which one can devise by using this framework are not simple repli-
cations of the findings of psychology but result from the interplay
between the assumptions about alternative institutional structures (or
more generally situational factors) and the explicit psychological
premises on the dispositions of individuals. This approach, I believe, can
give a fuller sense to methodological individualism, which is a central
and rightly cherished principle of analytical social science.[9]

About the Book

This book, including the present chapter, attempts to summarize the
research on institutions, institutional change and human behaviour that I
have undertaken since the late 1970s. It contains chapters which are
based on my earlier writings, published in Polish but not in English, and
chapters which largely replicate some of my earlier English publications.
All these chapters, although written at different times, were guided by
the analytical framework which I have sketched above.

The first part of the book, 'Socialism versus Capitalism', focuses on
the comparative analysis of the performance of the alternative institutional regimes. It also discusses problems of institutional compatibility
and the related problems of the necessary scope of institutional change
away from socialism and the compatibility of various political and
economic regimes.

The first six chapters replicate my English publications written in
1988–89. I have only deleted a few small parts in order to avoid
excessive repetition. Otherwise, I have preserved the original text – not
only in the hope that it has withstood the test of time, but also because
some readers may be interested in the ideas on economic systems and
their change of an author who was later brought into a position enabling
him to direct the economic transition from socialism in Poland in 1989–
91. The remaining two chapters were written in 1994 and 1995, but draw
on my earlier writings in Polish.

Part II, 'From Socialism to Capitalism', discusses institutional

---

[9] I would like to acknowledge my intellectual debt to Antoni Malewski, a brilliant
Polish social scientist who died prematurely in the 1970s. His 1975 book greatly influenced
my thinking on how to study human behaviour under various external conditions,
including institutional ones.

change, and focuses on the post-Communist transition, started in the late 1980s. It deals with the political and economic developments and the interplay between them. The chapters in this part are based on my publications written in 1993–95. I tried to blend in knowledge gained during my academic studies and insights obtained while holding a position of major responsibility during the period of 'extraordinary politics'.

Finally, the third part focuses on Poland's economic transformation and on the related political developments. Chapter 14 describes the reforms prior to the 1990 breakthrough. It was written in 1988 from the position of an academic. The next two chapters analyse the transition in 1989–93. They are based on my publications written in 1993 and 1994. The book ends with my personal recollections on Poland's reforms, written from the position of an insider.

In my research on which this book is based, I enjoyed the support of many people. Most of them I mention in the footnotes to the respective chapters. Here I cannot help but express my gratitude to my wife, Ewa Balcerowicz, for her patience, understanding and moral and intellectual support in the whole period when I was dealing with institutions and institutional change, both as an academic and as a policy-maker.

References

Akerlof, G.A. & Dickens, N.T. 1982 'The Economic Consequences of Cognitive Dissonance', *American Economic Review* 72, pp. 307–19.

Aranson, E. 1972 *Social Animal* (London: W.M. Freeman).

Balcerowicz, K. 1989 'Systemy gospodarcze. Elementy analizy porównawczej' (Warsaw: *SGPiS*).

Collard, D. 1978 *Altruism and the Economy* (Oxford: Martin Robertson).

Festinger, L. 1957 *A Theory of Cognitive Dissonance* (Evanston, Ill.: Row Peterson).

Gilad, B., Kaish, S. & Loeb, P. 1987 'Cognitive Dissonance and Utility Maximization', *Journal of Economic Behaviour and Organization* 8, pp. 61–73.

Hebb, D.O. 1971 'Drives and the NS Conceptual Nervous System', in D. Bindra & J. Stewart (eds.) *Motivation* (Harmondsworth, Midx.: Penguin), pp. 118–36.

Karyłowski, J. 1982 *O Dwoch rodzajach altruzmu* (Wroclaw: Ossolineum).

Kozielecki, J. 1987 'Motywacja Hubrystyczna – Krótka Rozprawa o Nienasyceniu', *Problemy* 8, pp. 11–18.

Levi-Strauss, C. 1983 *Le régard loigné* (Paris: Librairie Plon).

Madsen, K.B. 1968 *Modern Theories of Motivation* (Copenhagen: Munksgaard).

Malewski, A. 1975 *O nowy ksztalt nauk spolecznych. Pisma zebrane* (Warsaw: PWN).

McClelland, D. 1961 *The Achieving Society* (New York: Van Nostrand).

Putnam, R.D. 1993 *Making Democracy Work: Civic Traditions in Modern Italy* (Princeton, NJ: Princeton University Press).

Röpke, J. 1977 *Die Strategie der Innovation* (Tübingen: J. C. B. Mohr).

Simon, H. 1957 *Models of Man* (New York: Wiley).

Shiller, R.J., Boycko, M. & Korobov, V. 1991 'Popular Attitudes Toward Free Markets: The Soviet Union and the United States Compared', *American Economic Review* 81, pp. 386–400.

Weber, M.C. 1922 *Wirtschaft und Gesellschaft* (Tübingen: J. C. B. Mohr).

Williamson, O.E.C. 1975 *Markets and Hierarchies Analysis and Antitrust Implications* (New York: The Free Press).

Part I

Socialism versus Capitalism

2

Problems with the Definition of Socialism in Today's World

In discussing concepts, one is on much shakier ground than when analysing issues of causal relationships, for, in the latter case, reality can provide a filter to separate justified propositions from unfounded ones. This is the well-known Popperian falsification procedure. There is no such possibility in the former case. Definitions cannot be falsified. Only the claims made with respect to objects which are denoted by definitions can in some cases (if the propositions are properly formulated) be put to empirical tests, but these belong to the second category. How then can one distinguish 'scientific' definitions of socialism from 'unscientific' ones?

Without even hoping to give a precise answer to this question, I would suggest that any scientific definition should try to meet three rather modest and related conditions:

- It should not be value-loaded.
- It should not be completely arbitrary and changeable over time.
- It should have a certain rigour.

One can easily give examples of the explicit or implicit definitions of socialism which violate at least one of these conditions. With respect to the first requirement, let us note that there has been a widespread tendency in official language in the communist countries to refer to all kinds of negative phenomena as 'deviations from socialism'. In current

The text of this chapter was written in 1988 and first published in 1991 in *Socialism Today? The Changing Meaning of Socialism*, edited by Ota Šik (Basingstoke and London, Macmillan), pp. 65–74.

discussion in the USSR, some authors refuse to acknowledge that there was ever any socialism there, or at least up until 1985. A Polish author asked the rhetorical question: 'Where is there more socialism: in Sweden or in Rumania?' (Malanowski 1989). I think that behind all these pronouncements there is one general value-loaded concept of socialism as a state of universal happiness.[1] So if some events or developments are clearly negative they do not belong to socialism, they are completely independent of it, or happen despite socialism rather than because of it. Some representatives of this approach are all too ready to recognize Hitler's Germany as an extreme form of capitalism but are loath to acknowledge Stalinism as an extreme form of socialism. For 'socialism' is a sacred word for them.

The second condition implies that one should not remain satisfied with passively listing various definitions of socialism, or giving one's own definition, without stating some criteria which would restrict the uncritical expansion or manipulation of the meaning of this term.[2] In other words, socialism should not be an infinitely flexible concept if it is to have any meaning at all. A certain stability of the conceptual network is required if we are to register the changes in reality correctly.

There have, in my view, been two main reasons why a tendency towards an almost unlimited expansion of the concept of socialism has gained ground in the Comecon countries. First, 'socialism' has been the name of the official ideology of the ruling parties. Facing, on the one hand, a grave crisis in their countries but unwilling, on the other hand, to openly admit the failure of this ideology, some of these parties have recently been proposing radical changes, while claiming that they represent modifications of their (fundamentally unchanged) concept of socialism. This is probably meant to convey the impression that there was nothing basically wrong with official doctrine from the very beginning. Hence the ideological claim to keep power does not suffer too much.

As an example of this expansion of the official concept of socialism, let me quote a passage from the 1987 resolution of the Hungarian Workers' Party: 'The second economy and the private sector are integral

[1] The tendency to define socialism in such a way was noted by Sirc (1974, p. 170): 'socialism is often loosely used to mean a system in which everybody has a good life'. He then adds: 'If that is what it does mean, then we are all socialists . . . .'

[2] This should not be confused with the suggestion that there should be some ideological barriers to the systemic changes in the countries of 'real socialism'. The point is that – at least in scientific discussions – there should be a limit to recognizing just any kind of such changes as falling within the scope of 'socialism'.

parts of the *socialist* [author's emphasis] economy'.[3] Similarly, private agriculture has been recognized, by a special clause inserted in the Constitution in 1983, as an element of the *socialist* economy in Poland.

Along with the authorities, there are also some economists who propose radical changes (for example the introduction of a capital market, including a stock exchange) as a means of restructuring within the socialist economy. This probably reflects the desire to neutralize ideological attacks against such changes, and perhaps to provide some face-saving for the authorities, in the hope that they would then be more willing to accept the arrangements proposed. Muddling the concept of socialism seems to be a price worth paying for a (hopefully) increased chance of introducing them. I have some understanding of the motives of this tendency.[4] But I still think that in the interests of conceptual clarity, there should be some limit to arbitrariness in the use of the concept of socialism, at least in theoretical discussions. An additional reason for this restraint is that it appears doubtful whether the strategy of pushing all kinds of changes under the suitably enlarged umbrella of socialism can be effective, as it probably over-estimates the possibility of fooling its opponents.

The Uses of the Word 'Socialist'

In discussing the concept of socialism, it is worth distinguishing several broad categories with respect to which the word 'socialist' is often used:

- *Socialist ideals* or the desired states of society. There is a whole catalogue of these ideals, the main ones probably being economic justice, fair distribution of income and wealth, removal of poverty.[5]
- *Socialist economic systems*, that is certain types of country-wide arrangements regulating economic life.
- *Socialist doctrines*, that is, sets of propositions which aim at explaining how and why socialist systems are to emerge,[6] or focus

[3] Another interpretation is, however, also possible: that is that the word 'socialist' is meant to imply that although the private sector will be allowed to grow, it will have to remain in a minority (quoted as in Szelenyi 1988, p. 42).

[4] A similar approach consists of arguing that certain categories (for example, profit, market commercial banking and so on) previously considered to be 'capitalist', emerged long before capitalism. Thus they are not specifically 'capitalist' and are therefore acceptable in 'socialism'.

[5] For various formulations of socialist ideals see: Kolakowski & Hampshire (1974).

[6] Here, Marxian historical materialism is the main case in point.

on describing the properties of these systems and of their (allegedly) superior performance, including their special ability to realize socialist ideals.

- *Political parties and other organizations* which call themselves 'socialist' or profess allegiance to socialism.

An obvious point is that one should be extremely careful in any attempt at deriving the definition of the socialist system from the official programmes and pronouncements of the institutions included in the fourth category, otherwise one may easily fall victim to the political manipulation of concepts. I have already mentioned this danger while speaking about recent pronouncements of some ruling parties in the Comecon countries. But a similar danger exists with respect to organizations in the West which fall under the fourth category. There, the rules of the electoral game seem to be such that it is much easier to change the programme than to own up to it by changing the name of the party or that of its ideology.[7] The Spanish Socialist Party, which carries out a 'Thatcherite' economic policy, may serve as an example.

Another point is that one should avoid *defining* socialist economic systems in terms of the high degree of achievement of socialist ideals (and of other good things). Instead, they should be defined in terms of some institutional characteristics. Failure to respect this requirement leads to value-loaded definitions of socialism,[8] which, as I have already noted, should be rejected on methodological grounds. But there is another methodological reason for conceptually separating the socialist ideals and the socialist systems: only then the link between the two is a matter of theoretical and empirical analysis and not of mere definition. Such analyses may reveal that certain socialist ideals, for example narrowing income differentials, are realised to a large extent under some capitalist systems. Taiwan seems to be a case in point here (see Tsiang 1988). In order to be open to such findings, the believers in socialist ideals should free their minds of socialist doctrines which postulate a rigid link between certain institutional arrangements and a certain type of economic result.

---

[7] It may well be that changing the name of the party is like changing the name of the firm: in both cases there is a risk that because of the resulting confusion, some 'customers' may be lost.

[8] One example of this approach seems to be Lisichkin's proposal that 'criteria for the existence of socialism should be . . . such . . . as the level of labour productivity, the level of living standards, the level of welfare (for example infant mortality and life expectancy), and the extent of democratic freedoms' (quoted in Ellman 1989, p. 3).

Socialist Economic Systems

I will now focus on socialist economic systems. I have argued that they should be defined in terms of some institutional characteristics. But in which institutions should we see the distinctive features of these systems? What should be the criterion for choosing such institutional arrangements? I would suggest that in order to avoid arbitrarily stretching the concept of socialist systems, the basic criterion should be the preservation of at least some central elements of its original meaning. On this assumption, most of us probably agree that the distinctive feature of the socialist economy (one which gave rise to the very term 'socialism') is that it is based on the social ownership of the means of production.[9] The concept of this ownership is by no means clear and would require a longer discussion.[10] But whatever it means, it does not encompass private ownership. Indeed, social ownership was meant to be – in some sense – the opposite of private ownership.

There are two main reasons why it was proposed to replace private ownership with social ownership:

- Income derived from private ownership (property income) was considered to be 'unearned'. Only 'labour-income' was recognized as legitimate.[11] An unfortunate effect of this attitude is that instead of being concerned with the overall income differentials, regardless of their source, one may become obsessively pre-occupied with just one type of income, branded as an expression of exploitation.
- Private ownership of the means of production was regarded as the institutional basis for the free competitive market, which in turn

---

[9] One major exception from this definitional assumption is the definition of the socialist economic system solely in terms of the large extent of redistributive measures as performed by the welfare state. It is in this sense that, for example, the term 'Swedish socialism' is used. Such a usage was criticized by Diehl (1926, p. 580), who argued that it confuses the socialist order with the social reforms carried out under capitalism. *The Economist* seems to be of the same opinion when it says that 'the Social Democrats' model of society' is a 'welfare capitalism' ('New Paths for Socialism', 1985).

[10] I have tried to clarify this and the other concepts of ownership elsewhere (see Chapter 7 and also Balcerowicz 1987).

[11] The assessment of the various sources of income (and of income differentials) is always a value judgement, and this obviously applies to the socialists' appraisal of property income. In Marxism, however, this negative assessment is presented as though it were a scientific finding, when in fact it is simply based on Marx's arbitrary definition of 'surplus value'. For penetrating comments on this, see Sowell (1980, pp. 225–7).

was condemned as a wasteful and extremely inefficient mode of coordination in the economy.[12]

At the same time it was held possible to replace spontaneous market coordination by some superior, conscious harmonization of economic activity, that is, by overall economic planning. In this interpretation, the case for the replacement of private by social ownership is thus derived from the perceived link between the former and the free market, and from the belief that market coordination can be replaced by some superior non-market coordination. In this view, the core of the socialist economy is the overall economic planning, which substitutes for the market, and private property is condemned *because* it makes such planning impossible by giving rise to spontaneous, anarchic interactions in the economy.

This interpretation is typical of the majority of the early socialists, and it is central to Marx's vision of the socialist economic system.[13] What seems to me to be crucial in Marx's perception (or definition?) of private ownership of the means of production, is the 'separateness' of the respective producers, a feature which leads to their interacting in such a way that the 'anarchy of production', that is, the competitive market mechanisms, is the result. Indeed, this separateness appears to be the main reason why private was to be replaced by social ownership.[14] Hence any concept of the latter which would entail this separateness runs against the very core of Marx's vision of socialism. His hope might have been that harmonious non-market coordination could be achieved without centralization; by the free cooperation of the autonomous producers. But we know that this is impossible in any complex economy.[15] For in order to suppress the market, one must restrict the autonomy of enterprises, and this in turn creates a vacuum which must

[12] It is worth stressing that for most of the prominent early socialists (including Marx), it was the free competitive nature of the market, that is economic rivalry, which was viewed as the main evil, as the main source of disturbances in the economy. Market competition is thus incompatible with the socialist tradition. For the presentation of the views of some early socialists, see Kernig (1979). Their view of the free, competitive market was thus the exact opposite of Adam Smith's vision of the 'invisible hand'.

[13] In describing Marx's views on socialism I am largely drawing on Kloc (1980, pp. 1–160). For a similar interpretation to that contained in this work, see Nove (1983, pp. 1–60); Lavoie (1985, pp. 28–38).

[14] In support of this view, one may recall that Marx considered the growth of capitalist joint-stock companies to be an element of transition between capitalism and socialism because they were increasingly replacing the market mechanism by planned, non-market coordination.

[15] For a penetrating critique of the Utopian nature of the proposals for non-market, and at the same time non-hierarchical, coordination, see Lindbeck (1977).

be filled by centralist planning. Therefore, regardless of what Marx's dreams were, the only real form of social ownership compatible with his vision of socialism as a market-less economic system, is centralized state ownership. 'Real socialism' (and further, 'war communism') is thus in this respect in basic agreement with what Marx's vision of socialism really contains.[16] We may somewhat ironically look at it as an instance of the product becoming alienated from its producer.

New Models of Socialism

The disillusionment with the performance of the traditional Soviet-type economic system has given rise, in the countries burdened with it, to a search for new models of the socialist economy. There is no room here to discuss the evolution of these models. Let me just note that a significant step in this process was the presentation by Brus in 1961 of the 'decentralized model', whereby the decisions regarding current operations would be largely decentralized while the centre would retain direct control over new investment. This kind of model appears to have constituted a basic 'reform paradigm' in the 1960s and 1970s in Poland and Hungary; it was also popular in Yugoslavia (Ellman 1971, p. 20). The model constituted a partial departure from Marxist socialism, since it allowed some elements of the market to slip into the regulation of current production. But it could still be defended on Marxist grounds, as investment decisions were to remain largely the domain of central planning.

Today, however, most of the reform economists are rightly sceptical of the merits of investment centralization (this includes Brus, 1988). The prevailing view now is that efficiency enhancing reform must involve the introduction of genuine market mechanisms, which would include a capital market. However, most of the schemes presented so far still preserve the dominance of the social ownership of the means of production. This is why they are often regarded by their authors or

---

[16] It is sometimes objected that 'real socialism' offers no clues with respect to the performance of Marx's model of socialism, as Marx predicted that socialism would emerge in the most developed countries, but instead it was introduced into a backward state. But this argument completely misses the point. The problem is not only that the predictions were falsified by historical developments. The point is that if the attempt to introduce Marxian socialism had actually been undertaken in the most developed countries, it would have fared even worse, since the efficiency of hierarchical, non-market coordination declines with the growing complexity of the economy.

commentators as representing the 'socialist market economy'. This, however, provokes comment.

First of all, it should be noted that if such schemes are still to be regarded as socialist,[17] then they certainly belong to the non-Marxist variety.[18] For in a Marxist perspective, 'market socialism' is a contradiction in terms, and ownership is, in my interpretation of Marx, social to the extent that it overcomes the separateness of the producers, that is, their spontaneous market-type interactions.

Consequently, once one abandons the Marxist case against the market, one should also be ready to revise one's ideologically motivated hostility towards private ownership of the means of production.

But my reading of the schemes of market socialism is that for most of their authors and proponents, the adjective 'socialist' and the related insistence on social property do not express any ideological commitment. Rather, they express the perception of what is politically permissible and what is not. However, given the recent changes in the socialist camp, this may be to err on the side of excessive caution.[19] This is why I think that the set of the economic system envisaged should not be constrained by an -*ism*, and that reform discussion – at least among economists – should not be concerned with whether the respective schemes still comply with socialism. Instead, attention should be paid to their potential performance and their capability of solving the grave economic problems of the socialist countries.

---

[17] The following passage from Ludwig von Mises (1951, p. 141) shows that the schemes discussed, involving the decentralization of investment, represent a radical departure from what was traditionally understood by 'socialism': 'if it is to remain socialist, the socialist state cannot leave to other hands that disposition of capital which permits the enlargement of existing undertakings, the construction of others and the bringing into being of undertakings that are completely new. And it is scarcely to be assumed that socialists of whatever persuasion would seriously propose that this function should be made over to some group of people who would simply have the business of doing what capitalists and speculators do under capitalist conditions'.

[18] Indeed, some of the aforementioned schemes remind us of certain 'Utopian' socialists (for example, Owen or Lassalle), who advocated an economic system based on producer cooperatives.

[19] As an indication, let me cite the recent Polish discussion on the private sector in which many economists demanded that the limit on employment in a single private firm should be raised, and proposed various figures for the new limit. But then, after the change in government in 1988, a law was passed in January 1989, which abolished this limit altogether!

References

Balcerowicz, L. 1987 'Remarks on the Concept of Ownership', *Oeconomica Polona*, no. 1, pp. 75–95.

Brus, W. 1961 *Ogólne problemy funkcjonowania gospodarki socjalistycznej* (Warsaw); English version, *The Market in a Socialist Economy* (London: Routledge and Kegan Paul, 1971).

—— 1988 'From Revisionism to Pragmatism', paper presented at the 'Plan and-or Market' Conference in Vienna.

Diehl, K. 1926 'Socialismus and Kommunismus', *Handwörterbuch der Staatswissenschaften* (Jena: Gustav Fischer) pp. 578–611.

Ellman, M. 1971 *Soviet Planning Today* (Cambridge: Cambridge University Press).

—— 1989, 'Intellectual Barriers to Economic Reform in the USSR' (Sopron: mimeo).

Kernig, C. 1979 *Sozialismus. Ein Handbuch* (Stuttgart: W. Kohlhammer) vol. 1.

Kloc, K. 1980 'Plan i rynek w radzieckich dyskusjach ekonomicznych 1917–1929', dissertation (Warsaw).

Kolakowski, L. & Hampshire, S. (eds.) 1974 *The Socialist Idea* (London: Weidenfeld and Nicolson).

Lavoie, Don 1985 *Rivalry and Central Planning* (Cambridge: Cambridge University Press).

Lindbeck, A. 1977 *The Political Economy of the New Left: An Outsider's View* (New York: Harper and Row).

Malanowski, J. 1989 Interview in *Przeglad Tygodniowy*, no. 15.

Mises, L. von 1951 *Socialism: An Economic and Sociological Analysis* (New Haven: Yale University Press, German original published in 1922).

—— 1985 'New Paths for Socialism', *The Economist*, 21 December.

Nove, A. 1983 *The Economics of Feasible Socialism* (London: George Allen & Unwin).

Sirc, L. 1974 'Socialism and Ownership', in Kolakowski & Hampshire (eds) *The Socialist Idea*, pp. 170–83.

Sowell, T. 1980 *Knowledge and Decisions* (New York: Basic Books).

Szelenyi, I. 1988 'Eastern Europe in an Epoch of Transition Towards a Socialist Mixed Economy?' (Sopron: mimeo).

Tsiang, S.C. 1988 'Taiwan's Economic Success Demystified', *Journal of Economic Growth*, no. 1, pp. 21–36.

3

On the 'Socialist Market Economy'

The search for models of a market economy in the socialist countries with relatively the most reformed economic systems (Hungary, Yugoslavia, Poland) reflects the disillusion with their performance. They are rightly considered to be basically non-market systems, and this is thought to be the main reason for their disappointing results. On the other hand the adjective 'socialist', if it occurs at all in the reform debates, is then usually used to denote that the proposed market system should be different in some respects from capitalism. Thus we get the first approximation of where to locate a 'socialist market economy'. It should depart even further from the traditional Soviet model (i.e. further than the most reformed socialist economies actually did) but not as far as to fall within the scope of capitalism.

The second approximation is obtained after specifying what changes in the relatively most reformed socialist systems are necessary to transform them into 'market economies'. This obviously depends on what is meant by the term 'market economy'. In my view it is an economy where the market mechanism is the dominant mode of coordination in the sphere of private goods, that is, goods which can be distributed among individual users. A market mechanism is, by definition, a horizontal mode of coordination between supply and demand. This rules out any administrative interference in the terms of specific transactions, e.g. administrative prices or administrative rationing. The demand is thus not constrained by any official quotas and its changes can freely express themselves in prices. Furthermore, the

This chapter first appeared in *Acta Oeconomica* (Budapest) 40, Nos. 3–4 (1989), pp. 184–8, and was written in 1988 as a short response to a series of questions on the 'socialist' market economy sent to a group of selected economists.

supply is free to adapt to a changing demand, both in the short and in the longer run. The latter presupposes that the investment decisions are largely decentralized. Assuming that the decentralized investments cannot (and should not) be wholly financed out of the enterprises' retained profits, we conclude that the market mechanism includes some form of capital market, i.e., market for longer-term loanable funds.

There are still many elements of the most reformed socialist economies which are in clear contradiction with this description of the market mechanism, e.g.:

- the remnants or substitutes of the command or rationing mechanism, e.g. predominantly administrative allocation of foreign exchange, open or disguised administrative intervention in the structure of production and foreign trade,
- pervasive price controls,
- bureaucratic restrictions on enterprises' entry into new markets,
- massive inter-enterprise redistribution of financial means via the budget,
- party-state 'nomenklatura' for the appointment of the managers of enterprises, banks etc.

The transformation of socialist systems into market economies must, therefore, involve the elimination of these elements.

The third approximation is obtained after determining in what respects the socialist economy is different from the capitalist one. There is no unanimity on this issue. The differences largely stem from the varying propensities of different authors to stretch the concept of socialism in such a way as to be able to – seemingly – invalidate the criticism of it, or its earlier versions; at the same time, they often propose some radically new arrangements while claiming that they are still within the – suitably enlarged – framework of 'socialism'. The former tendency is usually motivated by unwillingness to concede defeat in the debates over the possible performances of socialism and capitalism. The latter often reflects the desire to neutralize the ideological attacks against the proposed changes. Muddling the concept of socialism is probably thought to be a price worth paying for the – hopefully – increased chance of introducing new arrangements. I have some understanding for the motives behind this tendency. However, I still think that in the interest of conceptual clarity there should be some limit to the arbitrariness in using the concept of socialism, at least in theoretical discussions. (This should not be confused with the limit on proposing changes with respect to socialist systems.) An additional reason for this restraint is that it appears doubtful whether the strategy of pushing all kinds of changes under the suitably enlarged shield of 'socialism' can be effective, as it probably overestimates the possibility of fooling opponents.

In order not to be arbitrary in the attempt to limit the arbitrariness in defining a socialist economy, I propose the following mental experiment: one should stop widening this concept at the point where its further expansion would provoke the greatest surprise among the most prominent early theoreticians of socialism, if they were alive. On this principle most of us will probably agree that socialism is *not* based on the classical private ownership of the means of production, i.e. an ownership whereby an enterprise is solely or largely owned by private persons other than the people working in it.

There are a number of models which appear to respect the above formulated restriction and which, at the same time, could be market systems. I can mention only the main ones here.

1. *Illyrian socialism,* or in other words genuine labour self-management of the Yugoslav type. 'Yugoslav' means that workers' rights to control an enterprise are not based on their shares in that enterprise, while 'genuine' emphasizes that – as distinct from Yugoslav practice – there is no hidden party–state control over the enterprises' managers (especially no nomenklatura).
2. *Workers' property.* Enterprises in this model are not only controlled by their employees but are also wholly owned by them, i.e. there are shares which belong entirely to the people working in a given firm.[1] Hence this is *property-based* labour self-management. One of its variants is cooperative socialism: the workers' enterprises take the form of classical producer cooperatives, where each member has equal formal rights in running the enterprise regardless of his share in its assets. Cooperative socialism is an old idea advocated by some prominent socialists (especially Ferdinand Lassalle) in the nineteenth century. It was, however, sharply criticized then by self-proclaimed 'scientific socialists' (Marx, Engels and their followers). Another variant of workers' property would allow the voting rights to rise with a worker's share in the enterprise's capital. However, this 'intra-enterprise capitalism' may be found to overstep the boundary of socialism.

---

[1] The shares, however, cannot be freely traded, as this would turn the workers' property into classical private ownership. The stock market with its various motivating and information functions has, therefore, no place in this model.

3. *Leasing the 'social' capital.* In this model natural resources and fixed assets are formally national property but are placed against the payment of rent at the disposal of private individuals or groups of people;[2] these people are then supposed to act as independent entrepreneurs. Such a concept of market socialism was proposed as early as 1922 by Boris Brutzkus, an outspoken critic of Marxism. Tibor Liska's 'entrepreneurial socialism' is another example (1982).

4. *Capitalist institutions without private capitalists.* This refers to the conception of an economic system in which enterprises would have the legal form of joint-stock companies owned by some non-private institutions. There would also exist a stock exchange on which the latter could buy and sell shares. Depending on what institutions are to be shareholders we get some more specific models. One of them heavily emphasizes the role of state holdings.[3] Another proposal additionally admits non-administrative institutions like banks, municipalities, universities etc. (Święcicki 1988).

One can envisage still another variant, where each enterprise is predominantly owned by some other enterprises, a minority share belonging to its own personnel as represented by the workers' council. Each enterprise would have a board of directors which, among other things, would nominate the professional management and which would represent the enterprise's shareholders, i.e. its own personnel and other enterprises. Each enterprise would derive some income from the dividends paid out by other firms, and thus would hopefully pressurize them for increased profits. In this way profit-orientation could perhaps be instilled in non-private firms.

5. *Mixed systems.* The above are pure models. However, one can also combine them in many different ways, e.g. by having workers' property and leasing in different sectors of the economy. Another type of mixed system is obtained when one allows the private sector to enter the scene. Yet the assumed concept of socialism condemns this sector to a marginal role, although it is impossible to say precisely at which point a further growth of this sector is already incompatible with that concept. In any case, if we accept it, then we are justified in being surprised when the economic successes due to the enlargement of this sector in the still predominantly socialist economies are attributed to socialism.

[2] These groups, however, do not have to be identical with the enterprise's personnel. Otherwise the leasing solution would fall within the scope of Illyrian socialism.

[3] This solution has been advocated by Márton Tardos.

Space permits me only a few general remarks on the above-mentioned models. Let me first suggest that three questions be posed.

First, is it possible to pass from socialist systems to these models, and what should the transition path be like? This question includes such important issues as how to overcome the resistance of those vested interests which are against a radical economic reform, or how to get rid of shortages without relapsing into high open inflation.

Second, if it were possible to introduce the envisaged systems, could they last? To put the question another way, do they not have some in-built tendency to transform themselves into some other system? I would venture a guess that these systems could last if their conceptions were suitably completed. This means, for example, that they would have to include a ban or at least severe restrictions on the foundation and development of enterprises with different legal forms than the ones on which a definition of a given system is based. The envisaged systems are thus characterized by what may be called a *closed* or *monopolizing* domestic property law.[4]

Finally, if these systems could be introduced and if they could last, how would they perform? Here one should first of all point out that it is difficult to make firm predictions, because the envisaged systems do not have any real counterparts so far. The propositions one can formulate are based, therefore, on very imperfect analogies with some parts of capitalist economies (e.g., the state holdings in Italy's public sector), on theoretical models which cannot be falsified for lack of empirical data (see the vast literature on Illyrian socialism), or finally on simple intuition and common sense. Interestingly enough, one can make much firmer predictions on how the socialist economies, with their relatively high human capital, would perform under capitalism. There are enough comparative studies (e.g. Czechoslovakia–Austria, Hungary–Austria, GDR–FRG) to warrant the conclusion that the overall efficiency of these economies, and consequently the average standard of living of their population, could be much higher than under their present system – albeit at some social cost, especially the danger of open unemployment.

However, one can still offer some conjectures on the performance of the envisaged schemes, assuming they could be introduced and that they would last. Each of them requires a separate treatment. Here I can make only a few points. It seems possible that at least some of these schemes could raise the overall efficiency of even the most reformed socialist economies. Such schemes would increase the autonomy of

---

[4] For more on this, see Balcerowicz 1987.

enterprises and create more scope for competition. However, these potential gains in efficiency appear to be lower than those achievable under capitalism. This is primarily due to the above-mentioned closed nature of the domestic property law under the envisaged schemes. This would limit the flow of the new enterprises (founded independently of the state and of already existing firms) and thus also limit the introduction of new ideas and new competition.[5] It is worth noting that in this respect the workers' property model fares better than the Illyrian socialism model or leasing model. This is because, in the former case, private persons would be able to found an enterprise at their own risk and on their own behalf, albeit only in the prescribed form of a workers' enterprise. This constraint would probably still limit the supply of entrepreneurs as compared to that possible under the open property law, where the would-be founders can freely choose between various legal forms of enterprises, including the private ones. For, under the form of a workers' enterprise, a potential founder might lose control over his own creation; therefore, maintaining control is probably an important consideration for would-be founders.

Apart from these (and other) general relative deficiences, each of the envisaged models might display some specific ones. For instance, Illyrian socialism is likely to face the problem of how to induce the enterprise's personnel to forgo the increases in their current income for the sake of intra-enterprise investment. The state holdings being the sole or main shareholders of enterprises might be the channel of the continued political interference into their affairs, etc.

Finally, one should mention that at least some of the deficiences of the capitalist market economy are likely to be present under the socialist one, too. This applies first of all to the danger of open unemployment. Indeed, under some market socialist schemes (especially Illyrian socialism) this danger might be greater than under capitalism.

Against this background and in the face of the grave economic problems in the CMEA countries, one wonders whether the search for the model of the market economy should be constrained by the adjective 'socialist'.

References

Balcerowicz, L. 1986 'Enterprises and economic systems, organizational adaptability and technical change', in H. Leipold & A. Schüller (eds), *Zur*

---

[5] For more on this, see Balcerowicz 1986.

Interdependenz von Unternehmens-und Wirtschaftsordnung, Gustav Fischer Verlag, Stuttgart, pp. 189–208.
—— 1987 'Remarks on the concept of ownership', *Oeconomica Polona*, no. 1.
Bársony, J. 1982 'Tibor Liska's concept of socialist entrepreneurship', *Acta Oeconomica* 28, nos 3–4, pp. 422–55.
Brutzkus, B. 1922 'Problemy narodnogo khoziaistva pri socialisticheskom stroje', *Ekonomist*, 2 (Moscow).
Święcicki, M. 1988 'Reforma własnościowa. Propozycje przekształceń polskiej gospodarki', mimeo.

4

The 'Socialist Calculation Debate' and Reform Discussions in Socialist Countries

The 'socialist calculation debate' (SCD) has been discussed in the economic literature many times (see, for example, Hoff 1949; Bergson 1948, 1967; Ward 1967; Delhaes 1983; Schoppe 1982; Neck 1982; Dore and Kaser 1984; Lavoie 1985; Bernholz 1987). It is known that before the Second World War the participants on the 'anti-socialist' side included Ludwig von Mises, Boris Brutzkus and Friedrich A. Hayek, and on the opposite side Fred A. Taylor, H.D. Dickinson, Oskar Lange, Joseph A. Schumpeter and Maurice Dobb.[1] The debate continued in the post-war period. Various mathematical procedures for decentralized planning, partly based on the previous proposals of the 'socialists', were then elaborated by Arrow and Hurwicz, Malinvaud and others (for a comprehensive analysis of these schemes, see Heal 1973). Some of the issues discussed during the SCD were generalized by Hurwicz (1960) in his concept of the 'allocation mechanisms'. The literature on this topic and on the related problem of 'incentive compatibility' has been growing very fast in recent years (for a review, see Radner 1987).

This chapter is based on work done between 1985 and 1988 and was written during the autumn of 1988 when I was a beneficiary of the Friedrich Ebert Foundation in West Germany. The financial assistance of the Foundation is gratefully acknowledged. It was first published in 1992 in *Reform and Transformation in Eastern Europe: Soviet-Type Economics on the Threshold of Change*, edited by János Mátyás Kovács & Márton Tardos (London, Routledge).

[1] For brevity, I will sometimes refer to the two sides of the SCD as 'anti-socialist' and 'socialist', respectively. These expressions denote the position taken during the debate and not necessarily the political sympathies of the participants.

Many participants in the SCD focused on the problem of rational calculation, or in other words, on the issue of the allocative efficiency of socialism. This is even more true of the commentators on the SCD. But it would be improper to reduce the SCD to the 'calculation debate' because some of the protagonists (mostly on the anti-socialist side) raised other issues as well.

In what follows, I will try to relate the SCD to the reform discussions in the socialist countries after the Second World War, that is, to investigate what kind of relationship (if any) exists between these two streams of economic thought. As far as the SCD is concerned, I will concentrate on the writings of the above-mentioned authors. With regard to the reform discussions, I shall focus my attention on those which have taken place in Poland and Hungary. I will disregard the question of to what extent the reform proposals (or the reform practice) in these countries have influenced the theoretical literature belonging to the SCD.[2] Finally, I will not try to trace the actual flow of ideas from the participants in the SCD to the reform economists, that is, to establish which of the latter were familiar with the SCD and which were not.

The relevant question is therefore this: did the contributions to the SCD contain anything of potential value to the reform economists?

The writings of the latter typically consist of two parts. One is a critical examination of the established (that is, Soviet-type) economic system. This may be called a diagnosis, as it aims at identifying the main weaknesses in the economic performance and at linking them to some aspects of the system. The second part is a description of the proposed new system, which, if established, would I hope eliminate the indicated weaknesses.[3]

I will first discuss the relevance of the SCD for the diagnostic part of the reform concepts and then for the reform proposals proper. One should, of course, remember that the diagnoses of the system may have an indirect impact on the reform proposals, as they influence the direction of the search for a better system.

---

[2] We may, however, mention some examples of this impact. The Soviet economic practice has heavily influenced the thinking of Dobb (1933). The quantity-guided planning schemes of Kornai and Lipták are theoretical models of the actual Soviet-type planning. The 1965 change in the system of material incentives in the Soviet Union spawned a sizeable analytical literature in the West (see Koont & Zimbalist 1984).

[3] Some reform concepts also contain the description of the transition path from the existing system to the reformed one. This is an issue of great practical importance, one that is relatively neglected in the literature on economic reforms.

The 'Socialist Calculation Debate' and the Diagnosis of the Failures of Socialism

THE PROBLEM OF ECONOMIC CALCULATION

This problem can be broken down into two broad issues:

1 The availability of proper economic data for comprehensive central planning.
2 The informational capacity of the centre; that is, the capacity to assimilate and process the data in such a way as to arrive at rational decisions with regard to the allocation of resources.

The original challenge of the anti-socialist critics centred on the first issue. One can distinguish here two problems. Brutzkus (1922b, pp. 167–70) was one of the few authors who pointed out that identifying consumer preferences and, consequently, determining the correct structure of the production of consumer goods in the absence of a market for these goods, may be a relatively easy task only at a very low level of economic development.[4] With income per capita rising, there would be, however, an increasing differentiation of consumer preferences and the problem would become very complex. Physiological norms as the basis for consumption planning would not do. Similar points were made by Hoff (1949, pp. 74–5, 182–3). In contrast, Mises, widely perceived as the main protagonist on the anti-socialist side of the SCD, did not pay much attention to the difficulties in the central determination of the structure of the production of consumer goods. He even stated (1935, p. 107) that 'the economic administration [in the socialist state] may know exactly what goods are most urgently needed'.

The second problem, which lay at the very heart of the calculation debate, was the alleged lack of proper economic data for identifying the optimal combination of resources to produce a given output, that is, to establish which production technique is the cheapest. This point was emphasized both by Brutzkus and Mises. Both authors derive this assertion from the lack of markets for the means of production in socialism (as envisaged by the Marxists), and both try to show why free market prices are the indispensable informational input for rational calculation. There is, however, one difference between them. Mises goes

---

[4] Brutzkus obviously assumed that socialist production is to be adapted to the consumers' preferences. This was an assumption that only few socialist participants of the SCD would contest. One of them was Dobb (1933, p. 591).

one step further and maintains that only the institutions typical of capitalism can ensure that proper market information will be generated,[5] while Brutzkus admits the possibility of an efficient 'market socialism' and even provides its outline (see the third section).

By contrast, Mises emphasizes that the problem of calculation only arises under the inherently dynamic, changing conditions of the real world (1951, p. 122):

> if we assume that the socialist system of production were based upon the last state of the system of economic freedom which it superseded, and that no changes were to take place in the future, we could indeed conceive a rational and economic Socialism. But only in theory. A stationary economic system can never exist. Things are continually changing, and the stationary state, although necessary as an aid to speculation, is a theoretical assumption to which there is no counterpart in reality.

Thus, contrary to the opinions of many later commentators, Mises's challenge as to the impossibility of rational calculation in socialism referred to the real world and not to the imaginary world of economic theory (cf. Lavoie 1985, pp. 48–77):

The main response on the socialist side to Mises's challenge was to propose procedures of iterative, price-guided planning, whereby the Central Planning Board takes the place of the Walrasian auctioneer by fixing the prices by trial and error and the enterprises' and industries' managers are instructed to follow the rules of welfare economics. Oskar Lange (1938) is widely considered to have elaborated the fullest non-mathematical version of these procedures. It was later formalized by Kenneth Arrow and Leonid Hurwicz (1960). Another version was elaborated by Malinvaud (1967). These economists concentrated on the convergence property of the proposed schemes and demonstrated that under some restrictive assumptions (for example, no incentive problem, no externalities, no increasing returns to scale) there is, within the framework of their mathematical models, a convergence to Pareto-satisfactory equilibrium.

However, as soon as one leaves the realm of pure theory and tries

[5] Mises argues that capitalist ownership is indispensable for rational calculation because it provides the necessary autonomy and the necessary incentives for the economic subjects to try to forecast future economic data, including future prices correctly. Capitalist institutions are also important for rational calculation because they separate – through the mechanism of bankruptcy – those which are especially competent in this forecasting activity from those who are not. Mises thus considers the capitalist institutions, which generate correct expectations and in turn shape the current market data, public goods (for more on this, see Murrell 1983).

to visualize the operation of these schemes in the real world, many doubts come to mind.[6] Most of them were formulated as early as 1940 by Hayek (1949, pp. 181–208). First, without dismissing the problem of the availability of proper data to the planning board, he emphasized its insufficient informational capacity, while referring to central price fixing by trial and error:

> when . . . one proceeds to consider the actual apparatus by which this sort of adjustment is to be brought about, one begins to wonder whether anyone should really be prepared to suggest that such a system will ever even distantly approach the efficiency of a system where the required changes are brought about by the spontaneous action of the persons immediately concerned.

Hayek adds, following Mises, that the difficulty arises out of the dynamic nature of the real world:

> If in the real world, we had to deal with approximately constant data . . ., then the proposal . . . would not be so entirely unreasonable. But this is far from being the situation in the real world, where constant change is the rule.

Other issues raised by Hayek include the omission of price expectations in the Lange-type scheme, and thus the disregarding of the problem of who is to bear the responsibility for the consequences of the decisions based on erroneous forecasts; the difficulty of identifying the marginal costs by the managers who are required to produce until these costs are just equal to the price of the good; the inability of the centre to set the prices in accordance with the differences in the quality of the goods, and so on.[7]

---

[6] This is not meant to be a critique of the post-war authors in mathematical planning, as if they were only interested in pure theory and refrained from making any claims as to the practical applicability of their models. This, however, cannot apply to Oskar Lange, who was directly responding to Mises's challenge. For Mises explicitly referred to the real world, and Lange responded with a proposal placed in the Walrasian world, thus assuming away most of the practical problems. Lange, it seems, either misread or ignored Mises's challenge (see Murell 1983). In an early critique of Lange's scheme, Hoff (1949) stated that 'Lange ought in any case, to have said that his alleged solution was not of practical value' (p. 188).

[7] In some other writings, including an earlier one (1935), Hayek also pointed out the problem of inarticulability of knowledge. He stressed that some of the knowledge possessed by the managers and relevant for decision-making cannot be articulated by them and, hence, communicated to the centre. This point has been recently developed by Lavoie (1986) (see also Sowell, 1980, pp. 218–20).

Hayek did not pay much attention to the question of why the socialist managers should follow the rules specified in the Lange-type schemes, which does not mean that he did not consider it as a problem. Rather, he wanted to show that *even if* the managers were perfectly willing to obey these rules, the procedure still could not work properly. Some other authors discussed *the incentive problem* related to these rules at greater length (see, for example, Bergson 1967; Ward 1967; Schoppe 1982; Pickersgill & Pickersgill 1974, pp. 310–14). The general point they make is that as soon as we abandon the unrealistic assumption of the harmony of interest between the managers and the centre, new difficulties emerge: the former may (a) misrepresent the input needs and production possibilities; (b) behave in a monopolistic way by limiting production and thus creating artificial shortages in order to get higher prices; (c) pressure the centre for more investment outlays than is economically rational; and so on.

Taking into account the conflict of interests means that one passes from the analysis in terms of the team-theory (in the Marschak-Radner sense) to the game-theory approaches. Indeed, such approaches to the analysis of central planning have been intensively developed in recent years. However, as John Roberts (1987, p. 350), who made a significant contribution to the formulation of this line of analysis, points out, the positive results in game-theory approaches to planning have been achieved by using at least one of a pair of unpalatable assumptions: 'a myopia assumption, that postulates that agents, in choosing their messages at any iteration, care only about the change in their utilities at the iteration', and the assumption of complete information. With regard to the latter he rightly comments: 'in reality one believes that individuals are not perfectly informed about one another; indeed, if they were, it is not clear why we would need any decentralized procedure'. This reminds us to some extent of the objections of Mises and Hayek to analysing the calculation problem in a static framework, which assumes away the informational complexities.

INITIATIVE, RISK-BEARING, INNOVATION

What would happen to actions involving risk, if the competitive market system based on private enterprises were replaced by comprehensive bureaucratic planning linked to the state ownership of the means of production? One difficulty noted both by Brutzkus (1922a, pp. 53–4; 1922c, p. 57) and Mises (1935, pp. 116–18) is how to make the socialist managers responsible for the losses incurred by their enterprises.

Both predicted that the lack of appropriate mechanisms of managers' financial responsibility would lead to a tendency to fill this gap by detailed bureaucratic regulations, constraining the initiative of the managers. The tendency for bureaucratization was also emphasized by Hayek (1949, pp. 198–9) in his analysis of the Lange-type schemes, whereby the managers are required to follow some centrally determined rules:

> From the point of view of the manager, it will be much more important that he should always be able to prove that in the light of knowledge he possessed the decision actually taken was the right one than that he should prove to be right in the end. If this will not lead to the worst forms of bureaucracy, I do not know what will.

The bureaucratic restrictions on the managers' initiatives were considered by Brutzkus (1922c, p. 57) to lead to poor innovative performance of the socialist economy, to 'technical inertia and conservatism'. He considered bureaucratization a sufficient reason for this, but also pointed out another potential barrier: the lack of sufficient material regards for the would-be inventors and innovators.

With regard to innovation, Hayek (1949, pp. 196–7) emphasized that it is competition that brings about the discovery of the new production techniques which result in the lowering of the level of costs. The socialist economy, based on planning that replaces the market, would therefore be deprived of the major innovative force. A somewhat related point was made by Hoff (1949, p. 89). He noticed that in a capitalist society there is always a number of persons 'irresistibly attracted' by risky investment in new technical developments. Such persons will also be found under socialism 'but it will not be possible to make use of their peculiar attributes and self-sacrifice, as the socialist community does not allow commercial activity on one's own account'. Hoff thus pointed out the direct link between the type of property rights and the innovative performance of the economy.

And what were the views of the prominent representatives of the social side of the SCD? Lange (1938, pp. 109–10) admitted that the bureaucratization of economic life may indeed be a danger under socialism, but he claimed that he couldn't see 'how the same, or even greater, danger can be avoided under monopolistic capitalism'.[8] It is also this allegedly growing monopolization which was responsible, in his

---

[8] For more on Lange's views on bureaucratization under socialism, see Kowalik 1992.

view, for capitalism's increasing inability to exploit new technological opportunities (pp. 112–15).[9]

Schumpeter (1962) was no less confident about the relatively innovative possibilities of socialism. He assumed that industrial managers would be instructed to produce as economically as possible, and as a result they would introduce new and more efficient pieces of machinery (p. 178). He also thought that 'in the socialist order every improvement would theoretically spread by decree and substandard practice could promptly be eliminated' (p. 196).[10]

CONSEQUENCES OF THE CENTRALIZATION OF INVESTMENT

In Lange's model, the centre was to determine only the overall volume of investment, while its allocation among the various industries and plants was to be left in the hands of lower-level managements. Hayek (1949, pp. 200–1) pointed out that any attempt at practical application of this model would most likely result in a widespread central control of investment. Lange himself changed his position and advocated that the centre should directly determine the allocation of investment. Hence, he joined his socialist critics (for example, Dobb, Baran and Sweezy) in the belief that direct central control over investment is the source of the basic superiority of socialism over capitalism. Such a control was thought to lead to a better coordination of investment (that is, avoiding the 'duplication' of the productive capacities). The centre was also regarded as being capable of foreseeing the technological developments and of ensuring that the selected investment projects would reflect the 'general interests' of the economy. Besides, the central determination of the rate of accumulation was to ensure a higher rate of growth,[11] for the individual consumers were considered notoriously short-sighted.

It was left to the anti-socialist critics to point out the dangers of the

---

[9] In comparing socialism with capitalism, Lange was thus using two different paradigms. While describing his proposed socialist system he was operating most of the time (except for the rare moments of realism as in the case of bureaucratization) within the Walrasian framework, where the most important practical problems of socialism were assumed away. However, in describing capitalism he was using the Marxist paradigm, according to which capitalism was inevitably developing into a monopolistic phase.

[10] It is not clear what Schumpeter meant by 'theoretically'. The following passage implies, however, that he had in mind a real possibility, that is, a possibility of socialism operating in the real world.

[11] Thus, even if allocative efficiency and consumer sovereignty suffered from the centralization of investment, the sheer volume of the investment outlays was thought to be sufficient to ensure that, in a relatively short time, the consumers would be better off than under the capitalist system starting from the same level of development.

centralization of investment. Brutzkus (1922b, pp. 170–2) emphasized that the investment decisions taken by the centre would be politically motivated and, therefore, of poor economic quality. He also predicted that the central distribution of the investment outlays would induce the lower levels, unconstrained by any fear of bankruptcy, to put enormous pressure on the centre in order to get as many means allocated as possible. As a result, the overall co-ordination of investment would be so poor as to make the 'capitalist anarchy' appear in perfect harmony (Brutzkus 1922b, p. 173). A similar point was made by Hoff (1949, p. 206), who also questioned the ability of the central authorities to display a greater foresight with regard to technical developments and the future preferences of consumers than the 'autonomous concerns in the capitalist society where managers and owners are more or less dependent for their living on the correctness of their judgment'. Hoff also contended that 'if a central authority should prove unwilling to admit to mistakes, the development will continue in the same false direction, so that final readjustment will be more painful than the trade fluctuations of the capitalist society'.

How to explain these differences in the various views on the consequences of the centralization of investment? They stem, it seems, from the profound divergence in the assumptions on the nature of the socialist state. The proponents of socialism implicitly assumed that central decision-makers would have no informational problems[12] and that they would only be interested in serving the 'social interest'. The anti-socialist critics had much more realistic views on the nature of the socialist state (and on all states, for that matter).

SHORTAGES

This phenomenon, characteristic of socialist economies, was not in the centre of the SCD. One can find, nevertheless, some penetrating observations on this topic, mostly made by the anti-socialist critics. Brutzkus (1922c, p. 57) stated, for example, that comprehensive planning replacing the market mechanism would lead to price rigidity and to the unresponsiveness of the supply of consumer goods to the changing demand for them. The resulting shortages of these goods would in turn

---

[12] Hayek (1949, p. 201) observed, with respect to the seemingly – decentralized schemes of Lange and Dickinson, that their authors console themselves, while describing the advantages of central control over investment, with hope for the 'omnipresent, omniscient organ of the collective community'.

weaken the incentives to work. Brutzkus (1922b, p. 172) also predicted that the administrative rationing of inputs would generate massive misallocation.

The issue of shortages was also raised by Hayek (1949, p. 193) in his critique of central price-setting, proposed in the Lange-type models. Hayek pointed out that, because of inevitable delays in this process, and due to the inability of the centre to fix prices in accordance with the differences in the quality of goods, 'a great many prices would be at most times substantially different from what they would be in a free market'. In other words, the administrative prices would often diverge from the market-clearing level. One should therefore not confuse a 'simulated' market with the real one.[13]

COMMENTS

Anyone familiar with the experiences of the socialist economies easily recognizes that the problems of socialism identified by its critics during the SCD[14] overlap, to a large extent, with the weaknesses of the Soviet-type economic system. These were pointed out during the reform discussions in the socialist countries and provided the rationale for the reform proposals.

In contrast, some of the prominent participants on the socialist side of the SCD formulated predictions as to the beneficial effects of socialist schemes, which, from the perspective of real socialism, appear rather naive. Apart from the aforementioned belief in the advantages of the centralization of investment, one may recall Lange's (1938, p. 48–107) claim that socialism would solve – thanks to the elimination of private

---

[13] This is why the term 'market socialism' should be used in my view only with respect to those models that envisage a genuine market, which includes free price-setting.

[14] The critics also raised other issues. Brutzkus (1922, pp. 58–61), for example, argued that the state ownership of the means of production and centralized planning are incompatible with civil and political liberties, a point developed later by Hayek. Brutzkus (1922c, p. 62) also contrasted two approaches to social problems: one which advocates a total overhaul of the existing institutions of capitalist society in the belief that the new system would ensure universal happiness, and another, more modest approach, which aims at combating concrete social evils. This reminds us of Hayek's critique of 'constructivism' and of Popper's critique of 'holistic' social engineering.

Mises (1951, p. 202) has some interesting thoughts to offer to those reform economists who think that the main economic problem of real socialism lies in the lack of political democracy and not in the nature of property rights, and who thus advocate a 'democratization' or 'socialization' of central planning. For Mises envisaged such a 'democratic socialism' and argued that in such a system 'the opposition will always be ready to prove that more could be assigned to immediate satisfactions and the government will not be disinclined to maintain itself longer in power by lavish spending'.

entrepreneurship, and central price-setting – the problem of externalities, or that only socialism can reap the benefits of free competition. Schumpeter (1962) was even more optimistic in attributing to socialism the possibilities for more rapid technical change, higher workers' discipline, quicker structural change and lower administrative expenses – as compared to capitalism.

The 'Socialist Calculation Debate' and the Reform Proposals

In taking up this issue, we may first recall that the main response on the socialist side to Mises's challenge was the elaboration by Taylor, Lange and others of the price-guided schemes of central planning, or, in other words, of the 'simulated' market. However, these schemes have never been adopted by the economists in the socialist countries as the basis for their reform proposals. This was very well put by Marschak (1973, p. 47):

> The practitioners of economic reform in socialist countries attempting to decentralize a command economy have rejected any idea of adopting in some practical way the classic proposals for a socialist economy in the western literature. The scheme of Lange and Lerner, with market-clearing price-setting by a central agency and profit maximizing production decisions by managers, and the many later schemes which are its offspring, appear to be treated with amusement, disdain, or total neglect.

We may add that this attitude towards practically-minded reforms is understandable. (Marschak himself names some of the reasons for this.) For these schemes, being the offshoots of orthodox neo-classical economics, disregarded essential complexities of the real world.[15] An attempt at applying them in practice was bound, therefore, to end up in complete failure or in the creation of an economic system very different from that envisaged in the schemes and quite similar to the traditional centralized planned economy (for more on the latter see Schoppe 1982). Hence, what has been considered the main socialist solution put

[15] For the critical assessment of the relevance of neo-classical economics to the comparative analysis of the real-world economic systems (and therefore, to reform economics), see Nelson 1981; Neck 1982; and Nove 1992. Some newer developments in Western economic theory might be, however, more relevant to the reform economists (see Grosfeld 1992; and Kovács 1993). This does not mean that these new concepts provide detailed blueprints for better systemic arrangements, but that they indicate in what directions one should look for them.

forward during the SCD did not find any counterpart in practically-oriented reform thinking in the socialist countries. By contrast, for a long time the reformers seemed to be in basic agreement with the socialist critics of Lange-type models as to the desirability of the centralization of basic investment decisions. This is clearly visible in the influential book by Włodzimierz Brus (1961), who proposed a decentralized model, whereby the decisions regarding the current operations of the firms would be largely decentralized but the central authorities would retain direct control over new investment. This kind of a model appears to constitute a basic 'reform paradigm' in the 1060s and 1970s in Poland and Hungary.[16] However, in the late 1980s not many reform economists in these countries believed in the merits of the centralization of investment.[17] (This scepticism is also shared not by the author of the 'decentralized model' – cf. Brus 1992). Thus, neither Lange-type schemes, nor those of his socialist opponents, are to be found nowadays among the reform proposals in the former socialist countries. The prevailing view in 1989 is that economic reform must involve the introduction of the genuine market mechanism.

Interestingly enough, this idea of economic reform can be found in Brutzkus (1922b, pp. 180–1), one of the most outspoken critics of Marxist and Soviet socialism. He envisaged a system in which natural resources and fixed assets were national property, but were placed at the disposal of independent groups of employees against payment of interest and rent. The community was to collect all non-labour incomes.[18] This was, in Brutzkus's view, not only desirable from the point of view of social equity, but also economically necessary because socialism, as he pointed out, reduces the propensity of individuals to save. The proposed system was to be based on the genuine market mechanism, comprising both consumer goods and the means of production. This vision of market socialism reminds us to some extent of the Tibor Liska's concept of 'entrepreneurial socialism' (see Bársony 1982). Leasing the state enterprises also constituted one of the preferred directions in recent economic reform proposals in the Soviet Union

---

[16] This paradigm was also popular in Yugoslavia (cf. Ellman 1971, p. 20).

[17] This scepticism is well founded. Besides the aforementioned doubts as to the economic rationality of central investment decisions, one could note the fact that the centralization of investment precludes the free entry by new competitors and makes difficult, if not impossible, the delineation of the financial responsibility of enterprises. For the latter can always claim that their financial difficulties are due to the mistaken investment decisions of the superior bodies.

[18] The payments for the entrepreneurial services were, however, to be included in labour incomes.

(Muzhin 1989). Leasing the state land to the farmers has been the backbone of the 'responsibility system' in Chinese agriculture since 1979 (see Erling 1984).

Some participants on the socialist side of the SCD also sketched out schemes of 'market socialism' (see Hoff 1949, pp. 139–46, 153–63). For example, Roper (1931, pp. 60–2, quoted in Hoff 1949, p. 140), after a critical examination of the system based on central price-fixing by trial and error, arrived at the following conclusion: 'the best chance for success of a socialist community lies in a decentralized organization which retains, so far as possible, the strong features of capitalism.'

This general proposition reminds us of the recent search in socialist countries for models of – what one could call – *'simulated capitalism'*, without private capitalists. The main idea here was to transform the present state enterprises into joint-stock companies exclusively, or predominantly, owned by some non-private institutions. There would also exist a stock exchange on which the latter could buy and sell shares. Depending on what institutions are to become shareholders, we get some more specific models. One of them heavily emphasizes the role of the state holdings. Another proposal additionally admits non-administrative institutions like banks, pension funds, municipalities, universities, and so on. One can envisage still another variant where each enterprise would be predominantly owned by some other enterprises, a minority share belonging to its own personnel as represented by the workers' council.[19]

Such proposals were often accompanied by demands to lift the restrictions on the founding and developing of private firms. Indeed, liberal laws with respect to the domestic private sector were passed in Poland and Hungary before 1989. There was also a considerable liberalization of foreign investment in these countries.

All these were signs of a – so much needed – economic pragmatism. But a student of the SCD cannot help but recall Mises's assertion (1951, pp. 217–20) that the effective reform of the socialist economic system entails, in fact, a return to capitalism. In any case one can – somewhat pointedly – subsume the development of the reform concepts in the countries of real socialism as 'the imitation of capitalism under increasingly relaxed constraints'.[20] The original Marxian model of socialism resembled one huge capitalist factory with all operations being centralized. Then there appeared the proposal for the decentralization of

---

[19] For various proposals of 'simulated capitalism' see, for example, Tardos 1992; Antal *et al.* (eds) (1987); Święcicki (1988); 'Privatising in China' (1989).
[20] The main departure from this trend is the model of the labour self-managed economy. But it has its own problems as the vast literature on 'Illyrian socialism' shows.

current operations with the basic investment decisions remaining in the hands of the centre, that is, there was no capital market included in the system. This resembles the large capitalist corporation. The next step was 'simulated capitalism', which allows for a capital market but bans or heavily restricts private shareholders. Freedom to establish private firms and the privatization of state enterprises are the final point in the whole process, thus fulfilling Mises's ironic prediction.

References

Antal, L., Bokros, L., Csillag, I., Lengyel, L. & Matolcsy, G. (eds) 1987 'Turnaround and reform', *Közgazdasági Szemle* 6.

Arrow, K.J., & Hurwicz, L. 1960 'Decentralization and computation in resource-allocation', in R.W. Pfouts (ed.) *Essays in Economics and Econometrics in Honour of Harold Hotelling*, Chapel Hill, NC, University of North Carolina Press.

Bársony, J. 1982 'Tibor Liska's concept of socialist entrepreneurship', *Acta Oeconomica* 3–4.

Bergson, A. 1948 'Socialist economics', in Howard Ellis (ed.) *Survey of Contemporary Economics*, Philadelphia, Blakiston.

Bergson, A. 1967 'Market socialism revisited', *Journal of Political Economy* 5, 655–73.

Bernholz, P. 1987 'Information, motivation, and the problem of rational calculation in socialism', in Svetozar Pejovich (ed.) *Socialism. Institutional, Philosophical and Economic Issues*, Dordrecht, Kluwer Academic Publishers, 147–75.

Brus, W. 1961 'Ogólne problemy funkcjonowania gospodarki socjalistycznej', Państwowe Wydawnictwo Naukowe Warszawa (English version (1972) *The Market in a Socialist Economy*, London, Routledge & Kegan Paul).

—— 1992 'From revisionism to pragmatism: sketches to a self-portrait of a "reform economist"', in Kovács & Tardos (eds), *Reform and Transformation in Eastern Europe*, 136–42.

Brutzkus, B. 1922a 'Problemy narodnogo khoziaistva pri socialisticheskom stroie' ('Problems of the national economy in a socialist system'), *Ekonomist* 1, 48–65 (Moscow).

—— 1922b 'Problemy narodnogo khoziaistva pri socialisticheskom stroie' ('Problems of the national economy in a socialist system'), *Ekonomist* 2, 163–83 (Moscow).

—— 1992c 'Problemy narodnogo khoziaistva pri socialistcheskom stroie', ('Problems of the national economy in a socialist system') *Ekonomist* 3, 54–72 (Moscow).

Delhaes, K 1983 'Zur Diskussion über die Funktion der Preise im Sozialismus', *Arbeitsberichte zum Systemvergleich* 4, Marburg, Forschungsstelle zum Vergleich wirtschaftlicher Lenkungssysteme.

Dobb, M 1933 'The economic theory and the problems of a socialist economy', *Economic Journal* 43, 588–98.

Dore, M.H.J., & Kaser, M.C. 1984 'The Millions of equations debate: seventy years after Barone', *Atlantic Economic Journal* 3, 30–44.

Ellman, M. 1971 *Soviet Planning Today*, University of Cambridge Department of Applied Economics, Cambridge University Press.

Erling, J. 1984 'Reformen in der Chinesischen Landwirtschaft', in T. Bergmann, P. Grey & W. Quaisser (eds) *Sozialistische Agrarpolitik*, Köln, Bund-Verlag, 214–31.

Grosfeld, I. 1992 'Reform economics and western economic theory: unexploited opportunities', in Kovács & Tardos (eds), *Reform and Transformation in Eastern Europe*, 62–79.

Hayek, F.A. 1935 'The present state of the debate', in F.A. Hayek (ed.) *Collectivist Economic Planning*, London, Routledge, 201–43.

—— 1949 'Socialist calculation III: the competitive "Solution"', in *Individualism and Economic Order*, London, Routledge & Kegan Paul, 181–208, reprinted from *Economica* VII (26) (1940).

Heal, G.M. 1973 *The Theory of Economic Planning*, Amsterdam, North Holland.

Hoff, T.J.B. 1949 *Economic Calculation in the Socialist Society*, London, William Hodge & Co. (Norwegian original published in 1938).

Hurwicz, L. 1960 'Optimality and informational efficiency in resource allocation mechanisms', in K. Arrow, S. Karlin & P. Suppes (eds) *Mathematical Methods in the Social Sciences*, Stanford, Calif., Stanford University Press.

Koont, S., & Zimbalist, A. 1984 'Incentive and elicitation schemes: a critique and an extension', in A. Zimbalist *Comparative Economic Systems: Present Views*, Boston, Kluwer – Nijhoff Publishing, 159–75.

Kovács, J.M. 1992 'Compassionate doubts about reform economics', in Kovács & Tardos (eds), *Reform and Transformation in Eastern Europe*, 299–334.

Kovács, J.M., & Tardos, M. (eds) 1992 *Reform and Transformation in Eastern Europe: Soviet-type Economics on the Threshold of Change*, London, Routledge.

Kowalik, T. 1992 'Reform economics and bureaucracy', in Kovács & Tardos (eds), *Reform and Transformation in Eastern Europe*, 164–76.

Lange, O. 1938 'On the economic theory of socialism', in B.J. Lippincott (ed.) *On the Economic Theory of Socialism*, Minneapolis, University of Minnesota Press, 55–120.

Lavoie, D. 1985 *Rivalry and Central Planning: The Socialist Calculation Debate Reconsidered*, Cambridge, Cambridge University Press.

—— 1986 'The Market as a procedure for discovery and conveyance of inarticulate knowledge', *Comparative Economic Studies* 28(1), 1–19.

Malinvaud, E. 1967 'Decentralised procedures for planning', in E. Malinvaud & M.O.L. Bacharach (eds) *Activity Analysis in the Theory of Growth and Planning*, London, Macmillan.

Marschak, Th.A. 1973 'Decentralizing the command economy: the study of a pragmatic strategy for reformers', in M. Bronstein (ed.) *Plan and Market. Economic Reform in Eastern Europe*, New Haven, Yale University Press, 23–64.

Mises, L. von 1935 'Economic calculation in the socialist commonwealth', in F.A. Hayek (ed.) *Collectivist Economic Planning*, London, Routledge, 87–130 (German original published in 1920).

—— 1951 *Socialism: an Economic and Sociological Analysis*, New Haven, Yale University Press (German original published in 1922).

Murrell, P. 1983 'Did the theory of market socialism answer the challenge of

Ludwig vom Mises? A reinterpretation of the socialist controversy', *History of Political Economy*, 92–105.

Muzhin, A.B. 1989 'Arenda gosudarstvennykh predpriatii v SSSR', mimeo, Sopron.

Neck, R. 1982 '"Die Sozialismusdebatte" im Lichte ausgewählter neurer Entwicklungen der ökonomischen Theorie', *Jahrbuch für Sozialwissenschaft* 2, 242–64.

Nelson, R.R. 1981 'Assessing private enterprise: an exegesis of tangled doctrine', *Bell Journal of Economics* 12(1), 93–111.

Nove, A. 1992 'Soviet reforms and western neo-classical economics', in Kovács & Tardos (eds), *Reform and Transformation in Eastern Europe*, 103–20.

Pickersgill, G., & Pickersgill, J.E. 1974 *Contemporary Economic Systems: A Comparative View*, Englewood Cliffs, NJ, Prentice-Hall.

'Privatising in China' 1989 *The Economist*, 11 February, 62.

Radner, R. 1987 'Decentralization and incentives', in T. Groves, R. Radner & S. Reiter (eds) *Information, Incentives and Economic Mechanisms: Essays in Honour of Leonid Hurwicz*, Oxford, Basil Blackwell, 4–47.

Roberts, J. 1987 in T. Groves *et al.* (eds) *Information, Incentives and Economic Mechanisms: Essays in Honour of Leonid Hurwicz*, Oxford, Basil Blackwell, 349–74.

Roper, W.C. 1931 *The Problem of Pricing in a Socialist State*, Cambridge, Mass., Harvard University Press.

Schoppe, S.G. 1982 'Das Problem der Wirtschaftsrechnung in einer Zentralverwaltungswirtschaft aus neuer burokratiethoeoretischer Sicht', *Jahrbuch für Sozialwissenschaft* 2, 225–41.

Schumpeter, J.A. 1962 (1st edn 1942) *Socialism, Capitalism, and Democracy*, New York, Harper & Row.

Sowell, Th. 1980 *Knowledge and Decisions*, New York, Basic Books.

Święcicki, M. 1988 'Reforma wlasnosciowa', mimeo, Warsaw.

Tardos, M. 1992 'The property rights in Hungary', in Kovács & Tardos (eds), *Reform and Transformation in Eastern Europe*, 283–296.

Ward, B. 1967 *The Socialist Economy: A Study of Organizational Alternatives*, New York, Random House.

5

On the Reformability of the Soviet-Type Economic Systems

There is now a general agreement that the Soviet-type economic system (STES) displays great resistance to change: most of its attempted reforms have been rejected and practically none of them has produced – while it lasted – a radical increase in overall economic efficiency. One way of conceptualizing the reasons for these failures is to say that the reforms did not reach a required 'critical mass' or – in other words – that they did not pass a necessary 'threshold'. This conveys the idea that one cannot depart from the STES by accumulating successive partial changes. For while the next such changes are envisaged, the previous ones remain ineffective or are simply discarded outright. Thus, the main problem is that the reform of the STES is largely indivisible.

The present chapter takes up this idea of indivisibility, beginning with a discussion of the structure of the STES. In what follows I will focus on the reform in the socialist sector outside agriculture, thus disregarding the question of to what extent it is possible to improve the economic performance under the STES by allowing the private sector to grow, and whether the 'Chinese way', i.e. first reforming agriculture and then tackling the rest of the economy, has a general applicability.

This chapter was written in 1988 and first published in 1990 in *The Evolution of Economic Systems: Essays in Honour of Ota Šik*, edited by Kurt Dopfer and Karl-F. Raible (London, Macmillan), pp. 193–201.

The 'Constructional Logic' of the Soviet-Type Economic System

This logic is manifested in the fact that the STES has certain basic characteristics which give rise to a number of derivative features. The distinction between these groups of traits is not based on their importance for economic performance, but that by definition the basic features generate, *regardless of the will of the economic actors*, the derivative features, not the other way round. The basic features themselves are interrelated, i.e. some of them are more important in shaping the STES than others.

One can distinguish four basic characteristics:

(1) The most essential basic feature is the command-rationing mechanism (CRM), i.e. the planning targets, administrative allocation of inputs, and the material balances which are meant to harmonize the first two instruments. All this is expressed in a comprehensive and relatively detailed central plan broken down during interlevel bargaining. In its coordinating and allocative functions the CRM replaces a product market.

(2) Given the inevitable human informational limitations, the CRM requires for its operation a special organizational system. Its principal features are: the hierarchical subordination of the lower echelon managers to the superior state and party bodies (the nomenklatura mechanism);[1] a highly developed central and intermediate administration; and an extreme organizational concentration whereby smaller enterprises exist mostly as parts of huge centralized organizations.

(3) To maintain this system of organization, the centralization of rights to create, restructure and dissolve organizations is in turn necessary. Private individuals and enterprise managers are thus largely barred from taking these actions. This is especially true of creating new enterprises. Other mandatory features include the assignment of enterprises to specific branches; the prohibition of independent ties between different organizations and the elimination of enterprises through administrative procedures rather than through bankruptcy. This *centralization of organizational rights* precludes the spontaneous

---

[1] A nomenklatura mechanism is largely operated by the party apparatus. It should be noted, however, that in the monoparty system of the Soviet type the distinction between the party and state administration is a fiction. Party apparatus should be regarded, therefore, as a prominent part of a – conceptually broadened – apparatus of the state.

evolution of the organizational system and ensures that it preserves the basic form necessary for the operation of the CRM.

The centralization of organizational rights is an essential aspect of what may be called the closed or monopolizing domestic property law, i.e. the law which tries to ensure the monopoly of one particular form of the ownership of the means of production by barring other forms (Balcerowicz 1987). In the STES the favoured form is state ownership, but it could also be some type of the self-management solution as in Yugoslavia.

(4) Specific bureaucratic financial institutions carrying out massive inter-enterprise redistribution of funds are a necessary supplement to (1) and (3) and a substitute for the capital market. These institutions include: (a) a non-commercial banking system (a monobank), which distributes credit according to the stipulations of the central plan and not to the criteria of financial viability; and (b) an overgrown state budget which could be automatically financed by the monobank. There is no place for a securities market.

Various combinations of basic features lead to a number of interrelated derivative traits, for example:

- Administrative price fixing which in turn produces informationally defective prices;
- The isolation of domestic producers from foreign markets, stemming among other things from the domestic prices being unrelated to the world prices; the protectionist bureaucratic regulation of imports (licences, quotas, etc.) and a tendency for import substitution. They are, in my view, to a large extent by-products of command central planning, as planners seek to reduce the sources of uncertainty;
- Enterprises' soft budget constraint (Kornai 1986) resulting from the extensive government intervention, defective prices and the lack of commercial financial institutions;
- Extreme monopolization due among other things to the extreme organizational concentration, the centralization of organizational rights (which precludes free market entry), the lack of foreign competition and the soft budget constraint, which makes suppliers insensitive to a possible drop in demand.

Basic and derivative characteristics produce, given certain psycho-social invariants (the dominance of self-centred motivation, informational limitations of the decision-makers), a number of features of economic performance typical under the STES: low cost efficiency, low innovativeness, chronic shortages, etc.

The indicated links within the basic features, between them and the derivative characteristics, and among the latter themselves, may be called the *functional necessities*.[2] For these links are in force regardless of the will of the human actors. For example, if the CRM is to be maintained, a special hierarchical organizational system must be preserved too, regardless of whether one wants it or not. Thus only the abolition of the CRM makes possible – although in no way ensures – the transition to a radically different system of organization. The functional necessities largely stem from human informational limitations, either directly or indirectly. An example of the direct relationship is that the CRM requires a hierarchical organizational system, as it reduces the informational burden on the central decision-makers. To maintain this system the centralization of organizational rights is in turn necessary; this demonstrates how the informational limitations indirectly generate the functional necessities.

Besides these necessities there are also *motivational factors* that make the STES a highly indivisible whole. The problem here is that the STES – as with any other economic system – creates its own social structure, and that in the course of an economic reform certain powerful constitutent groups are bound to lose some of their power, prestige or income, or be subject to additional effort. It is, therefore, reasonable to expect that these groups will try to prevent or obstruct the reforms, for example, by using the nomenklatura mechanism informally to maintain direct control over the enterprises. This is why radical systemic changes are needed at the very beginning, as they reduce the danger of the rejection of the reform by neutralizing the groups which oppose it, and by creating or strengthening the groups which support it. But such steps are, of course, politically very difficult.[3]

---

[2] The study of these necessities belongs, in my view, to a hugely neglected field of the analysis of the economic systems, which should aim at establishing and explaining what country-wide combination of the systemic arrangements are empirically possible, what are empirically impossible and what are necessary. The knowledge of these relationships is obviously relevant for the study of the possible evolution of the respective economic systems, and for building their realistic typologies. It is also often necessary in explaining the impact of the selected systemic arrangements on the economic performance, since one should consider not only direct but also indirect influence of a given arrangement, i.e. an influence via other arrangements which are linked to it by functional necessities.

[3] This is why a radical economic reform is much more difficult to introduce than to maintain (disregarding the possibility of external liquidation of the reform). The reverse is true of the superficial reform.

The Reform Thresholds and Types of Economic Reform

From the 'constructional logic' of the STES we can now proceed to the reform thresholds. They are illustrated as 'stylized facts' in Figure 5.1 where r denotes the degree of radicalism of the economic reform,[4] e is the overall economic efficiency[5] and t is time measured from the start of the reform.

RT_1 signifies the first reform threshold. By definition it is passed when the CRM is largely replaced by other mechanisms of coordination but the remaining basic features of the STES are preserved. The second threshold, RT_2, is passed when all four basic characteristics are abolished. The left side of Figure 5.1 illustrates three types of economic reforms, or more precisely, their dynamics. On the right side, there is a function $e = e(r)$, which shows the maximum efficiency possible under the increasingly reformed economic systems. The shape of this function illustrates the basic problem of the reform: only radical changes enable a substantial increase in e, i.e. the achievement of the most important economic goal of the reform. Small steps give very little or practically nothing.

Economic reforms of the first type, ER_1, are below the RT_1, i.e. maintain all the basic features of the STES. These reforms attempt, for example, to replace the gross indicators with net ones – while preserving the command planning; to reduce the number of the binding targets; to shift some competence from the ministerial level to the regional bodies; to create new types of compulsory associations of enterprises, etc. (see Šik 1987, pp. 82–5). ER_1 have so far largely prevailed in socialist countries.[6] As illustrated by Figure 5.1, ER_1 have two characteristics. First, the new systemic arrangements brought about by them are largely subject to inevitable rejection. For these arrangements create additional tensions which are dealt with by recourse to the old directive methods, and these are used because the reform, being so superficial, preserves the institutional possibilities for using them (the principle of the directive planning, party–state nomenklatura). A related reason for the rejection of the ER_1 is that it leaves virtually untouched the bureaucratic apparatus opposing reform. The main motive for this

---

[4] The reform is, by definition, the more radical the wider is the application of the new arrangements and the more they depart from the STES.

[5] As measures, e.g. by the potential long-run rate of growth of aggregate consumption (cf. Schumpeter 1947, p. 190).

[6] The latest Soviet economic reform belongs so far, in my view, to ER_1. For analysis corroborating this assertion see Schüller & Peterhoff 1988.

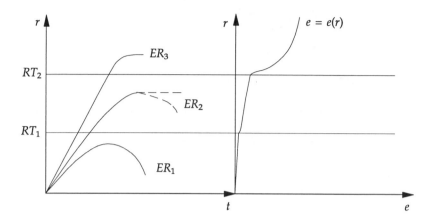

Fig. 5.1 *Reform thresholds*

resistance is, in the case of ER_1, as distinct from more radical reforms, not so much the fear that the reform will infringe upon material interests, power or ideology but the fact that under the ER_1 the main function of the apparatus remains the balancing of the material flows in the economy. However, some elements of the ER_1 make the performance of this function more difficult (Kantorovich 1988).

Second, during their short existence, the ER_1 can bring at most a minimal increase in e.[7] For these reforms preserve all the basic causes of low efficiency: the CRM, extreme monopolization, distorted prices, soft budget constraint, etc. With the persisting low efficiency, ER_1 is not able to improve the economic situation of the population and cannot count, therefore, on its support. There is thus a link between the economic performance of the reform and its capacity for survival.

The reforms ER_2 largely abolish the CRM – without, however, doing away with all the basic features of the STES. The Hungarian economic reform of 1968 and the Yugoslav reforms in the 1950s and 1960s are the main cases in point. Figure 5.1 illustrates two main characteristics of ER_2. First, they are also susceptible to the rejection process, although perhaps not so inevitably as ER_1. The recentralization in Hungary in 1973–79 and the hidden return to a quasi-administrative system in Yugoslavia in the 1970s (Mercinger 1985) demonstrate that

---

[7] This assessment is on the safe side. Some observers (cf. Kantorovich 1988) argue that the discussed reforms worsened the economic performance.

this is a real possibility. For the ER_2 still preserve a strong institutional potential for recentralization, especially a party–state nomenklatura.

Second, the systems brought about by ER_2 can be more efficient then the STES and the short-lived systems produced by ER_1 (see, e.g., Slama 1984). The basic reason for this is, in my view, the abandonment of the CRM. However, the possible increase in e brought about by ER_2 is still quite small. For having preserved some of the basic features of the STES – e.g., party-state nomenklatura, centralization of organizational rights, lack of a capital market – the ER_2 are still not able to eliminate two phenomena which rule out high efficiency: strong monopolization and the pervasive rent-seeking, i.e. the tendency of enterprises to concentrate on bargaining with superior bodies for the most convenient terms of activity. Thus, even the more radical reforms are not radical enough to solve the efficiency problem of real socialism.

This brings us to ER_3: economic reforms which would pass the RT_2 and therefore replace all the basic features of the STES with market-type systemic arrangements. It is there that the solution to the efficiency problem seems to lie. The category of ER_3 is, however, so far empirically empty, and the big question is how to get there. Another important problem is whether ER_3 include only reforms based on massive privatization, i.e. return to capitalism in the Marxist sense, or whether there is an equally efficient 'Third Way'. These questions require a separate treatment.

Concluding Remarks

The basic difficulty of the reform of the STES is that in order to be successful, i.e. to be able to survive and to produce a substantial increase in economic efficiency, it has to be very radical, or – in other words – it must pass a high threshold in a short time. One wonders, therefore, whether Popper's (1957, pp. 64–70) advocacy of 'piecemeal social engineering' applies to systems created by the previous 'holistic engineering'.

The concept of the reform thresholds suggests a useful approach to the analysis of the attempted reforms of the STES, one which could perhaps be better structured than some others. After establishing just what these thresholds are one should use them as a yardstick to assess the chances of the given reform, by inquiring whether the balance of socio-political forces is such that the necessary threshold can be passed. Space does not permit me to discuss this second issue. But it is obvious that the passing of this threshold requires quite extraordinary social and political circumstances.[8] Anybody familiar with the difficulties of introducing partial systemic changes, e.g. tax reforms in the West, will easily comprehend the political complexity of a successful economic reform of the STES.

The thesis about the high reform threshold suggests that in assessing the chances of the proposed reforms in socialist countries, one should be wary of using the hitherto popular formulation that a given proposal is 'a step in the right direction'. For this misses the essential issue of the magnitude of the step. It may well be that a proposed reform, although more radical than its predecessors, is still not enough to propel it beyond the minimum threshold. There would be then no difference between the two, as far as the final outcome is concerned: both would fail. Another popular idea to be avoided is that 'reform is a process'. This is a dangerous truism, as it may be taken to imply that the dynamic of the reform does not count. But we know that in order to be successful the reform must have a special dynamic: its first step has to be very big – if it is to get beyond the reach of the functional necessities within the STES and create a balance of socio-political forces favourable to the further existence and development of the reformed system.

References

Balcerowicz, L. 1987 'Remarks on the Concept of Ownership', *Oeconomica Polona*, no. 1, pp. 75–95.
Kantorovich, V. 1988 'Lessons of the 1965 Soviet Economic Reform', *Soviet Studies*, no. 2, pp. 308–16.
Kornai, J. 1986 'The Soft Budget Constraint', *Kyklos*, no. 1, pp. 3–30.
Mercinger, J. 1985 'Yugoslav Economic System and Performance of the Economy in the Seventies and Early Eighties', in P. Gey, J. Kosta & W. Quaisser (eds), *Sozialismus und Industrialisierung*, Frankfurt, Campus.
Popper, K. 1957 *The Poverty of Historicism*, Boston, Beacon Press.
Schüller, A., & Peterhoff, R. 1988 'Gorbatschov Reform – Modell für Osteuropa?', in H. Giger & W. Linder (eds), *Sozialismus-Ende einer Illusion*, Zürich, None Zürcher Zeitung.
Schumpeter, J.A. 1947 *Capitalism, Socialism, and Democracy*, New York, Harper & Row.
Sik, O. 1987 *Wirtschaftssysteme. Vergleiche – Theorie – Kritik*, Berlin, Springer.
Slama, J. 1984 'Empirische Prüfung der Wirkung der Reformen in den planwirtschaftlichen Ländern', *Jahrbücher für Nationalökonomie und Statistik*, vol. 6, pp. 537–56.

[8] In the case of the smaller socialist countries, as distinct from the USSR, it is not only the internal political developments but also the external ones (i.e. the evolution of the Soviet constraint) which determine just how radical the economic reform will be.

6

The Soviet-Type Economic System, Reformed Systems and Innovativeness

A Framework for Analysis

One of the basic weaknesses of the economies under the Soviet-type economic system (STE) is low innovativeness in the sphere of civilian technology relative to Western economies and even some NICs. This is shown by many studies, e.g., Amann 1983: Bergson 1983 and 1987; Hanson & Pavitt 1987; Poznanski 1984; Vogel 1983; Welfens 1987. The purpose of this chapter is to join these and other economists in trying to explain the innovative weakness of the STE. A few words about the impact of economic reforms on innovativeness follow but first some clarification of the basic concepts and relationships is in order.

'Innovation' is understood here in a broad sense, comprising not only the first but also subsequent introductions of a new product or production technique in a given country. In other words (technical) innovation results, if successful, in a technological element which is new at least to the introducing enterprise. 'New' does not necessarily mean 'beneficial' or 'effective' from a social point of view.

Innovativeness (I) is a concept often used but rarely defined. I shall try to do this by means of two other concepts: the rate of innovations (R) and their social efficiency.

This chapter summarizes my long-standing interest in the links between technical change and the economic systems, and was completed shortly before I entered the government in September 1989. It was originally published in *Communist Economies* 2, no. 1 (1990), pp. 3–23.

R expresses the relative scope or frequency of the innovative activity in a country. It may be defined in operational terms as the number of innovations introduced during a given time, or the total costs of innovative activity, both divided by some suitable measure, e.g., national product, in order to make R independent of the size of the economy.

Social efficiency (utility) refers to the social effects of the innovative activity, and is a much more difficult concept to define. For these effects could be of different kinds: changes in the level of aggregate consumption, in the size of involuntary unemployment, in working conditions, in environmental quality. Some of these changes are difficult to measure and any attempt to aggregate the partial indicators into a single one is always arbitrary. To simplify the problem I will focus only on the 'consumption' efficiency of innovations (CE), as measured by their direct and indirect contribution to the level of aggregate consumption (*cf.* Schumpeter 1962, p. 190).

This of course, makes, our analysis incomplete by leaving aside the important question of to what extent economic systems conducive to this type of efficiency have to sacrifice some other dimensions (e.g., full employment).

I define I as follows:

$$I = R.CE, \quad \text{where } R \gtreqless 0; \ CE \geq 0^{[1]} \tag{1}$$

This formula displays two fundamental cases of low innovativeness. In the first case R is low. In the most extreme situation: $R \approx 0$ and $I \approx 0$. This would refer to so-called traditional societies with stationary technology. In the second case CE is low owing to a poor choice of project and/or their inefficient execution.

By proposing the above definition of innovativeness I want to emphasize that the analysis of innovative activity under the varying economic systems should not be limited to its quantititative aspect, i.e., the R. For the differences in the social 'quality' of the selected innovations may be equally or more relevant to consumers' welfare

---

[1] In the case of innovations aimed at new production techniques and/or new machinery the CE may be defined as rising with the input savings made possible by these innovations, net of their costs. It is much more difficult to measure the CE of innovations in the consumer goods sphere. For there appears a difficult problem of evaluating the changes in the range and quality of these goods. An ideal solution would be to apply the 'hedonic prices', pioneered by Griliches (Stigler 1966, p. 78). For our purposes it suffices to assume that the CE is higher the greater the improvement in the quality, and the smaller the increase in the unit cost of the new product as compared to some previous one. Innovations bringing an increase in costs without any improvement in the quality should obviously be considered as having a negative value of CE.

(*cf.* Pejovich 1984, p. 429). This is especially true, as I will try to show, of comparisons between liberal competitive capitalism and traditional Soviet socialism.

There are, in my view, two basic determinants of an economy's level of R: the size of its human capital (H) and the type of economic system (ES). The role of H has been stressed, among others, by Schultz, who pointed out that a certain level of education is necessary to enable people to see new technological possibilities (Siebert 1985, p. 53). Mansfield (1968, p. 147) indicated in turn that it increases the adaptability of employees to new conditions of work. No simple relationship exists, however, between H and R, for there is an intervening variable, i.e., ES. Taking H and ES together one can formulate the following propositions:

(1) There is a critically low level of H denoted by H_{min} such that if $H \leq H_{min}$ then $I \approx 0$, regardless of ES. This is because a widespread lack of elementary modern knowledge renders innovative undertakings impossible ($R \approx 0$). The necessary condition for a positive I in backward countries is, therefore, investment in education.

(2) For any given $H > H_{min}$, the maximum value of I depends on ES.[2] For human capital constitutes only an innovative potential and ES determines how this potential is used.[3] Two countries with a similar H but different economic systems can therefore have quite divergent levels of I.

I will develop point (2) in the next section by showing how the STE limits innovativeness to a level much lower than is achievable with a similar level of H under competitive capitalism.

The problem of the impact of ES upon I can be reduced to two questions (1) What technical projects are selected under a given economic system? (2) How effectively can the chosen projects be executed? Question (1) involves both R (choosing between routine production and innovations) and CE (choosing between various kinds of innovation). Question (2) concerns only the latter. The CE rises with the efficiency of implementation of the selected projects, except when their choice is so poor that the introduction of the related new products or production

---

[2] This maximum value, which may be called the innovativeness frontier, can lie above the innovativeness actually achieved, if an erroneous economic policy is pursued.

[3] The type of economic system also influences to some extent the state of H, since the knowledge acquired in the institutions of formal education is later developed or depreciated depending on ES.

techniques would reduce consumer welfare. In this case, slow execution could be better than rapid execution.

Turning to question (1), we note that the choice made by any given agent depends on: (a) the availability to him of information about alternative actions; (b) his preferential ordering of various kinds of actions, i.e., their expected relative utility. A given action will be chosen only if it is known to an agent and if it has an appropriately high expected utility relative to other actions.

The distribution of information across alternative actions, i.e., which projects are known and which are not, depends to a large extent on the preferences of an agent. Routine, i.e., non-innovative, activity is always known to its executor. It is thus only the innovations which may be affected by the information barrier. To what extent this is the case depends on an agent's willingness to *search* for the innovative projects (or at least to assimilate the information channelled to him). This is why projects belonging to a class of actions which has a low expected relative utility are also likely to be largely unknown to an agent and therefore would not be selected. But even if they were known, they would be rejected. It is thus appropriate to focus on the relative expected utility of innovations to the relevant agents in the economy.

The preferences of any actor depend on: (a) his utility function; (b) his socio-institutional environment. Factor (a) determines what factors are motivationally relevant to an actor, i.e., what his motivators are; (b) shapes the actual and expected distribution of different variables across alternative kinds of actions, including variables which by virtue of (a) are motivators. In the multi-agent world (a) and (b) are interrelated. The utility function of any actor, by shaping its behaviour, influences the environment of some other actors, which in turn may influence the behaviour of the first actor, etc. Thus, by changing the utility function of a large class of domestic enterprises by nationalizing or privatizing them, we are also changing the environment facing each of them.

In every economic system it is the decision-makers in the enterprises[4] who ultimately decide whether to innovate and, if so, what the nature of those innovations will be. We may thus focus on the relative expected utility of innovations to an enterprise's managers. Their utility function, in a general form appropriate for the discussion of innovativeness, should be conceived as:

---

[4] This refers both to established enterprises and to potential ones, i.e., possible new entrants.

$$U = (E, IM, EM).\tag{2}$$

E stands for managerial effort. I shall realistically assume that under any economic system less is preferred over more of it, i.e.

$$\frac{\delta U}{\delta E} < 0.$$

IM refers to intrinsic motivation, linked solely to the performing of certain actions (e.g., achievement motivation, satisfaction from good work). Differences in *IM* stem from the varying personalities of managers. This allows us to disregard *IM*, on the assumption that the managers in the STE are in this respect not basically different from their counterparts under competitive capitalism.[5]

Ignoring *IM*, however, is only admissible with respect to the managers of established enterprises. In every society there are potentially innovative new entrants for whom the intrinsic satisfaction of implementing their own ideas may be especially great. It matters, therefore, to what extent an economic system allows such persons to act. (We shall return to this point later.)

Finally, *EM* signifies external motivators, i.e., income or managerial career. The nature of these motivators is largely independent of the economic system. The impact of the *ES* consists instead in varying the factors to which *EM* are linked and in shaping the form of this linkage.[6]

The expected relative utility of an innovation to an enterprise may be expressed as:

$$\Delta EU = EU_i - EU_c,\tag{3}$$

where EU_i stands for the expected utility of an innovation and EU_c for that of the routine production. An innovation will be chosen if $EU_i > EU_c$. It is obvious that EU_i may vary over time. For example, for a capitalist enterprise under competition it will be lower (and possibly negative) just after introducing a product innovation than when much time has already elapsed since the previous one. We may deal with this time dimension by asking how often, on average, (if at all) enterprises under the different economic systems perceive: $EU_i > EU_c$. An economic

---

[5] This assumption is rather on the safe side given the nomenklatura mechanism in the STE, which gives political loyalty a prominent place in selecting managers.

[6] We may write it as: $EM = S(x)$ where x is (are) the system-specific variable(s) to which *EM* are linked and S is the system-specific functional form of this linkage (including the would-be constraints on x). In simplified analyses, x (e.g., profit in the case of a private enterprise) is often directly treated as a determinant of the managers' utility function.

system with a higher frequency of this type is likely to display a higher R but not necessarily a higher I, for I depends not only on R but also on CE.

Let us now turn to the determinants of ΔEU_i; Formula (3) shows that ΔEU_i is higher, the lower is EU_c. Therefore, an economy in which enterprise managers expect to be – somehow – punished for not innovating, i.e., for relying on routine production, will, given the level of EU_i, display a higher ΔEU_i than an economic system where enterprises enjoy a permanently easy life. One can thus expect a higher R in the first case than in the second. Another point is that the decline of EU_c reduces, *ceteris paribus*, the level of EU_i, and consequently the level of EM, necessary for meeting the condition $EU_i > EU_c$. Hence, inducing enterprises to innovate may be 'cheaper' in an economic system with penalties for not innovating than in a system without such penalties.

Let us now consider managerial effort and denote by ΔE the perceived difference in this factor between an innovation and continuation. It may be assumed for any economic system that ΔE is positive and that on average it increases with an innovation's CE (for more on this, see Balcerowicz 1988, pp. 36–8). We recall that

$$\frac{\delta U}{\delta E} < 0.$$

We may further assume that – at least for the managers of established enterprises – the difference in the intrinsic motivation (IM) associated with innovations is not sufficient to offset ΔE. All this implies that, if innovations are to be undertaken by established enterprises in any economic system, positive and appropriately large *differential external incentives*, D_i, must be expected by the managers and that they must grow with CE. I define D_i as:

$$D_i = EEM_i - EEM_c \tag{4}$$

where EEM_i stands for the expected value of EM_i under innovation and EEM_c that under continuation. Let us now denote by ΔEM_i the difference between the highest level of EM which a firm can hope to get by choosing an innovation (i.e., the most optimistic variant of its outcome), and the most likely level of EM under routine production. We may safely assume that $D_i > 0$ only if $\Delta EM_i > 0$. In other words, if, by innovating, the firm cannot hope to gain more than it is most likely to achieve without innovation, the additional effort, ΔE, will not be offset and innovation will be rejected.

But this is not the end of the story. For the value of ΔE is much larger – for any given innovation – in some economic systems (owing to various institutional and real constraints on enterprises' actions) than in others.[7] Hence the values of D_i and ΔEM_i necessary for $EU_i > EU_c$, must – other things being equal – be larger in the first case than in the second. I will return to this below.

Another feature of innovations, besides additional effort, ΔE, is that – in contrast to the routine activity, which is already mastered – they may end in technical failure. Apart from this possible negative outcome, the very process of carrying out an innovation may disrupt the operation of an enterprise. To the extent that such events (technical failure, disruptions) give rise to penalties, i.e., reductions in EM, to the managers, innovations are *risky* to them. This risk tends, of course, to lower D_i and EU_i.[8] To offset this impact the value of ΔEM_i must rise still further above the level required to make up for ΔE. Furthermore, since the aforementioned events leading to risk are much more likely to be associated with highly efficient innovations than with inefficient ones, the necessary rise in the level of ΔEM_i is much higher in the first case than in the second. Finally, similarly to ΔE, the probability of the above-mentioned events, and the size of the penalties related to them, also vary – for any given class of innovations – with the economic system.

In concluding this section let us emphasize that it is much easier to elicit a high rate of innovation than high innovativeness. To achieve the first goal, all that is needed is a large ΔEM_i just for innovating. This requires that each enterprise's environment includes agents with a large rewarding or punishing potential (i.e., the ability to vary EM). However, if a high ΔEM_i were attached to any innovation, then enterprises would choose the easiest, most trivial and, therefore, least efficient projects. And with a low (possibly negative) CE, innovativeness could not be

---

[7] One can distinguish here between barriers to innovation perceived as surmountable and those perceived as insurmountable. The former can be expressed through ΔE and through the subjective probability of the technical success of innovation (p) having the value: $0 < p < 1$. In the latter case, besides increased ΔE, there is $p = 0$. This tends to lower ΔEU_i, especially if the technical failure is expected to lead to some penalties or if technical success is expected to bring high rewards.

[8] One may envisage an incentive system in which the risk of innovation is completely eliminated. Such systems, however, would not be conducive to high innovativeness, although they may induce a high rate of innovation. For the complete elimination of risk of innovating would cause moral hazard problems, i.e., induce enterprises to be reckless in their choice and execution of innovative projects. (For more on this see Balcerowicz 1988, pp. 38–43).

high. Hence a high level of I can be achieved only if D_i and EM_i are large for highly efficient innovations (radical cost reductions, sharp improvements in the quality of the products at relatively low cost), and small for inefficient ones (with opposite characteristics). This presupposes that agents who shape the EM obtained by enterprises not only have a large potential to reward or punish but also the ability to distinguish between innovations with different levels of CE. It is the lack of this selection capacity (and not the inability to vary EM) which is the main reason for the low innovativeness in the STE.

Characteristics of the Soviet-Type Economic System

The STE has a particular 'constructional logic', i.e., some basic characteristics which, given certain psycho-social invariants (e.g., dominance of self-centred motivation, information limitations of the decision-makers), are interrelated and give rise to a number of derivative features.

Both groups of characteristics were described in the previous chapter. Let us recall that the basic features include: (1) the command-rationing mechanism (CRM) usually called directive central planning; (2) a multilevel heirarchical organizational system with an extreme organizational concentration which rules out any competition among the suppliers; (3) the centralization of rights to create, restructure and dissolve orgnaizations, i.e., barring private persons from taking these actions; this centralization is an essential aspect of a closed regime of property rights; (4) massive centralistic redistribution of funds between enterprises via the budget and the monobank.

Various combinations of these features lead to a number of inter-related derivative traits, such as administrative price-fixing, enterprises' soft budget constraints, extreme monopolization, etc.

The basic and derivative characteristics generate a number of typical features of economic performance in the STE. One is low innovativeness – our dependent variable here. But there are many others, including some that have a great impact on I.

Chronic shortages are the most important element of the latter group. There is still much disagreement over what features of the STE generate shortages and how they do this, but there is little doubt that the responsible factors are systemic (see, e.g., Beksiak & Libura 1972; Kornai 1980; Gomulka 1986; Soos 1984). In my view they are the basic characteristics of the STE acting both directly and through some derivative elements, especially rigid prices and enterprises' soft budget constraint.[9]

The Soviet-Type Economic System and Innovativeness

Let us now see whether the condition for high innovativeness we formulated above can be met in the STE. We may first note that the additional effort, ΔE, is much bigger for any innovation in the STE than under liberal capitalism, and that this difference is especially large in the case of highly efficient innovations. The main reasons for this are input shortages and bureaucratic import protectionism. Innovations, as distinct from mere continuation, require qualitatively new inputs, and – on average – the more so, the more efficient they are to be. Obtaining these inputs under these conditions requires, however, much more additional effort than is the case with market clearing and free access to imports (see Berliner 1976, pp. 73–4).[10] An additional reason for the increased ΔE is the overall bureaucratization: changes in an enterprise's activity, especially significant ones, require a lot of paperwork (*cf.* Bergson 1983, p. 59).

The unreliability of domestic supplies and the closed nature of the economy must also make the enterprises' managers uncertain whether the new inputs necessary for an innovation will be available. As a result

[9] Generally speaking, rigid prices are, however, more important, as they are a sufficient condition for generating shortages while the soft budget constraint might not lead to them if prices were sufficiently flexible (*cf.* Gomulka 1986). But this refers only to shortages understood as the malfunctioning of the distribution system, i.e., various manifestations of not fully satisfied demand (queues, etc.). Such shortages should be distinguished from the disturbances in the sphere of production (and consumption) resulting from the lack of the right quantities of complementary goods. Typical examples of the second type of shortages are bottlenecks and forced substitution, i.e., breaching the requirements of complementarity by using technically unsuitable inputs for lack of the right ones. The distinction between these two types of spheres of shortages is analytically important, as it is generally easier to remove the first than the second. To do away with queues, a large increase in prices may be sufficient (at least for a while). But such an increase would not – in itself – eliminate the bottlenecks. In the second case flexible supply is of crucial importance, and such supply is impossible in the STE because of CRM and other basic characteristics of the STE. Rigid supply is, of course, also an important reason for shortages of the first type.

[10] In addition, shortages, i.e., unreliability of external supplies, give way to users' tendency to undertake production of the necessary inputs on their own. This is often small-scale production, where it is impossible to use specialized machinery; high unit cost and a low degree of standardization are the results (see Samborsky 1973, pp. 200–5.) Shortages also lead to what may be called 'forced' innovations, aimed at replacing the technically required but non-available inputs with imperfect substitutes. This helps to keep up production but usually at the cost of the quality of the products.

the subjective probability of such events as technical failure or disturbances in the course of an innovation must be higher for managers in the STE than for their counterparts under liberal capitalism. This difference in probability is again likely to be especially large in the case of highly efficient innovations. To the extent that the managers must expect some penalties for the aforementioned events – as indeed is the case in the STE (see later) – this increased probability further lowers the relative utility, ΔEU_i, for innovations with a high CE. Therefore, to offset the negative impact of increased E and increased technical risk upon ΔEU_i, a particularly high value of ΔEM_i must be associated with these innovations. But can this condition be met?

In considering this question let us first recall the extreme power of suppliers *vis-à-vis* buyers. This enables enterprises, in the absence of effective counter-measures, to achieve satisfactory sales and financial results by relying on the *status quo* production or on relatively inefficient innovations which sometimes lead to quality and price combinations that are worse than the previous ones from the point of view of the buyers (Borozdin 1975, p. 33). For under extreme monopolization the buyers are incapable of punishing the sellers by moving their demand to alternative sources of supply. This holds for monopoly under any economic system. But the monopolies in the STE, besides being incomparably stronger and more pervasive, are in one respect worse than their private counterparts. The latter are interested to some extent in cost-reducing innovations by virtue of their utility function alone (profit-linked EM), i.e., without competition. This is not the case for monopolies in the STE, for their EM are linked to plan fulfilment (see below).[11]

However, the proper, i.e., profit-based, utility function for enterprises cannot in itself, i.e., without competition, induce high innovativeness. First, because competition increases the relative expected utility of cost-reducing innovations by providing penalties for routine production and thus lowering its utility to the enterprise's management.[12] Second, because competition is absolutely crucial for the frequency and quality

---

[11] To make matters worse, the massive bureaucratic redistribution of enterprises' financial resources eliminates the possibility (not very likely in any case) that some of them could take up highly efficient innovations and autonomously grow 'around' them, bringing extraordinary financial rewards to persons involved in this process.

[12] But on the other hand, the increase in the number of actual and potential competitors may decrease the utility of innovation, EU_i, for each of them. Thus, as noted by Schumpeter (1962), some degree of temporary market power may offer the largest relative incentives to innovate. (For discussion of this issue see, e.g., Tandon 1984.) However, such temporary market power has little in common with the permanent monopoly that I have in mind above.

of product innovations, i.e., their *CE*. Profit-oriented monopoly can maintain a high level of utility for itself without such innovations or by making only negligible changes in the products, as it does not need to fear losing its customers.

Let us, however, return to the STE and note that shortages are doubly harmful to the relative utility of highly efficient innovations. On the one hand, the expected problems with getting the necessary inputs raise the ΔE and the risk associated with such innovations and thus call for an especially high level of ΔEM_i. On the other hand, widespread shortages are sufficient to eliminate competition among suppliers. This rules out the possibility of a high level of ΔEM_i resulting from the spontaneous interplay of buyers and sellers. There emerges, therefore, the need for widespread central regulation to remedy this situation and ensure a high relative utility of socially efficient innovations for enterprises. But is such regulation, substituting for the effects of competition, possible in the STE (or in any real economic system, for that matter)? To answer this question we have first to consider the incentive mechanism related to the *CRM*, i.e., to central planning. Let us start with the impact of this mechanism on the ΔEU_i of radical *cost-saving innovations*.

Under the CRM, the *EM* depend on plan fulfilment. The probability (f) of fulfilling a future plan decreases with its expected tautness (t), as measured by the ratio of output targets to input allocations. This means that getting easy plans, i.e., plans with the level of t low enough to ensure plan fulfilment ($f \approx 1$), offers enterprise managers a high utility.

The managers also know that the superior authorities, lacking other information, tend to base each subsequent plan on the performance revealed during the execution of the previous one (and partly on this plan itself). This well-known ratchet mechanism additionally strengthens the incentives to bargain for an easy plan in each period, as the managers are not short-sighted and look ahead to more than one period. During the plan bargaining, the expected relative utility of more radical cost-cutting, including cost-saving innovations, must therefore be very low.[13] If the enterprises succeed in getting easy plans, because of their superior information about their own possibilities, as is often the case,

---

[13] It is worth noting that ΔEU_i of such innovations is low not only because they may fail and thus obstruct the fulfilment of the current plan but also because they may succeed, i.e., lower unit costs, and therefore lead to the imposition of a tauter plan in the next period (the ratchet mechanism). The latter could be avoided if the reduction in unit cost attributable to an innovation could somehow be hidden from the superior bodies (*cf.* Pejovich 1983, pp. 48–9). But this does not seem to be very likely.

ΔEU_i will also remain low during plan execution, and no such innovations will be forthcoming.

Let us, however, assume that the superior bodies disregard the protests from the enterprises and impose upon them taut plans, linked to strong penalties for non-fulfilment. Would such a strategy substantially increase the ΔEU_i of radical cost-saving innovations by reducing the utility of not innovating? The answer, in my view, is negative.

First, because – as noted earlier – in the STE such innovations require a large additional effort, ΔE. What is more, by imposing taut plans, the superior bodies would magnify input shortages and this would further increase ΔE and correspondingly decrease ΔEU_i of socially efficient process innovations. Besides, in the STE such innovations are burdened with a risk of obstructing plan fulfilment, as they may disrupt the production process or end in failure because of the non-availability of the necessary new inputs. And this risk again rises with t. So, if the plan is easy, there is no need to undertake the cost-reducing innovations, and if it is taut, they are especially risky, burdensome and often impossible to implement for lack of required inputs.

Second, there are usually much easier and less risky ways of – ostensibly – fulfilling a taut plan: lowering the quality of goods, increased manipulation of the product mix (which would intensify shortages), and the like. These forms of behaviour are difficult to control owing to the information limitations of the superior bodies and the impotence of buyers. Increasing the tautness of the plans would, therefore, magnify such behaviour (cf. Keren 1979) instead of inducing radical cost-saving innovations.

Finally, even if the aforementioned ways of (ostensibly) fulfilling the taut plans were somehow excluded, the strategy of imposing such plans under the threat of strong penalties could still not be relied upon to generate these innovations. For in this situation the managers would have a choice between not innovating and thus certainly suffering the penalties for non-fulfilment of the plan, and trying to implement innovations which – under a taut plan – are burdened with extreme ΔE and with a particularly high risk of failure, i.e., of also suffering these penalties. Such a situation would make the jobs of managers so unattractive that the authorities would sooner or later have to relax the plans for lack of suitable candidates for managerial positions.

This problem would not arise if the fulfilment of the taut plans were related to rewards rather than penalties. Then, granted that these rewards were very high, and that managers had no possibilities of ostensibly fulfilling the plans, some radical cost-reducing innovations could appear. But, as already noted, the second assumption is unrealistic.[14] Linking high rewards to the fulfilment of taut plans would also intensify various manipulations by the enterprises rather than induce them to undertake socially efficient process innovations. All in all, neither easy not taut plans can give such innovations an appropriately high relative utility in the eyes of enterprise managers.

Let us now turn to *product innovations*. As in the case of changes in production techniques, highly efficient product innovations require incomparably bigger ΔE and are much more likely to fail and thus obstruct the fulfilment of the plan that innovations with a low level of CE.[15] The former innovations demand, therefore, a very large ΔEM_i relative to that for the latter. But this condition cannot be met in the STE. To see why not, we must consider the administrative price setting in this system.

The traditional method is cost-based pricing: the prices of new products are based on their individual cost, as reported by the enterprises. Given extreme monopolization and the inherent informational weakness of the administrative quality and cost control, such pricing enables the enterprises to get favourably high prices (and thus a positive ΔEM_i) for new goods with only negligible, if any, quality improvements but rising unit cost as compared to their predecessors. Such new goods are bound, of course, to have a low, possibly negative, value of CE. However, they may spread quite rapidly in the STE.[16] This suggests that the usual conclusion about slow diffusion of new technologies in the East relative to the West holds only for some types of innovation – those with a high average CE. But there is the other side of the coin: innovations with a low CE, which may be diffused rapidly in the East, but slowly, if at all, in the West.

Cost-based pricing in the STE not only leads to innovations of doubtful social utility having a positive ΔEM_i but also makes the value

[14] This is why the theoretical incentive schemes (e.g., variants of the principal-agent model) which deal with the incentive problems in the STE but assume one product or just 'output' do not offer practical solutions. For they assume away the important complexities of the real STE related to the manipulations of the quality of products and of the product-mix. For other limitations of the applicability of theoretical incentive schemes, see Grosfeld (1988, pp. 12–13).

[15] One can argue that – on average – socially efficient product innovations are even more burdensome and risky in the STE, and thus have still lower ΔEU_i than radical process innovations. The main reason for this is that the former usually require more new inputs than the latter.

[16] One example is the technology of building flats from prefabricated concrete panels. Despite warnings that it has higher input intensities than the existing technologies, it spread rapidly in Poland in the 1970s; this contributed greatly to the present crisis in housing.

of ΔEM_i for highly efficient innovations equal to zero or even negative. The latter is certainly true of new products which would have lower unit costs than their predecessors. For such innovations would reduce the achieved level of the gross indicators (e.g., the value of sales) and thus obstruct the fulfilment of the plan.

These deficiencies of cost-based pricing of new products have led to the application of other price-setting rules. They generally aim at linking the prices of such products to the users' benefits, as estimated by the administrative bodies, and at reducing the initial prices after a certain preannounced time. (For more on these methods see Berliner 1976, pp. 308–54; Mann 1975; Lozinov & Felzenbaum 1975.) The snag is, however, that such methods claim much more time and effort from the administrative bodies than the traditional cost-based pricing; and because of this rise in agency costs, they are avoided (Moore 1981). What is more important, these methods cannot be effective and may be even harmful to innovativeness, for they are based on information which can be even more easily manipulated by the enterprises (Berliner 1976, p. 317; Mujżel 1978; Hanson & Pavitt 1987, p. 32). As a result, these pricing rules create still more scope for faked product innovations having a high level of ΔEM_i (and thus of ΔEU_i) to the enterprises. The rate of such innovations will tend to increase with t, as such rules create an additional possibility for – ostensibly – meeting taut plans.

The inefficiency of central planning as an instrument for inducing innovativeness has brought about the tendency to introduce a host of special measures aimed at increasing the level of I. But these too are unsatisfactory solutions. All these instruments fall into one of two categories:

(1) those that do not address the main problem, i.e., the low utility to the enterprise of highly efficient innovations relative to that of inefficient ones and of routine production;
(2) those which do address this problem but are bound to be just as ineffective (and sometimes even harmful) in stimulating innovativeness as is the basic incentive mechanism of the CRM.

The first category includes:

- Providing generous financing for innovations. This is like trying to get a car with a defective engine moving by pumping more petrol into its tank.
- Developing institutions aimed at providing enterprises with information about the available inventions. When highly efficient

projects have a low priority on the enterprises' scale, it does not matter whether these projects are known to them or not. In the first case they are rejected outright; in the second they would have been, if they were known. In both cases they are not chosen.

- Ending the traditional separation of the R&D and the producer organizations. Such an integration may speed up the flow of information between the two, and accelerate the innovation process. However, in the STE it creates an insoluble dilemma. The stronger the ties, the higher the chances of achieving these effects but the greater the negative influence by producers on the directions of R&D. With looser ties between R&D and production, on the other hand, there are greater possibilities for the choice of R&D projects that have little chance of implementation by domestic producers.
- Raising the financial rewards for inventors. This must mainly result in increasing the stock of inventions not implemented by domestic enterprises.
- Reducing or completely eliminating – through special insurance funds – the financial risk linked to the failure of an innovation. This misses the main point, as the basic kind of risk in the STE is not financial but a danger that an innovation may obstruct the fulfilment of the plan. Besides, eliminating the financial risk of innovation is likely to create some moral hazard problems with respect to the choice and implementation of technical projects (see footnote 8).

The second category of special instruments includes:

- Special pricing rules for new products (see above).
- Offering the enterprise's employees engaged in an innovation rewards based on its estimated social benefits. The basic incentive system of central planning and other features of the STE prevent this instrument from inducing enterprises to choose highly efficient innovations. At the same time, it is likely to encourage firms to select innovations of doubtful social value. For, given the inherent informational weaknesses of the superior bodies, the estimates of an innovation's benefits may easily be manipulated by the enterprise (*cf.* Berliner 1976, p. 493).
- Supplementing the general plans for enterprises with special targets for technical change. Some of these targets, e.g., the directive for general cost reduction or taut technical norms for use of the respective inputs, constitute additional instruments increasing the tautness of the plan and thus must share all the basic weaknesses of

this strategy already discussed. Other targets, e.g., the number of new products or new production techniques, face the fundamental problem of the superior bodies' inability to distinguish – on any large scale – between more and less efficient projects and to see whether the former are feasible. Hence, such targets – like the special reward schemes – are likely to stimulate innovations with a low level of CE.[17]

All in all, no special instruments can substantially increase enterprises' innovativeness in the STE. At the same time most of them increase agency costs and burden enterprises with additional paperwork.

The enterprises' resistance to highly efficient innovations, combined with the superior bodies' inability to overcome it, are together a *sufficient* reason for a low level of I. But the problem does not end here; superior bodies themselves are likely to take actions detrimental to innovativeness. A fuller explanation, for which there is no place in this chapter, would require an examination of the utility functions of the officials in these organizations and their institutional environment. However, for our purposes here, it may be sufficient to point out that the superior bodies consist of the centre – the redistributor of society's resources and the ultimate decision-maker with respect to big investment projects – and the powerful branch and regional institutions (party–state apparatus) which try to influence its decisions. This generates a continual struggle for resources (especially investment funds), having little to do with considerations of economic efficiency. Under these conditions the central authorities are likely to take many poor decisions, directly resulting in innovations of dubious social value, i.e., wrong investment projects, or in increased shortages, which indirectly affect innovativeness.[18] However, even if the central authorities somehow managed to select the best investment proposals, there would still remain the basic problem that centrally created new plants must operate under the system that makes them successfully resist highly efficient innovations. This applies, among other things, to new plants based on imported technology.

---

[17] Indeed, as Volkov (1975, p. 17) writes, enterprises' plans for technical change in the Soviet Union included undertakings detrimental to social efficiency.

[18] The extent to which this actually happens, i.e., the quality of economic policy, depends on the personal characteristics of the leadership. This is a variable responsible for a large part of variation in economic performance in the STE. But I would argue that even exceptionally competent people at the top could not raise its innovativeness above the mediocre, while incompetent and irresponsible leaders can bring about an economic disaster.

I have so far focused on the already established enterprises and their interplay with the superior bodies, thus neglecting dynamic organizational processes such as the creation of new independent enterprises (newcomers) or entry by existing ones into new markets (outsiders). These processes are essential for high innovativeness and should be at least briefly mentioned here.[19]

First, the very possibility of entry increases the competitive threat faced by established enterprises in a given market and thus raises the pressure on them to innovate. Second, in many fields major breakthroughs are not made by well-established enterprises, but by those entering the market. Therefore, the new entrants are an important direct vehicle for major innovations, and – through this – they make the overall competition more technology-oriented. Without new entrants (especially without innovative newcomers), competition would probably centre more on price. Furthermore, its intensity would decline in the longer run.

The special role of new entrants with respect to radical innovations may be due to some important motivational forces (Boulding 1974, pp. 457–8). For example, the intrinsic satisfaction that an inventor derives from putting his own idea into practice in his newly founded firm is likely to be much greater than the intrinsic rewards associated with the same project and expected by the manager of an established enterprise. Besides, new entrants are not biased by the production experience in the field they are to enter. Finally, not having yet operated in this field, they do not have to fear – in contrast to the incumbents – that their innovation would reduce the demand for established products (this applies only to product innovations).

The STE bars independent new entrants and thus suppresses an important innovative force. This is due first of all to the centralization of rights to set up new enterprises, an important feature of the predominant state ownership of the means of production. This ownership is typical not only for the STE but also for most other models of socialism. They thus all have the same innovative weakness. This was pointed out by Hoff (1949, p. 89), who noticed that in capitalist society there is always a number of persons 'irresistibly attracted' to risky investment in new technical developments. Such persons will also be found under socialism, 'but it will not be possible to make use of their peculiar attributes and self-sacrifice, as the socialist community does not allow commercial activity on one's own account'.

---

[19] I have discussed the impact of these processes on innovativeness elsewhere (Balcerowicz 1986). For an interesting broader analysis of the organizational dynamics see Pelikan (1986).

In addition, the STE – as distinct from more decentralized models of socialism – is characterized by the rigid hierarchical system of organization necessary for operating the CRM. This includes ascribing each enterprise to a given branch, and thus largely barring diversification and related entry by outsiders. The impossibility of diversifying also blocks the use of inventions that are made in a given enterprise but happen to fall outside its – administratively established – field of activity.

The STE is responsible not only for the poor choice of technical projects but also for their *ineffective execution*: slow average pace, large discrepancies between original and achieved technical parameters and excessive costs.

Slow pace results from chronic shortages, interrupting the execution of projects, and the inflexible decision-making, stemming from overall bureaucratization. As a result projects can become obsolete even at the R&D stage.

Shortages are also the main cause of discrepancies between original and achieved technical parameters, since the unavailability of some planned inputs quite often leads to their replacement by technically inferior ones.

Finally, excessive costs of projects are basically due to the low productivity prevailing in all the stages of the innovation process. Besides, there are some special factors operating in the manufacturing start-up phase, where 'learning by doing' takes place and the unit cost of successive product batches falls. This is reflected in the so-called learning curve (see e.g. Anderes 1954; Baloff 1970). The area between this curve and the level of unit costs after the learning process is over constitutes the learning costs – which should be considered an important part of total innovation cost (Balcerowicz 1976). The learning cost in the STE is bound to be much higher than that in the market economy, owing to shortages which interrupt the learning process, and a slower pace of learning, resulting from less experience in introducing innovations. Another likely reason is the propensity of the STE to concentrate on building big plants (Ehrlich *et al.* 1982): the manufacturing start-up in one huge plant may be more complicated and costly than the same process in two smaller plants with the same joint production capacity as the first one (Samborsky 1973, p. 188; *Petrochemical Industries*, 1970, p. 57).

Reformed Economic Systems and Innovativeness

Dissatisfaction with the poor innovative performance in the STE is one of the main reasons for the economic reforms so frequently attempted in the CMEA countries. Space does not permit me a longer discussion of these reforms and of their impact on innovativeness. In what follows I shall limit myself to a few remarks.

The reforms which had been tried up to 1989 (see Chapter 5) can be broadly divided into:

(1) those which left the command-rationing mechanism (CRM) and all other basic features of the STE generally intact;
(2) those which largely abolished at least the CRM without, however, replacing all the remaining basic characteristics of the STE with the arrangements typical of the market economy.

The reforms of type (1) consist, for example, in changes in the number and composition of the plan directives; in shifting some rights to operate the CRM from central to regional bodies; in various reorganizations within the framework of the multilevel hierarchical system. Such reforms aim at 'perfecting' the STE. They prevailed in the CMEA countries until the 1980s. All these reforms turned out to be short-lived; this is sufficient reason why they cannot be relied upon to increase innovativeness substantially. Moreover, even while they last, they are still not able to achieve this objective. For, being so superficial, they simply leave intact all the main features of the STE responsible for the low level of *I*: the CRM with its perverse incentive mechanism, extreme monopolization, widespread shortages, centralization of rights to set up new enterprises, etc.

The more radical reforms (type 2) attempt a break with directive central planning but leave largely intact at least some of the other basic features of the STE: hierarchical organizational system, centralization of organizational rights, the basically non-commercial financial institutions performing a massive inter-enterprise redistribution of monetary resources. The main examples of such reforms include the Hungarian New Economic Mechanism of 1968, the Yugoslav reforms after the break with Stalin and until the early 1970s and – to a lesser extent – the Polish economic reform of 1982. Even these more radical reforms are not immune to the rejection process, as indicated by the recentralization in Hungary in 1973–79, or the institutional changes in Yugoslavia in the 1970s, which turned its economic system into a regionally decentralized but quasi-adminstrative economy (Mencinger 1986). The reasons for this tendency for rejection would require separate treatment. Let us instead focus on the innovative performance of the more radically reformed system.

There are no indications that this performance under the NEM in

Hungary has been substantially higher than that in countries with more traditional systems (see, e.g., Marer 1986, pp. 182, 195, 220; Iles 1986; Poznanski 1982). Hungarian economists point to many phenomena, typical of the STE and indicative of poor innovativeness: enterprises are interested – at the most – in small and easy innovations (Balázs 1987, p. 20); inefficient use of machinery imported from the West (Hoch 1987, pp. 73–5); unsatisfactory post-licensing R&D (Garami 1981), etc.

One may, of course, wonder to what extent the poor actual innovativeness under the NEM was due to the NEM itself, and to what extent to other factors, e.g., erroneous government policies or the impact of the CMEA. In other words, one may ask whether the maximum (potential) innovativeness achievable under the NEM is not much higher than the actual level. It is very difficult to answer this question empirically. Instead, I will argue, looking at the NEM itself, that this maximum level of I under the NEM can only be slightly higher than that for the STE, and must certainly be much lower than that typical of liberal capitalism. Hence, NEM-like economic systems are not the proper answer to the innovative weakness of the STE. We shall see this by following the analytical framework we have applied above and looking first at the relative expected utility of highly efficient innovations to enterprises' managers.

The expected additional effort, ΔE, associated with such innovations must be much higher under the NEM than in free market economies. For the NEM has remained a shortage economy (Laki 1980; Antal 1979, pp. 264, 268).[20] Therefore, buyers seeking new inputs and new suppliers must experience especially great difficulties. Besides, the foreign trade regime, although more relaxed than that typical of the STE, still relies on bureaucratic import restrictions (Nagy 1988; Oblath 1988). This increases the effort of getting the necessary new inputs from abroad. Finally, there has still been a great deal of bureaucratic regulation restricting enterprises' autonomy (Marer 1986, p. 215).

The supply difficulties on the domestic market and difficult access to imports must also increase the probability that a radical innovation may be impossible to implement at all or during a required time because of the unavailability of the necessary inputs; thus the volume of production may suffer. This in turn is risky to an enterprise's managers

---

[20] The reasons for the continued shortages in the NEM require separate treatment. Here I can only mention that shortages seem to be caused not only (and not so much) by the enterprises' soft budget constraint but also by price rigidity – owing to the pervasive price controls – and by the rigidity of supply. The latter results mainly from the absence of profit orientation by producers, from the continued monopolization and from many institutional constraints on enterprises' activity.

as they have been informally held responsible for production and sales in their respective fields (Tardos 1984, p. 24; Bauer 1983, p. 308). The system of enterprises' 'responsibility for supply', based on the continued dependence of the managers on the state and party bodies (Tardos 1987, p. 127; Marer 1986, p. 209), therefore produces similar detrimental effects on their willingness to innovate as does the CRM in the STE. The main difference is that these effects may be smaller in the NEM to the extent that the 'responsibility for supply' mechanism is less rigid than that of the CRM. But, all in all, because of the high level of ΔE and of the aforementioned risk associated with highly efficient innovations, a relatively large 'incentive counterbalance', ΔEM_i, must be expected for such innovations, if they are to be selected by enterprises. However, this condition can rarely be met in the NEM.

The sufficient reason for this is the permanent absence of the competitive threat to the domestic producers. This absence is caused by factors similar to those in the STE: bureaucratic import protectionism, extreme industrial concentration, excess demand – the obverse of shortages, restrictions on entry by newcomers (see later), and enterprises' soft budget constraint.[21]

I have remarked above that a profit-oriented monopolist, in contrast to the monopolist in the STE, may be interested to some extent in cost-reducing innovations by virtue of the utility function alone. The producers in the NEM are much closer in this respect to the latter case than to the former. They cannot be very profit-oriented; first, because the 'responsibility for supply' focuses their attention on production and sales variables; and, second, because there is widespread inter-enterprise redistribution of profits via the centre, whereby the ultimate financial situation of enterprises is largely 'evened out' (Nyers & Tardos 1978, p. 36; Marer 1986, p. 209). The second factor additionally reduces the financial autonomy of enterprises and thus diminishes the possibilities that an enterprise may autonomously grow around a successful innovation.

This brings us to the role of the central bodies. The crucial fact here is that the centre continued to dominate – directly or indirectly – the investment decisions (Nyers & Tardos 1978, p. 36; Balassa 1977, p. 66; Deak 1978; Marer 1986, p. 209). This corresponded to the initial concept

---

[21] The reasons for the soft budget constraint seem to be similar to those in the STE. The continued widespread state intervention in the affairs of enterprises, which includes centralization of the major investment decisions, makes it unlikely that the superior bodies would fail to help enterprises in financial difficulties, as these difficulties may be due to the state interference itself. The administrative – and thus distorted – prices make the financial results a very imperfect indicator of true efficiency; this must further reduce the readiness of the state to let insolvent enterprises go bankrupt.

of the NEM according to which current operations should be decentralized but the longer-run development decisions should largely remain in state hands (Szamuely 1984, p. 60). However, the central investment decisions are not likely to be of high economic quality because of the utility function of the central decision-makers (the priority of political considerations) and the pressures exerted upon them by the groups and institutions lobbying for investment.

The prominent role of the central bodies in setting up new plants also precluded any larger role for independent newcomers, an important potential innovative force. They were also largely banned because of the related dominance of state ownership of the means of production. The situation in this respect changed only in the early 1980s, when the restrictions on private activity were relaxed somewhat.

I have focused so far on the choice of technical projects. The execution of the selected projects cannot be much more efficient in the NEM than the STE either. For in both cases there exist the same main factors which must make the pace of implementation slow: large discrepancies between original and achieved technical parameters and excessive costs; and shortages and bureaucratic decision-making, especially with respect to investment.

All in all, we may conclude that innovativeness in the NEM cannot be much higher than in the STE. Notwithstanding all the partial changes and the enthusiasm of many early observers, the NEM has simply – at least until recently – not departed far enough from the STE to be able to produce a breakthrough in innovativeness.

This is even more true of the Polish economic reform after 1981 (see Chapter 14). For it has had all the features of the NEM that preclude a high level of I. In addition, the Polish post-1981 economic system has preserved more elements of the traditional CRM: widespread administrative rationing of inputs and – related to that – output targets in the form of the so-called government contracts and operational programmes. Under these conditions innovativeness was bound to remain low. This is confirmed by empirical studies (see, e.g., Krajewska 1984 and 1987) and by the official evaluations of the reform (*Ocena* . . . 1988, pp. 41, 58).

Therefore, even more radical economic reforms attempted so far have not been radical enough to solve the problem of low innovativeness.[22] It

---

[22] Space limitations do not permit me to complete the picture by analysing the impact of the Yugoslav economic system on innovativeness. I can only add that I share Pejovich's (1984, p. 445) belief that the incentives to innovate under that system are significantly greater than in other socialist countries, but significantly smaller than in the capitalist West. However, this refers, in my view, to the Yugoslav system before the early 1970s' changes.

seems that it cannot be solved without fundamental changes in the property rights and ownership structure, and in the foreign trade regime. Recent developments in Poland and in Hungary (increased freedom for the private sector, proposals to privatize state enterprises, introduction of the two-tier banking system, more liberal foreign trade regulations, etc.) suggest that at least these two countries may head in this direction. But the difficult initial economic situation and the unprecedented scope of the required changes make the outcome of this new generation of reforms uncertain.

References

Amman, T. 1983 'Technical progress and political change in the Soviet Union;, in A. Schüller, H. Leipold & H. Hammel (eds), *Innovationsprobleme in Ost und West*, Stuttgart, Fischer Verlag, pp. 197–213.

Anderes, F.J. 1954 'The learning curve as a production tool', *Harvard Business Review*, January–February.

Antal, L. 1979 'Development – with some digression: the Hungarian economic mechanism in the seventies', *Acta Oeconomica* 3–4, pp. 257–73.

Balassa, A. 1977 'Achievements and lessons from the medium-term planning in the Hungarian enterprises', *Acta Oeconomica* 1, pp. 53–68.

Balázs, K. 1987 'Market oriented science on the non-equilibrium market', Budapest, mimeo.

Balcerowicz, L. 1976 'Koszty rozruchu produkcji nowego wyrobu', *Ekonomista* 6.

—— 1986 'Enterprises and economic systems: organizational adaptability and technical innovativeness', in H. Leipold & A. Schüller (eds), *Zur Interdependenz von Unternehemens- und Wirtschaftsordnung*, Stuttgart, Fischer Verlag, pp. 189–208.

—— 1988 'Innovationspexifika und die Innovarionsleistung von Wirtschaftssystemen', in P.J. Welfens & L. Balcerowicz (eds), *Innovationsdynamik im Systemvergleich*, Heidelberg, Physica Verlag, pp. 28–77.

Baloff, N. 1970 'Startup management', *IEEE Transactions on Engineering Management*, November.

Bauer, T. 1983 'The Hungarian alternative to Soviet-type planning', *Journal of Comparative Economics* 7, pp. 304–16.

Beksiak, J., & Libura, U. 1972 *Równowaga gospodarcza w socjalizmie*, Warsaw, PWN.

Bergson, A. 1983 'Technological progress', in A. Bergson & H.S. Levine (eds), *The Soviet Economy: Towards the Year 2000*, London, George Allen & Unwin, pp. 34–78.

—— 1987 'Comparative productivity: the USRR, Eastern Europe, and the West', *American Economic Review*, June, pp. 342–57.

Berliner, J. 1976 *The Innovation Decision in Soviet Industry*, Cambridge, Mass., MIT Press.

Borozdin, J.V. 1975 *Tsenoobrazovanie i potrebitel'skaya stoimost' produktsii* (Moscow, Nauka).

Boulding, K. 1974 'The interplay of technology and values: the emerging superstructure', in L.D. Siegal (ed.), *Collected Papers*, Vol. IV, Boulder, Colo., Westview, pp. 453–67.

Deak, A. 1978 'Enterprise investment decisions and economic efficiency in Hungary, *Acta Oeconomica* 1–2, pp. 63–82.

Ehrlich, E., *et al.*, 1982 'Establishment and enterprise size in manufacturing: and East–West comparison', Wiener Institut für Internationale Wirtsxhaftsvergleich, 80.

Garami, O. 1981 'Adopting foreign technology and the domestic R and D', *Abstracts of Hungarian Economic Literature* 3, p. 224.

Gomulka, S. 1986 *Growth, Innovation and Reform in Eastern Europe*, Brighton, Sussex, Wheatsheaf.

Grosfeld, I. 1988 'Reform economics and Western economic theory', Vienna, mimeo

Hanson, O., & Pavitt, K. 1987 *The Comparative Economics of Research, Development and Innovation in East and West: A Survey*, London, Harwood Academic Publishers.

Hoch, R. 1987 'Technological development and management', in *Alternative Models of Socialist Economic Systems*, Budapest, Institute of World Economy, pp. 73–5.

Hoff, T.J.B. 1949 *Economic Calculation in the Socialist Society*, London, William Hodge.

Iles, I. 1986 'Structural changes in the Hungarian economy (1979–1985)', *Acta Oeconomica* 1–2, pp. 21–33.

Keren, M. 1979 'The incentive effects of plan targets and priorities in a disaggregated model', *Journal of Comparative Economics* 1, pp. 1–26.

Kornai, J. 1980 *Economics of Shortage*, Amsterdam, North Holland.

—— 1986 'The soft budget constraint', *Kyklos*, 39.

Krajewska, A. 1984 'Innowacje w przedsiebiorstwach', *Życie Gospodarcze* 29, p. 14.

—— 1987 'Postawy wobec innowacji i ich uwarunkowania', *Gospodarka Planowa* 1, pp. 19–23.

Laki, M. 1980 'End-year rush-work in Hungarian industry and foreign trade', *Acta Oeconomica* 1–2, pp. 37–65.

Lozinov, V. & Felzenbaum, V. 1975 'Planovyi i fakticheskii effekt novoi tekhniki, *Voprosy ekonomiki* 11, pp. 80–91.

Mann, H. 1975 'Die Planmässige Preisbildung als Instrument zur Förderung des Wissenschaftlichtechnischen Fortschrittes', *Wirtschaftswissensschaft* 6, pp. 826–42.

Mansfield, E. 1968 *The Economics of Technological Change* (New York, Norton).

Marer, P. 1986 *East–West Technology Transfer: A Study of Hungary 1968–1984*, Paris, OECD.

Mencinger, J. 1986 'Yugoslav economic system and performance of the economy in the seventies and early eighties', in P. Gey, J. Kosta & W. Quaisser (eds), *Sozialismus und Industrialisierung*, Frankfurt, Campus Verlag.

Moore, I.H. 1982 'Agency costs, technological change and Soviet central planning', *Journal of Law and Economics* 2, pp. 184–215.

Mujżel, J. 1978 'Ceny w planowym kierowaniu organizacjami gospodacrzymi', *Gospodarka Planowa* 11, pp. 550–5.

Nagy, A. 1988 'Why does not it work?' in *World Economic Environment and the Hungarian Economy*, special issue of *Acta Oeconomica*, pp. 23–44.

Nyers, R., & Tardos, M. 1978 'Enterprises in Hungary before and after the economic reform', *Acta Oeconomica* 1–2, pp. 21–44.

Oblath, G. 1988 'Exchange rate policy in the reform package', in *World Economic Environment and the Hungarian Economy*, special issue of *Acta Oeconomica*, pp. 81–94.

Ocena przebiegu i wynikow wdrażania reformy gospodarczej w 1987 r. 1988 Warsaw Komisja Planowania przy Radzie Ministrow.

Pejovich, S. 1983 'Innovations and alternative property rights', in A. Schüller, H. Leipold & H. Hammel (eds), *Innovationsprobleme in Ost und West*, Stuttgart, Fischer Verlag, pp. 41–50.

—— 1984 'The incentives to innovate under alternative property rights', *Cato Journal* 4, pp. 427–55.

Pelikan, P. 1986 'How do new technologies fare under different institutional rules?', Stockholm, Industrial Institute for Economic and Social Research, Paper 169.

Petrochemical Industries in Developing Countries, 1, 1970, UNIDO, New York.

Poznanski, K. 1982 'Problemy innowacji w przemyśle węgierskim', *Ekonomista*, 1–2, pp. 95–120.

Poznanski, K. 1984 'The management of technological change in the Soviet Union and Eastern Europe', draft for the World Bank, mimeo.

Samborsky, G.I. 1973 *Spetsializatsiya v usloviyakh nauchnotekhnicheskoi revolyutsii*, Moscow, Nauka.

Schumpeter, J. 1962 *Capitalism, Socialism and Democracy*, New York, Harper & Row.

Siebert, W.S. 1985 'Development in the economics of human capital', in D.C.S. Carline, C.S. Pissarides, W.S. Siebert & P.J. Sloane (eds), *Labour Economics*, London, Longman.

Soos, K.A. 1984 'A propos the explanation of shortage phenomena: volume of demand and structural inelasticity', *Acta Oeconomica* 3–4.

Stigler, G. 1966 *The Theory of Price*, New York, Macmillan.

Szamuely, L. 1984 'The second wave of the economic mechanism debate and the 1968 reform in Hungary', *Acta Oeconomica* 1–2, pp. 43–67.

Tandon, P. 1984 'Innovation, market structure and welfare', *American Economic Review* 3, pp. 394–403.

Tardos, M. 1984 'How to create efficient markets in socialism', Budapest, mimeo.

—— 1987 'The role of money in Hungary', *European Economic Review* 31, pp. 125–31.

Vogel, H. 1983 'Vergleichende Analyse der Innovationskraft in West und Ost', in A. Schüller, H. Leipold & H. Hammel (eds), *Innovationsprobleme in Ost und West*, Stuttgart, Fischer Verlag.

Volkov, O.I. 1975 *Planovoe upravlenie nauchnotekhnicheskom protsessom*, Moscow, Nauka.

Welfens, P.J.J. 1987 'Growth, innovation and international competitiveness', *Intereconomics*, 22.

7

Towards an Analysis of Ownership

Property rights are one of the most intensively discussed topics in institutional economics. Some excellent summaries of the extensive literature are available (see, for example, Furubotn & Pejovich 1972; De Alessi 1983). However, I believe that a clear and comprehensive analytical framework has not yet been fully developed, and I find some conceptual approaches to property rights rather deficient. This includes the dichotomy of 'well-defined' versus 'ill-defined' property rights or a 'strong' versus a 'weak' regime of these rights. These categories are not sufficiently precise and are too broad. Another widespread deficiency is the failure to distinguish between the general institutional framework and the concrete institutional arrangements. A clearer conceptualization of the ownership factor is needed, I believe, and it should take the form of a set of more specific and interrelated variables. Such a conceptual framework would help to elucidate the channels through which ownership influences the economic performance. We would then also better understand the consequences of the changes in this factor, including the most important one in the contemporary world: privatization.

The purpose of this chapter is to outline such an analytical framework and to use it to formulate a number of testable hypotheses. I start by relating the property right problem to the demand side and the supply side of the economy. I then discuss the main ownership variables on the supply side. Section 3 focuses on the enterprises' ownership types. I then move to the issue of the regimes of entrepreneurship and

This chapter is largely based on my earlier writings (Balcerowicz, 1986, 1987, 1989) and was prepared when I was E. L. Wiegand Distinguished Visiting Professor of Democratization at Georgetown University in Washington, DC, in March 1995. I am grateful to Amanda Klekowski for her help in editing this chapter.

their relationship to the ownership structure of the economy and inter-agent distribution of property rights. This is followed by the discussion of the level of enforcement of these rights. Based on all this, I outline the main channels through which ownership influences economic performance.

1. The Ownership Factor and the Supply and Demand Sides

The discussion of property rights usually focuses on the supply side of the economy, i.e., on what types of organizations can be created, what their ownership forms are, and what the impact of both on economic performance is. This is an extremely important aspect of analysis which I will follow in the next sections. But I would like to mention here that the property rights problem can also be related to the demand side of the economy. The relevant question is then how 'private' the purchasing power in the economy is, i.e., to what extent it is concentrated in the hands of the state institutions (state bureaucracy and the state enterprises) and to what extent it is owned by non-state agents (private consumers, non-state organizations). The differences in this state–private distribution of global demand may have important consequences for the economy. For example, the state bureaucracies may display some specific spending pattern, i.e., try to use their budgetary allocations before the end of each fiscal year in order to avoid the ratchet effect. Or the state enterprises, being subject to a softer budget constraint and less interested in profits, may not drive as hard a bargain in their purchasing activity as the private firms. Therefore, a large share of the state organizations in the total demand may reduce the price elasticity of demand. This would have important inflationary consequences.

In analysing the demand aspect of property rights one should distinguish state organizations' spending which is based on taxation (government bureaux) from that financed by the revenues from sales (state enterprises).[1] In the former case, the 'privatization' of demand is achieved through cuts in both spending and taxation which increases the net income of the citizens. Another way of shifting the spending power from the state bureaucracy to private individuals is to preserve

---

[1] The third component of state spending, i.e. transfers, does not seem to have important direct macroeconomic consequences as the money is ultimately spent by the private individual. However, large transfers may affect the composition of final demand and consequently that of supply.

the public financing of certain services, but to allocate it to the individual beneficiaries via vouchers (e.g., educational vouchers).

In the latter case, demand is 'privatized' when the state enterprises are privatized; obviously, firms are suppliers in one market and buyers in other markets. These demand effects may be regarded as indirect results of the change in the ownership structure of some parts of the supply side of the economy. The markets where such demand effects are especially important include the labour market; private firms may be expected, given their profit orientation, to link nominal wage increases much more strongly to the growth of productivity than the state firms. Another case in point is the credit market, where the state firms, given their softer budget constraint, may be less sensitive to interest rates. Hence, the credit market dominated by state debtors is likely to display much more credit rationing than that in which the private firms prevail.

2. The Ownership Variables: The General View

Let us now focus on the ownership factor in relation to the supply side. As a first approximation, it is useful to conceptualize this factor as a set of more specific variables which constitute a sort of multidimensional 'ownership space'. This space contains various alternative *ownership systems*, each system being a combination of specific states of the ownership variables.

Only some such combinations, however, are empirically possible, and one of the tasks of institutional economics is to identify them, and to explain what forces make them into such options.

The first step in developing this analytical scheme is to distinguish the *general institutions* of ownership (the ownership law) from the *concrete ownership arrangements (structures)*.[2] The former, by definition, provides the menu of legal possibilities articulated with reference to the abstract persons. The latter are – to some extent – the concrete manifestations of these legal options implemented by specific agents in a given society.

The basic building blocks in defining the ownership law are the concepts of scarce private goods (money, physical objects, legal titles,

---

[2] This distinction is sometimes phrased, following Douglass North (1990), in terms of 'institutions' versus 'organizations'. However, I find this wording misleading as the term 'institutions' is normally understood to cover organizations, too. For more on the distinction between general framework and specific arrangements, see Balcerowicz (1989), Pelikan (1992).

social positions) and of the rights to these goods. The ownership problem arises only because of the presence of scarce private goods, and only in a multi-agent world. In the world of plenty or on a Robinson Crusoe island, the ownership problem would not exist. In the real world with scarce goods and many people, the ownership law may be defined as a set of socially sanctioned rules governing the access of people to those goods. The function of these rules is to establish relationships between scarce goods and agents, and those links may be called the property rights. The components (types) or property rights are conceptualized in various ways. The traditional conceptualization derived from Roman law lists the right to use an asset, to change its form and substance, and to transfer all rights in the asset through, for example, sales, or some rights through, for example, rental (Furubotn & Pejovich 1972, 1139–40). The newer conceptualization distinguishes between the decision-making rights or control rights and the right to derive economic benefits, more narrowly called the cash-flow rights (Grossman & Hart 1986; Balcerowicz 1986). These two approaches are not in conflict. They differ in their breadth: the first is more general and the second is more suited to the analysis of the ownership problem with regard to the means of productions and firms.

According to the above definition, the property law as a social device which links scarce private goods – via property rights – to people in a given society may take various forms, i.e., it is a variable. One may distinguish three basic aspects of its variability: the structure, the clarity and the level of enforcement.

The structure dimension can be best discussed by starting with the most important historical case of the ownership law, i.e., Roman Law. It had three distinguishing features: (1) it was *individualistic* – the agent to which the rights were ascribed was an individual (or a family), (2) it was *liberal* – this agent could have the maximum possible set of rights, including the right to transfer the rights, (3) because of (1) and (2) it was *exclusive*: it sharply divided the society, with respect to a given good, into owners and non-owners. Roman law was resurrected by modern Western states (Lloyd 1977). They picked up and developed the construct of a legal person, i.e., that of an organization or association which has all the legal rights, except those that only a real person can enjoy. This evolution included the development of company law and of various legal types of companies which had separate legal rights to assets which their management controlled – a development of immense practical consequences, as it allowed the accumulation of capital and set the stage for the 'separation of ownership and control'.

Roman law and its Western offspring in their most liberal form achieved in the nineteenth century what may be jointly called a *classical private property law*. It is this law which provides the necessary point of reference to the frequently discussed 'attenuation' of property rights or of their 'weakening'. This attenuation should be distinguished from its replacement by other variants of the ownership law. The attenuation refers to decision-making (for example, labour, safety, environmental regulation) and the curtailment of the effective right to economic benefits through taxation of profits or through price controls. The weakening of control rights tends to indirectly reduce cash-flow rights, as it may eliminate the most profitable uses of a scarce good (see also Furubotn & Pejovich 1972, p. 1140).

It is obviously the structure dimension of ownership law and of its applications (i.e., the concrete ownership forms) which are referred to where 'well-structured' property rights are contrasted with other variants of these rights (see, for example, Shleifer 1994). What is meant here is a basic quality of the ownership law, that is, how it channels human energy and shapes human actions, given certain motivational and informational invariants (self-centred motivation, informational limitations of human beings).

The structure dimension of the ownership law should be distinguished from its clarity aspect. A law may be badly structured, i.e., may induce people to engage in behaviour which produces poor economic outcomes, but may be very clear. State ownership is the case in point.

The third dimension of the ownership law, the level of enforcement, should be discussed in relation to this structure and not completely separately. For this level partly depends on the type of structure: some structures are more difficult to enforce than others.

Also, normative judgements about the importance of the degree of enforcement cannot be formulated independently from the structure of the ownership law. Beneficial economic outcomes of well-structured property law tend to increase with the level of its enforcement. But is this also true of badly structured property rights?

In discussing the impact of the structure dimension of the ownership law on the economic outcomes, we must assume a certain level of enforcement. The point is also to distinguish the impact of the structure and that of the extent of enforcement of the ownership law (to the degree that they are not correlated). This can be done if we imagine that each alternative structure of the ownership law has a range of alternative enforcement levels, and these ranges are not identical: some high levels are possible with respect to a certain structure of the ownership law, but not with regard to other structures. By implication, there is also an 'overlapping' part of the range of enforcement levels, common to all the structures of the ownership law. This conceptualization allows us to distinguish three types of changes (or differences) in the ownership law:

(1) Changes in the structure of the law, given the level of enforcement.
(2) Changes in the level of enforcement (while the structure is unchanged).
(3) Changes in both.

The property rights literature usually focuses on the change (difference) in the structure of the ownership law without mentioning the related problem of enforcement or implicitly assuming that its level remains unchanged (Case 1). However, in real life, a major shift in the structure is likely to be accompanied by a change in the level of enforcement, as each structure requires a different enforcement apparatus, and it takes more time to build a new one than to enact new legislation.[3] It is especially true of the transition from state-dominated property rights to classical private ownership law (see Shleifer 1994). In this case a two-stage transition is likely. In the first stage a radical change in the structure of the ownership law is accompanied by the decline in its enforcement level (Case 3), while in the second stage this level may be increased (Case 2). It seems, therefore, that the first type of change (shift in the structure while the degree of enforcement is constant) is an analytically useful but empirically empty category, except for minor changes in the structure of the ownership law.

However, the second category of change in the ownership law is empirically very relevant. It covers not only the second stage of the institutional developments in post-socialist economies but also changes in some developing countries where the initial level of enforcement of private property rights was very low due to the lack of formal ownership titles and to intrusive and corrupt state bureaucracy. Hernando de Soto (1988) has drawn our attention to the enormous practical importance of moving away from this situation towards higher degrees of enforcement of these rights. Such a shift certainly merits being regarded as a separate important category of change in the ownership law.

---

[3] This is just one instance of the important implications of the differences in the speed of various processes of institutional change which are discussed at greater length in Chapters 10 and 13.

Let us now return to the structural aspect of this law. We may distinguish in it two parts: one rules the consumption activity and the other the production activity in society, i.e., refers to the scarce goods which generate a stream of income. The property rights literature focuses on the second part; this is justified – it is here that the greatest variation has taken place, which has had enormous consequences for economic welfare. However, the reasons why the variation of the ownership law in the consumption sphere has been less than that with respect to production and what arrangements in the latter sector can co-exist with what solutions in the former sphere also merit attention. We will take up these issues later.

Before we do that, however, we must introduce our important concept of the *regime of entrepreneurship* (or property rights regime).[4] By definition, it is that part of the overall ownership law which determines what type of firm can be legally founded and developed. The differences in this regime have enormous consequences for the economic outcomes, both directly and via their impact on other ownership variables. I will develop this theme in section 4.

And this brings me to the second set of these variables, that is, the concrete ownership arrangements or structures. At the most elementary level, these arrangements can be conceptualized as a network in which firms are linked – by property rights – to different types of owners and are distributed across various sectors of the economy. One can distinguish the following main variable aspects of this network:

(1) The ownership structure: the shares of firms representing various ownership types in the economy. A set of firms of the same ownership type constitutes an ownership sector.
(2) The inter-sectoral distribution of various ownership sectors. This variable is distinct from (1) and it matters on its own, as the magnitude of the public–private efficiency differential depends on the sector.[5] The reasons for the differences in the size of this differential are not yet fully explained, but it is an empirical fact. Therefore, the same ownership structure but different inter-sectoral distributions of ownership sectors would produce different economic results. For example, the damage to the economy is less if the state sector is concentrated in the distribution of electricity than if it dominates agriculture.

---

[4] In the earlier chapters of this book, this concept was also referred to as the type of ownership law (open or closed).

[5] The same goes for the efficiency differential between private and labour-managed firms.

(3) Firms conventionally included in the same category of ownership: private firms, which may have different *constellations of owners*, i.e., different types and/or shares of agents which have the property rights to them.[6] Some of these differences can be important; they gave rise to a huge literature on the 'separation of ownership and control', 'managerial capitalism', and alternative types of financial systems (the German–Japanese model versus the Anglo-Saxon model, for example). They are also analysed under a newer catchword of 'corporate governance'. This concept refers either to the alternative constellations of large enterprises' owners or – more broadly – to the alternative constellations of agents and mechanisms which monitor and motivate the management of large corporations.

(4) Focusing on the owner component of the enterprises–owners network, we may distinguish the inter-agent distribution of property rights to enterprises. The relevant question here is the degree of concentration of the decision-making power and of wealth; this matters not only from the economic but also from the political point of view. An even more important question, from both points of view, is that of turnover within the ownership ·elite.

I have distinguished overall seven ownership variables. The first three variables, the structure, the clarity and the level of enforcement, refer to the ownership law. The remaining four, discussed above, describe the concrete ownership arrangements. The analysis of property rights should clarify the links between these variables so as to make a distinction between those systems of ownership which are empirically possible and those which are ruled out on empirical grounds. This helps with the second major task, that of explaining the economic impact of the alternative systems of ownership, and of the respective ownership variables.

In the following sections, I attempt to take some steps in this direction and to develop certain issues which I have mentioned in this section: the regimes of entrepreneurship, the relationship between these regimes and the ownership structure and the inter-personal distribution of property rights, the enforcement of the ownership law in relation to its structure, the main channels through which the main ownership variables influence economic behaviour and the economic outcomes. But first there is a section devoted to the ownership type of enterprise, because this concept constitutes the main building block for other concepts which I have introduced.

[6] I borrow the expression from John Scott (1985).

3. Types of Ownership of Enterprises

I will start with two preliminary clarifications and then formulate the criteria for defining the alternative ownership types of enterprises. Based on these criteria I will discuss the concept of a classical private enterprise, the non-classical private enterprise and the related issue of the constellation of owners and – more generally – of monitors of large corporations. The analysis of the main types of non-private enterprises will complete this section.

Three types of organization can be distinguished from the economic point of view: bureaux financed by budgetary allocations; non-profit-making organizations, financed largely by donations and endowments; and enterprises, which, at least in principle, are financed by sales revenues. The problem of the alternative ownership form exists, first of all, with respect to enterprises. Non-profit-making organizations are – in a certain sense – always private, while bureaux are usually state-owned and first have to be transformed into enterprises if they are to change their ownership form. The theory of ownership should include the comparative analysis of non-profit organizations and private enterprises, and the transformation of bureaux into other organizational forms. However, in this chapter I will focus on the main issue, the ownership type of enterprises.

These types denote two things. First, they refer to the legal models contained in, say, company law. These are the options among which the enterprises' founders may choose (if there is a choice). Second, an ownership type refers to the results of the application of these legal models in economic life, e.g., to the actual enterprises which represent various legal ownership types. In the latter case, we must disregard all the characteristics of an enterprise which are not related to the given legal model but to other factors, e.g., a special company history, the personality of its founder, etc. I will use the concept of the ownership type of enterprises in one of these two senses or in both depending on the issue under the discussion.

My second preliminary remark concerns three criteria which should be used to define the various ownership types of enterprises:

(1) *The nature of the ownership title.* The ownership title, by definition, denotes alternative bundles of the property rights with respect to an enterprise. I will distinguish here the capitalist ownership title from the non-capitalist one. The former combines control rights with cash-flow rights, and both tend to rise in proportion to the share in the enterprise's capital. In addition, capitalist ownership titles are

transferable. Non-capitalist ownership titles do not have these characteristics. A cooperative ownership title, for example, decouples the formal decision-making rights of a member from her or his share in the enterprise assets (one person, one vote); the same is true of mutual companies. The transferability of non-capitalist ownership titles is usually limited, too.

(2) *The nature of the owners.* This is a criterion independent from the nature of the ownership title. If the main owner is the state, then we would not recognize a company as private even if the state formally has a capitalist ownership title (i.e., the firm has the legal form of a corporation in which the state is the main or the only shareholder). This well-established intuition helps us to avoid confusing corporatization with privatization. This intuition has rational roots. The nature of the owners matters in and of itself. The theory of ownership is to some extent the theory of owners – an important class of enterprises' principals. The state has some special characteristics which make it a bad owner (see section 3.4).

(3) *The enterprise autonomy.* The differences or changes in this dimension result, of course, in the changes (differences) in the decision-making rights of owners, and indirectly – in their effective rights to the enterprises' residual income.

These three criteria are sufficient to define the main ownership types of enterprises clearly. But it is useful to add a fourth criterion: the enterprises' maximand, i.e., an economic variable (or variables related to the firm's activity) which is of main interest to its management and thus provides the main criterion for selecting the type and direction of action.[7] In doing this one moves beyond mere definitions and adds some substantive propositions, i.e., bits of theory. For the propositions on enterprises' maximands should not be simply assumed, but should be deduced from the assumptions regarding the behaviour of the respective types of owners and the definitional characteristics of the ownership types of enterprises. The propositions with regard to the behaviour of the owners should, in turn, be based on a well-reasoned and verified theory. Thus, for example, a theory of the behaviour of state enterprises needs a theory of the state.

---

[7] I am consciously defining the enterprise maximand in such general terms to avoid a discussion of whether firms maximize or engage in satisficing behaviour. For our purposes, it is sufficient to establish the kinds of variables they are mainly interested in.

3.1 CLASSICAL PRIVATE ENTERPRISE

The classical private enterprise is an owner-management enterprise. More specifically, it is an enterprise whose owner is a physical person[8] who has a capitalist ownership title to the whole of the enterprise's capital. In addition, the owner-manager hires labour and the firm enjoys full external autonomy.

Combining these definitional characteristics with some realistic assumptions on the human motivation which bear on the behaviour of the classical private owners, one can easily deduce the powerful profit orientation of classical private firms and the related drive for economic efficiency. This is why the classical private firm raises few controversies among economists of various theoretical orientations. And indeed, the economic success of some places (e.g., Northern Italy, West Germany, Taiwan, Japan) may be at least partly due to a high share of small or medium-size firms of this type. Some developments in Western countries, such as management buy-outs, may be interpreted as a return to a classical private firm.

3.2 NON-CLASSICAL PRIVATE FIRMS: TOPOLOGY OF OWNERS

This ownership type results from three institutional developments:

(1) Large corporations tend to be managed by professional managers who have small (if any) ownership stakes.
(2) Among the owners of these corporations, the share of various institutions has been rapidly increasing and that of physical persons rapidly declining. However, the share and, even more, the composition of institutional investors, differs across the Western countries.
(3) Some 'ultimate' owners, especially physical persons and pension funds, hire professional 'surrogate' owners (such as banks, fund managers). Thus, a market for ownership services (as distinct from that for property rights) is being developed. The nature of the contracts which govern this market deserves more research effort.

It is the first tendency which has caught most attention and is the subject of a huge and unresolved controversy ranging in time from Adam Smith to the contemporary institutional economists.[9] The type

---

[8] The definition may be extended to cover a small dominant group of owner-managers.
[9] This controversy is discussed in depth by Mueller (1993).

and magnitude of the behavioural deviations of large,modern corporations from profit maximization as assumed for a classical private enterprise is under debate and, even more fundamentally, so is the question of whether the expansion of the corporate sector improves or worsens the performance of a capitalist economy. There is not enough room here to enter this debate in detail. I would only like to stress that the other two tendencies may be no less important than the first one and should attract more attention. At this stage of our discussion, it is sufficient to define a non-classical private enterprise as an ownership type which departs from the classical firm in at least one of two respects: those who manage are not the main owners but are hired by the owners, and owners; include (non-state) institutions or, more precisely, individuals who do not represent themselves but certain organizations, the behaviour of whom is thus constrained and shaped by their institutional roles. The latter remark suggests that to explain the behaviour of corporations dominated by institutional shareholders, we need a theory of the behaviour of individuals in various institutional roles. This theory should be based on the general methodological principle of deriving propositions regarding individual behaviour from some realistic assumptions with respect to the motivational and informational characteristics of individuals, and the definitional characteristics of the respective roles.

A preliminary step in this direction is the *typology of owners*; it can be structured along three dimensions:

First, we may distinguish physical persons, the state and local authorities, and the non-public organizations. The last group can be broken down into enterprises and non-profit institutions, and enterprises into the financial and non-financial ones. The financial firms, in turn, are usefully divided into banks and non-banking institutions.

Second, the owners may be divided into passive and active (or in other words, 'strategic'); the latter, by definition, exert a direct influence upon the enterprise's management because they have a sufficiently large share and the appropriate competence. An interesting empirical question is what types of agents prevail among the active owners. We may mention some entrepreneurial capitalists, banks, endowments and venture-capital funds. The latter represent an important category of *professional* active owners, i.e., those who specialize in playing this role in successive enterprises and not in just one firm.

Third, we may distinguish agents whose natural role is in conflict with the ownership functions (i.e., inducing and pressing the management to maximize profits). This category includes above all, the state authorities, for reasons to be discussed later. Banks which play the double role of shareholders and creditors with respect to the same enterprises are another, and more controversial, example of this category. Generally speaking, a sharp conflict between the natural role and the ownership function should be regarded as a strong indication that the affected agent may be a bad owner (and/or that it may compromise its natural role).

A good owner, by definition, induces the enterprises to increase profits through productivity increases. I think an agent must simultaneously meet two conditions to qualify as a good owner:

(1) It must be an active owner;
(2) It should display a strong pecuniary orientation.

A strong pecuniary orientation (combined with other kinds of self-centred orientation, such as an achievement motivation) is a natural feature of most physical persons, and those who become owners are certainly not short of it. This is why the classical private firms have such a powerful profit orientation. The pecuniary orientation cannot be so naturally expected from individuals in the institutional roles, even if in their private capacity they care greatly about (private) money. The key issue is whether the institutional role allows for or precludes the linkage of the individual's income to the profits of the enterprise in which the institution he or she represents is a shareholder. This linkage is officially banned in the case of the public institutions (state or municipal authorities), and its appearance in the form of corruption is in sharp conflict with the natural role of these institutions. This is one of the reasons why public bodies tend to be bad owners. This linkage may officially exist in the case of enterprises as owners of other enterprises.[10] We should also allow for the possibility that individuals may very strongly identify with the goals of organizations they represent on the governing bodies of an enterprise and correspondingly press its management for increased profits. This is perhaps true of individuals representing some non-profit institutions which may attract strongly motivated people.[11] Hence, an interesting possibility emerges: non-profit institutions in the role of

[10] In this case, however, extensive cross-shareholding would reduce the intensity of the ownership monitoring. But such shareholding is not a necessary feature of enterprises as owners.
[11] This analysis should consider the possibility that non-profit organizations whose membership is based on self-selection may attract people with some special motivational characteristics (Niskanen 1992). This is one of the few instances when the assumption of some special psychological characteristics in explaining the impact of institutional variables may be justified.

owners can perhaps be included among guardians of the profit motive in the capitalist economy (cf. Kornai 1995). But the problem is, of course, whether their members have enough competence in their ownership roles.

Let us now return to the non-classical private enterprises. They share with the classical private firms the capitalist ownership titles, which, by definition, are not held by the public authorities but by a combination of non-public agents. It is this feature which ensures that the basic behavioural orientation of non-classical private firms may be regarded as being closer to that of classical ones than to the behavioural tendencies displayed by firms belonging to other ownership types. As a result, notwithstanding all the differences between classical and non-classical private firms, it is justified, I think, to group them in one general category of private enterprises.

The capitalist ownership titles held by non-public agents give rise to a number of mechanisms of *ownership monitoring* which tend to make the enterprise's profit an important variable to the managers of the non-classical firms. These mechanisms have been discussed at great length in the relevant literature; therefore, I will only list them here. They include the monitoring function of the stock exchange, the takeover mechanism, the market for managers, the managerial contracts based on stock options, and direct monitoring by active owners. Various constellations of enterprises' owners produce different configurations of these mechanisms, and one of the important tasks of institutional economics is to assess the quality of the respective configurations. This task may be expanded, as is often the case, to include monitoring by creditors. The comparative analysis then focuses on various combinations of the mechanisms of monitoring by owners and that done by creditors. In a further and final extension, all the remaining parts of the enterprises' institutional environment are added (for example, the markets on which they buy and those on which they sell) and analysed as sources of signals which, by virtue of the enterprises' maximands, become in their eyes the utility information, i.e., shape the preferential ordering of various kinds of actions.[12] Only in this broad perspective can we clearly see the important relationships between the respective monitoring mechanisms and identify those which determine the quality of most other incentive mechanisms. Product market competition seems to be such a crucial monitoring force. Only when it is present may one expect the other monitoring mechanisms to induce the enterprises to engage in

---

[12] For an example of such analysis, see Chapter 6.

socially optimal actions. However, it should be added that the intensity of this competition depends partly on the enterprises' ownership form and on the related mechanisms of the monitoring by owners (see section 6).

Let us finish this section with a generalized definition of a private enterprise. Such an enterprise: (1) has a non-public owner or owners who, (2) hold(s) the capitalist ownership titles; (3) enjoys large autonomy *vis-à-vis* the state. Going beyond a definition we add that: (4) private enterprise displays stronger profit orientation than enterprises representing other types of enterprises; this results either from the nature of its owner (classical private firm) or from the operation of the mechanisms of ownership monitoring (the non-classical firm).

This description provides a useful point of reference for defining the various types of non-private firms: such enterprises depart from at least one of the above definitional conditions of a private firm.

3.3 PSEUDO-PRIVATE ENTERPRISES

This ownership type meets all the definitional conditions of a private enterprise except one: its autonomy is drastically constrained by state regulation, and, therefore, the effective decision-making rights of owners are correspondingly reduced. There are formally private owners holding capitalist ownership titles but without much say; the control is largely shifted to the government bureaucracy.

Three empirical cases fall in this category: first, the nominally private enterprises subjected to the war economy command mechanism (see, for example, Eucken (1965) for Germany, and J. K. Galbraith (1980) for the United States); second, firms in the heavily interventionist and regulated developing countries of which, until the recent liberalizing reforms,India provided a striking illustration; third, heavily regulated public utilities in the OECD countries (until a recent wave of deregulation).

Many call these ownership forms 'private'. This is based on the – usually silent – assumption that the existence of non-public owners who hold the capitalist ownership titles is a sufficient condition for recognizing a firm as private, regardless of its autonomy. However, such a conceptual convention violates one of the fundamental aspects of the original notion of private property: economic freedom. Private enterprise then becomes an extremely broad category and includes ownership forms which are close to centralized state ownership. This, in turn, leads to claims that ownership in itself does not matter very much, as it may co-exist with various modes of coordination, both market and non-market, and may produce very different economic outcomes. All these assertions follow from the discussed definition of the private enterprise which disregards the autonomy dimension.

Therefore, such a definition should be rejected as analytically misleading, and a narrower concept of the private enterprise, based on the assumption of the firm's autonomy, adopted. As a corollary, I propose to call firms which depart from this definition of the private firm, in that they are radically constrained by state regulations, 'pseudo-private'; nominally private firms subject to milder forms of regulation should perhaps be called 'quasi-private'.

Breaking the traditional concept of the private enterprise down into the genuinely private and pseudo-private or quasi-private forms has important analytical consequences. Liberalizing an economy composed of the latter enterprises can then be regarded as an important process of privatization, as it restores private enterprises. This was the case in many developing countries but not in the socialist economies, which were devoid of even pseudo-private firms. Therefore, the overlap between the domains of the concepts of liberalization and privatization is much smaller in the case of post-socialist transition than in the case of market-oriented reforms in the developing countries.[13]

Liberalizing an economy which consists of pseudo-private firms can have dramatic and beneficial economic consequences. First, because it shifts the focus of profit orientation from rent-seeking activities to the improvement of economic performance, i.e., increasing productivity, reducing costs and introducing innovation. Second, because it releases an important source of non-pecuniary motivation, i.e., achievement; this motivation operates whenever decision-makers have enough autonomy. This second change strengthens the efficiency-enhancing impact of the first.

3.4 STATE ENTERPRISES

This ownership type is defined by its owner: the state. Having the state as an owner produces other departures from the conditions which define the private enterprise.

The state is a very special owner. It differs from other owners in at least five interwoven respects. The first and most crucial is that the state is a political organization; those who occupy the higher positions in this

---

[13] This is why a distinction between stabilization, liberalization and deep institutional restructuring which includes privatization (see Chapters 9 and 10) is especially useful with respect to the post-socialist economic transition.

organization and execute the ultimate ownership rights are subject to the incentive system which differs radically from that of private owners. As a result of this system, typical politicians would tend to maintain popular support regardless of whether the state is democratic or non-democratic. Combining this tendency with control rights to enterprises must produce serious deviations from the profit orientation in state-owned firms. Some actions which are politically popular (such as investing in economically depressed regions and increasing employ-ment) could reduce profits, and many others which make economic sense (for example, restructuring enterprises) are politically unpopular. This politicization 'from above' is likely to be strengthened by the politicization 'from below' – by the pressures from employees and their trade unions, aimed at preserving the status quo or getting the financial compensation for the effects of politicization from above. Such a compensation means, of course, that state enterprises tend to face a 'soft budget constraint' in Kornai's sense. Besides, by absorbing a country's savings, state enterprises crowd out the private sector (see Kikri, Nellis & Shirley 1994).

Second, the contemporary state has the monopoly on the creation of money. Subsidization of state enterprises may thus be carried out in an inflationary way.[14] Third, the state also has the monopoly on legislation; it may therefore bias the legal framework so as to protect the state enterprises. Fourth, people who execute the control rights of the state, the politicians and the public officials, cannot and should not have the legal rights to the state enterprise's profits. Corruption is a very imperfect substitute for such rights and it undermines the main public functions of the state (cf. Shleifer 1994).

Fifth, state enterprises cannot be subject to the mechanisms of ownership monitoring, as these are based on the transfer of capitalist ownership titles. Such titles, if they exist, must remain in the hands of the state if the enterprise is to continue being state-owned. The vacuum created by the lack of these mechanisms tends to be filled with bureau-cratic regulations, all the more since the state supervising administration is usually a large organization.

Summing up: the political nature of the state combined with its special powers make it a bad owner of enterprises. As a result, firms owned by the state are likely to be inefficient and display only a weak profit orientation. To assume that the state can systematically behave

---

[14] This danger would be reduced by the presence of an independent central bank, held responsible for the stability of money. However, the political conditions which produce a large state sector are not very likely to allow the emergence of such a bank.

like a private owner, and thus that the state enterprises can behave and perform like private ones, is to deny that differences in institutions and incentives matter.

To be sure, the strength of the described behavioural specificities of the state owner and of state-owned enterprises (SOEs) varies, depending on several factors that determine the power of the countervailing forces. The first factor is the share of the state sector: the higher it is, the less likely it is that competitive and other pressures will come from the private sector, and more inefficiency would be displayed by the SOEs. Therefore, the lessons from the relatively small state sector are not indicative for a large state sector. More specifically, if a small state sector, as is the case, is inefficient, then even more inefficiency can be expected in a state-dominated economy. The second factor which matters is the size of a country. A large state sector in a small country may face more competition in export markets than proportionally the same state sector in a large country. Moreover, a small closed economy dominated by the state invites disaster. The third factor is the sectoral location of the SOEs. As I have already mentioned, the state–private efficiency differential varies depending on the sector. The reasons for this difference require more research. Behind it probably lie the inter-sectoral differences in the required flexibility of supply, in the minimum efficient size of an enterprise and in the scope for radical, highly risky and uncertain innovations. The state enterprises are at a special disadvantage in sectors characterized by highly flexible supply, small enterprise size, and wide scope for innovation, which conflict with the discussed specifications of state ownership. Furthermore, centralized state ownership as it existed under the Soviet-type economic system was especially damaging to efficiency (see Chapter 6).

Finally, the normal behaviour of the state owners and thus of the state-owned enterprises may be suspended after a great change in the political system, during a short period of extraordinary politics (see Chapter 9). The powers of the state-owners may then be reduced[15] or the new political team would be disinclined to use them. Such a situation cannot last. Granted that these powers are not removed altogether, i.e., the enterprises are not privatized, the political influences with respect to the inherited state sector would return, only in the new

---

[15] If these powers are eliminated but the enterprises do not get private owners and if their managers are not expecting privatization imminently, the nominally state enterprise turns into a sort of post-socialist, 'managerial' firm. Such enterprises are likely to engage in the worst excesses predicted for managerial corporations (such as diversion of supplies, excessive growth) as the former are not constrained by the mechanisms of ownership monitoring which operate with respect to the latter firms.

forms related to a changed political system. The politicians believing in a liberal state would either be removed from office (or resign) as they would not have much choice but to act in accordance with the political incentive system.

3.5 LABOUR-MANAGED ENTERPRISES

In this ownership form, the formal decision-making rights, by definition, are equally distributed among the employees (one person, one vote principle), and therefore nobody has the capitalist ownership title to the enterprise. The labour-managed enterprise may either be a producer cooperative in which all the employees are members who may have different shares but the same voting rights (the cooperative ownership title), or an Illyrian enterprise in which there are no shares and the decision-making rights are related to the status of an employee.[16] In both cases, and this is crucial, these rights are in the hands of the *non-capitalist insiders*, i.e., persons whose main income is not related to the enterprise's profits (revenues minus all costs, including wages).

The actual decision-making is, of course, not as equally distributed as the formal decision-making rights. The gap between the two is due to unequal distribution of information among the members and also to the fact that they delegate many powers to the workers' council. This council also hires and dismisses the management. However, even with all these caveats, the non-capitalist insiders must have a significant impact upon the choice of directions and actions of their enterprise, especially if it is small.

Now, assuming such a significant impact of the non-capitalist insiders, whose pecuniary interests are not related to the enterprise's profits, we must conclude that profits cannot be a maximand of a labour-managed firm. This role is played by another economic variable which better reflects the interests of the non-capitalist insiders: the value added per capita in the firm. Such a maximand produces a different choice of actions than that by a comparable private, profit-oriented enterprise. Here we encounter a huge theoretical literature on the comparative behaviour and performance of these two types of enterprises, started by Ward in 1958, Meade in 1972 and others. The

---

[16] The Illyrian form is a theoretical model which corresponds to the self-management doctrine in former Yugoslavia. The actual competences of the self-management bodies were much more limited than those in this model by the powers of the party apparatus, especially with respect to the nomination and the dismissal of the enterprise's directors, the division of its income, and with regard to investment (see Lydall 1984).

predictions of these theoretical works cannot easily be falsified for lack of real-life labour-managed firms which would be sufficiently close to their theoretical models.[17] However, most of these predictions make intuitive sense. The most important prediction is probably the one that says that the labour-managed firms would create fewer jobs than their private counterparts. An economic system dominated by such enterprises would thus be plagued by high unemployment. This prediction is not surprising in the light of the insider–outsider theory of unemployment, which links its level to the power of the insiders, i.e., those who already have jobs. A labour-managed enterprise may be regarded as an extreme case of the dominance of the non-capitalist insiders within a firm.

3.6 BETWEEN THE LABOUR-MANAGED AND THE CLASSICAL PRIVATE ENTERPRISE

I am referring here to a range of ownership types of enterprises in which the employees (including the managers) have the capitalist ownership titles. At the one extreme of this range there is an egalitarian partnership where all the partners have equal shares and thus equal decision-making rights, and in which there is no hired labour. This form is fundamentally similar to a classical producer cooperative. However, the capitalist ownership titles allow unequal shares and, correspondingly, unequal decision-making and cash-flow rights to the enterprise's insiders. Hence, they can be divided into non-capitalist and capitalist ones. The former derive their main income from wages, the latter from the enterprise's profits. Different proportions of these two groups produce a different balance of forces and, therefore, a different behavioural orientation of the firm. Distributions may exist whereby neither of these groups would have a clearly dominant voice. These distributions would produce a sphere of indeterminacy with regard to the enterprise orientation. However, once the capitalist ownership titles are sufficiently concentrated in the hands of a small group of capitalist insiders, and the remaining persons have – in total – much smaller shares, a private firm

---

[17] One should distinguish here between labour-managed firms acting in a predominantly capitalist environment and economic systems dominated by such firms. The former category has some empirical counterparts, for example, producer-cooperatives in Western countries. Such firms, however, import wage restraint and other disciplining pressures from their capitalist environment and, therefore, are not representative of labour-managed systems. One can, however, expect that the deficiencies of such firms acting in the capitalist environment would be even more pronounced if they dominated the whole economy.

with workers' co-ownership emerges. This can be an efficient ownership type, as it combines a strong profit orientation with the possibility of having cooperative relationships within the firm.

Finally, once the capitalist ownership titles are amassed by a small group of insider-managers (or by just one manager) we reach another extreme of the range – a classical private firm.

4. The Entrepreneurship Regime, the Ownership Structure and the Distribution of Property Rights

The entrepreneurship regime (ER) denotes, by definition, that part of the overall ownership law which determines the kind of firm, by ownership type, that can legally be founded and developed. Three main types of ER can be distinguished in the contemporary world: closed (ER_c), open or liberal (ER_o) and restrictive (ER_r).

ER_c, by definition, tends to ensure the monopoly of just one ownership type by banning all other types, or heavily restricting their development. Historically speaking, the preferred type was either a state firm, as in the Comecon countries, or a formally managed labour firm, as in former Yugoslavia. Going beyond the historical experience, one can also imagine a closed entrepreneurship regime which favours producer-cooperatives. The result would then be a sort of cooperative socialism. It would differ from other variants of ER_c in that it would allow the private persons to set up enterprises but only in the prescribed form of a cooperative. Generally speaking, an ER_c always favours one type of non-private enterprise by banning the private ones. There has been no ER_c which would tend to ensure the dominance of the private firms by banning the non-private ones. It is no accident: the private enterprises do not need such legal protection to prevail in the economy. Their predominance is based on the logic of individual choice, a point to which we will return later.

The open regime of entrepreneurship, ER_o, ensures the choice among many types of enterprises, both private and non-private, e.g., the cooperatives. ER_o has been typical for the OECD countries and for some developing countries. The recent liberalizing reforms have vastly increased its scope.

Finally, the restrictive regime of entrepreneurship, ER_r, ensured the monopoly for the state firms in some selected sectors of the economy ('the commanding heights', the 'strategic' sectors) but allowed the founding and development of private enterprises in other sectors. However, countries which operated the ER_r often maintained cumbersome and time-consuming procedures governing the setting up and functioning of nominally private companies. Economic systems of such countries, therefore, were characterized by the privileged position of state firms and such extensive government regulations that nominally private enterprises were in fact pseudo-private or quasi-private (see section 3). No wonder these systems were very inefficient.

There are two basic questions with respect to the *ER*. The first treats it as a dependent variable and inquires why and how different variants of the *ER* come into being. This is the domain of the history of the political, legal and economic developments and of the theory of politics which tries to explain its main output: legislation. In more concrete terms, the first problem includes the transition from feudalism to free market capitalism in the eighteenth and nineteenth centuries, the Communist revolutions – first in Russia after the First World War and then its exported transplants in Central and Eastern Europe after the Second World War, as well as the quasi-autonomous Communist revolution in China in the 1940s. It further includes the theory of legislation and regulation in democratic capitalism and finally the pro-capitalist revolutions in the former socialist countries in the past few years.

Each of these developments presents a challenging analytical problem and one may doubt whether there is one unified theory which is capable of explaining, and even less likely, predicting them. Major shifts in history are fundamentally unpredictable, given an enormous element of chance and the changing patterns of interaction between the main variables. The most one can do, I think, is to elaborate an explanatory scheme which would identify at least some of the main determinants of major institutional change. They include the role of some powerful anti-capitalist doctrines, such as Marxism, which instilled quasi-religious beliefs in the group of determined early followers. This, plus the historical chance factors and the use of force, largely explains the Communist revolutions in Russia and in China. Further Communist revolutions are easy to explain by the use of Soviet force. Once the command economic system was established, forces of the functional necessities started to operate. This system had a certain 'constitutional' logic: the command mechanism of coordination required a special organizational structure, and this structure could be maintained only under a closed regime of entrepreneurship (see Chapter 5).

The rapidity and timing of pro-capitalist and pro-democratic revolutions in the former socialist countries caught everyone by surprise, so nobody can pretend to have had a good predictive theory of the socialist (and post-socialist) world. But, again, some *ex post facto* explanation is possible. It can be structured, I think, in terms of the interplay between some systematic forces and the chance factors. The former include the growing conflict between the claims of the official doctrine and reality, made more visible by the modern mass media. The chance factors refer to the ascension to power of personalities (most importantly, Gorbachev), who recognized this gap and embarked upon the reforms which were, however, not intended to completely dismantle the system. Nevertheless, once the developments – surprising to the main actors – were heading in this direction, force was not used to block it, probably because of the preferences of the top decision-makers, and not because it was too late. The historical chance factors had acted again. The pro-capitalist and pro-democratic revolutions in the smaller socialist countries were strongly linked to the developments in the former Soviet Union and the related disappearance of the Soviet threat. This link was the weakest in Poland, where the Solidarity era in 1980–81 preceded the Gorbachev reforms and might have contributed to serious rethinking of the whole ideology and policy.

The major shifts referred to above included radical change in the entrepreneurship regime. Other changes in these regimes, such as the recent transition from the ER_r to ER_o which has occurred in many developing countries, can largely be explained by the combination of their economic crises produced by the statist economic policy; the perception of the positive experience of the liberalizing reforms in other countries (e.g., in Chile), which is an example of cultural diffusion; the changed economic doctrine of development which stresses the importance of private enterprise and of free markets – which is largely a return to classical truths; and finally, by the fact that this 'new' old doctrine entered the conditionality of the international financial institutions which offered precious financial assistance. This last factor was also instrumental in those postsocialist countries where the internal political forces were not sufficiently strong to set them on the course of economic liberalization.

The second question treats the ER as an independent (exogenous) factor and asks how it shapes other institutional variables. I consider this question as belonging to the core of theoretical institutional economics. It allows clear and falsifiable predictions with respect to two other previously mentioned ownership factors: the ownership structure (OS) and the inter-agent distribution of property rights (AD).

The ownership structure varies depending on the share of the private and non-private sectors. One can distinguish three main types of OS – capitalist, OS_c (dominated by the private sector), socialist, OS_s (dominated by socialist enterprises, i.e., state-owned or labour-managed forms) and mixed, OS_m, which is an intermediate form.

Let us denote by OS^0 the initial state of the OS, and by OS^n its end-state, say, after a couple of years from time t_0. And let ER^T stand for the entrepreneurship regime which is in force from at least t_0 until at least t_n (T denoting the period between t_0 and t_n). We can now formulate the following propositions relating ER and OS:

Proposition (1)   If $OS^0 = OS^0_c$ and $ER^T = ER^T_o$, and there are no periodic nationalizations, then $OS^n = OS^n_c$.

Putting this simply: the open regime of entrepreneurship is a sufficient condition for preserving the inherited capitalist ownership structure.

Proposition (2)   If $OS^0 = OS^0_s$ or OS^0_m, and $ER^T = ER^T_o$, and there are no periodic nationalizations, then $OS^n \rightarrow OS^n_c$.

The open regime of entrepreneurship tends to transform the inherited socialist or mixed ownership structure into a capitalist one.

Proposition (3)   If $OS^0 = OS^0_s$ and $ER^T = ER^T_c$, then $OS^n = OS^T_c$.

A closed regime of entrepreneurship is a necessary and sufficient condition for preserving the inherited (or introduced) socialist ownership structure. Similarly:

Proposition (4)   If $OS^0 = OS^0_m$ and $ER^T = ER^T_r$, then $OS^n = OS^n_m$.

A restrictive regime of entrepreneurship is required to preserve the inherited mixed ownership structure.

Proposition (5)   If $OS^0 = OS^0_c$ but $ER^T = ER^T_c$, then $OS^n \rightarrow OS^n_m$ or OS^n_s.

Blocking private entrepreneurship would tend to transform the inherited capitalist ownership structure into a mixed or socialist one, for such a situation presupposes that the state assumes the monopoly of the new investment.

At the heart of these propositions lies the logic of individual choice: whenever the private founders are free to choose among the private and non-private ownership types, they tend to select the private one, as it gives them the most control and cash-flow rights. Therefore, ER_o naturally preserves or produces OS_c, if only the state does not expropriate the private owners. There is no need to ban non-private ownership forms in order to obtain the capitalist ownership structure. It will emerge spontaneously if people are free to choose. In this sense, a private enterprise economy is a natural state of society. There is no contemporary culture in which ER_o would not produce a supply of private entrepreneurs and a stream of private enterprises.[18] Cultural factors are, therefore, secondary in this regard to the institutional determinants, i.e., the *ER*.

A qualification is needed with respect to Proposition (2) which states that ER_o tends to transform the inherited socialist (or mixed) ownership structure into a capitalist one. The period required for such a transformation may be a long one, and the inherited dominant state sector is likely to absorb much of society's savings. Therefore, the introduction of ER_o should be accompanied by the transformation of the SOEs into the private firms, i.e., by narrowly defined privatization.

Proposition (3) describes the nature of the socialist revolution: the simultaneous nationalization and banning of the private entrepreneurship sector in order to avoid the re-emergence of the private sector (i.e., the switch to the situation described by Proposition (2)). The essence of socialism was, therefore, to deprive people of their economic rights and thus to prevent the return to a natural state of society in the economic realm.

Let us now focus for a while on the relationship between *ER* and the related *OS*, on the one hand, and the inter-agent distribution of property rights to enterprises on the other. Here, one can formulate several propositions which consider the initial distribution of these rights (AD^0):

> *Proposition (6)*   If the AD^0 is highly concentrated and $ER = ER_r$ and includes barriers to private entry, then this unequal distribution tends to be perpetuated across generations.

This describes the situation in some Latin American countries. The wealthy families do not face much private competition and may achieve large gains from rent-seeking.

> *Proposition (7)*   Less concentrated AD^0 combined with ER_o tends to produce less concentrated distributions in the future and ones which are less entrenched across generations.

[18] See, for example, studies which show the dynamism of African entrepreneurs where they are allowed to operate (Marsden, 1990).

High positions in these distributions may be occupied thanks to free entry, by a changing set of persons over time.

Proposition (8)   As a corollary from (6) and (7) we may point out the importance of reducing the inherited high concentration of *AD*, which is usually a product of special historical developments.

One measure is an inter-agent redistribution of property rights to some class of assets, carried out within the framework of private ownership law. Land reform is the most important example here. Such an operation should be sharply distinguished from the change of *ER*. A successful redistribution of private property rights, combined with a liberal regime of entrepreneurship and a good educational system focuses the energy of the people on productive activities instead of wasting it in redistributive struggles and in rent-seeking. Rapid growth with relative equity may then result. This seems to be one of the basic lessons from the East Asian success.

Proposition (9)   A highly equitable initial distribution of property rights to enterprises achievable during the post-socialist transition thanks to voucher privatization is not likely to be maintained.

People differ in their attitudes towards risk and those who are more risk-averse will trade their ownership titles for safer assets. Lasting popular capitalism is, therefore, an unachievable ideal. However, this should not be regretted as long as developments away from the initial equitable distribution of property rights are based on voluntary and well-informed choice.

Proposition (10)   The closed regime of entrepreneurship and the resulting socialist ownership structure, the central features of socialism, unavoidably produce an enormous concentration of the control rights in the hands of the state bureaucracy.

Those who occupied the leadership in this hierarchy enjoyed an economic power unparalleled by any capitalist dynasties. The extent to which this power was linked to the economic gains depended, however, on personality factors and, perhaps, on national culture.

Let us conclude this section with some observations on the ownership law in the sphere of consumer goods. As I already noted, the variability of legal arrangements in this domain has been much less than that with regard to the means of production and enterprises. The open regime of entrepreneurship and the related capitalist ownership structure always co-existed with private property rights with respect to consumer goods. Other combinations would quite simply be inconsistent. The incentives needed to operate private enterprises and to engage in private entrepreneurship would disappear if the sphere of consumer goods were collectivized. However, even the closed regime of entrepreneurship and the related socialist ownership structure co-existed with a wide range of consumer goods, subject to private property rights. To be sure, there were some goods which during certain periods in certain countries could not be privately owned, for example urban one-family houses or cars. These exceptions aside, legal private ownership of consumer goods was allowed even though private entrepreneurship was banned. This can be explained by two factors. First, public ownership of most consumer goods is technically impossible – food and toothbrushes cannot be nationalized. This was pointed out by Ludwig von Mises (1981). Second, ideological objections to private ownership of consumer goods were much less pronounced than those directed against private property in the sphere of production. The former was assumed to produce much less inequality of power among the people than the latter. Overlooked, however, was the fact that state dominance in production unavoidably produces much more of this inequality than capitalist ownership.

5. The Enforcement Level and the Structure of Property Rights

The enforcement level can be expressed by the strength of the expectations of the owners that their rights not be infringed by the non-owners. The enforcement is usually discussed with regard to just one type of ownership law – the classical private one. However, this is an unjustified limitation. The problem of enforcement should be analysed in relation to the various types of this law. Then, we see that the level of enforcement depends on the structure of the ownership law. This is just a special case of a more general relationship between the content of a law and the degree to which it is binding.

Consider first the simplest case – that of a well-structured classical private ownership law. We are on safe ground here since, by definition, this law channels human energy in the right directions; the more it is enforced, the better for economic performance.

There are cases when the enforcement of such a law is very

deficient. One of them happens during the breakdown of the state, the usual result of a civil war, such as, for example, in Lebanon in the 1980s. Another takes place in the early phases of post-socialist transition. A massive legislative change from a state-dominated to a private owner- ship law cannot be accompanied by an equally radical restructuring and strengthening of the legal infrastructure and the enforcement apparatus. As a result, the initial level of enforcement of the newly acquired private property rights tends to be low. Given a concentrated effort, it can be increased in the next stages. This is one of the reasons why the economic efficiency of the transition economy may increase with the passage of time. Finally, there was the case of many developing countries, so vividly described by Hernando de Soto (1989). Here, the overwhelming majority of people operated in the informal sector, lacked the formal ownership titles to land and real estate and did not enjoy the protection of their rights by the state enforcement apparatus. The economy was predominantly private, but the society was divided into a small minority whose rights were well protected, and the vast majority who enjoyed title protection. To remedy this situation makes both economic and social sense.

Let us now consider a state-dominated ownership law, such as existed in the former socialist countries. There was a constant struggle to enforce this law: that is to bar people from engaging in private economic activity which was declared illegal. Much harsher penalties were provided for the violation of what was called 'social' ownership than that of the remaining private one. But this was an uphill battle, as witnessed by widespread petty theft within the state enterprises, other forms of informal privatization and the extensive black market. The malfunctioning of a socialist economy created both opportunities and demands to engage in private economic activity. In addition, the legal norms of 'social' ownership could not be sufficiently internalized. And it was by no means guaranteed that a higher degree of enforcement of state-dominated property rights (if it were possible) would have improved the overall performance of the economy. The opposite could well have been true, as it would have deprived the economy of much needed flexibility.

6. Ownership and Economic Performance

Based on the previous sections we can point out that the analysis of the ownership factor includes the following main problems:

(1) Changes in the entrepreneurship regime (*ER*);
(2) The relationship between the *ER* and the ownership structure (*OS*);
(3) The impact of *ER* and *OS* on the inter-agent distribution of property rights (*AD*);
(4) Changes in the level of enforcement of the property rights and their impact on economic performance;
(5) The impact of the *ER* and the related *OS* on economic performance;
(6) Given an open regime of entrepreneurship (ER_o) and the resulting capitalist ownership structure (OS_c), explaining the differences and changes in the composition of private firms, i.e., shares of classical versus non-classical private enterprises, types of non-classical firms (e.g., differences in the constellations of their owners) and in the mechanisms of corporate governance;
(7) Explaining the impact on economic performance of these intra-capitalism differences or development.

These problems constitute a huge inter-disciplinary research agenda. We have briefly discussed some of them. Problems (1), (2) and (3) were dealt with in section 3, and problem (4) in section 4. Problems (6) and (7) require a separate treatment. I would like to make a few remarks here. It should be emphasized that they belong to the core of analytical institutional economics and are of great practical relevance. Non-capitalist economic systems have been disappearing from the real world and the focus should shift to the intra-capitalism differences and developments. The discipline of comparative economic systems has lost much of its relevance, but comparative institutional economics centred on capitalism has correspondingly gained in importance.

Despite a huge literature on the 'separation of ownership and control', managerial capitalism, corporate governance, alternative models of financial systems, etc., the research on the origins and consequences of the intra-capitalism differences and developments is still in early stages. There is too much theoretical speculation and too little solid empirical investigation, guided by a clear and precise analytical framework. One should not take it for granted, for example, that the much discussed models of capitalism (Anglo-Saxon versus German-Japanese) emerged as a result of anybody's plan or as a result of efficiency-increasing institutional evolution. Historical chance factors instead might have played a decisive role. The relatively small role of banks as institutional owners in the United States can be largely explained by the operation of the Glass–Steagall Act, which resulted in turn from a populist distrust of the large financial institutions in the thirties (Roe 1993). A larger role of banks in the ownership constellations in Japan is due to the fact that the American occupying forces dissolved the large *zaibatsu* but for some unknown reasons left the ownership positions of the large banks intact (Scott 1985). The relative weakness of the mechanisms of ownership monitoring related to the stock exchange and the correspondingly larger role of banks in the whole corporate governance in Germany, Austria, France and some other countries of Western Europe might have largely resulted from the underdevelopment of the private pension funds, which are important players in these mechanisms.

They were crowded out by the expansion of the state-run pay-as-you-go pension system. The fiscal crisis of these systems has created the pressure and the scope for the development of the funded system which may ultimately increase the role of the mechanisms of ownership monitoring related to the stock exchange in countries with the Japanese-German model' nowadays (Davies 1993).

These remarks referred to problem (6), i.e., explaining the differences in the constellations of owners and in the related mechanisms of the corporate governance. Another aspect of this problem, and one which deserves much more attention, are the differences in the share of the classical private enterprises. Comparative studies are needed to explain these differences by looking at such variables as the regulatory regimes, the complexity of the tax system, the nature of the financial system (how much access to finance depends on the size and the enterprise), the state of the venture capital institutions, etc. Much more careful research is also needed with regard to problem (7), i.e., the impact of the discussed intra-capitalism differences in the ownership arrangements on the economic performance. It is ironic that features such as the large direct role of banks and reduced role of the stock exchange, which were claimed to explain the strength of German and Japanese economies when they performed above average, started to be regarded as weaknesses once these economies had run into trouble. And it may well be that both views were wrong, as other institutional factors were probably much more important in shaping the economic performance of both countries.[19]

In the following, I would like to focus on problem (5), i.e., the impact of some fundamental differences in ownership on economic performance, or – in other words – why and how ownership matters. A systematic discussion of this issue requires: (1) a careful definition of the ownership variable; (2) similar definitions of the selected

---

[19] These factors might have included the share of the classical private firms, the tax/GDP ratio, the export orientation, the flexibility of the labour market.

performance variables; (3) specifying the mechanisms through which ownership affects these variables; (4) identifying other determinants of the same economic outcomes so that we can assess the significance of ownership.

Building on the results of section 4, we conceptualize the ownership as a regime of entrepreneurship (ER) and ownership structure (OS). Three consistent ownership regimes can thus be considered: competitive capitalism (ER_o, OS_c), command socialism (ER_c, OS_s dominated by the centralized state companies), market socialism (ER_c, OS_s dominated by the labour-managed firms). For the purposes of this discussion, I will take the level of enforcement as given.

The most important performance variables affected by ER and OS are various dimensions of economic efficiency which can jointly be measured by the long-term growth of the total factor productivity; this, in turn, influences the rate of the – appropriately defined – economic growth.[20] Other performance variables which can be linked to ER and OS include the level of unemployment understood as the difference between the labour force and *productive* employment,[21] and inflation.

Among the types of economic efficiency affected by ER and OS one should list above all innovativeness, defined in Chapter 6 as a product of the rate of innovation and its social utility. Static (allocative) efficiency is also affected, to the extent that differences in ER and OS lead – via the autonomy dimension – to different distributions of decision-making in the economy, i.e., various levels of centralization. One should add efficiency of coordination, a performance variable which has not been considered so far in the mainstream literature, but which is important for economic welfare and is strongly related to ER and OS. I have discussed this variable and its institutional determinants at length in other works (Balcerowicz 1985, 1989). By definition, it is inversely related to the losses resulting from the violation of the complementarity requirements in production and in the use of the consumer durables. Such losses result, among other things, from the disturbances in the inter-enterprise supplies of complementary inputs, from the lack of the technically required spare parts, and from overcapacities.[22] Efficiency of

---

[20] One possible measure is the long-term growth of aggregate consumption (see Schumpeter 1962).

[21] Such unemployment consists both of open and disguised unemployment.

[22] R. R. Nelson (1981) has in mind a similar variable when he speaks of 'responsiveness'. However, he reaches, in my opinion, a wrong conclusion when he emphasizes the coordination problems of the private market economy and disregards the much larger problems of the centralized state-dominated economy.

coordination is strongly influenced by the flexibility of supply, which in turn can be clearly linked to ER and OS.

Another new efficiency component which should be considered is *ecological efficiency*; it can be measured by the ratio of the emission of pollutants to the GDP.[23] Finally, X-efficiency in Leibenstein's sense can be related to ER and OS, too.

Figure 7.1 presents, in a highly simplified fashion, the main mechanisms through which ER and OS affect the selected performance variables. There are two main intermediate variables, i.e., those shaped by ER and OS, and which, in turn, influence performance. One of these is competition: the type of competition, i.e., whether competition predominates among the buyers (producers' market) or among the suppliers (buyers' market) and if the second is the case, what is the degree of intensity.

Competition as an incentive mechanism depends on three variable conditions: the ease with which demand can shift among the alternative sources of supply; the existence of at least some suppliers who undertake actions resulting in outcomes which attract demand and thus provoke these shifts (the intensity of the competitive threat); and the extent to which increases or decreases in sales have serious consequences for the affected suppliers (e.g., whether there exists an effective bankruptcy mechanism or enterprises' losses are subsidized).[24] All these conditions must be met for competition among suppliers to operate.

The second intermediate variable is the mode of coordination: market versus non-market, and if market mechanism is the case, what are its properties? These two intermediate variables are interrelated as non-market coordination implies a producers' market. However, market coordination may display various levels of competition among suppliers depending on ER, OS and the foreign trade regime.

In the following text I will formulate several propositions linking ownership to economic performance. No extended proofs will be provided as the purpose here is to sketch the map of channels through which ownership affects the economic outcomes.

Proposition (1) ER determines potential competition with respect to the suppliers as it shapes the scope of new entry.

[23] Alternatively, one could use an 'ecologically corrected' GDP by subtracting the monetary equivalent of the losses due to pollution from the conventional GDP.

[24] The notorious subsidization of enterprises' losses is captured by the notion of Kornai's soft budget constraint.

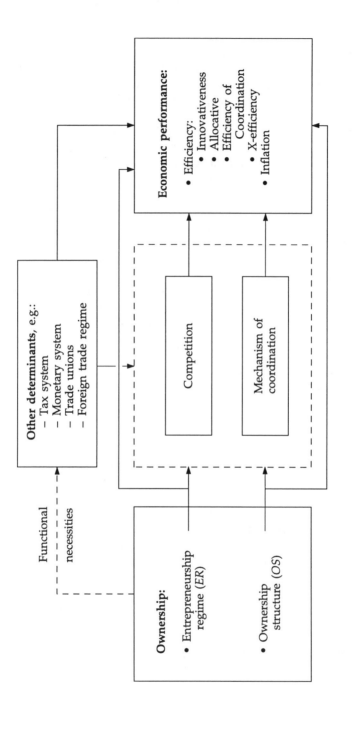

Fig. 7.1 *Ownership and economic performance*

Proposition (2) OS determines the type and intensity of actual competition.

Capitalist ownership structure (OS_c) creates much more competition than does the socialist one (OS_s) as the differences in the enterprises' maximands lead to different intensity of actions resulting in competitive threats (cf. Jasiński 1992). Also, the state-dominated ownership structure undermines competition among suppliers through the related soft budget constraint. Finally, massive state ownership in the centralized form eliminates this competition through the related organizational concentration (see Chapter 5).

These propositions point out that the popular claim 'competition matters more than ownership' can make sense only with respect to situations where competition is independent of ownership, for the latter is regarded as given. A typical case usually discussed in the literature is a small public sector in a predominantly capitalist economy. Increased competition, due, for example, to deregulation or foreign trade liberalization, may then produce visible efficiency gains.[25] However, if the share of the state sector is large, such increased competition is likely to be reversed given the danger of politicization (see section 3.4). Furthermore, it cannot be assumed *a priori* that privatization without competition is incapable of increasing efficiency. The empirical research points to the contrary (Kikori *et al.* 1994). But, most importantly, privatization should and, in most cases, can be combined with increased competition thanks to the increased competitive threat, hardening of the enterprises' budget constraint and foreign trade liberalization. The first two effects are due to privatization itself. The efficiency differential between a privatized economy subject to competition and the previous state-dominated economy, incapable of introducing or maintaining competition, could be huge, indeed.

Proposition (3) ER and OS determine the mode of the coordination in the economy.

A closed entrepreneurship regime and ownership structure dominated by the state firms in a centralized form eliminate the market mechanism. The demand for coordination must then be met by some

---

[25] But even such gains are not sufficient to establish the validity of the discussed claim, as one should compare them with efficiency gains from privatizing the public firms without introducing competition. In practice, one should, of course, both privatize and introduce competition.

form of bureaucratic mechanism which unavoidably displays low flexibility of supply and shortages. As a result, the efficiency of coordination is much lower under command socialism than that obtainable under competitive capitalism. The insufficient coordination of the expansion of productive capabilities in the respective industries, a weakness which is sometimes linked only to the latter system (cf. Nelson 1981) paradoxically may be much more serious under central planning, given the tendency to falsify information in the intermediate bureaucratic bargaining and the political nature of the decision-making with respect to investment.[26] Command socialism, as distinct from competitive capitalism, is also plagued by massive losses due to the violation of the requirements of technical complementarity in current production and consumption, i.e., in the process of using the productive capacities and stock of consumer durables by households.

Market socialism is an intermediate case, as it – theoretically – allows a limited market mechanism but blocks free entry and, therefore, limits the flexibility of supply. This flexibility would be lower then that under competitive capitalism also because of the different reactions of the enterprises, due to a difference in their maximands (for more on this see Balcerowicz 1989).

Proposition (4) Large differences in ER and OS lead to large differences in the level of innovativeness.

Chapter 6 provides an analysis of command socialism, reformed socialism and competitive capitalism. I would only recall here that both indirect and direct influences of ER and OS are at work here. The former operate through the differences in competition (see propositions (1) and (2) and through the mode and efficiency of coordination (see (3)): shortages radically lower both the propensity and ability of firms to undertake socially useful innovations. The direct effects include the impact of ER, i.e., whether the potential innovators who exist in every society can set up and develop enterprises. Another direct effect is due to the differences in firms' maximands. Profit orientation is a much

---

[26] Indeed, those who claim the superiority of centralized coordination unwittingly adhere to an idealized theory of a state, which is typical of old-fashioned welfare economics. However, it should be emphasized that the coordination of investment under market capitalism is still not fully explained. For example, one can inquire what the respective roles of some not yet completely known properties of the market mechanism itself are, and of its complements, e.g. the dissemination of information by various industrial associations. For an interesting view on this issue, see Richardson 1972.

stronger driving force for innovativeness then the criteria applied in a large state sector.

The innovativeness of market socialism may be higher than that under command socialism, thanks to more enterprise autonomy and fewer shortages than under command socialism. However, it must be lower than that achievable under competitive capitalism. The main reasons for this innovative differential include differences in the scope of entry, in the intensity of competition, and in the enterprises' maximands. Also, the labour-managed firms would be more prone to risk avoidance than their private counterparts (see Bergson 1982).

Proposition (5)   Large differences in ER and OS lead to large differences in the level of X-efficiency.

ER and OS affect the type and intensity of competition, and competition is decisive in influencing this level. An additional factor, present under command socialism, is the excessive demand for labour which rules out a strong work discipline.

Generally speaking, X-efficiency depends on intra-enterprise incentive systems and these systems are crucially dependent on the firms external monitoring environment. An environment without competition among the suppliers, a product of certain states of ER and OS, precludes a widespread existence of such intra-firm incentive mechanisms which can produce a high level of X-efficiency.

Proposition (6)   Contrary to certain claims, the problem of negative externalities exists under any economic system, as defined by ER and OS.

This problem does not depend on ownership factors, but is caused by the fundamental fact that human motivation tends to be self-centred. Thus people do not usually consider as costs those phenomena which are negative side effects of the activity which brings them benefits, but which affect others.

Therefore, all economic systems face the task of reducing the negative spill-overs of economic activity by introducing their costs into the calculus of the self-centred economic agents. This problem can be solved much more successfully under competitive capitalism than under socialism, especially in its state-dominated form. First, in the former system, firms are much more sensitive to cost increases than their counterparts under socialism. This results from differences in competition and in the enterprises' maximands. The profit orientation, given an appropriate regulation, can be put to the service of ecology and produce large savings in the use of the environment. Second, private firms are obviously much less intertwined with the state than are state-owned enterprises. The capitalist state can, therefore, enforce environmental regulation much more decisively than the socialist one.[27] Due to both these factors, competitive capitalism can display much higher environmental efficiency than socialism, especially in its command form.

> *Proposition (7)* Unemployment, defined as the difference between the labour force and the number in productive employment, may be linked to ER and OS.

Competitive capitalism is likely to produce less such unemployment than both command and market socialism. Command socialism generates much hidden unemployment and market socialism creates fewer jobs than competitive capitalism (see section 3.5).

> *Proposition (8)* Some forms of socialism – if not all – are likely to experience a stronger wage push, i.e., nominal wage increases ahead of the productivity growth, than competitive capitalism.

As a result, the former systems would tend to be plagued by stronger inflationary pressures. This is especially likely to be a problem in labour-managed systems, where firms are dominated by non-capitalist insiders. A decentralized (reformed) state socialism where managers are given more autonomy would have this weakness. Not being owners and not subject to effective mechanisms of ownership monitoring, they would be less willing to resist and less capable of resisting excessive wage pressure. To remedy this situation wage controls would have to be maintained or reintroduced. However, they cannot be fully effective, and produce microeconomic distortions in the long run.

To assess the relative importance of ownership for economic performance, one should discuss the impact of other determinants, i.e., those which are not included in the definitions of ER and OS. Examples include the tax system, the monetary system, the labour-market institutions, and the foreign trade regime. Ideally, all the important institutional determinants of economic outcomes should be considered.

---

[27] The same goes for any regulation, including the regulation of natural monopolies (see Jasiński 1992). An additional factor is the nature of the political regime. A democratic state is much more susceptible to the pressures of environmental groups than the non-democratic one. However, it appears that democracy can co-exist extensively with capitalism but not with socialism (see Chapter 8).

One should specify the forms (or states) each variable can assume and link these forms to the various levels of economic performance, say, rates of economic growth. The institutional forms which make the most rapid growth possible could be called its institutional fundamentals. Our analysis points out that ER_o and OS_c are such fundamentals, as far as ownership is concerned.

Having the ownership factor and the list of other institutional determinants, one should find out what forms of ER and OS can co-exist with other variables, or what states of these other variables they require. This is the compatibility analysis discussed in Chapter 1. Such analysis would indicate, for example, that a closed entrepreneurship regime and a socialist ownership structure dominated by the centralized state enterprises can co-exist only with a restrictive and protectionist foreign trade regime (Balcerowicz 1989). The same rigidity exists with respect to the form of the labour-market institutions or a tax system. In contrast, ER_o and OS_c can be combined with various forms of institutional factors other than ownership. As a result, command socialism (ER_c, OS_s) displays much less variability in economic performance than market capitalism (ER_o, OS_c). In the latter case, the high efficiency and growth potential of ER_o and OS_c can be used to a different extent, depending on the form of other institutional variables. Such factors as rigid labour markets, high indirect labour costs or high direct taxation may be responsible for the low level of its utilization. This obviously does not undermine the importance of ER_o and OS_c but points to the importance of a proper shaping of other institutional factors.

One of the central tasks of institutional economics is to work out an institutional theory of economic growth. Such a theory would show, I believe, that countries which are growing especially rapidly differ from other countries in that the former have had more institutional fundamentals such as an open regime of entrepreneurship, a capitalist ownership structure, flexible labour markets, a low or moderate tax/GDP ratio, a stable macroeconomy, and a stable political system. It is the existence of an especially large scope of such fundamentals and not any single factor, say, a special type of government intervention or a special type of investment, which explains economic miracles, be it in West Germany in the 1950s or East Asia since the early 1960s.

References

Balcerowicz, L. 1985 'Adaptacyjność organizacyjna systemów gospodarczych', *Ekonomista* 6.

—— 1986 'Uwagi o pojmuś własności', *Studia Filozoficzne* 4, pp. 105–25.
—— 1987 'Remarks on the concept of ownership', *Oeconomica Polona*, no. 1, pp. 75–95.
—— 1989 *Systemy gospodarcze. Elementy analizy porównowczej* (Warsaw: SGPiS).
Bergson, A. 1982 'Entrepreneurship under labour participation: the Yugoslav case', in J. Ronen (ed.), *Entrepreneurship* (Lexington, Mass.: Lexington Books).
Davies, E. P. C. 1993 'The development of pension funds: an approaching financial revolution for Continental Europe', in R.O'Brian (ed.) *Financial and International Economy* (Oxford: Oxford University Press for the *Amex Bank Review*), pp. 108–27.
De Allesi, C. 1983 'Property Rights, Transaction Costs, and *X*-Efficiency: An Essay in Economic Theory', *American Economic Review*, March, pp. 64–81.
De Soto, H. 1989 *The Other Path* (New York: Harper and Row).
Eucken, W. 1965 'On the theory of the centrally administered economy', in M. Bernstein (ed.) *Comparative Economic Systems* (Homewood: Illinois University Press).
Furubotn, E. G. & Pejovich, S. 1972 'Property rights and economic theory: a survey of recent literature' *Journal of Economic Literature* 10, pp. 1137–62.
Galbraith, J. K. 1980 *A Theory of Price Control: The Classic Account* (Cambridge, Mass.: Harvard University Press).
Grossman, S. J. & Hart, O. 1985 'The costs and benefits of ownership: a theory of vertical and lateral integration', *Journal of Political Economy* 94, pp. 691–719.
Jasiński, P. 1992 'The transfer and redefinition of property rights: theoretical analysis of transferring property rights and transformational privatization in the Port-STES', *Communist Economies and Economic Transformation* 4, pp. 163–89.
Kikori, S., Nellis, J. & Shirley, M. 1994 'Privatization: lessons from market economies', *World Bank Observer* 9, pp. 241–72.
Kornai, J. 1995 'The Principles of Privatization in Eastern Europe', in Kazimierz Z. Poznanski (ed.), *The Evolutionary Transition to Capitalism* (Boulder, Colo.: Westview Press), pp. 31–56.
Lloyd, D. 1977 *The Idea of Law* (Harmondsworth, Midx.: Penguin Books).
Lydall, H. 1984 *Yugoslav Socialism: Theory and Practice* (Oxford: Clarendon Press).
Marsden, K. 1990 'African entrepreneurs: pioneers of development', Discussion Paper No. 9, JFC, Washington, DC.
Mises, L. von 1981 *Socialism: An Economic and Political Analysis* (Indianapolis: Liberty Classics).
Mueller, C. D. 1993 'The corporation and the economist', *International Journal of Industrial Organization* 102, reprinted in *Economics Alert*, no. 3, pp. 1–3.
Niskanen, W. 1992 'Guidelines for delineating the private and the government sector', in H. Siebert (ed.) *Privatization: Essays in Honour of Herbert Giersch* (Kiel: Institut für Weltwirtshaft an der Universitat Kiel)..
Nelson, R. R. 1981 'Assessing private enterprise: an exegesis of tangled doctrine', *Bell Journal of Economics* 12, pp. 93–111.
North, D. 1990 *Institutions, Institutional Change, and Economic Performance*, (Cambridge: Cambridge University Press).
Pelikan, P. 1992 'The dynamics of economic systems, or how to transform a failed socialist economy', *Journal of Evolutionary Economics* 2, pp. 39–63.

Richardson, G. B. 1972 'Organization of industry', *Economic Journal* 88, pp. 883–96.

Roe, J. M. 1993 'Some differences in corporate structure in Germany, Japan, and the United States', *Yale Law Journal*, no. 1, pp. 1000–161.

Schumpeter, J. A. 1962 *Capitalism, Socialism, and Democracy* (New York: Harper and Row).

Shleifer, A. C. 1994 'Establishing property rights', Annual World Bank Conference on Development Economics, Washington, DC.

Scott, J. 1985 *Capitalist Property and Financial Power: A Comparative Study of Britain, the United States and Japan* (Brighton: Wheatsheaf).

8

Political and Economic Regimes: Problems of Compatibility and Performance

This chapter revisits some of the classical issues, i.e. is socialism compatible with democracy? Is democracy a substitute for capitalism? Does capitalism undermine democracy? These issues have been debated for a long time, but recent developments in the post-socialist countries and in many parts of the Third World, as well as the political and economic problems of the OECD countries make them especially relevant and urgent. I am, of course, not able to provide definitive answers to these fundamental questions. However, I hope to be able to put them in a clear analytical framework and to clarify at least some of them.

1. Political versus Economic Systems

The totality of a country's institutions constitute its institutional system (see Chapter 1). One can distinguish various subsystems within this system, including the political and economic ones. There is no

The first draft of this chapter was presented at the seminar at the Institute for Human Sciences in Vienna in September 1994 during my stay as a visiting fellow. It was extended and presented at the seminar at the European Bank for Reconstruction and Development in February 1995 when I was a visiting fellow in the Chief Economist's office of the Bank. The present version was written in April 1995 during my stay as E. L. Wiegand Distinguished Visiting Professor of Democratization at Georgetown University in Washington, DC. I would like to thank Amanda Klekowski for her help in editing this chapter.

universally recognized and precise dividing line between these two regimes. The best one can do is to follow certain established definitional conventions. In adopting this approach, I would include in the political regime all the institutions which are directly related to the change and execution of power within the state. This includes some parts of the general legal framework, e.g. constitutional rules, determining the division of power and cooperation within the state, laws governing electoral campaigns and elections, laws regulating lobbying, and laws on political parties determining their creation and functioning. The political parties (if they exist) are the main type of political institution which belongs to the second category, that of institutional structures. The economic system, in turn, consists of institutions which shape decision-making and the implementation of decisions with respect to production, income, saving, investment and consumption (Lindbeck 1977).

These are some unavoidable overlaps: certain institutions are present – performing different activities – in both political and economic systems. For example, a trade union or an employers' association which tries to influence the relevant legislation is part of a political regime. The same organizations when participating in collective bargaining belong to the economic system. The state itself – depending on its organs and activities – is also present in both political and economic systems. The state institutions involved in the processes, which generate outputs such as legislation, can be regarded as parts of the political regime. This is the political economy dimension of the state, analysed, for example, by the theory of public choice with respect to the democratic regimes in normal times.[1] The state institutions involved in the implementation of economic policies belong to the economic system.

2. Varieties of Political Systems

Debates about political regimes largely centre on the classical distinction between their democratic and non-democratic varieties. I will follow this important convention, but with some qualifications. *Democracy* is understood here as an institutional arrangement whereby those who rule are chosen in regular, free and fair elections, based on the principle of one person, one vote. This presupposes, in any large group, the

---

[1] This theory does not deal with the operation of non-democratic regimes nor with political systems after the liberalizing breakthroughs which produce a short period of 'extraordinary politics'. For the latter, see Chapters 9 and 15.

freedom of speech and association which, however, may also exist – to some extent – without democracy (e.g. in a constitutional monarchy). The essence of democracy is, therefore, a regular, legal and non-violent contestability of the ruling positions, and the related possibility of the peaceful removal of those who rule. This procedural definition of democracy proposed by Schumpeter (1962) is not widely and rightly regarded as being logically superior to the alternative definitions in terms of either source of authority (the will of the people) or purposes (the common good). For these definitions are plagued by problems of ambiguity and imprecision (see Popper 1988; Huntington 1991). Besides, they are value-loaded, and as such they settle by assumption important problems which should only be decided by analysis.[2] Such idealistic definitions may also have some dangerous practical consequences. Given the unavoidable gaps between the ideals they hold as criteria for democracy and reality, they may breed disillusionment with the form of government, which, however imperfect, can still be the best available in the real world.

In large groups, including nation-states, democracy can only be representative and not direct. Depending on what proportion of the adult population has electoral rights, we can speak of numerically limited democracy where only a fraction of such a population has those rights, or of a mass democracy, where practically all the adults have them. Nowadays, only the latter variant is called a 'democracy' and henceforth I will follow this convention.

The concept of democracy based on procedural definition allows the investigation of what variable properties of democratic regimes influence its quality, as measured, for example, by the quality of decisions they produce, and what changes should be introduced in the democratic framework in order to improve this quality. This issue is related to the problem of the sources of variation within the class of democratic regimes. For example, democracies differ in the locus of authority (presidential versus parliamentary systems), in electoral laws and in related party systems, in the power of the bureaucracy versus the elected politicians, in the type and strength of the interest groups, etc.

An interesting framework for the positive and normative analysis of democracy was proposed by Fishkin (1991). He distinguishes, following the American Federalists Madison and Hamilton, three criteria for comparative analysis and assessment of democratic regimes: political equality, non-tyranny and deliberation. Political equality is at its

[2] There is a certain analogy between the value-loaded definitions of socialism (see Chapter 2) and these definitions of democracy.

maximum in a system 'which grants equal consideration to everyone's preferences and which grants everyone approximately equal opportunities to formulate preferences on the issues under consideration' (Fishkin 1991, pp. 30–1). The minimum condition, which distinguishes democracy from non-democracy, is equal formal voting rights. Besides, the fulfilment of the equality conditions may vary depending on 'the background conditions' that set the stage for the use of these formal rights. These conditions include, for example, potential differences in the size of electoral districts which differentiate the number of voters per representative, access to media, the extent to which voters are influenced by threats or bargains outside the political sphere (for example, political clientelism or promised rewards in an afterlife), the impact of economic inequalities on the possibilities of political participation, etc.

Tyranny is defined as 'the choice of policy that imposes severe deprivations when an alternative policy could have been chosen that would have imposed no severe deprivations on anyone' (Fishkin, 1991, p. 834). In the context of democracy, non-tyranny means, therefore, the avoidance of 'the tyranny of majority'. Finally, deliberation refers to the role of knowledge and reason versus that of the emotions and unreflective preferences in the various processes of democratic decision-making: in the choice of the candidates for elective offices, in the work of the elected officials and in such forms of direct democracy as referendums. Deliberation is obviously crucial for the quality of decisions.

Fishkin points out that most of the institutional arrangements that further one or two of these conditions involve sacrifices of the remaining criterion or criteria. He focuses on the dangers of the 'plebiscitarian' form of democracy based on frequent opinion polls, referendums and television campaigns in which the candidates' appearances are reduced to sound bites.[3] This form of democracy, which is one the rise in most countries, may increase political equality, but only at great cost to deliberation.

Non-democracy, by definition, refers to the political systems where the succession of the rulers is based on mechanisms other than regular and free elections, e.g. hereditary succession, a *coup d'état*, bargaining behind closed doors within the monopolistic ruling party, etc. Some non-democracies, such as former socialist countries, organized elections, but they served to rubber-stamp decisions taken previously and to verify the obedience of the people. The non-democracies which exist in

---

[3] The average sound bite or block of uninterrupted speech fell from 42.3 seconds for presidential candidates in the United States in 1968 to only 9.8 seconds in 1988 (Adato (1990) quoted in Fishkin (1991), p. 62).

the real world vary even more than the democracies, perhaps because the former allow – by their very nature – a greater scope for the operation of differences in the personalities of the leadership. The institutional differences among non-democracies include, for example, the role of the army versus the monopolistic party, the position of the government *vis-à-vis* private business as compared to its position with respect to the trade unions, etc.

Besides the variation within democracies and non-democracies, there are some variables which may cut across these categories, for example the quality of public administration.

3. Varieties of Economic Systems

I will base the typology of economic systems on three related institutional variables: the type of entrepreneurship regime (ER), the ownership structure (OS), the mechanism of coordination (MC). These variables were discussed in the previous chapter. Let us only recall that ER denotes this part of the general legal framework which determines what types of enterprises can be legally established and developed. There have been three main types of ER: closed (ER_c), open or liberal (ER_o) and restrictive (ER_r).

ER_c, by definition, bans the private enterprise in order to ensure the monopoly of another type of firm: this preferred type was either the state firm or a labour-managed enterprise. ER_o ensures a choice among many types of enterprises, both private and non-private, such as cooperatives. ER_r ensured a monopoly for the state firms for some selected sectors of the economy ('the commanding heights' or the 'strategic' sectors). In addition, the procedures for setting up private firms were often cumbersome, time-consuming and costly.

One can distinguish three main types of OS: capitalist: OS_c (dominated by the private sector), socialist: OS_s (dominated by socialist enterprises, i.e. state-owned or labour-managed) and 'mixed', OS_m, which is an intermediate form. As I have pointed out in Chapter 7, there is a strong link between ER and OS:

$$ER_o \longrightarrow OS_c$$
$$ER_c \longrightarrow OS_s$$
$$ER_r \longrightarrow OS_m$$

ER and OS determine the mode of coordination. The *market mechanism* as a mode of coordination within the sphere of private goods

Table 8.1 *Types of economic systems*

Regime of entrepreneurship (ER)	Ownership structure (OS)	Mechanism of coordination (MC)	Type of system
Open	Capitalist	Market	Market capitalism
Closed	Socialist	Command	Command socialism
Closed	Socialist	Limited market	Market socialism
Restrictive	'Mixed'	Distorted market	Distorted or quasi-capitalism
Open	Changing from socialism to capitalism	Immature market	Liberal transition economy
Restrictive	Slow change	Neither plan nor market	Heavily regulated transition economy

presupposes freedom of supply, prices and demand (ER_o, OS_c). The alternative, the *command mechanism*, is based on supply targets, administrative rationing of goods which constrains demand, and on controlled prices (ER_c, OS_s dominated by the centralized state firm). There are some intermediate modes of coordination ('neither plan nor market') which rely on extensive licensing, government 'contracts' which substitute for commands and the controlled prices of the basic inputs and of consumption goods.

ER_c and OS_s, which is dominated by some variant of labour-managed firms, would give rise to a limited market, both in the sense of limited competition (see Chapter 7) and the exclusion of equity markets. ER_r and OS_m combined with restrictions on entry would produce a distorted market. Finally, post-socialist economies which introduce radical liberalization would, in the early phases of their market-oriented reforms, have a sort of an immature market mechanism. This immaturity results from the fact that institutions necessary for a well-functioning market, e.g. legal infrastructure, enforcement apparatus, financial intermediaries, take more time to develop than the liberalization itself (for more on this, see Chapter 10).

Table 8.1 presents a typology of economic systems based on the three discussed institutional variables. It should be stressed that the table disregards some important dimensions of differentiation within the respective types. Economies belonging to market capitalism differ, for example, in the degree of budgetary redistribution and in the related scope and forms of the welfare state, in the corporate governance structure, in the form of their financial system, in the role of the central bank, in the presence or absence of corporatist elements, etc.

4. Politico-Economic systems: Three Basic Questions

Let us now see what the theoretically possible combinations of the above displayed variants of the political and economic regimes are. Table 8.2 is the result of this exercise:

Several comments are in order. First, the models presented in this table should be interpreted as stylized facts which do not represent all the real politico-economic systems. For example, some Western economies with extensive welfare states, regulated labour markets and anti-market protectionism in agriculture are closer to the category of distorted capitalism than that of market capitalism. Among the transition economies, Russia until 1995 falls between the model of a liberal transition economy and that of a heavily regulated economy.

Second, as I already noted, democracies differ in some important respects. However, this is not considered in the table as I was unable to link the types of that form of government with the indicated types of the economic system. The same goes for non-democracies. I will return to the variation of both categories of political regimes in section 7.

I noted in Chapter 1 that the study of institutions should focus on the problems of their compatibility, performance and dynamics. These three basic questions can be asked with respect to the displayed combinations of political and economic regimes:

(1) Which pairs of these regimes are mutually compatible and which are not, i.e. have a built-in tendency to collapse or to turn into another system?
(2) What is the performance of the respective politico-economic systems?
(3) What are the determinants and properties of transitions from one politico-economic system into another?

The compatibility problem includes the following main questions:

- Can socialism co-exist with democracy?
- Does capitalism undermine democracy?
- Does democracy weaken market capitalism?

Table 8.2 *Politico-economic systems*

Political system	Economic system	Empirical examples
Democracy	Market capitalism	Some OECD countries; some developing economies
Democracy	Distorted capitalism	India, until recently
Democracy	Socialism	No lasting example so far
Non-democracy	Market capitalism	East Asia until recently
Non-democracy	Distorted or quasi-capitalism	Latin American until recently
Non-democracy	Command socialism	Former Comecon countries
Non-democracy	Market socialism	No good empirical example; former Yugoslavia comes the closest
Early democracy	Liberal transition economy	Central Europe, the Baltics until 1995
Chaotic pluralism	Heavily regulated transition economy	Most of the former USSR until 1995

The performance problem comprises such issues as:

- Is the type of political regime (democracy versus non-democracy) important for economic growth?
- The political performance of modern mass democracy, as measured by the popular participation and the level of popular dissatisfaction with respect to the political process and the politicians.

The problem of the systems' dynamics includes both great societal shifts and intra-regime changes, e.g. the evolution of modern capitalism. I will discuss some issues of institutional change in the following chapters of this book which focus on the postcommunist transition.

In the remaining sections of this chapter I will briefly discuss some of the compatibility and performance problems.

5. Can Socialism Co-exist with Democracy?

This question is or great importance for those postsocialist countries which have at least pluralist (if not yet democratic) political systems but are in the early stages of market-oriented reforms which are in danger of being blocked. What could happen to their political system if this situation continues in their economic regime? If history is to be trusted, then the answer would be that the above combination of the political and economic systems is unlikely to exist, for so far there is no example of a socialist economy co-existing, for a significant amount of time, with democracy. However, one could rightly argue that historical experience alone cannot be relied upon to supply proofs of impossibility of the enduring co-existence of these two regimes. History moves only on some possible trajectories. The fact that something has not yet existed does not imply that it cannot exist. For example, one can claim that the exclusive co-existence of democracy with capitalism has resulted from a peculiar historical sequence. The countries which at present combine both regimes, first became capitalist, then capitalism brought about economic development, and economic development brought about – via increased education and growing demand from the working classes for political rights – the transition to democracy. However, this sequence is not the only possible one. As a matter of fact, the post-socialist countries first made decisive moves towards democracy in the political sphere before they could have become capitalist (see Chapter 9). Why should the preservation of the non-capitalist economy endanger these democratic gains? We are back at the initial question. Therefore, we have to look at the theoretical arguments regarding the relationship of socialism and democracy. I can see three forces which make the enduring co-existence of socialism and democracy rather unlikely. To see their operation clearly, let us envisage a system which combines democracy and socialism and ask what would happen to socialism or to democracy:

(1) Socialism produces only poor economic results relative to com-
    petitive market capitalism: the deficiencies of command socialism
    are well known,[4] and were discussed in Chapters 3, 4 and 6. Market
    socialism would suffer from more unemployment and less inno-
    vativeness, i.e. less growth of aggregate consumption (see Chapter
    7).[5] This poor relative economic performance would be common
    knowledge thanks to liberties related to democracy (free mass
    media, freedom to travel, etc.), and would, therefore, breed popular

---

[4] Besides, command socialism, given its enormous concentration of power at the upper levels of the economic hierarchy, would be directly incompatible with democracy.

[5] Shleifer (1994) also argues that democracy under market socialism would endanger the economic performance via the politicization of the economy. This danger was already pointed out by von Mises (1951, p. 202).

discontent. This discontent would either have to be suppressed, which would mean an end to democracy, or it would lead to economic liberalization, i.e. transition to capitalism.[6]

(2) A democratic political order would include liberal parties which would demand that the closed entrepreneurship regime (ER_c) be replaced by an open one (ER_o). They would either have to be banned, which would make a sham of democracy, or – after an appropriately long economic crisis (see Proposition (1)) – they would succeed, i.e. and initiate the transition to capitalism.

(3) Democracy requires a certain social structure which is at least partly related to the institutions of capitalism (private entrepreneurs, free professions). Blocking the development of capitalism, i.e., preserving socialism, would prevent, therefore, the emergence of a social base necessary for enduring democracy.

These arguments show why Schumpeter's (1962) assertion that socialism is perfectly compatible with democracy should be regarded sceptically. First, he claimed wrongly (see Chapter 4) that socialism can be economically superior to capitalism, so he eliminated problems (1) and (2). He additionally ruled out problem (2) by assuming that socialism can be successfully introduced and maintained if 'things and souls' are ripe (p. 220), which may be interpreted to mean if people in democracies are against private entrepreneurship. In any case, it is a fallacy to assume something which is central to the proposition one advances. Finally, he disregarded problem (3).

Against the background of the three arguments above, the latecomers in the post-communist tradition would be advised to speed up their economic reforms not only in the interests of economic development but also for the sake of democracy.

6. Can Capitalism Co-Exist with Democracy?

This question may appear absurd as what we call 'democracy' has existed *only* in conjunction with capitalism. But it signals in a somewhat

[6] Let us note a paradox here. Imagine a country which is initially both democratic and capitalist and in which – in the name of democracy – the so-called 'economic democracy' is introduced, i.e. private enterprises are turned into labour-managed ones (on the basis of the principle of one person, one vote) and private entrepreneurship is banned. Given the poor relative performance of labour-managed market socialism, this would either lead to the suppression of democracy in the political sphere or to the return to capitalism in the economic one.

pointed form some real tensions and dilemmas relating to the role of money in contemporary politics. It was Karl Marx who referred to them in the following exaggerated fashion: democracy is impossible under capitalism since under capitalism it is the capitalists who rule. The government is simply an executive committee of the bourgeoisie. Democracy is only 'formal' or, in other words, a sham.

History has falsified this extreme view. Marx's view disregarded, among other things, the internal divisions among the 'capitalists' and the growing role of the other social classes, including the workers, which has been made possible thanks to the liberal foundations (civil society) of capitalist society, so neglected by Marx. But, as with every caricature, this view contains some grains of truth, which may be interpreted as warnings. They refer to the manner in which the sponsors of political parties influence the selection of candidates for political positions, the choice of the political agenda, political behaviour, etc. These and other issues are discussed by Dahl (1989), Fishkin (1991) and other analysts of contemporary democracy.

However, it should be noted that such influences are by no means limited to business circles. Trade unions and professional associations are often a powerful political force. Therefore, general responses are needed. They should include, for example, complete transparency of the party finances – parties should perhaps be subject to similar auditing requirements as publicly quoted companies and to regulations limiting lobbying. The latter seems to be also necessary to deal with one of the performance problems: a growing public disillusionment with the practices of contemporary democracy. Other reforms would refer to the role of the mass media, especially television, and to the procedures which would increase the scope for deliberation in contemporary mass democracy (see Fishkin 1991).

Another claim regarding the tension between capitalism and democracy centres on economic inequalities. It is rightly argued that very large inequalities of this type lead to unequal possibilities of political participation and thus are in conflict with, at least, the spirit of democracy. But are economic inequalities under capitalism unavoidably very large? The answer is that they differ widely depending on the type of capitalism. Distorted capitalism of a statist-oligarchic variety which prevailed until recently in many Latin American countries produces much larger economic inequalities than an export-oriented and much more private capitalism of an East Asian type (see World Bank 1993). The latter generated much more rapid economic growth than the former. A rather optimistic conclusion then emerges: the economic model most conducive to economic growth also creates the best economic conditions (i.e. relatively modest inequalities) for democracy.[7]

7. The Type of Political Regime and Economic Growth

I will follow the classical conceptualization of political regimes in terms of democracy versus non-democracy – introduced in section 2 – and ask the question: how important is democracy compared with non-democracy for economic growth, other things being equal? This question is especially relevant to the countries of Eastern Europe and the former Soviet Union, which were given the historical chance to make a transition to *both* democracy and the capitalist market economy. The understanding of what can be expected from each of these systems is clearly important to the people of these countries.

From the methodological point of view, the problem of the importance of the type of political regime for economic growth can be reduced to two comparisons:

(1) (democracy, socialism) versus (non-democracy, socialism);
(2) (democracy, capitalism) versus (non-democracy, capitalism).

However, as we noted in section 5, only non-democratic socialism has existed and there are strong grounds to believe that democratic socialism is not possible as a stable system. The negative result of the compatibility analysis, therefore, eliminates the performance issue in accordance with a principle formulated in Chapter 1. We can thus focus on the second comparison.

There have been many empirical studies during the last twenty years on the link between the type of political regime and the rate of economic growth among the non-socialist countries. These studies have been reviewed by Sirowy & Inkeles (1990). They reach the conclusion that 'at best . . . democracy does not widely and directly facilitate more rapid economic growth net of other factors' (p. 1501). Helliwell, in a

---

[7] Scully (1991) makes a general point that regimes which provide wide scope of economic freedom, in terms of individual rights, and ensure an equal distribution of these rights, can achieve both high economic efficiency and relatively equal income distribution.

meticulous study of 125 countries over the period 1960 to 1985, ends with a similar conclusion: 'it is still not possible to identify any systematic net effects of democracy on subsequent economic growth'. Alesina & Perotti (1994) reach substantially the same, although a differently worded, conclusion: 'there is no evidence that on average, a democracy with civil liberties is costly in terms of economic development'. They add: 'If anything, it may be the other way around, that democracy with civil liberties promotes economic development' (p. 354). However, in this second sentence they go beyond the empirical findings and they confuse democracy as such (elective government) with its institutional correlate. In doing that, they disregard the question of how the scope of various liberties is related to the type of political regime and what liberties matter the most for economic growth.

However, empirical research is subject to some methodological objections (see, for example, Przeworski & Limongi 1993). Let us, therefore, turn to theoretical debates. These are also inconclusive and have been carried out in a rather peculiar way: the proponents of the claim of superiority of non-democracy over democracy emphasize the advantages which may be present only in *some* non-democratic regimes as though they were typical of *all* of them. These advantages include greater capacity to mobilize savings and to focus the energy of the nation on the goal of long-term economic growth. It is also claimed that authoritarian regimes are more resistant to the pressures of the interest groups which are a by-product of democracy and hamper growth.

The proponents of the economic superiority of democracy over non-democracy argue, in turn, that private property rights would be more secure under democracy than non-democracy (Olson, 1993; Niskanen, 1992). But this assertion is based on a very specific modelling of a utility function of a dictator. The name given to him by Mancur Olson speaks for itself – 'a stationary bandit'. It is assumed that a dictator maximizes his private wealth and nothing else. All the conclusions about the economic inferiority of non-democracy compared to democracy follow from this assumption. I have no sympathy for dictators but on methodological grounds, I cannot help but remark that not all autocrats are of the Bokassa-type. Self-interest cannot always be reduced to the utility function which has only one argument: personal wealth. Other motives may matter, too, for example, self-esteem, which could take the form of vanity, prestige, achievement motivation, etc. And the assumption on the utility function of the individual who – by the nature of his/her institutional position – drives the whole country, is absolutely crucial for the conclusions of the models of non-democratic regimes.[8] Besides, even granting that personal wealth is a central motivating factor and therefore a central argument in the related utility function, but assuming that instead of maximization, satisficing in Simon's sense (1959) takes place, would undermine the conclusions of these models. Therefore, the proponents of the economic superiority of democracy over non-democracy commit the same logical mistake as the proponents of the opposite claim: they treat something specific to only some non-democracies as though it were typical for all of them. They treat very heterogeneous categories as though they were homogeneous. This points to a limited analytical usefulness of conducting comparative analysis in such general terms as democracy and non-democracy.

The above suggests that the whole problem of the relationship between political regimes and economic growth (and other aspects of economic performance) should be reformulated and analysed in a different framework. This new framework should be provided by the theory of the institutional determinants of economic growth, determinants which underline such proximate causes of this process as the rate of savings and investment and the rate of productivity growth (see Chapter 7). One should try to link some variable aspects of the political sphere to those institutional determinants. Some of the former would overlap with the latter, other political variables would have to be related – via clearly elaborated causal mechanisms – to the institutional determinants of economic growth as included in the theory.

Political variables should not be limited to the general dichotomy: democracy versus non-democracy. Various types of democracies should be distinguished. In searching for the variable aspects of democracy which matter for economic growth one should consider: (1) the scope of deliberation provided by the procedures of democratic decision-making (see Fishkin 1991); (2) the constitutional framework regulating the economic policy, e.g. whether there are constraints on the monetary financing of the budget deficit or whether economic liberties are protected (see for example, Gwartney & Wagner 1988); (3) the strength of narrowly focused and aggressive interest groups (see Olson 1982). A typology of non-democracies, based as much as possible on similar criteria, should be worked out, too. Ideally, one would arrive at a set of

---

[8] In principle, the theory of the economic behaviour of non-democratic regimes should be based on the probability distributions of the various utility functions of the dictators. The empirical strength of the conclusions of the above models should then be measured by the probability of the occurrence of the personal wealth maximizing dictators, multiplied by the probability that they would choose ways of wealth maximization postulated by these theories. It appears that the product of these two probabilities is closer to zero than to one.

variables describing the political sphere, P_1, P_2, ... P_j, and two related typologies: one for democracy: D_1 D_2, ... D_k, and another one for non-democracy: non-D_1, non-D_2, ... non-D_n.

This approach would probably show that what really matters for economic growth is not just the general juxtaposition, democracy versus non-democracy, but the types of each of these regimes. One should try to link various types of democracy and non-democracy to the rates of economic growth they are likely or able to produce.[9] By ascribing frequencies to those various types of democracy and non-democracy one would get statistical distributions of the growth performance of democracy and non-democracy.[10] One could go one step further and interpret those frequencies as probabilities of the occurrence of a given type.[11]

The proposed approach would reveal that various types of non-democracy differ much more in growth performance than various types of democracy. Even casual observation confirms this proposition. It can be explained by two factors. First, there is much more scope for differences in the quality of political decisions under non-democracy than democracy as the former allows much more scope for the operation of the personality variables than the latter.[12] More importantly, the variation of the institutional forms of non-democracy seems to be much larger than that under democracy.

Second, there is the relationship between democracy and non-democracy, and the institutional determinants of economic growth which are not included in the definitions of those two political regimes.

[9] The first rate would show the average performance; the second, the maximum possible one. The divergence between the two rates could be largely explained by the variation of economic policy possible under a given type of democracy and non-democracy. One may expect this variation to be larger under non-democracy than democracy, given the larger scope for the operation of the personality factors in the former case.

[10] These frequencies could be based on the relative number of countries which may be regarded as the empirical counterparts of the respective types.

[11] By interpreting frequencies in these distributions as probabilities of occurrence of a certain type of democracy or non-democracy, one would get the expected values of the economic growth performance of these types. A certain type of non-democracy, say, South Korean pro-capitalist autocracy, may have a very high absolute value for economic growth but its expected value may be quite low, given a low probability of the occurrence of this type. One should distinguish those probabilities from those of switching, say, from a badly performing democracy to a well-performing autocracy. Such a probability may be practically zero; instead a probability that a country with a badly performing democracy, if it abandoned the democratic range, would get a badly performing autocracy, would be quite high.

[12] It could be contested that people who become leaders under non-democracy are for some reason psychologically more homogeneous than those who assume similar positions under democracy. This issue would have to be settled by in-depth psychological research. Casual observations suggest that the opposite is the case.

The point is that the variation of those factors can be much larger under non-democracy than under democracy; this produces, of course, much larger differences in the growth performance under non-democracy than those under democracy. The scope of economic freedom is the institutional variable, which is crucial for the economic growth. This variable can be conceptualized as the regime of entrepreneurship and as related to ownership structure (see Chapter 7). Experience shows that non-democracies were related to all the possible main forms of these variables: to the closed *ER* and the socialist ownership structure dominated by the state companies (typical socialist autocracies), to the closed *ER* and *OS* determined by the – formally – labour-managed firms (socialist autocracy in the former Yugoslavia), to the restrictive *ER* and the mixed ownership structure (populist autocracies which existed in Latin America) and finally – to the open *ER* and the capitalist ownership structure. The last category includes the pro-capitalist autocracies which until recently existed in East Asia[13] and proved to be capable of exceptional growth.[14] In contrast, if we disregard the transition countries, then we note that democracies co-exist with only two variants of *ER* and *OS*: open *ER* and the capitalist *OS* (most of OECD countries) and restrictive *ER* and rather mixed ownership structure (India until recently, at least). It appears that other institutionally based determinants of economic growth, e.g. macroeconomic stability, the tax system, the type and role of the trade unions and of business associations, may be much more varied under non-democracy than democracy, given much greater variety of the non-democratic regimes.

There exists perhaps a special type of non-democracy, say an East Asian pro-capitalist autocracy (Balcerowicz 1994) which is capable of a better growth performance than any type of democracy acting under comparable conditions. This proposition has to be tested by a rigorous comparison of the growth performance of the non-democratic East Asian tigers since, the early 1960s, with that of some very fast growing democracies in the 1950s (Japan, West Germany, Italy). This comparison would reveal certain institutional similarities which cut across the dichotomy: democracy versus non-democracy. The indicated groups of countries were characterized, I think, by an unusual accumulation of the institutional fundamentals of economic growth: very open regime of entrepreneurship, a capitalist ownership structure with an important

[13] For more on these types of non-democracies, see Balcerowicz (1994).

[14] This performance can be explained – at the level of proximate determinants – by the high rate of growth of productivity and the unusually high rate of savings and investment.

role for classical private firms, a low tax/GDP ratio and flexible labour markets.

Another comparison which one can use to test the above proposition would centre on East Asian countries before and after their democratization. In both comparisons one should control, of course, for the impact of the differences in the initial level of per capita income and in the external determinants of economic growth.

I do not want to pre-empt the results of these comparisons, but I would like to formulate one conditional proposition: if highly performing non-democracies turn out to be superior – in the area of economic growth – to the highly performing democracies, then it will mostly be attributed to the capacity of the former to achieve a very high rate of savings and investment without sacrificing the rate of productivity. The latter rate would be similarly high in both groups of countries – this would result from a similarly large amount of economic freedom. The potential superiority of highly performing non-democracies can be expected, therefore, to be due to their special capacity to mobilize savings. It is probably here that the difference between democracies and non-democracies eventually matters.

However, even if the above propositions are confirmed, in no case do they imply that the post-socialist countries which started the transition both to democracy and capitalism should abandon the former in the interest of the latter. There are several reasons for rejecting such a proposition. First, democracy, although it is not a substitute for capitalism, matters for non-economic reasons: it ensures – under contemporary conditions – the highest degree of social legitimization for those who rule, and the highest respect for the dignity of those who are ruled. Second, an attempt to switch to a non-democratic regime from a position of an immature democracy is not likely to result in a highly performing non-democracy of the East Asian type. For such regimes are very rare and they originate under very special conditions. A move away from immature democracy would most likely end in a populist autocracy which could be even worse for economic performance than the former regime.

Hence, the conclusions for the postsocialist countries are clear. They should try to strengthen the democracy in the political sphere: by increasing the scope for deliberation, by shaping a constitutional framework which would limit the possibilities of engaging in populist economic policies, by enacting electoral laws which would reduce the excessive number of political parties, etc. These reforms would help to speed up the transition to capitalism, and this transition in turn would strengthen democracy.

References

Adato, K. 1990 'The incredible shrinking sound bite', Cambridge, Mass., Joan Shorenstein Baronce Center of the John F. Kennedy School of Government, Harvard University, Research Paper No. 2, June.

Alesina, A. & Perotti, R. 1994 'The political economy of growth: a critical survey of the recent literature', *World Bank Economic Review* 8, pp. 351–72.

Balcerowicz, L. 1994 'Democracia y capitalismo en el mundo conterporaneo', in R. de Urquía & Enrique M. Ureña (eds), *Economia y Dinamica Socia* (Madrid: Union Editorial).

Dahl, R. 1989 *Democracy and Its Critics* (New Haven, Conn.: Yale University Press).

Fishkin, J. S. 1991 *Democracy and Deliberation: New Directions for Democratic Reform* (New Haven, Conn.: Yale University Press).

Gwartney, J. D. & Wagner, R. E. (eds) 1988 *Public Choice and Constitutional Economics* (London: JAI Press).

Huntington, S. P. 1991 *The Third Wave: Democratization in the Late Twentieth Century* (London: University of Oklahoma Press).

Helliwell, J. F. 1992 'Empirical linkages between democracy and economic growth', National Bureau of Economic Research, Working Paper No. 4066, May.

Lindbeck, A-C. 1977 *The Political Economy of the New Left* (New York: Harper and Row.

Mises, L. von 1951 *Socialism: An Economic and Sociological Analysis* (New Haven, Conn.: Yale University Press (German original published in 1922)).

Przeworski, A. & Limongi, F. 1993 'Political regimes and economic growth', *Journal of Economic Perspectives* 7, pp. 51–69.

Niskanen, W. A. 1992 'Autocratic, democratic, and optimal government' (paper submitted to the Third Schumpeter Prize Competition, March).

Olson, M. 1993 'Dictatorship, democracy and development', *American Political Science Review* 87, pp. 567–76.

—— 1982 *The Rise and Decline of Nations: Economic Growth, Stagflation and Social Rigidities* (New Haven, Conn.: Yale University Press).

Scully, G. W. 1991 'Rights, equity and economic efficiency', *Public Choice* 68, pp. 195–215.

Shleifer, A. 1994 'The politics of market socialism', *Journal of Economic Perspectives* 8, pp. 165–76.

Simon, H. 1959 'Theories of decision-making in economics and behavioural science', *American Economic Review* 49, pp. 253–83.

Sirowy, L. & Inkeles, A. 1990 'The effects of democracy on economic growth and inequality: a review', *Studies in Comparative International Development* 25, pp. 126–57.

World Bank 1993 *The East Asian Miracle: Economic Growth and Public Policy* (Oxford: Oxford University Press).

Part II

From Socialism to Capitalism

9

Understanding Post-Communist Transitions

The Specificity of Post-Communist Transition

The specific nature of the transition from communism in Central and Eastern Europe becomes clear when we compare it with other major shifts from one stable state of society to another potentially stable state. Other types of transition include (1) *classical transition*, meaning the extension of democracy in advanced capitalist countries between 1860 and 1920; (2) *neoclassical transition*, referring to democratizations in basically capitalist countries after the Second World War (West Germany, Italy, and Japan in the 1940s; Spain and Portugal in the 1970s; some Latin American countries in the 1970s and 1980s; South Korea and Taiwan in the 1980s); (3) *market-oriented reform* in non-communist countries (West Germany and other Western countries after the Second World War; South Korea and Taiwan in the early 1960s; Chile in the 1970s; Turkey and Mexico in the 1980s; Argentina in the 1990s); and (4) *Asian post-communist transition* (China since the late 1970s and Vietnam since the late 1980s). There is, of course, much internal variety, especially within the first two categories. We will, however, disregard it here in order to focus on the fundamental differences *between* rather than *within* the respective types of transitions.

I was assisted in the empirical research for this chapter by Christopher Giessing, and obtained useful comments from Marek Jaśkiewicz and Edmund Wnuk-Lipiński. It was completed while I was a Visiting Fellow at the Institute for Human Sciences in Vienna where Kelly Music helped me to edit it. An abbreviated version of this chapter was published in the *Journal of Democracy* 5, No. 4 (October 1995), pp. 75–89 (The Johns Hopkins University Press).

A number of features distinguish the post-communist transition in Central and Eastern Europe as we can see from Table 9.1.

First, the scope of change is exceptionally large. Both physical and economic systems are affected, and changes in these systems in turn interact with changes in the social structure. All these internal changes in the respective countries came about due to and in the framework of the dissolution of the Soviet Empire. Most of the post-Soviet countries faced the additional transition problems of defining their territorial as well as social and cultural boundaries, and of building their institutional machineries.[1]

In all other cases of radical transition, there was either a focus on the political system while the economic system remained basically unchanged (as in classical and neoclassical transitions), or a focus on the economy while the political regime (usually non-democratic) was unaffected. The unprecedented scope of changes in Eastern and Central Europe means, among other things, an extreme information overload for top decision-makers. Errors and delays are hardly surprising, especially since decision-makers must work with a public administration largely inherited from the old regime. Massive administrative turnover proved possible only in the former East Germany after reunification, an option obviously not open to other post-communist countries.

Second, although the changes in the political and economic systems *started* at about the same time, it is misleading to speak of 'simultaneous transitions' in post-communist Europe. It takes more time to privatize the bulk of the state-dominated economy than to organize free elections and at least some rudiments of political parties. Given the largely simultaneous beginnings of the political and economic transitions, this asymmetry in speed *produces a historically new sequence*: mass democracy (or at least political pluralism, i.e., some degree of legal political competition) first, and market capitalism later.[2]

Third, this sequence implies that market-oriented reforms, which must be exceptionally comprehensive because of the socialist economic legacy, have to be introduced under democratic, or at least pluralistic, political arrangements. Most other market-oriented reforms were introduced under non-democratic regimes (the third and fourth types of transition). Within this group, it is hard to find any case of economic transition that both approached the comprehensive of what occurred in post-communist Europe and was carried out under a democratic regime. Indeed, all the radical economic reforms elsewhere were introduced

[1] See Offe 1991; and Schmitter 1994.
[2] Bunce & Csanadi 1993.

Table 9.1 *Major societal transitions*

	Classical	Neoclassical	Non-communist economic reforms	Post-communist transition: China	Post-communist transition: Eastern Europe
INITIAL CONDITIONS					
Political system					
• In general	Restricted democracy	Authoritarian regimes	Varied: military dictatorship (Chile, Turkey); Occupying forces (West Germany, Japan); Authoritarian regimes (S. Korea, Taiwan); Quasi-authoritarian regime (Mexico); New democracy (Argentina)	Communist party-state	Communist party-state
• Party system	Relatively developed	Suppressed	Suppressed	Suppressed	Suppressed
Economic system					
• In general	Capitalist	Capitalist	'Suspended' capitalism (e.g. West Germany in 1948); or distorted capitalism (other countries)	Socialist, i.e. 'destroyed' capitalism	Socialist, i.e. 'destroyed' capitalism

Continued overleaf

Table 9.1 *Continued*

	Classical	Neoclassical	Non-communist economic reforms	Post-communist transition: China	Post-communist transition: Eastern Europe
• Level of redistribution through the budget (social expenditure, welfare state)	Very low	Low or moderate	Rather low	Rather low	Very high
Socio-economic structure	Relatively industrialized	Varied: but most countries were relatively industrialized	Varied: from little industry to relatively industrialized	High share of easily privatizable agriculture	High share of socialist industry
FEATURES OF TRANSITION					
Scope	Only political system	Only political system	Only or mostly economic system	Only economic system	*Both* political and economic system
Speed	Gradual or step-wise extension of suffrage	Rather rapid shift from non-democratic regime to mass democracy	Rather rapid stabilization, liberalization, often accompanied by privatization	Rather rapid liberalization and privatization accompanied by periodical stabilizations of the overheated economy	Rapid shift from non-democratic to the pluralist political arrangements, speed of economic reform differs

Sequence	First capitalism, then mass democracy	First capitalism, then democracy	First capitalism, then mass democracy	First capitalism, then mass democracy or at least political pluralism	First mass democracy or at least political pluralism then – capitalism?
Extent of violence	Occasionally violent	In some cases occasionally violent	In some cases occasionally violent	Occasionally violent (Tiananmen Square)	Largely peaceful so far
Role of the mass media	Limited (no radio, no TV)	Important (radio, TV) a large *increase* in the role of mass media	Usually suppressed or controlled, except for economic reforms under new democracy (e.g. Argentina)	Suppressed	Large *increase* in the role of all mass media especially radio and TV (visibility effect)
Role of external factors	Rather limited except for the cultural impact of the British model	Important: mass democracy became a dominant model of the political organization (cultural diffusion)	Rather important: stable, liberal and outward-looking capitalist economy increasingly became a model in the 1970s and the 1980s	Limited; possibly authoritarian 'Asian Tigers' as a model	Very important for countries other than the former USSR: without the collapse of the Soviet empire the transition in those countries would have been impossible; in addition: democratic capitalism as a model

under clearly autocratic and rather oppressive regimes (Chile in the 1970s, China since the final years of that decade).[3] There were some economic reforms carried out under democracy in the 1980s, including privatization programmes in certain developed Western countries and stabilizations and structural adjustments in developing economies. Problems attributable to the democratic political environment did arise during these transitions, perhaps warning of similar hazards lurking in the much more comprehensive and complicated transitions of Eastern and Central Europe.

These complications are, of course, far from being a sufficient argument for falling back on authoritarian solutions. This is so not only because of democracy's intrinsic importance to human dignity, but also because authoritarian regimes do not invariably promote rapid economic development (as they have done in South Korea and Taiwan); many (such as Juan Peron's regime in Argentina) have disastrous effects on the economy.

A fourth exceptional feature of Eastern Central European economic and political transitions is their lack of violence. Other parts of the old communist-dominated East – in particular Yugoslavia, the Caucasus, and areas of what used to be Soviet Central Asia – have seen terrible bloodshed over the last few years even as Eastern and Central Europe have undergone a peaceful revolution, with massive changes in political and economic institutions resulting from negotiations between the outgoing communist elite and the leaders of the opposition. (The only case of violent transition in Eastern or Central Europe took place in Romania, where there were no negotiations prior to the transfer of power.) Negotiations would never have taken place (or, had they taken place, never would have borne fruit) had not the Soviet threat been gradually eliminated by Gorbachev's *glasnost'* and *perestroika*. These negotiated changes were not based on any explicit political pact and contained a large element of surprise for all the main actors. However, they would not have come about if the members of the old elite had felt physically threatened or even if they had not believed that they would be free to seek favourable positions in whatever new system would emerge. In this sense one can speak of a tacit political pact.

The non-violent nature of the transition in Eastern-Central Europe, related to such tacit political pacts, has had important implications for

---

[3] The case that comes relatively close to a comprehensive economic reform conducted under democracy is that of Argentina since 1989. Even there, however, the amount of necessary economic change was much less than in the post-socialist economies, as capitalism in Eastern Central Europe had been destroyed, not merely distorted as in Argentina and other Latin American countries.

other aspects of the transition. First, the old ruling elites are intact and stand ready to profit electorally from the dissatisfaction of a part of the population – a dissatisfaction which, paradoxically, is likely to be greater in proportion to the economic desolation that these old elites wrought while in power. Second, the newly emerging capitalist class is likely to include many of the former elites, a circumstance that tends to reduce the legitimacy of the whole capitalist transition and may fuel attacks by one part of the former opposition against the part currently in office. Such conflicts within the former opposition are good news for the forces of the old regime.

Post-Communist Democratization Compared

Any consideration of the political transition in Eastern-Central Europe should keep in mind that democracy means the institutionalized practice of peacefully choosing rulers through regular, free and fair elections based on the principle of one person, one vote. This presupposes freedom of speech and association, which may also exist, however, under certain non-democratic regimes (e.g., constitutional monarchies). In large societies, democracy cannot be direct, but has to be representative. Depending on what proportion of the adult population has the franchise, we can speak of *limited democracy*, in which only a fraction of the populace has the vote, or of *mass democracy*, in which practically all adults can vote. Stable and lasting mass democracy requires mass political parties.

We can isolate a number of peculiarities of the political transition in Eastern-Central Europe by comparing it with the classical model of democratic transition. Eastern-Central Europe's experience of a sudden shift from a clearly non-democratic regime to a mass democracy was quite distinct from the classical pattern of democratization, which features a gradual extension of suffrage under limited democracy until mass democracy becomes the new reality. Therefore, these two democratizations differed in both point of departure and speed. The classical model of gradually widening suffrage allowed more time for learning democratic practices than is possible when a sudden shift to mass democracy occurs. The new democracies of Eastern-Central Europe are thus likely to require more learning-by-doing than the earlier mass democracies of the West.[4]

[4] Exception to this hypothesis may be those countries that have strong traditions of well-functioning democracy dating back to before the Second World War. In Eastern Central Europe, only the Czech Republic meets this condition.

This difference may be bolstered by the absence of competitive party systems prior to the post-communist democratization; the classical model involved the mobilization of previously established working-class organizations into electoral competition with other parties. The exclusive beneficiaries of the gradual extension of suffrage in the West were the subordinate classes, especially the workers; thus, they were likely to feel a strong attachment to the democratic system.[5] This may be less true of the post-communist working classes, who share the suddenly gained mass democracy with all other groups. In post-communist countries, it is the intellectuals (whose standing in society is much higher than it was in the West a century ago) who are most likely to esteem democracy. The intelligentsia, on average, benefits more than other groups from political opening, which means newfound access to information, foreign travel, and the like.

Two other differences are also of great importance. The classical model of democratization harks back to a time when the idea of using national budgets as engines of economic redistribution was fresh; there was much scope for the inauguration of social programmes whose beneficiaries could be enlisted as friends of democracy.[6] The situation today in post-communist lands is very different. They have inherited an extensive and increasingly inefficient 'socialist welfare state' characterized by high ratios of budgetary expenditure to GDP. Successful market-oriented reform, moreover, far from allowing any further increases in budgetary redistribution, actually demands the opposite.

A further difference concerns the role of the mass media, or more precisely the interaction of the mass media's role with developments in the economy and society at large. During the era of classical democratization there was a rather liberal press, no broadcast media, and no fundamental change in the economy. The post-communist transition, combining both political and economic openings begun under difficult economic conditions, came about in the age of powerful broadcast media (especially television). Under communism – especially before *glasnost'* – the tightly controlled media did not report on negative aspects of the system. When political liberalization freed these media, they naturally focused on once-forbidden negative stories, a tendency strengthened by the generally low level of professionalism displayed by journalists trained under communism. As a result, there was a sudden increase in the public's exposure to negative mass-media coverage, and

[5] This is pointed out in Rueschemeyer *et al.* 1992.
[6] For a summary article investigating to what extent the growth of public expenditure has been related to the expansion of suffrage and to what extent to other factors, see Mueller 1987.

viewers often mistook the increased visibility of undesirable phenomena like crime and poverty for their true growth. This 'visibility effect', absent in classical democratizations, was likely to encourage unfavourable assessments of the whole transition and, consequently, to influence electoral outcomes and the subsequent direction or pace of the economic transition.[7]

If we compare the post-communist with the neoclassical transition, the visibility effect operates in both cases, but its dangers are smaller in the neoclassical case, which typically presupposes an already established capitalist economy. The economy at the start of the neoclassical transition was usually healthier than a post-communist economy, while the level of pre-existing redistribution in the former was usually much lower than in the latter.

The Web of Interactions

Let us now focus on economic and political transition in Eastern-Central Europe. Figure 9.1 presents a simple scheme for such an analysis. Figure 9.1 shows how the economic and political transition depends on (1) initial states of the economy and of the socio-political sphere (E_0, SP_0); (2) external developments (ED); and (3) policies (P). Initial conditions are given by history and external conditions by external forces; both are beyond the control of a single country undergoing transition. Policies are a potentially controllable factor. However, the degree of their controllability and also their direction depend on SP, which interacts with E. We are dealing with complex interactions containing large elements of chance, which should be analysed in a *dynamic* framework: initial conditions and chance (e.g., who is responsible for economic reform) determine the initial policies, which, together with uncontrollable external developments, shape E_1. E_1, in turn, influences $E_2, \ldots, E_n$, and eventually the final outcome of economic transition. This transition is also shaped by political developments, which are to some extent 'contained' in SP_0 (e.g., the visibility effect, mentioned before). Finally, economic developments determined, among other things, by earlier policies (which are influenced by SP) may in turn influence future political developments, etc.

---

[7] The visibility effect may be conceptualized in economic terms as a mechanism producing false utility information and thus likely to lead to wrong decisions. False utility information is also supplied by most economists in post-socialist countries, as official economics was heavily politicized and no better than the economy. Some Western experts and politicians are also engaged in producing false utility information.

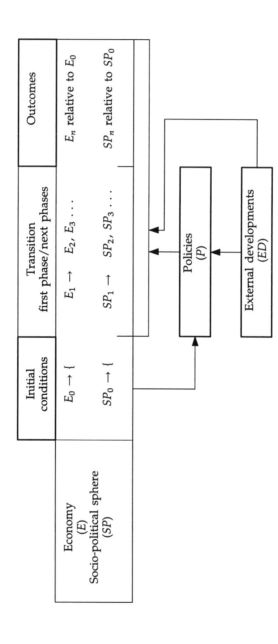

Fig. 9.1 *Transition: a simple analytical scheme*

Special Features of Post-Communist Economic Transition

Let us try to disentangle this web of complex and dynamic interactions by focusing first on economic transition in Eastern-Central Europe, and then on its interactions with political factors.

The post-1989 economic reforms in Eastern-Central Europe are fundamentally different from those in the past in that they go beyond socialism, as defined by the overwhelming dominance of the state sector in the economy. (This fundamental change is best illustrated by the privatization process in Russia.) The general direction of present Eastern-Central European economic transition is, therefore, basically in line with the economic reforms elsewhere: 'less state, more private enterprise and market'. But there are important differences between these two economic transitions. This can best be explained by pointing out that in the context of market-oriented reform there are three main types (fields) of economic policy (Balcerowicz 1993; and see further in Chapter 12):

(1) Macroeconomic stabilization (S policy), by means of macroeconomic policy;
(2) Microeconomic liberalization (L policy), that is enlarging the scope of economic freedom by removing various restrictions imposed by the state. L policy includes changing the general framework (e.g., liberalizing the regime of property rights) and removing more specific regulations (e.g., price controls, commands and rationing of goods);
(3) Fundamental institutional restructuring (I policy): making changes to existing institutions (privatizing state enterprises, reforming the tax system, etc.) and creating new ones (e.g., the stock exchange). L and I policies taken together may be called *systemic transformation* (*ST*).

Eastern-Central European economic reforms are different from other reforms in that the former require an unprecedented amount of I, if they are to reach market capitalism. This is due to the specificity of their initial economic conditions (E_0). Capitalism in Eastern-Central Europe was *destroyed* and not merely *suspended* (as in Germany before 1948) or *distorted* (as in Latin America or India before their liberalizing reforms). Besides, Eastern-Central European reforms have to contain an exceptional amount of L, as their economies were not only non-capitalist but also non-market, i.e., coordinated by the command rationing mechanism or – in other words – the central plan.[8] The required scope of L can be compared to dismantling the war economy mechanisms in Western countries after the Second World War. It is much larger than the L typical of recent market-oriented reforms in Latin America.

An unusually large scope of necessary systemic change is an invariant feature of all Eastern-Central European reforms, due to the common elements of their initial conditions. Another common characteristic is the possibility of a relatively rapid implementation of that part of systemic transformation which depends on quick spontaneous learning of specific new knowledge and skills (e.g., marketing, finance). This possibility results from a high level of general education (human capital), one of the few positive legacies of the previous regime.

However, there were also some serious differences in E_0, which have had important implications for the economic transition:

- some socialist economies inherited extreme macroeconomic imbalance (open/or repressed inflation). This group included Poland in 1989, and the former Soviet Union and Albania in 1990–91. There was, by contrast, relatively little macroeconomic instability in Czechoslovakia and Hungary. Bulgaria and Romania were in the intermediate situation (see Chapter 11 for more on this subject). Countries with extreme macroeconomic imbalance faced the double challenge of stabilizing and of changing the economic system at the same time. Countries with a much less serious stabilization problem had to tackle the issue of how to maintain and strengthen the macroeconomic stability while liberalizing prices and implementing other systemic reforms.
- Every Eastern–Central European economy was distorted by many years of import substitution, centralized investment decisions, dependence on the Soviet economy for exports and for imports of oil and gas. These distortions can be expressed by the notion of *pure socialist output*, i.e., that part of the total output which could be maintained, if at all, only under a socialist economic order and the related existence of the CMEA. The economic structure in Eastern-Central European countries was, on average, worse than that in China with respect to the difficulty and costs of economic transition. The former contained a very high share of distorted socialist industry, while the Chinese economy had a high share of technologically simple and, therefore, easily privatizable

---

[8] Hungary and Poland had fewer commands and control in their economies before 1989, but were still heavily controlled and distorted.

agriculture.[9] However, the share of pure socialist output differed across Eastern-Central European countries. It was exceptionally high in Bulgaria and in most non-Russian countries of the former Soviet Union because of the very strong dependence of these economies on the Russian economy for exports. Within the former Czechoslovakia, it was much higher in Slovakia than in the Czech Republic.

• Poland, Bulgaria and Hungary inherited much *foreign debt*, while Czechoslovakia and Romania were largely debt-free. Within the former USSR, Russia has taken over a sizeable Soviet debt.

Three Helpful Propositions

Here are three propositions to provide help in understanding both the challenges that post-communist Eastern-Central Europe faces and the relative merits of various economic policy options:

(1) *An extreme case of inherited macroeconomic instability calls for the rapid implementation of a tough stabilization programme.* Delay will only worsen the macroeconomic situation, and a gradual or mild stabilization programme will most likely fail to overcome inflationary inertia and expectations. A large macroeconomic imbalance, containing elements of hyperinflation, may be compared to a fire: it is very dangerous to delay putting it out, or to put it out slowly.

(2) *There are important interlinkages and synergies within the package of market-oriented reforms.* Radical price liberalization is needed to eliminate massive shortages; the elimination of shortages is in turn necessary to ensure the more efficient operation of enterprises. Rapid price decontrol (including substantial adjustments of distorted administrative prices, e.g., of energy) is also necessary in order to obtain more rational relative prices. Price liberalization, however, has to be linked to comprehensive foreign-trade liberalization so that increased enterprise autonomy is accompanied by an increase in competitive pressure on the newly freed enterprises. Widespread price controls and other forms of detailed state intervention will tempt enterprises to lobby for hidden or open subsidies, which may threaten macroeconomic stability. Thus liberalization aids stabilization, which in turn is conducive to meaningful institutional change. This is the link between stabilization-cum-liberalization on the one hand, and institutional restructuring on the other. Institutional

---

[9] Besides, the Chinese economy at the start of the reforms, i.e., in the late 1970s, displayed relatively little macroeconomic instability.

changes including tax reform, social security reform, privatization, and enterprise restructuring are necessary not only in order to improve efficiency, but also to bolster macroeconomic stability. There is, therefore, a link between deep institutional restructuring and the longer-term sustainability of the macroeconomic balance.

(3) *Different processes of economic reform have different maximum possible speeds.* Stabilization and liberalization policies, for instance, will bear fruit much more rapidly than institutional changes like reform of the tax system or privatization of a large public sector. Decision-makers should remain mindful that the third runs on a slower clock than the first two, and should plan accordingly. Reformers face a choice between quickly stabilizing and liberalizing a still-socialist economy or implementing such changes at a slower pace in order to allow time for the institutional dismantling of socialism to 'catch up'.

Radical liberalization can be expected to spur a rise in the number of private firms that outstrips the ability to keep pace with the inherited tax system (designed to deal with just a handful of large state firms). A rise in tax evasion is thus an unavoidable by-product of sweeping liberalization. (There may be even more tax evasion if liberalization is limited and the tax system is full of various breaks and preferences.) The danger is that increased tax evasion at a time of unavoidably growing budgetary expenditures will reduce the legitimacy of the capitalist transition and the governments and parties supporting it.

The Timing of Reform

Let us now look at economic policy as a variable that may differ along three dimensions: time of launching, phasing and pace. Time of launching refers to the interval between a political breakthrough and the start of economic reform; phasing describes the relative timing of stabilization, liberalization and institutional-restructuring policies; pace describes the implementation rate for each of these main components of reform.

By applying criteria drawn from these three dimensions we may identify many theoretical variants of economic policy, but for brevity's sake we will mention just two general types.[10] The first is a radical and comprehensive economic programme, in which stabilizing, liberalizing and restructuring measures are launched at about the same time and implemented at close to the maximum possible speeds. Such programmes

---

[10] For a more comprehensive typology of economic policy options in the transition economies, see Gomulka 1994.

may be launched very quickly following a political breakthrough or after some delay. The second type consists of non-radical economic programs, defined here at those in which stabilization, liberalization and restructuring are not launched simultaneously, or are implemented at a slower pace than they might be, or are even interrupted (e.g., stabilization in Russia in mid-1992).[11]

Under the economic conditions existing at the time of communism's demise in Eastern-Central Europe, radical economic reforms, resolutely pursued, were the best choice for bringing about disinflation, structural change, and the takeoff into economic growth and market capitalism. Empirical analysis tends to confirm this hypothesis, as there is so far no example of highly successful non-radical reform.[12]

Given the naturally slower pace at which institutional restructuring (including privatization) must proceed, even the most energetically implemented transition to a market economy will require two stages. In the first stage, the economy undergoes liberalization and stabilization but remains more 'market socialist' than capitalist. In a second stage – assuming that it is successful – the gains of liberalization and stabilization are consolidated, and the transition to market capitalism is completed and institutionalized.

Given the challenging initial conditions and unfavourable external developments (especially the collapse of trade within the Comecon) that faced each country in Eastern-Central Europe during the post-communist transition, each class of reform measures was bound to generate discontent in some section of the populace. Predictably, the intensity of these currents of discontent was directly proportional to the adversity of initial conditions and external developments. For example, the same set of economic policies produced four times more open unemployment in Slovakia than in the Czech Republic in 1992 because 'pure socialist output' accounted for a much higher share of the Slovak economy.

In addition to turning disguised unemployment into open unemployment, radical economic reform also increases discontent simply by broadening the scope of general economic freedom. Since only some people can directly take advantage of the new opportunities, others may feel resentment, especially if they view the new winners as undeserving. Rapid shifts will occur in the relative pay and prestige of various occupations and professional groups as markets replace the planned

[11] But the actual rate of implementation may differ between two countries because of differences in their initial conditions. For example, substantial previous price liberalization or an initially balanced macroeconomy may require only limited further price decontrol or macroeconomic tightening. This was the case in Hungary.

[12] See, for example, Chapter 12.

socialist economy. Miners, heavy-industrial workers and other groups that see themselves as 'losers' – even if only in relative terms – are likely to be dissatisfied. There is an unavoidable trade-off, moreover, between opportunity and security. This hard truth may be poorly understood and bitterly disliked, especially by those who experience a much larger increase in insecurity than in perceived opportunities.

Given the same difficult initial and external conditions sketched above, non-radical reform will also produce discontent, though in different ways. If the initial macroeconomic situation is highly unstable, non-radical economic reform will find itself immediately bedevilled by high and growing inflation, which produces its own version of severe economic insecurity. Non-radical reform programmes do this by preferring hidden over open unemployment. Hidden unemployment is less psychologically painful to the persons concerned, but it must be financed through fiscal or quasi-fiscal subsidies, which in turn spur inflation.[13] The result is inflation-bred insecurity and disaffection. Moreover, it must be kept in mind that any future attempts at macroeconomic stabilization will flush hidden unemployment out into the open.

Non-radical programmes, which typically feature less liberalization and correspondingly more state intervention, also give rise to new economic inequalities, with the 'winners' being those who can successfully lobby the government. In practice, this means members of the old communist elite, who are more experienced, better organized, and better connected than others. The inequalities generated by their lobbying are less justified by economic performance than those that stem from radical reform programmes, and rankle the 'losers' even more. Finally, by channelling entrepreneurial and managerial energies into rent seeking and corruption rather than the search for greater efficiency, non-radical programmes that avoid liberalization destroy the prospects for economic development. Anyone willing to take the longer view, then, should realize that the discontents and drawbacks associated with non-radical reform outweigh the problems brought by sustained and radical efforts at comprehensive liberalization, stabilization and institutional restructuring.

The Period of 'Extraordinary Politics'

The key to understanding the interaction between the political and economic dimensions of post-communist transitions is to realize that any

[13] Another way to finance increased hidden unemployment is to accept reduced average productivity of labour, but this means a corresponding reduction in average real wages, and falling wages cut buying power as surely as do rising prices.

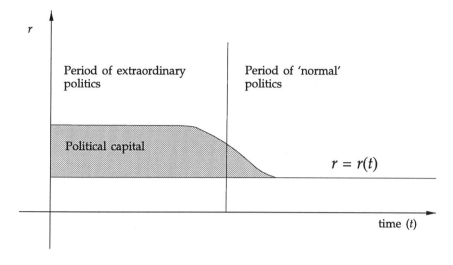

Fig. 9.2 *A two-stage model of politics*

great political breakthrough in a country's history is followed by a period of 'extraordinary politics' that soon gives way to 'normal politics.'

Figure 9.2 presents this two-stage model in a highly simplified form. The function $r=r(t)$ expresses the level of readiness to accept radical economic measures, starting at the moment immediately following the epochal political change – in this case, the fall of communism. It is based on the assumption that liberation from foreign domination and domestic political liberalization produce a special state of mass psychology and corresponding political opportunities: the new political structures are fluid and the older political elite is discredited. Both leaders and ordinary citizens feel a stronger-than-normal tendency to think and act in terms of the common good. All of this is reflected in an exceptionally high level of r.

Extraordinary politics, however, quickly gives way to the more mundane politics of contending parties and interest groups (as described, for instance, by Nobel laureate James Buchanan and other theorists of the public-choice school). It is in this second period that certain features of political contention which are common in established democracies become much stronger (parties searching for an agenda and an ideological profile, the ensuing politicization of major issues, and so on). These features superimpose themselves on the developments typical of a new democracy – the visibility effect, the appearance of an inchoate party system, and the like – and then normal politics in the fledgling democracy comes to seem unattractive and levels of r drop sharply.

Variations in sociopolitical characteristics from one country to another can be reflected in the initial level of r, the duration of 'extraordinary politics', the downward slope of $r=r(t)$ after this period, the subsequent level of r persisting under 'normal' political conditions, and so on.

The brevity of the exceptional period means that a radical economic programme, launched as quickly as possible after the breakthrough, has a much greater chance of being accepted than either a delayed radical programme or a non-radical alternative that introduces difficult measures (e.g., price increases) in piecemeal fashion. Bitter medicine is easier to take in one dose than in a prolonged series of doses.[14]

Each of the clearly radical economic programmes in post-communist Eastern-Central Europe was the handiwork of a government representing new political forces. This is true of Poland, the former Czechoslovakia, Bulgaria, Estonia and Latvia. Yet new political forces did not launch such programmes everywhere that they were in control. Lithuania in 1992–93 was radical with regard to privatization but hesitant with regard to stabilization, while Hungary in 1990–94 pursued a 'gradualism' that was partly due to the weight of previously accumulated changes and partly deliberate.

By contrast, whenever the political system remained dominated in the first phase of transition by the forces of the past, only non-radical economic options were pursued. The clearest examples are Belarus and Ukraine, and to a lesser extent Romania. In each of the two former cases (as in Russia), the post-Soviet legislature erected formidable barriers to radical economic reform.

Countries that did not take advantage of the period of 'extraordinary politics' to launch a radical economic programme still face the challenge of making the transition to market capitalist, but now under more difficult political and economic conditions. From the point of view of economic development, the radical strategy is the best option, regardless of when it is deployed. Yet countries that have missed the first period are in danger of going from one kind of non-market economy (central planning) to another characterized by pervasive

---

[14] As to the likelihood of difficult economic measures being accepted, the 'political capital' existing during the period of 'extraordinary politics' may be regarded as a counterpart to the use of force in the authoritarian regimes that implemented radical economic programmes. Given the relatively short duration of this period, however, some of these regimes (i.e. procapitalist autocracies) may have a comparative advantage in sustaining and completing such reforms.

macroeconomic instability, detailed but chaotic state regulation, and related massive rent seeking. This is especially likely if the legislatures in these countries continue to be dominated by industrial and agricultural interest groups even after the second cycle of free elections.

Given the evanescence of 'extraordinary politics', time-consuming institutional reforms (e.g., privatization, social security reform, health reform, and the like) are likely to meet more resistance than quickly implemented stabilizing and liberalizing measures. One must therefore expect delays in institutional restructuring, for reform of this nature is simply out of sync with the brevity of the 'extraordinary' interval.

If a country has been operating under difficult initial and external conditions, it is a mistake to blame social discontent on a particular type of economic programme. Attributing widespread dissatisfaction to 'shock therapy' for instance, is erroneous because under conditions grave enough to elicit such radical measures, *any* economic policy package will generate discontent. There is no *a priori* reason to expect that the dissatisfaction attendant upon radical reforms will be greater than that attendant upon non-radical ones.

Indeed, the reverse could well be the case. Even cursory examination of the Eastern-Central European experience shows no clear link between the intensity of displays of social discontent (strikes, demonstrations, and so on) and the type of economic programme pursued. Poland, Bulgaria and Romania have seen the worst displays of discontent, yet the former two countries pressed radical reforms while Romania followed a stop-and-go gradualism. Hungary, Czechoslovakia (and later the Czech Republic and Slovakia), Estonia and Latvia have had few manifestations of discontent. Hungary never adopted a radical economic programme, while all the others did.

The Importance of Initial Conditions

The foregoing suggests that one should seek to explain differences in social discontent and political instability from one country to another by first of all examining the conditions present as the transition got under way. A paucity of open unemployment during the transition is a great help, as officials in the Czech Republic can testify. The intensity of labour unrest seems to depend on the presence of militant workers like the miners of Poland and Romania, as well as on the existence of influential trade unions that played a large role in toppling communism only to turn increasingly populist (Solidarity in Poland, Podkrepa in Bulgaria).

The character of the country's political class is also relevant. Demagogues presumably exist everywhere, but clearly they are not equally mobilized and vocal in all countries. The relative extent of their presence, along with the intensity of the visibility effect, may have a serious impact upon popular attitudes and behaviour in different countries during the economic transition.

If it is erroneous to blame unrest on this or that type of economic reform, it is equally mistaken to attribute the electoral defeats of the political forces that ruled during the first stage of post-communist transition to one sort of economic programme. Such defeats happened in 1993 in Poland – a radical reformer – but also in Lithuania, Russia and Hungary, where radical reform never came close to being adopted. Thus causes other than the type of economic programme must underlie these outcomes. Among these causes are phenomena that are present everywhere but operate with varying force depending on circumstances.

The visibility effect is one such phenomenon; it strengthens the usual tendency of a part of the electorate to blame problems on whatever government is in power. In reality, the magnitude of these problems as well as the prospects for quickly solving them depended on a given post-communist country's initial situation, and this varied greatly across the region. Another important variable is the type and composition of the political class, especially the relative importance of its populist component. Also significant is the extent to which opposition to the government's economic policy becomes linked to the popular position on certain emotional issues such as the loss of empire in Russia, the status of the Hungarian minority in Romania, or the role of the Catholic Church in Poland.

Finally, the pre-election strategies adopted by the various political forces matter as well. For example, in Poland in 1993, the ruling parties of the moment committed the grave mistake of going through the elections separately even as their chief rivals, the ex-communists, were agreeing to run together under the banner of a single coalition. With help from a new electoral law, the ex-communists obtained about 21 per cent of the vote and 33 per cent of the seats in Parliament, making them Poland's largest single political force.[15]

Even if for some of the aforementioned reasons the political forces that launched radical economic reform suffer an electoral defeat, the economy is likely to be in much better shape than would have been the case had other approaches been adopted. Furthermore, radical reform

[15] On Poland's September 1993 elections, see Smolar & Król 1994.

tends to leave behind certain legacies – currency convertibility, an independent central bank, a large private sector – that even ostensible opponents are likely to respect.

From our analysis, a clear conclusion emerges. Given the typical initial conditions of a socialist economy, a country will be better off politically and economically in the medium-to-long run if it adopts a radical and comprehensive economic reform programme as quickly as possible after the political transition, implements as much of this programme as possible during the brief period of extraordinary politics, and then stays the course of reform by implementing far-reaching institutional changes.

References

Berg, Andrew 1993 'Does macroeconomic reform cause structural adjustment? Lessons from Poland', International Monetary Fund, Washington, DC.

Bunce, Valerie, & Csanadi, Maria 1993 'Uncertainty in the transition: post-communism in Hungary', *East European Politics and Societies*, 7, no. 2.

Gomułka, Stanisław 1994 'Economic and political constraints during transition', *Europe-Asia Studies*, 46, no. 1.

Mueller, Dennis C. 1987 'The growth of government', *IMF Staff Papers*, March, pp. 115–49.

Offe, Claus 1991 'Capitalism by democratic design? Democratic theory facing the triple transition in East Central Europe', *Social Research*, 58, no. 4, Winter.

Rueschemeyer, Dietrich, Stephens, Evelyne Huber & Stephens, John 1992 *Capitalist Development and Democracy*, Chicago, University of Chicago Press.

Sachs, Jeffrey, & Wing Thye Woo 1993 'Structural factors in the economic reforms in China, Eastern Europe and the former Soviet Union', mimeo.

Schmitter, Philippe C. 1994 'Dangers and dilemmas of democracy', *Journal of Democracy*, March.

Smolar, Aleksander, & Król, Marcin 1994 'A Communist Comeback?', *Journal of Democracy*, January.

10

Economic Transition in Central and Eastern Europe: Comparisons and Lessons

This chapter discusses in a comparative perspective some important general issues involved in the transition to a market economy in Central and Eastern Europe.

I begin with the section on how, I think, one should analyse economic transitions. This section presents a simple analytical framework and some relationships between its constituent variables. Then follows a section dedicated to the much-debated issue of the role of the state in the economic transition. Next I discuss the equally debated issue of gradualism versus 'Big Bang' in the transition to a market economy. I conclude with some lessons learned.

How to Analyse the Economic Transition

Any transition from one state of a certain system to another potentially stable state can be usefully analysed by means of an analytical scheme which consists of four variables: (1) initial or inherited conditions; (2) conditions external to a given transition and influencing it or, in other

This chapter is largely based on the International Finance Corporation Annual Lecture in Washington which I gave on 1 December 1993 and which was published in *Australian Economic Review*, 1st Quarter 1994, pp. 47–59. Useful comments were made by Anthony Doran, Guy Pfefferman, Brian Pinto and Bertrand Renaud on the first draft of this lecture. The usual caveats apply. The author also thanks Derek Cross and Mark M. Michalski for their help in editing it.

words, its exogenous determinants; (3) policies; and (4) outcomes. In the previous chapter, I applied this simple model to the analysis of the overall transition in the post-communist countries, discussing changes both in the economic and socio-political sphere and the interplay between them. In this section, I will discuss its application to the economic transition.

An economy can be defined as being represented by several variables: (1) the economic system (i.e., institutions affecting the decision-making and the implementation of decisions with respect to production, savings, investment and consumption); (2) the economic structure (the territorial and branch composition of output); (3) the macroeconomic situation; (4) the physical capital; (5) the human capital; (6) size; (7) location. It is usually assumed by definition that the essence of economic transition is the change in the economic system, i.e. systemic transformation, and the changes in other indicated variables are included in the 'economic transition' to the extent that they are related to this transformation. On this definition, market-oriented reform is a special (and currently almost the exclusive) case of economic transition. Sometimes it is macroeconomic stabilization, if required by the initial conditions, which is regarded as an essential component of 'economic transition'. Therefore, a change in the economy which does not include the systemic transformation in conjunction, if necessary, with macroeconomic stabilization, is not regarded as 'economic transition'. For example, a change in the economic structure or in physical capital resulting from the government's policies pursued within a given institutional framework falls beyond the conceptual scope of 'economic transition'. However, structural change and the systemic change to which it is related are both part of this economic transition.

Inherited conditions are the initial states of the factors which constitute the economy. They may be divided into those which may be changing during the subsequent transition (e.g. the economic system, the macroeconomic situation, the economic structure, the physical and human capital) and those which endure, e.g. location or size of the country. Exogenous determinants of economic transition thus include those lasting inherited factors to the extent that they influence the transition. External economic developments constitute another part of those determinants of economic transition in a given country. They are independent from any smaller economy but obviously affect it.

Still another and more controversial subset of exogenous determinants of economic transition would consist of domestic political developments. They influence the economic transition both directly and via economic policy. The first channel includes, for example, an increase in inflationary and wage pressures and the slowing down of restructuring in enterprises. Both result from the frequent electoral campaigns with their promises of monetary relaxation, enterprises' supports and protectionism. These signals must affect, to some extent, the expectations and subsequently the actions of the economic agents. Some learning is, perhaps, possible especially on the part of enterprises' managers: if the political parties which made these promises do not fulfil them after gaining power and largely continue the previous tough policies, the managers may be more resistant next time to political demagogy. Therefore the direct economic harm done by demagogic and populist electoral campaigns in the transition countries may be decreasing with the passage of time. However, this optimistic conclusion is based on the assumption that the right economic policy is continued regardless of who is in the driving seat. This continuity may be due to a hidden consensus on the economic policy between the competing political parties or to the powerful constraints keeping the economic policy on the narrow path of economic virtue. Both conditions may be only partially met which leaves some scope for harm to the macroeconomic discipline by adverse political developments. And such developments can surely affect the economic transition via the second channel, i.e. the economic policy. Even in the best case when the basic strategy is right and remains in place, the frequent changes of ministers responsible for major reforms, e.g. privatization, pension reform, health service reform, must interrupt and slow down its implementation. And reality may be much worse than this scenario.

So there is not much doubt that the domestic political developments may affect the economic transition. But are they independent of the changes in the economy, so that they can be included in the same category as their exogenous determinants? Is it not often argued that political complications have resulted from economic difficulties during the economic transition in East and Central Europe? In addition, some observers link these difficulties and thus the political complications to only one type of economic programme, which they usually call 'shock therapy'. This second argument, however, can be easily falsified. As I have already pointed out in the previous chapter, the magnitude of social and political complications during the economic transition in the post-socialist countries was not related to the type of economic programme (for more on this see Chapter 13).

As to the alleged link between the economic transition and the political difficulties, those who emphasize it implicitly assume that no transition, i.e. no systemic transformation and the related changes in the economy, would produce fewer economic difficulties and correspondingly fewer political complications. However, such an assumption is highly suspect. Given the typically difficult inherited conditions in the post-socialist economies, the lack of transition was bound to produce – at least after a certain time – more economic difficulties than a well-structured and executed market-oriented reform. Finally, one can also question another implicit assumption, namely that the adverse political developments were exclusively or mostly due to the economic difficulties. Even a brief examination of the transition countries shows that the political developments there have had their own dynamics, driven by political competition and the resulting conflicts and splits in the political parties and within the whole emerging pluralistic political system (this was certainly the case in Poland in 1990–2 – see Chapter 15). All in all it is justified, I think, to include domestic political developments in the category of exogenous determinants of economic transition in the post-socialist economies.

The next variable in our simple scheme, that is, the *economic policy* in transition economies, has already been defined in the previous chapter as consisting of macroeconomic stabilization, microeconomic liberalization and fundamental institutional restructuring. The last two policies taken together constitute the already mentioned systemic transformation. We will return to these three components of economic policy.

Finally, the last variable, the *economic outcomes*. They should always be defined as *changes* in the factors which are subject to economic transition, or – to be more specific – as the state of the economic system, the macroeconomy, the economic structure, etc. after a certain time, the length of time to be *relative* to the inherited states of these variables. For example, the economic outcome is a change in the proportion of free prices, in the share in the private sector or in the inflation rate (disinflation or more inflation).

Among the four discussed factors, the economic outcomes constitute the dependent variable, while the inherited conditions, external factors and economic policy are its determinants. Among these determinants, in turn, the first two are beyond the control of a single transition economy. Therefore, the economic policy is the only controllable factor. However, its direction and the degree of controllability depend mostly on political developments and personality factors, which are subject to chance. The political economy dimension of the economic policy is, therefore, crucial.

Economic transition is largely the result of the interplay between the uncontrollable inherited and external conditions and the controllable economic policy. This interplay resembles the interactions between a person's genes and environment in shaping that person's characteristics and behaviour. In both cases the uncontrollable factors determine the range of possibilities, while the potentially controllable variables decide which of these possibilities are activated, i.e. become a reality. In the case of economic transition, the inherited conditions also influence the costs and benefits of a given economic policy option.

The *location* of a country illustrates the first type of interplay between the inherited conditions and policies nicely. Under an autarchic economic policy the location does not matter very much. Things change radically, however, under liberalization, i.e. a market-oriented reform. It then becomes essential which are the neighbouring countries. For example, the Czech Republic, a relatively small country, is the only transition economy which has borders with two Western countries – Germany and Austria. During the economic transition this location has a powerful job-and-income-creation effect (not necessarily in the formal economy), which partly explains the low level of recorded unemployment in that country.

Estonia, which has borders with Finland, and Poland, thanks to its border with Germany, also profited from some favourable location effects. However, their relative impact on Poland must have been smaller than in other cases because of the much larger size of the Polish economy.

In contrast, countries like Ukraine, which are far larger and do not border on any Western economy, are devoid of such special and beneficial location effects during the economic transition. Generalizing, one can say that the inherited conditions may include some 'hidden treasures' which are activated during the appropriate liberalizing market-oriented reforms and thus support them. These 'hidden treasures' should be distinguished from other assets a country may possess, the use of which do not depend so much on an appropriate change in the economic system. Mineral deposits are a case in point here. Another example of 'hidden treasures' would be foreign tourist attractions, bringing a surge in revenue under political and economic liberalization. Prague, with millions of Germans and other foreign tourists after 1989, is again a good illustration. Albania may also benefit from such a 'hidden treasure'.

A 'hidden treasure' may be a 'composite' of such enduring inherited conditions as small size and favourable location, i.e. close to Western economies. This is typical of the Czech Republic, Hungary, Estonia, Slovenia and Slovakia, but not, for example of Kirghizstan, a most radical reformer in post-Soviet Central Asia. This composite generates two favourable economic effects, given the right economic policies: (1) a relatively small chunk of foreign direct investment makes a large contribution to the efficient privatization of the economy; (2) foreign trade liberalization can play a much larger role in introducing the discipline of competition than in the larger countries, thus neutralizing – to a larger extent – the tendency towards inefficiency, displayed by the inherited ownership structure, dominated by non-private firms.

A 'hidden treasure' which is typical, however, of most European post-socialist countries is a relatively high level of general education (human capital) which distinguishes them from many developing economies. This enables a rapid increase in the level of innovation once the economic system starts to move in the market direction. For as I argued in Chapter 6, an appropriately high level of human capital and a competitive market system are both required for a country to achieve a high level of innovativeness. The socialist countries met the first condition but were failing miserably on the second. A market-oriented reform thus unblocks the innovative potential contained in much human capital. A high level of general education also makes it possible for people rapidly to pick up specific skills that were not necessary under a command economy but are crucial in the market system, i.e. marketing, finance, modern management, business law. However, as with other 'hidden treasures', relatively high levels of general education can be fully used only under some economic policies, i.e. those which make decisive strides towards a competitive market system and thus create an increase in demand for labour with specific market economy-related skills and correspondingly high returns to education. But there is one crucial difference between such assets as good location or possession of attractive tourist centres, on one hand, and abundant human capital, on the other: the former are immobile while the latter can be eroded: the political liberalization accompanying the economic reform makes it possible for the best people to emigrate. Their willingness to do so would depend on their perception of the direction the country is taking and on the perceived demand for their services. The only controllable factor which influences the changes and indirectly their perceptions is the economic policy. Therefore, wrong policies are much more dangerous with respect to mobile than immobile 'hidden treasures'. Such policies block the use of both of these inherited assets. In addition they endanger the existence of the second one.

The opposite of 'hidden treasures' are those parts of aspects of inherited conditions which are revealed as *burdens* during the economic transition. These are factors which produce economic and social costs; e.g. a surge in hidden and open unemployment, a wage and inflationary pressure. They may be the source of the social complications, such as strikes and other manifestations of social discontent. A heavy dependence on exports to the Soviet market (or on any market which collapses not necessarily because of transition but during the transition) is probably the most important example of this category. Another example would be an important and inefficient regionally concentrated mining sector and a correspondingly high proportion of miners among the active population. This sort of structural burden, combined with political liberalization, tends to produce a strong wage push and thus contributes to inflation throughout the economy, while the related strikes may present a serious threat to political stability. The existence or absence of a large but inefficient mining sector is thus an important variable differentiating the starting position of post-socialist economies.

The costs and benefits which emerge in transition depend very much on the relative weight of 'hidden treasures' and burdens that a transition country inherits. A certain asymmetry seems to be present here. The effects of the burdens may be impossible to avoid, i.e. no feasible economic policy option might be available to prevent them from being activated. This was certainly true of the collapse of intra-Comecon trade which was related to the essence of economic transition, the timing of which depended on the decision of one country, the former Soviet Union. By contrast, the economic policies that block the use of the 'hidden treasures' are foolish.

The role of positive versus negative legacies has been especially pronounced in the case of the inherited economic structure. I have already mentioned the main examples of structural burdens. A 'hidden treasure' of this kind might be an economy that is easily and efficiently privatizable. China at the start of her reforms in the late 1970s provided a striking example of such an asset. A important role in the Chinese economy was played by the simple and easily divisible agriculture at that time organized in absurdly egalitarian Maoist communes. It was technologically easy to privatize them. Such privatization actually happened and set in motion powerful processes of market-oriented economic change which involved the majority of the Chinese population. In addition de-collectivization of Chinese agriculture must have been immensely popular among the peasants. The 'Chinese scenario' could not be repeated with so successfully in Russia, where agriculture played a much smaller role, was technologically much less divisible and where collectivization was politically much more entrenched (for more on that see Chapter 5). In addition China did not depend on exports to the Comecon countries and thus did not suffer a powerful external shock during her market-oriented reforms. These and other differences in the inherited conditions seem to explain much more of China's economic success than any superiority of Chinese transition strategy. Generally speaking, less industrialized socialist economies with large agricultural sectors seem to have a much easier ride towards the market economy than more industrialized and thus more distorted socialist economies with collectivized and technologically complex agriculture. Any comparison between Asian and European post-communist economic transitions must compare this important difference in the starting conditions. And among the European socialist economies small countries heavily dependent on the Soviet economy (Bulgaria and the smaller republics of the former USSR) inherited enormous burdens.

A structural legacy, typical of some post-socialist economies, was that the military sector constituted a large part of total output. This is revealed as a burden during the transition of any country which had previously exported a large share of this output so as to buy civilian goods in exchange. During the transition these exports would collapse. Such a situation appeared in smaller countries like Slovakia or Kirghizstan. The situation of Russia was, however, different: her military output was mostly for internal use, and – according with the statistical conventions was recorded as making a large contribution to the GDP. However, it went far beyond what was necessary for defence purposes; this 'excess' was – from the point of view of the welfare of the society – an enormous waste.[1] Nevertheless, the subsequent reduction of this excess makes a large contribution to the decline in GDP, which, in turn, is regarded by many as a collapse in welfare. All this means, of course, that Russia's statistics should be interpreted with special care.[2]

Finally, let us note that inherited economic conditions determine the scope of the required economic policies. Countries which inherited little inflation need much less macroeconomic stabilization than countries which start their transition with a highly unbalanced economy. The differences in this respect are discussed in Chapter 12. Another important difference refers to the type of economic system existing at the start of a market-oriented reform, and the related scope of the required systemic transformation. One can distinguish here three 'stylized' models. The first is the 'destroyed capitalism' model which characterizes the industrialized socialist economy. This economy was subject to massive central controls and regulations either in the form of traditional central planning (command mechanism) or its modified forms (reformed economies). Consequently, massive liberalization was required. In addition, all the

---

[1] This implies that the share of military spending was much lower than the share of military output in the GDP.

[2] One possibility would be to eliminate the 'excess' military spending before transition, and to subtract if from the official GDP figures. This would make the decline in the corrected GDP much smaller.

important institutions of capitalism (a liberal regime of property rights, private enterprises, a truly commercial banking system, and a suitable tax system) were abolished. Therefore, an unusually large amount of fundamental institutional restructuring was required. On top of that, some post-socialist countries inherited a highly unstable economy which called for massive macroeconomic stabilization.

Another model is that of 'suspended' capitalism. This describes the economic system which emerged from the war and existed at the start of the market-oriented reforms in Western countries in the late 1940s. This model called for radical macroeconomic stabilization and microeconomic liberalization, i.e. the dismantling of the war economy. However, little institutional restructuring was required as capitalist institutions were merely 'suspended' and not destroyed.

The intermediate case is that of 'distorted' capitalism. This occurs in many developing countries (e.g. India, Latin America) at the start of their economic transition. The distortions may be due to extensive state intervention and to a substantial state sector. The state share, however, may be much below what it was for the first case. Therefore, distorted capitalism calls for much less institutional restructuring than destroyed capitalism. The differences in the required liberalization are smaller. However, more work in this respect is typically needed in the post-socialist economy.

The Role of the State in Transition

The issue of the 'state versus the market' is one of the most divisive in economic debate. It is particularly complex in debates regarding the post-socialist countries. It is ironic that, although these countries have experienced the bankruptcy of an exaggerated economic role for the state, this resulted in debates characterized by a strong *pro-statist bias*, as expressed in demands for various forms of state policy (agricultural, industrial, transport etc.) as remedies for all kinds of problems. This pro-statist bias has three main sources.

First, is the erroneous belief, borrowed – not necessarily knowingly – from old-fashioned welfare economics, that to identify a market failure is enough to justify state intervention. In fact, market failure is only a necessary condition for envisaging a public intervention, as the deficiency of the 'visible hand' may be larger than that of the 'invisible' one. This simple truth is largely ignored in political and popular discussions. The voluminous amount of literature on state failures is either not widely known or disregarded.

Second, many people, including politicians, operate predominantly on emotional grounds. They expect quick solutions to various urgent problems, and for these solutions they look to the most obvious institution – the state. This emotional link between a genuine preoccupation with problems and an expectation that the solution must come from the *most obvious* organizations has also existed, I think, in many developing countries, contributing to widespread statism. Nor is it absent from electoral debates in the developed economies. An activist stand probably has greater political appeal than recourse to impersonal market forces.

Third, some participants in the debate on the economic role of the state in the post-socialist countries are influenced by their understanding of the 'Japanese model'. They attribute Japanese economic success mainly to some special role of the state (MITI is often regarded as the main driving force behind the economic development of Japan), instead of looking to the unique combination of factors present in Japan since the early 1950s that produced a positive synergy: a very small public sector, intense domestic competition, export-oriented growth, a conservative macroeconomic policy, a limited budget, labour relations centred on labour productivity and not on excessive wage increases and – at least until recently – a long-lasting political stability. This need to connect economic success to a state institution is a manifestation of the popular tendency to attribute the cause of some exceptional achievement to a single, striking phenomenon rather than to a combination of impersonal dispersed mechanisms.[3] The reverse of this tendency is to seek the reason for serious difficulties or failures in a single but hidden factor – manipulation by the IMF or the World Bank, for example.

The above remarks refer to factors that, I think, lie at the bottom of genuinely held but deeply mistaken *beliefs* about the state's role in the economy. But of course behind excessive state intervention lie the hidden *interests* of various groups, which are always presented in the guise of the public good and expounded by various lobbies. And some politicians use these mistaken beliefs or special interests to gain political influence.

The proper view of the state's economic role should be based, among other things, on the following simple premises.

---

[3] Even if, which is debatable, a particular organization were to some extent instrumental in achieving economic success in a particular country, it is an open question whether it can be sufficiently replicated in other countries – for example, whether the competent economic administration and the special culture of government–business relationship present in South Korea or Japan could be quickly reproduced in other places.

- The state, like most other goods, is a *limited resource* in terms of time, administrative and political competence, and money. Indeed, many popular discussions of the state's role are based on an *implicit* assumption that the state is an unlimited resource. Given that this is not so, any proposed state intervention should be analysed in terms of opportunity costs – that is, forgoing other possible activities.
- The capacity of the state to deal with different problems varies, mainly because of varying informational requirements. On this basis, one can distinguish on the one hand, the *sphere of the state's natural competence* (legislating and enforcing the law, dealing with other states, for example) and on the other hand its *sphere of natural incompetence* (a massive and detailed industrial policy, for example). The state funding, but not necessarily production, of certain services (elementary health service, education, unemployment benefits, social safety net etc.) may also be included in the first sphere – to the extent that it can be shown that private markets inevitably fail to provide these goods, that such goods generate important positive externalities, and that the amount and form in which they are produced do not harm macroeconomic stability and the structures of incentive, which are the basic requirements of long-running economic development.

These two arguments are largely sufficient to establish the rational – that is, not doctrinaire – case for a limited state. But there are two other arguments that strengthen the case.

- The rules of the game in the political system may be such that they normally select people with *competencies* other than those required for rational economic decision-making.
- The *criteria for success* that prevail in the political system may in some respects vary from those relevant to long-term economic development (for example, subsidizing or protecting inefficient or declining industries may make short-term political sense, but not economic sense). This is why the politicization of the economy is so harmful socially.

All these arguments apply with greater force to the role of the state in economies in transition than in established market economies. First, because within the economies in transition *state resources* are limited, there are fewer competent people in public administration, and there is less money due to a lower level of economic development and to a less efficient mechanism of collecting taxes. Second, some of the tasks that belong to the state's sphere of competence are incomparably greater than in established market economies. The task of institutional transformation is far greater than any reform being undertaken in the West and the task of maintaining stabilization is urgent. This leaves fewer state resources for other functions, most of which – especially massive and detailed intervention – exceed the realistically defined competence of *any* state.

In view of the above, it is a mistake to characterize the economic transition in the Central and East European countries – as some observers do – in terms of a 'pendulum' swinging from one extreme, i.e. an excessive state presence in the economy, to the other, i.e. 'unfettered private markets'. In my view, the main problem in most of these countries, especially the former Soviet Union, is a strong pro-statist bias and the associated excessive regulations, particularly in foreign trade, which – as in many developing countries – breed inefficiency and rent-seeking.

Powerful forces of ignorance and of special interests push the state towards the sphere of its natural incompetence. There are no foolproof safeguards against this tendency – we witness these problems even in highly developed market economies. But there are some institutional barriers that are especially important to countries in transition. These institutions should be established early in the process of transition. One is to establish an independent central bank, which should be made constitutionally responsible for the stability of domestic currency. Another is to ban the monetary financing of the budget deficit. These arrangements apply to the monetary and fiscal instruments, which, being the domain of a modern state, are easily politicized.

By limiting the possibilities of budgetary deficits, one also reduces the scope of state interventionism, which consists of granting fiscal privileges – that is, subsidies or tax preferences – to various interests and pressure groups. But there is the danger of another kind of interventionism, that of limiting foreign competition faced by groups of domestic producers. Such protectionism can be reduced by introducing a uniform tariff early in the transition process – when the interest groups are not yet strong – and then binding it to GATT. But this is only a partial solution, as there are many possible non-tariff barriers to trade, and most developed countries provide a bad example in this respect.

Besides the monetary, fiscal and foreign trade systems, the financial sector, especially the banks, can easily be manipulated politically. This has been amply demonstrated in many developing countries. Bank management should be made independent of political bodies by introducing non-political supervisory boards as a sort of protective shield in the case of banks that are still state-owned. Also the banks should be privatized.

Gradualism Versus 'Big Bang' in Economic Transition

This issue is subject to many misunderstandings, partly due to the emotional implications of the terminology. Many people react negatively when they hear the expression 'shock therapy'. Thus, they may become susceptible to the opposite therapies, which in some circumstances may be akin to putting out the fire slowly. Another source of misunderstanding is the lack of conceptual clarity when discussing the desirable speed of transition. An elementary step here is to break down this complex process into the subordinate processes of transition. There are, of course, many possible subdivisions, the usefulness of which depends on the particular purpose. A division I have already introduced and that I find especially helpful breaks the whole process of transition down into three elements:

- macroeconomic stabilization mainly by means of macroeconomic policy;
- microeconomic liberalization, that is, enlarging the scope of economic freedom by removing restrictions on setting up the developing private firms; eliminating price controls and restrictions on foreign trade; introducing currency convertibility, etc. Liberalization includes changing the general framework (liberalizing the regime of property rights, for example) and more specific regulations (removing controls on interest rates, for example); in the West the latter is usually called 'deregulation';
- fundamental institutional restructuring which consists of making changes to existing institutions (privatizing state enterprises, reorganizing the state administration, or reforming the tax system, for example) and creating new ones (the stock exchange, for example).

Some sectoral reforms include elements of both liberalization and institutional restructuring. For example, the reform of the financial sector centres around the total or partial removal of interest rate controls and the fundamental reform of banking as well as the setting up of a stock exchange and equity finance institutions.

Now we must introduce the concept of the maximum possible speed of a given process of change, as measured by the minimum time that must elapse between starting the process and reaching a particular outcome. These maximum speeds are not as easily defined as the laws of nature, such as the gestation period of an animal, but they are no less real.

An interesting question is what determines – for any assumed outcome – the maximum speed of a process of institutional or economic change. All I can point out here is that at the core are *ultimately* the inherent human limitations of information processing and learning. The maximum possible speed for the respective countries (that is, the country-specific reform possibility frontier) may – to a varying extent – deviate from this ultimate frontier because of differences in the relevant knowledge possessed by individuals in key positions or because of differing legislative constraints. The *actual* speed in any country may in turn be slower than this country-specific maximum speed because of its chosen transformation strategy or because of political complications.

A pure shock-type, or radical, transition to a private market economy may be defined as a transition whereby all the constituent processes are implemented with their maximum possible speed. As is usually the case with pure categories, it is difficult to find an exact empirical counterpart for such a transition. Probably the nearest possible empirical approximation is the economic transition in East Germany. But it is a mistake to use the catastrophic effect of the East German transition (massive unemployment, sudden decline in the GDP) as an argument for gradualism and against the radical approach. The catastrophic consequences in East Germany were mostly due to disastrous macro-economic changes, especially the wage explosion after the reunification, which need not be part of other radical transitions to a market economy.[4]

Another empirical example of the radical approach is the Polish economic transition of 1990 to 1991, which has often been analysed, sometimes in a caricatured way. Therefore, it is worth stressing the *radical, but non-dogmatic, nature* of the Polish economic reform.[5] It was radical because many important processes were implemented almost at top speed, but it was non-dogmatic because market-type mechanisms were not introduced during the first stages of the reform in those fields where the necessary institutional conditions for them were clearly absent and where transitional non-market arrangements appeared to be better. Wage setting was not deregulated. On the contrary, wage controls were strengthened because of the inherited hyperinflation and the dominant public sector. Interest rates were raised sharply from their deeply

---

[4] For more on this see Chapter 13.
[5] The Polish economic transformation is analysed in Chapter 16.

negative real level, but not fully liberalized in the first stage. Quantitative foreign trade barriers were largely abolished but customs duties were maintained, albeit at a reduced level. The hugely distorted prices of energy and other utilities had been brought to their proper level in several steps and not in one huge jump, for fear of overstretching the adaptive capacity of the economy.

What processes of transition should be implemented at a speed close to maximum if the goal is a fast *long-run* economic development? I can think of at least three kinds of changes.

The first is *macroeconomic stabilization*. If a country inherits hyperinflation, the safest approach is to introduce a *radical therapy*, as it is the most likely way to reduce inflamed inflationary expectations and thus to break the mechanism of self-fulfilling prophecy on which hyperinflation is based. The rational expectation school theorists would argue that a cold-turkey approach is also the best with regard to moderate inflation. But here the scope for disagreement is wider. This shows that the issue of gradualism versus 'big bang' depends on initial conditions – that is, the proper diagnosis of the disease the patient suffers from. For example, Poland at the start of its reforms suffered from 2000 per cent annualized inflation in the second half of 1989 and from massive shortages, while the former Czechoslovakia had only 10 per cent inflation, and Hungary 30 per cent. In addition, both these countries had relatively few shortages.

The second kind of change is *microeconomic liberalization*. All bureaucratic and fiscal restrictions on founding and developing private firms should be removed as fast as possible. In addition, a comprehensive price liberalization should be introduced in order to remove the inherited shortages in the economy and the related inefficiency, and to eliminate the price distortions that prevent rational economic calculation. Such liberalization calls in turn for comprehensive foreign trade liberalization in order to control domestic producers. A desirable complement to foreign trade liberalization is the unification of the exchange rate and the convertibility of currency, at least within the current account operations. As one can see, there is a certain indivisibility of liberalization.[6]

The third kind of change is *privatization* of the economy – that is, increasing the share of the private sector. One should distinguish here between the spontaneous growth of private firms and privatization, which involves shifting the assets from the state to the private sector. The latter could be done through privatization of whole state firms or

[6] See also Chapter 13.

through the transfer (sale or leasing) of their assets without changing the enterprises' legal structures, at least for the time being.[7]

The spontaneous growth of the private sector should be as fast as possible, as it is the main engine of growth and flexibility in the transition to a market economy. This is why a radical dismantling of barriers to setting up and developing private firms belongs to the group of transition processes where maximum speed is desirable. A more disputed question is the optimal pace of privatization. Some people fear a radical reduction in employment will follow the privatization of state enterprises and therefore advocate a go-slow approach. The concern with unemployment is a legitimate one. However, the link between the growth of unemployment and the pace of privatization is far from being so simple. One should always compare the development of unemployment in the longer run under alternative speeds of privatization – that is, different mixes of the public–private sectors – and under the same macroeconomic policy.[8] Then we notice that, given the hardened macroeconomic environment and competition, state firms, too, would reduce employment, probably with a certain delay.

Yet the reduction of employment could also take place quite abruptly because the delay of privatization may bring state firms to the brink of bankruptcy. Private firms, having a greater capacity to generate profits, also have a greater capacity to finance investment and create jobs. Besides, one should avoid the popular tendency of noticing only actual unemployment and ignoring the disguised one, or what some people call 'unemployment on the job'. Different speeds of privatization under similar conditions may produce different combinations of actual and disguised unemployment: a slower pace may, at least initially, produce less of the first, and more of the second. But disguised unemployment (or pseudo-employment) has negative fiscal effects similar to those of actual unemployment, often in a hidden form of quasi-fiscal deficits in the banking sector (bad loans). And people affected by disguised unemployment must suffer from the erosion of their skills and a drop in morale, and thus it becomes increasingly difficult for them to be truly employed. Economists call this phenomenon 'hysteresis'. To my knowledge, they have linked it exclusively to actual unemployment.[9]

[7] For more on privatization, see Chapter 11.

[8] However, a large share of the public sector surpassing a certain threshold produces the tendency for the politicization of the economic policy and thus over the longer run may undermine the hard macroeconomic policy. There is a link between the institutional structure and the macroeconomic environment.

[9] The pace of this drop in morale and skills and therefore the intensity of the hysteresis mentioned below may be larger in the case of actual unemployment than disguised unemployment. But this is an empirical question.

But there is another argument that, in my view, tilts the balance towards fast privatization of the state sector. This sector is by its very nature linked to political bodies (state institutions, sometimes political parties) and this entails the danger of its politicization, which is harmful to long-term economic development. The degree of an economy's politicization depends on, among other things, the overall nature of the political regime, as expressed by Myrdal's dichotomy of soft versus hard states, and the relative size of the public sector. The degree of politicization of this sector, and of the whole economy, seems to grow with the share of the public sector but probably in a non-linear way: there is a certain threshold share beyond which the political impact upon economic decisions becomes – sooner or later – very strong. The countries of Central and Eastern Europe started with a dominant state sector. Therefore, they need fast privatization in order to get below this critical size in a relatively short time. Otherwise, the political influences would be perpetuated, or they would reappear in new forms related to the newly democratized political systems. Fast privatization calls in turn for the use of non-conventional privatization methods (vouchers, special privatization funds etc.).

To be sure, a low public sector share offers only a chance, but not a guarantee, that there will not be a high degree of political influence in the economy. But a high public sector share seems to guarantee – sooner or later – such a situation.

Macroeconomic stabilization, microeconomic liberalization (except in the labour market and possibly the credit market), and privatization are the main processes of change where the radical approach seems to work best. But there are others, including tax reform and the early establishment of genuine local government, which are important from both an economic and a political point of view. However, in the case of these institutional changes, as distinct from privatization, there are no shortcuts in the form of non-conventional methods.

I have discussed so far the economic arguments for a radical strategy to transition. But there are also non-economic arguments in favour of such a strategy. A great political breakthrough, like the one that happened in Central and Eastern Europe in 1989, creates a special atmosphere of thinking and acting in terms of the common good. And the common good is relatively easy to define if the country inherits a macroeconomic catastrophe. But this period of 'extraordinary' politics gives way rather quickly to 'normal' politics of political parties and of special interests. It is, therefore, advisable to concentrate on difficult measures in the first period, when the probability that these measures will be accepted is much higher than it will be later. Finally, social psychology tells us that people are more prone to adjust their attitudes to the surrounding environment when this environment has undergone profound change than when it is going through gradual change.[10]

The Lessons Learned

Let me start with some general lessons regarding the economic transition.

The initial economic conditions *do* matter, as far as the pace and the effects of the transition are concerned. Therefore, one should frame assessments of the results of this process in the context of *initial conditions*. This rather obvious requirement is not always met in economic debates, as misunderstandings relating to the alleged general superiority of the 'Chinese way' of economic reform would indicate. The most important initial conditions are the inherited economic structure (the share of simple and easily divisible collectivized agriculture, the burden of heavy industry and the military industrial sector), the type of non-market economic system ('suspended' capitalism of the West German type in 1948 versus destroyed capitalism of the post-socialist countries in the late 1980s), and the degree of macroeconomic instability. Countries that at the start had a large share of easily privatizable agriculture (China, for example) can make a quicker and less painful economic transition than those in which such agriculture occupies a much less important place and which are burdened by a large socialist heavy industry (Russia, for example). The same goes for countries that inherited a relatively stable macroeconomic situation (again, China in the late 1970s, Czechoslovakia and Hungary in the late 1980s) as distinct from countries that had to start their economic transition under extreme macroeconomic instability (Poland, for example, and to some extent Russia and other countries of the former Soviet Union). Finally, it is much easier to arrive at a competitive capitalist market economy where capitalism was merely suspended than where capitalism was destroyed. Other important differences in the initial conditions include the level of the foreign debt and the importance and militancy of the trade unions.

The process and outcome of economic transition can be seen as *an interplay of internal and external factors*. These two groups of factors should be seen as complements: both must have an appropriate form if economic success is to be ensured, and a very unfavourable shape of one of them may be sufficient to bring about an economic failure. Thus no

---

[10] For more on this see Chapter 13.

amount of external aid, which is very limited in any case, can offset an inflationary macroeconomic policy, but a persistent protectionism blocking access to Western markets is likely to reduce substantially the chances for success, even of the most sensible economic programmes, and undermine the political position of those who pursue them. I will return to this issue in a moment.

The *choice of strategy* for economic transition depends in part on the initial conditions and especially on the degree of inherited macro-economic instability. A radical and comprehensive economic programme introduced in an initially socialist economy under extremely difficult macroeconomic conditions can be successful in spite of powerful external shocks. This seems to be the lesson from the Polish experience, as well as that of Estonia, Latvia and perhaps Albania. Being radical and comprehensive, such programmes are able to break down the inertia and structures of the inherited economic system and benefit from the political capital of increased tolerance for painful economic measures that emerges after great political breakthroughs.

Alternative strategies of tolerating high inflation (or, even more, of increasing it) and of very limited liberalization have practically no chance for economic success. And although they may appear less risky from social and political points of view, they are in fact extremely dangerous in these respects. Harsh measures would be necessary later, in a much worse economic and social situation. Postponing such measures can bring the country into a spiral of mutually reinforcing and destructive economic, social, and political tensions.

Forming economic policy is an art that requires making timely decisions with incomplete and imperfect *information*. This is especially true of the radical approach to a market economy during economic crisis and under powerful external shocks. One can distinguish here two kinds of informational premises for decision-making: those regarding the target model of the economy – that is, the outcome of the transition process – and those referring to the transition path. The first kind is much fuller and stronger than the second, if one assumes that the target system has to ensure fast long-term economic development. There is no doubt that one should then introduce a macroeconomically stable, outward-looking, competitive capitalist market economy, which pre-supposes a limited state focused on its sphere of natural competence. But, of course, there are open questions about the target system, too – for example, how universal the banks should be, which type of financial system best serves the interests of long-run economic growth, whether corporatist elements are an obstacle or, on the contrary, an asset in economic development.

There is much more uncertainty with respect to the transition path. However, one cannot say that all questions are open. One could reasonably expect, for example, that tough macroeconomic stabilization is the best way to overcome inherited hyperinflation or that a radical and comprehensive stabilization–liberalization programme has the greatest chance of removing massive shortages and, therefore, of increasing the overall economic efficiency. These beliefs have been strengthened by the experiences of countries that have implemented such programmes.

11

Various Roads to a Private Market Economy

Privatization is usually conceived in a narrow sense as a transformation of the ownership of state firms. This concept of privatization emerged in the developed economies in the 1970s and 1980s and reflected the reality of these countries. It is, however, unsuitable for a comparative analysis of various groups of countries, and especially for the discussion of the institutional transformation of the post-socialist economies.

For these purposes a concept of privatization of the economy is appropriate (Bornstein 1992; Balcerowicz 1994; Kornai 1995). This concept denotes a transition from the less to more private economy, as measured by the share of the private sector.[1] Privatization of the economy may result from various privatization processes, and the set of these processes depends on the inherited conditions in the economy. This relationship is discussed in the next section, which also examines the specificity of the post-socialist privatization in a comparative perspective. Various privatization processes, in turn, result from different economic policies, and some of these policies, especially macroeconomic stabilization and microeconomic liberalization, would appear at the first sight not to be very relevant for privatization. In fact, however, they may be very important instruments of privatization of the economy.

Three main types of privatization processes in Central and Eastern Europe, spontaneous growth of the private sector, asset privatization

This chapter was partly written when I was E. E. Wiegand Distinguished Visiting Professor of Democratization at Georgetown University in Washington, DC, in April 1995. I am grateful to Michał Meller for his help in editing this chapter.

[1] The private sector in production can be measured by the share of the private enterprises in GDP.

and the transformational privatization, are defined and discussed in this chapter, and an attempt is made to clarify the links between these processes. Drawing on this I analyse the problem of the optimal rates of decline of the state sector and of the optimal rates of growth of the private sector and the privatized one. Then I take issue with the 'evolutionary' approaches to privatization that criticize rapid transformational privatization, especially that which is based on non-conventional techniques (e.g. privatization vouchers).

1. The Inherited Conditions for Privatization and Some Privatization Scenarios

There are at least six interrelated variables which describe the initial conditions that have mattered for the subsequent privatization of the economy in various countries:[2]

(1) the extent of entrepreneurship in the regime (ER) and the related scope of the private sector;
(2) what type of government controls existed and the consequences for the extent of the resulting quasi- or pseudo-private sector;
(3) the development of the capital market;
(4) the development of the legal infrastructure and of the enforcement apparatus;
(5) the size of proportions of the economy and type of state sector;[3]
(6) the macroeconomic situation.

Based on these variables, we can distinguish five broad privatization scenarios related to five groups of countries.

The first category includes the OECD countries at the start of their rounds of privatization in the late 1970s. They inherited an open regime of entrepreneurship (ER_o) and the related capitalist ownership structure (SO_c). Therefore, the proportion of the economy in the state sector available to be privatized was small. Typically, it accounted for less than 20 per cent of GDP. These countries also had well-developed capital markets and strong legal infrastructure and enforcement apparatus. Consequently, even if the size of the state sector had been large, its privatization could have been carried out rapidly by conventional means (trade sales, public offerings, etc.) without producing any major legal

[2] For the definitions of these variables, see Chapter 7.
[3] Excluding education and the health system, which deserve separate treatment.

complications. The initial macroeconomic situation was stable, so the governments could focus on privatization and there were no interactions between the inherited monetary overhang, stabilization policy and the privatization processes so typical for some post-socialist economies. Finally, except for public utilities, the regulatory environment was relatively liberal. Therefore, there was no quasi- or pseudo-private sector which could be turned into a private one by a massive deregulation. Summing up, the privatization of the economy in the OECD countries could have been reduced to conventional privatization processes operating with a relatively small state sector.

The second category consists of more developed economies of the Third World such as Chile, Mexico and Argentina. Their entrepreneurship regime was usually fairly restrictive in nature (ER_r), so privatization policies had to include the liberalization of this regime. This opened the way for foreign direct investment and for the development of the domestic private sector. Government controls were typically much more extensive than in the OECD countries; they were responsible for the existence of a quasi-private sector, which could be turned into a private one once these restrictions had been lifted. Liberalization policy, i.e., the transition from ER_r to ER_o, and deregulation were, therefore, important for the privatization of the economy in these countries. The state sector was relatively more extensive than in the OECD countries but its size relative to the potential of the capital market, and that of the legal infrastructure, still enabled conventional privatization techniques to be applied without causing any major logistical or legal problems. However, the macroeconomic situation was typically much more unstable than in the developed economies. Privatization thus began under much more difficult macroeconomic circumstances and – through its fiscal implications – could have had important implications for macroeconomic stabilization.

The third category includes most of the less developed countries of the Third World. The importance of liberalization for privatization of the economy was even greater here than in the second group. This is especially true for India, which accounted for 20 per cent of the population of the developing countries.[4] The proportion of the economy

---

[4] India's economy before the recent liberalizing reforms did not possess a private sector, only a pseudo-private one. This, and an important but even more constrained and inefficient state sector, largely explains India's poor economic performance compared with China, especially in the 1980s when China carried out massive liberalizing and privatizing reforms. Therefore, to regard India as an example of capitalism and to compare its performance to China in order to draw the conclusion that socialism can work better than capitalism is a spectacular fallacy.

in the state sector was also higher in the third group; in infrastructure and in banking it was sometimes almost as high as in the socialist economies of Europe and Asia. However, unlike those latter countries, their agriculture and trade was not under state control. The capital market and the legal infrastructure were less developed than in the second group countries. This, as well as a relatively high proportion of the economy in the public sector, made rapid conventional privatization – on average – a much more difficult logistical and legal problem than in the second group countries, except in those cases where foreign direct investment provided a solution.

The fourth category was that of the Asian post-socialist countries: China since the late 1970s and Vietnam since the late 1980s. They had closed entrepreneurship regimes with socialist ownership structures. Hence, there was extremely wide scope for privatization via the liberalization of the economy. As a distinction from the third group, agriculture and trade in those fourth group countries were also nationalized and, therefore, the overall proportion in the economy in the non-private sector was much higher, and similar to that in the post-socialist economies of Europe in the late 1980s. However, agriculture was much more important in the Asian socialist economies and their system of agriculture was technically much easier to privatize than turned out to be the case in most European socialist economies. This explains much of the difference in privatization and in the overall economic transition between these two groups of post-socialist countries (see Chapter 13). Also, the initial macroeconomic situation in China was much more stable than it was in Poland, Romania and the former Soviet Union (see Chapter 12), though Vietnam started its economic transition with an extreme macroeconomic imbalance.

There was no capital market either in the Asian or in the European socialist economies, and the legal infrastructure for private ownership was extremely weak in both cases. However, these facts were less of an obstacle to privatization of the inherited state sector in the former than in the latter case. For, given the differences in the level of economic development, the state sector in the European socialist economies was much more concentrated in manufacturing than was the case in the socialist countries of Asia. And the conventional privatization of manufacturing is much more dependent on the capital market and the legal infrastructure than that of agriculture.[5]

---

[5] The lack of privatization of manufacturing in the Asian post-socialist economies cannot, therefore, be attributed only to technical barriers but rather to political factors – their regimes are still officially based on socialist ideology.

Finally, let us turn to the post-socialist economies in Europe, which are our main focus here. The previous categories have provided useful points of reference which bring the specific inherited conditions for privatization of the economy in these countries clearly into perspective. As in the Asian case, liberalization policy was extremely important for privatization in post-socialist Europe as it was to pave the way for the spontaneous development of the legal private sector which was almost non-existent at the start of the transition. The inherited proportion of the economy in the state sector was extremely high in both cases. However, as has just been noted, this sector differed sharply in its structure: a much lower proportion of easily privatizable agriculture and much higher proportion of manufacturing in the state sector in Eastern Europe made its privatization a much more complex technical problem than was the case in Asian post-socialist countries. In both cases the legal infrastructure and the enforcement apparatus which existed at the start of economic transition were linked to the state-dominated ownership law and thus not adapted to the needs of a growing private economy.

The rate of growth of the private sector during the first period after decisive liberalization is faster than that of the restructuring and building of the legal apparatus required for private property rights. And the situation was made more difficult in most European post-socialist economies by conflicting claims resulting from the restitution of property, a problem that did not usually emerge during the privatization stage in other groups of countries.[6]

Finally, as distinct from the Asian post-socialist privatizations, many countries of Eastern Europe and all the countries of the former Soviet Union started their privatizations with a very serious macroeconomic imbalance.

The inherited conditions, therefore, made privatization of the European post-socialist economies a unique challenge. A closed regime of entrepreneurship and the related lack of a legal private sector was one part of the legacy. This called for the transition to a open *ER* in order to clear the way for spontaneous growth of the private sector.

Having an extremely high proportion of the economy in the state sector, which was dominated by manufacturing, which in turn was dominated by large SOEs, constituted a much more difficult part of the post-socialist legacy. Here was the real challenge.

There were also some important differences in the inherited

---

[6] The post-socialist economies also differed in this respect. The restitution problem did not arise in the former Soviet Union, except for the Baltics. Other countries had to face it.

conditions for privatization among the European post-socialist economies. Probably the most important one referred to the power of labour within the state enterprises. This power was especially pronounced in Slovenia, Croatia and Poland because of the previous socialist economic reforms based on workers' self-management. An additional factor in Poland was the strong position of trade unions within the state enterprises and within the socio-political system at large.

The strong position of labour within the state enterprises ruled out a top-down approach to privatization. Instead, the privatization of the respective enterprises and the very enactment of the privatization programmes required lengthy negotiations with the labour organizations. Countries which had not launched syndicalist reforms under socialism and had inherited a centralized economy were – temporarily – in this respect in a better situation.

Another difference lay in the size of the inherited nominally private sector, which typically hardly existed. But there were some partial exceptions, mainly Hungary and Poland. In these two countries the socialist authorities had allowed a margin for private entrepreneurs to develop, especially in the second half of the 1980s (see Chapter 14 for Poland). However, this margin was still small and the nominally private sector was distorted by the conditions of the socialist economy under which it operated. On the one hand it was subjected to many bureaucratic conditions, but on the other it profited from the shortage economy and the deficiencies of the dominant state sector. Thus, this nominally private sector was in fact a pseudo- or quasi-private one, as in many countries of the Third World. The comprehensive liberalization of the economy in Poland and Hungary during the early phases of economic transition gave the firms in this sector a chance to operate as genuinely private ones. But only some of them were able to cope with competition as it emerged.

2. The Policies and Processes of Privatization in Central and Eastern Europe

Let us now discuss in a more analytical way the privatization problem faced by governments of the European post-socialist countries. The spontaneous growth of the private sector is the least controversial part of the whole privatization process. It is widely and rightly assumed that its pace should be as fast as possible, except perhaps for those sectors where new entrants need to be controlled because of an especially large difference between social and private risks (such as banking and insurance). It is also obvious that, to put in motion the rapid growth of the new private sector, entrepreneurs must be set free. Building a strong legal infrastructure for the law of private property is another requirement.

Much more controversial and misunderstood has been the privatiz-ation of the huge inherited state sector. The key distinction here is between two broad classes of privatization processes. The first is *asset privatization*, which results from the spontaneous downsizing of the state enterprises carried out by their managers, through sub-contracting,[7] through bankruptcy liquidations (as distinct from the bankruptcy reorganization), with respect to the state enterprises, and from so-called 'small' privatization, e.g. selling or leasing shops or restaurants belonging to a state cooperative organizations. To the extent that assets are transferred to the private sector through leasing or sales, asset privatization fuels the spontaneous development of this sector. The intensity of asset privatization depends on the stabilization (S) and liberalization (L) policies,[8] which determine, through changes in the enterprises' budget constraints and in the number of their potential competitors, the increase in the intensity of competition faced by the state enterprises. Different S–L policies bring about different flows of assets from the state to the legal private sector.[9] Also, by shaping enterprises' macro- and microeconomic environments, S–L policies have an important impact upon the quality of the newly emerging private and privatized firms, i.e. their potential. Therefore, these policies influence both the pace and structure of privatization in the economy and the quality of its products.

Asset privatization is often overlooked in the debates on privatiz-ation, perhaps because it is less spectacular than that of the whole state enterprises and it does not reduce their number (except in bankruptcy liquidations). However, asset privatization goes beyond the traditional concept of privatization found in the developed countries. It has played an important role in the overall privatization process among the more

---

[7] Subcontracting leads to asset privatization when a unit in the public organization (such as the laundry in a hospital) is set up as a private firm which performs the services on a contractual basis. If the contract goes to a firm other then the former unit of a public organization, then this unit will be liquidated and at least some of its physical assets may be transferred via sales or leasing to the private sector.

[8] Liberalization policy includes the liberalization both of the entrepreneurship regime and of prices, foreign trade and other operations.

[9] It should be emphasized that 'soft' S–L policies, with uncertain prospects for privatization, formally freeze the assets in the state sector but in fact are likely to give rise to widespread 'wild' privatization, e.g. asset stripping. Different S–L policies combined with different prospects of privatization produce, therefore, sharply different qualities of asset privatization.

radical reformers in Central and Eastern Europe; it may be regarded as one of the most important characteristics of that privatization.[10]

The second class of privatization processes with respect to the inherited state sector aims at transforming the state-owned enterprises into the private companies as going concerns. We might call this *transformational privatization* (cf. Jasiński, 1992). It is this type of privatization which has been identified, not completely correctly, as privatization *per se*, and which has attracted the most attention.

Spontaneous growth of the private sector is usually taken for granted as a desirable kind of privatization of the economy which should proceed as fast as possible; asset privatization is often overlooked and the debate on transformational privatization is full of controversies. They focus especially on the two related issues of the desirable pace of and appropriate methods for privatization, i.e. whether non-conventional techniques of mass privatization should be used in order to carry it out faster than if conventional techniques were used alone. These and other issues can be discussed only in an analytical framework which clearly states what are the criteria of success (goals, objectives) to be used in choosing or assessing privatization strategies and considering the links between various privatization processes.

Let us assume that the main goal of privatization is to maximize long-run economic growth. This criterion can be largely reduced to the requirement that enterprises which result from various privatization processes display the highest possible potential growth of productivity.[11] This productivity potential can be regarded as a measure of the quality of the privatization products; i.e. privatized enterprises. Let us denote by ΔST_t, ΔPS_t and ΔPRV_t, the rate of change of the size of the state, and of the private and privatized sectors in the respective periods: $t = 1, 2, \ldots$ n. At the start of transition the state sector almost totally dominated the economy, the private sector was extremely small and the privatized sector did not exist. ΔPS_t results from the spontaneous growth of the private sector and from asset privatization, ΔPRV_t is due to the transformational privatization.

Theoretically, one can envisage many different combinations of ΔST_t, ΔPS_t and ΔPRV_t, resulting from different mixes of privatization policies. The main differences would refer to the rate of decline of the

---

[10] This is fine, especially for the spontaneous downsizing of SOEs.

[11] An additional criterion emphasized by Kornai (1995) is that privatization be structured in such a way as to contribute as much as possible to the development of the middle class. To the extent that this development depends on the spontaneous growth of the private sector, the two criteria – economic growth and changes in the social structure – overlap.

inherited state sector and to the extent to which this decline is due – respectively – to asset privatization fuelling the growth in PS_t and to transformational privatization which leads to the ΔPRV_t.

Which combination of ΔST_t, ΔPS_t and ΔPRV_t ensures the fastest possible growth of the economy? There is no precise *a priori* answer to this question, but one can make some general points.

It appears reasonable to assume that this optimal combination includes the fastest possible ΔPS_t. The main reason for that is that the new private sector consists of the smaller classical owner-managed private firms driven by a simple and powerful incentive system, while the privatized firms are burdened with the problems of weak corporate governance which are even more serious than those faced by Western corporations (for the latter see, e.g. Coffe 1994, Grey & Hanson 1993). Also, private firms founded during the economic transition do not inherit the structural and cultural burden of the privatized (i.e. former state) enterprises which originated under socialism. I have in mind here the location, organizational structures, incentive systems, composition of labour and the work ethic. Accepting the argument that the fastest possible transformation to the private sector constitutes an essential part of the optimal strategy of privatizing the economy obviously has important implications for the economic policies which determine this growth. The transition from a closed to an open entrepreneurship regime appears again as extremely important, along with building the legal infrastructure for private ownership law. *S–L* policies are another crucial set of determinants. For they affect the pace of asset privatization in the state sector which, as noted, fuels the growth of the private sector. Besides, stabilization policy shapes the macroeconomic environment (e.g. the level of macroeconomic instability and of real interest rates) and this importantly influences the rate of growth and the structure of the private sector. If the country inherited a highly unstable and controlled economy, then a comprehensive and tough *S–L* package is crucial for the rapid growth of the private sector (Rostowski 1993; Johnson & Loveman 1995).

What about the other components of the privatization strategy: the rate of decline in the inherited state sector and the rate of growth of the privatized sector due to transformational privatization? If the new private sector has such important advantages over the privatized sector, should we bother at all with these two other processes? It is here that an important theoretical controversy rages, between proponents of the 'evolutionary' approach to institutional transformation and other theorists. Some of the former emphasize, as we just have done, the advantages of the newly founded private firms. But above all they contrast the 'organic' growth of the private sector with the 'artificial' nature of the transformation of the state sector, especially if it were to take the form of non-conventional mass privatization. In doing this they point out that capitalism originated in a spontaneous manner and not by government design, and that engaging in government-organized mass privatization schemes could be regarded as a spectacular instance of 'constructivism', which has been greatly criticized by Friedrich A. Hayek. Finally, some 'evolutionary' theorists emphasize that if the private sector continues to grow at a rapid pace and the state sector were to stagnate, then the differential dynamics so introduced would take care of the privatization of the economy without any massive transformational privatization (Kornai 1995).

I think these arguments do not stand up to critical analysis. The criticism based on the juxtaposition of 'organic' versus 'artificial' is an instance of playing on the emotional undertones of the selected words and represents a fallacy (for more on this see Chapter 13). The state can engage in various actions and assessments of those actions, which should not be based on the emotionally-loaded and inherently imprecise juxtaposition of 'artificial' and 'organic', but on careful analysis which assumes that the state has a limited overall capacity and that its ability to cope with various problems differs sharply from the ability of other potential agents, depending mainly on informational considerations.

The argument about 'constructivism' is, in my view, an example of imprecise and dogmatic thinking which is no substitute for the kind of analysis I have just mentioned. Which state's actions can be regarded as falling into this category and which are free of such a reproach? Was Britain's pioneer privatization designed and carried out by Margaret Thatcher's government an example of 'constructivism' and, if so, what does that imply?

More attention should be paid to the assertion that rapid 'organic' development of the private sector suffices to solve the problem of the privatization of a post-socialist economy, and, therefore, one should not worry about the decline in the size of the inherited state sector and about the pace of transformational privatization. I think this argument is based on several implicit but erroneous assumptions.

The basic error is to assume that the rate of growth of the private sector can be regarded as independent of the rate of decline of the inherited state sector. Only on this assumption can one show – in a simple, mechanistic way – that the rapid and sustained development of the private sector solves the problem of the privatization of the economy even if the state sector does not shrink and there is no transformational privatization. I have already explained the importance of asset privatization, i.e. the reduction in the size of the state sector which results from a tough and comprehensive S–L package, for the growth of the private sector. However, the scope for asset privatization is not unlimited but will be exhausted with the passage of time; there can be more of this privatization in the early phases of economic transition, and less and less in the later ones. These dynamics contribute to the decline in the rate of growth of the private sector. Therefore, this rate cannot be regarded as constant and independent of the rate of decline of the inherited state sector.

However, the quality of asset privatization is as relevant as its quantity. It matters for economic growth whether asset privatization consists of indiscriminate asset stripping by the incumbent managers or is part of a well-designed organizational and physical restructuring of an enterprise. The one factor which seems to influence most of these decisions is the managers' expectation of a fairly rapid transformational privatization of their enterprise and of their further career in it after privatization. The presence of such widespread expectations may induce an efficiency-enhancing restructuring (see Pinto *et al.* 1993). Their absence would produce the reverse, i.e. an asset-stripping type of asset privatization.[12] Obviously managers' expectations depend on actual transformational privatization. One cannot fool them just by announcing plans which are not fulfilled. And the strength of managers' prioritization expectations depends on the perceived probability that their enterprise would be privatized in the near future, and that depends – on average – on the pace of transformational privatization. Summing up: the quality of asset privatization is positively related to the pace of transformational privatization.

There is another important link between this pace and the related decline of the size of the state sector, on the one hand, and the rate of growth of the private sector, on the other. Even after the scope for asset privatization is exhausted, the state sector would remain very large. Let us assume that there is very little transformational privatization so that a large state sector would persist. How would this affect the development of the private sector and the overall economic efficiency and growth? The most likely scenario would consist of continuing or returning politicization of the state enterprises and financial losses in those

---

[12] This is what seems to be happening in Bulgaria where formal privatization was blocked and the state still formally controls 90 per cent of the economy. Given this lack of progress, so-called 'hidden privatization' takes place (Nelson 1994).

enterprises as a result.[13] These losses would absorb the country's savings and thus a large state sector would tend to crowd out the development of the private sector.[14] In an extreme case the development of the private sector would come to a standstill and the country would be caught in a very inefficient equilibrium with a large and wasteful state sector.

The above remarks suggest that rapid transformational privatization is an important component of the optimal privatization strategy. However, how can such a rapid pace be achieved? Can this be done by relying exclusively on the time-consuming conventional methods which were used outside the post-socialist world or is it necessary to combine these techniques with the non-conventional ones (various types of massive, free or quasi-free transformational privatization)? I have already noted the huge relative size of the inherited state sector in the post-socialist economies and the lack of capital markets at the start of transition. This ruled out rapid transformational privatization exclusively based on the conventional methods and called for some use of the less time-consuming non-traditional techniques. The relative importance of these techniques for rapid transformational privatization was inversely related to the relative importance of privatization based on direct foreign investment (DFI) and the latter depended on the size and location of the country. Therefore, Estonia, for example, could rely more on DFI as a vehicle for privatizing its economy than, say, Russia, Ukraine or Poland. But even small post-socialist countries would not be rapidly privatized without non-conventional mass privatization.

However, it is sometimes argued that though non-traditional privatization achieves a faster pace, it is only at the cost of the quality of the privatization produce as compared to conventional privatization. This claim is mostly based on the assumption that the latter may ensure a much better corporate governance structure than the former, and this difference will be reflected in the different potential growth rates of the enterprises' productivity. This is an important point which, however, should not be accepted at face value. At least three comments are in order.

---

[13] Continuing politicization of the state sector (and the related financial loss) has taken place in China where the state enterprises were not subjected to a tough S–L programme. Countries which introduced such programmes but are very slow with transformational privatization may face a return of politicization to the SOEs. Besides, the lack of privatization would – through the enterprises financial losses – undermine macroeconomic stability.

[14] For the empirical evidence of such crowding out, see Kikori *et al.* (1994). Irena Grosfeld (1995) raises this crowding out argument in her critique of the 'evolutionary' approach to privatization.

First, the size of the potential gap between the quality of the corporate governance obtainable – on average – under purely conventional privatization and that achievable under some mixtures of conventional and non-conventional techniques may vary, depending on the exact mixture of the privatization process. For example, with respect to large privatized enterprises a mix of privatization techniques could be used whereby they would acquire strategic investors under conventional privatization.

Second, analysing a possible trade-off between the pace of privatization resulting in the number of enterprises privatized, say, per year, and the quality of these enterprises, we need to see the latter factor in a dynamic perspective. What matters is not only the quality achieved upon privatization but also its later developments. These consequential developments may be seen as a series of average increases in the potential productivity growth rate of an enterprise following privatization. The baseline is what the average level of productivity would have been without privatization, i.e. if the firm had remained state-owned. There is a pace–quality trade-off: a slower conventional privatization is assumed to ensure a higher initial level of the quality of its product which remains constant; a non-conventional privatization (which at least partially includes, say, the use of vouchers) generates an initially lower quality which, however, converges to that produced by the conventional privatization. The difference in the impact on national economic growth would depend on the differences in the pace of privatization and the differences in the quality differential. The larger the first difference is relative to the second one, the stronger the case is for the economic superiority of the type of privatization involving the use of the non-traditional methods over the purely conventional one.

I think there are strong grounds for believing that this is actually the case. Non-conventional privatization may be very fast while the conventional kind is bound to be slow, given the already mentioned imbalance between the huge size of the inherited state sector and the underdeveloped infrastructure for conventional privatization. Furthermore, conventional privatization is in danger of being slowed down over time. In the extreme case, a country may find itself in an inefficient equilibrium with a large and wasteful state sector.[15] Case by case privatization becomes easily politicized as the country moves from 'extraordinary' to 'normal' politics (see Chapter 9). This danger is especially acute in the case of 'strategic' sectors (e.g. infrastructure,

---

[15] This was very likely to happen in Russia, for example, had the massive privatization not been introduced (see Shleifer 1994).

mining) which are very much in need of privatization.[16] Superimposed upon the danger of increasing politicization is the fact that purely conventional privatization usually starts with the best enterprises and moves to the increasingly inefficient ones.

The full picture of the effects of various privatization strategies should consider the developments in the remaining state sector, which would shrink at a different pace, depending on the strategy adopted. As I already mentioned, the slow decline in the size of this sector which would result from purely conventional privatization is likely to result in a renewed tendency for politicization of that sector, in the related inefficiencies and in 'wild' privatization. This would not necessarily be the case under the much faster mass privatization process.

One could object that privatization involving the use of non-conventional methods would not ensure the enterprises' productivity potential converging on that which is possible under the purely conventional privatization. If this were the case, then the two privatizations, if completed, would generate two different steady states: conventional privatization would eventually ensure a faster rate of growth of productivity and the related faster economic growth. However, it is hard to prove that such a productivity differential must inevitably emerge. Even if non-conventional privatization produces initially worse corporate governance structures than that available (for small groups of enterprises) under purely conventional privatization, the development of the secondary equity market and the related institutional investors is likely to remedy this situation.

Finally, the *completed* conventional privatization may simply not be an option, given the already mentioned dangers of the political blockage. In that case, even if the non-conventional privatization eventually produced a corporate governance structure worse than some theoretical or empirical models, it would still be the only and, therefore, the best privatization option for the country concerned.

Conclusions

The set of various processes which bring about the privatization of the economy depends on the inherited economic conditions. In the developed economies this set could have been reduced to a classical

[16] Including these sectors in non-conventional privatization may be the best, if not the only, way of avoiding a political deadlock.

transformational privatization; in the less developed countries it had to be supplemented by widespread liberalization. There was, however, usually no need to launch massive non-conventional privatization measures. The specificity of the inherited conditions in the post-socialist economy: the widespread government controls, the almost total dominance of the state sector, the lack of a capital market and the legal infrastructure for the private sector, and often a highly unstable macroeconomic situation, demanded an unusual set of economic policies if privatization of the economy was to be successfully completed and rapid economic growth ensured. As I have argued in this chapter, this set of policies included a comprehensive and thorough liberalization–stabilization package combined with a possibly rapid transformational privatization. In the inherited conditions of the European post-socialist economies a rapid rate of transformational privatization can only be achieved if the techniques of massive privatization are used.

References

Balcerowicz, L. 1994 'Determinaty i kierunki prywatyzacji w Polsce: Próba przegladu zagadnień' in J. Bossak (ed.) *Prywatyzacja w Polsce Szanse i Zagrozcnia* (Warsaw: SGH), pp. 3–17.

Bernstein, M. 1992 'Privatization in Eastern Europe', *Communist Economies and Economic Transformation* 4, No. 3, pp. 283–320.

Coffe Jr., J. C. 1994 'Investment Privatization Funds: The Czech Experience', a paper presented at the Conference on Corporate Governance in Central Europe and Russia, Transition Economics Division, Policy Research Department, The World Bank, Washington, DC.

Grey, C. & Hanson, R. J. 1993 'Corporate Governance in Central and Eastern Europe: Lessons from Advanced Market Economies', Working Papers, Policy Research Department, The World Bank, Washington, DC.

Grosfeld, I. 1995 'Triggering Evolution: The Case for a Breakthrough in Privatization' in K. Z. Poznanski (ed.), *The Evolutionary Transition to Capitalism* (Boulder, Colo.: Westview Press), pp. 211–28.

Jasiński, P. 1992 'The Transfer and Redefinition of Property Rights: Theoretical Analysis of Transferring Property Rights and Transformational Privatization in the Port-STES', *Communist Economies and Economic Transformation* 4, No. 2, pp. 163–89.

Johnson, S. & Loveman, G. W. 1995 *Starting Over in Eastern Europe: Entrepreneurship and Economic Renewal* (Cambridge, Mass.: Harvard Business School Press).

Kikori, S., Nellis, J. & Shirley, M. 1994 'Privatization: Lessons from Market Economies', *World Bank Observer* 9, No. 2, pp. 241–72.

Kornai, J. 1995 'The Principles of Privatization in Eastern Europe', in K. Z. Poznanski (ed.) *The Evolutionary Transition to Capitalism* (Boulder, Colo.: Westview Press), pp. 211–28.

Nelson, M. M. 1994 'State Sell-off Shifts Gears', *Central European Economic Review*, Autumn, pp. 8–10.

Pinto, B., Belka, M. & Krajewski, S. 1993 'Transforming State Enterprises in Poland: Evidence on Adjustment by Manufacturing Firms', *Brookings Papers on Economic Activity*, No. 1.

Rostowski, J. 1993 'The Implications of Very Rapid Private Sector Growth in Poland' (University of London, unpublished paper).

Shleifer, A. C. 1994 'Establishing Property Rights', Annual Conference on Development Economics, April, Washington, DC.

12

Macropolicies in Transition to a Market Economy: A Three-Year Perspective

Leszek Balcerowicz and Alan Gelb

Countries in transition to market economies have had to implement macroeconomic stabilization programmes at the same time as they were engaged in massive changes to their political institutions and the systemic framework of their economies. How have stabilization, economic liberalization and deep institutional reform interacted in the countries of Eastern Europe, and in particular, what was the relationship between initial conditions, political developments, reform strategies, and outcomes? Experience in Eastern Europe suggests that when there is a political breakthrough (as in the countries under review) a radical stabilization–liberalization strategy is probably the least risky approach to reform and will not constrain output or structural reform over the medium term. Even stabilization that is initially successful in containing inflation will later come under pressure because of social policies and the structural transitions impelled by reform. Several factors are identified that affect the credibility of reforms, and lessons are

Alan Gelb is division chief, Transition Economics Division, at the World Bank. The authors gratefully acknowledged the contributions of staff of the World Bank, the International Monetary Fund, the Bank for International Settlements, and Planecon and the assistance of Raquel Artecona and Nikolay Gueorguiev. Responsibility for errors and shortcomings is that of the authors alone. This chapter first appeared in *Proceedings of the World Bank Annual Conference on Development Economics 1994* (Washington, DC, 1995), pp. 21–44. It is reproduced here by permission. The views and interpretations expressed do not necessarily represent the views of the World Bank or its member countries and should not be attributed to the World Bank or its affiliated organizations.

derived both for countries that have stabilized and for those that still face this task.

The collapse of party and state domination of society and the economy left the countries of Eastern Europe and the former Soviet Union facing a daunting dual challenge: to move toward competitive market economies while at the same time maintaining and strengthening newly gained democracies. The economic transition in these countries is viewed here as having three elements: macroeconomic stabilization; liberalization of prices, markets, and entry; and deep institutional change. This chapter focuses on the problem of achieving macroeconomic stability and sustaining macroeconomic balance through the transition.

Countries in transition must implement stabilization policies in the midst of deep changes in political institutions and in the systemic framework of their economies. In the context of such large changes, outcomes usually ascribed to macroeconomic policies can strongly influence systemic and political developments. Conversely, macroeconomic policies can have a large impact on outcomes traditionally attributed to structural or institutional policies. We therefore emphasize the pattern of interaction between macroeconomic policies, systemic changes, and political developments – rather than the details of individual programmes and outcomes, which are, in any event, subject to unusually large measurement problems. The core countries in the analysis are those in Eastern Europe with longer post-1989 reform experience – Bulgaria, Czechoslovakia and its successors, Hungary, Poland, and Romania – but comparisons are made with other countries as appropriate.

'Destroyed Capitalism': Initial Conditions and Measurement Problems

> 'There's no use trying,' she said, 'one can't believe impossible things.' 'I daresay you haven't had much practice,' said the Queen . . . 'Why, sometimes I've believed as much as six impossible things before breakfast.'
>
> – Lewis Carroll, *Through the Looking Glass*

THE COMMON LEGACY . . .

After forty or more years of communism the 'destroyed capitalism' of Eastern Europe and the Soviet Union differed from both the temporarily 'suspended capitalism' of postwar Germany and the 'distorted capitalism' embraced by Latin American and other *dirigiste* economies. In the economies characterized by destroyed capitalism, institutions reflected a fundamentally different system of organization and incentives (Kornai 1992). With few exceptions private activity was severely repressed, and private ownership of assets was limited to savings deposits and part of the housing stock.

The restricted role of the private sector had important implications for economic institutions, including the operation of factor markets. Medium-size and large state enterprises dominated output and employment. Industry was overbuilt, especially machine building and heavy industry; services, particularly trade and distribution, were underdeveloped and highly constrained. Government played a major financial role, intermediating between enterprises and between households through subsidies and transfer programmes, and spending accounted for more than half of gross domestic product (GDP). Much of the revenue base was provided by the enterprise sector, where surpluses were concentrated among relatively few firms (in contrast, in market economies state enterprises are usually a fiscal drain).

The features of destroyed capitalism shaped many institutions and professions, including those of the legal system. Statistical systems were not adapted to dealing with large numbers of small firms or individual taxpayers, and enterprises had primitive marketing and accounting capabilities. But nowhere was the legacy of destroyed capitalism more pronounced than in the financial sector. Banking systems may have been 'deep' (as measured by the ratio of balances to output), but financial flows accommodated decisions on the real economy. There was no experience of indirect, market-based monetary policy. Payments systems were primitive. Passive, monopolistic state banks lacked the capability to evaluate creditworthiness, and risk was socialized.

Foreign trade was dominated by a few monopolistic organizations. Autarkic trade patterns emphasized bilateral exchange between the members of the Council for Mutual Economic Assistance (CMEA), with increasingly adverse implications for product quality, as shown, for example, by the low prices of Soviet automobiles on Western markets (Roberts 1993). Relative prices were distorted; prices on energy and essential goods and services were heavily subsidized so that cash wages (subject to centralized norms) could be kept low and investment levels high. Official trade margins were tightly controlled.

Repressed inflation was widespread, reflecting an absence of broad commodity markets and a 'shortage' economy, where demand for goods (and labour) often exceeded supply at controlled prices. Queuing, rationing and hoarding were common responses, although use of these practices differed among countries and over time. The prevalence of 'seller's markets' had profound implications for behaviour. Enterprise managers set production goals to meet the requirements of bureaucratic bargaining processes (including spurious quality improvements) rather than those of markets and clients. Parallel prices often were multiples of official prices. Input stocks were hoarded, and inventories of unfinished investments were large.

. . . AND ITS IMPLICATIONS FOR MEASUREMENT

Even in established market economies standard statistical data provide only an incomplete description of economic reality, but in countries in transition data deficiencies and biases are much more serious (for more extensive discussions, see Lipton & Sachs 1990; Berg & Sachs 1992; Berg 1993a,b; Bratkowski 1993; and Chapter 13). The statistical system inherited by the transition countries focuses on the contracting public sector rather than on the expanding private sector, and while output was overreported before transition, now there are strong tax incentives to underreport. Conventional statistics fail to reflect the sharp improvement in the quality and range of goods and in the composition of output stemming from market-oriented reform, instead applying the same 'welfare weights' to pre- and post-reform aggregates. And when prices are freed, conventional statistics overstate increases in the price level relative to an initial situation with unsatisfied demand at official prices. This bias distorts all deflated variables, particularly wages, which appear to fall more, relative to a consumer price index (CPI), than do real purchasing power and consumption. And conventional statistics do not measure welfare gains from the elimination of queuing, which may be considerable.

Reported unemployment data also are problematic. They are heavily influenced by incentives to report and typically are smaller than true labour redundancy, including that hidden within enterprises; indeed, the relation between unemployment and redundancy may vary a great deal among countries.[1] Cross-border transactions are poorly reported, giving rise to sometimes massive errors in trade data; there is

[1] For example, in 1992 a third of Hungary's registered unemployed workers (12 per cent of the labour force) may have been working, but in Russia, where registered unemployment is only 1 per cent, actual unemployment has been estimated at 10 per cent.

still no perfect way to compare rouble and hard currency trade, and so to distinguish the impact of the collapse of CMEA markets from that of the reforms themselves. Reported fiscal deficits can seriously understate true consolidated government deficits, particularly where the central bank supports enterprises with cheap credit (although, at the same time, enterprises may assume some functions of government, including providing unemployment benefits and social services) for an extended period. Finally, such basic statistics as stock-building and enterprise markups and profits are severely distorted by inflation and rapid disinflation, and bank profits can by spurious because of inadequate loan-loss provisioning.

These data biases are not neutral with respect to types of reform programme. Although many benefits of reform will be more seriously underreported the faster the economy moves away from the inherited statistical system, the swifter the reforms are the more rapidly will the inefficiencies of the old economic system be revealed. These inefficiencies include hidden unemployment, inefficient investments, excessive input stocks, repressed inflation and the associated costs of queuing, and 'purely socialist' output for which demand can be maintained (if at all) only in a socialist economy. Instituting market-based monetary policies will make subsidies and losses more transparent. Invariably, the fiscal budget becomes the repository for the losses of the previous system.

Country-Specific Factors and the Stabilization Problem

Despite the commonalities of their heritage, the transition economies inherited very different macroeconomic, structural and systemic conditions. These conditions determined the environment in which these countries began reform and thus the relative difficulty of achieving stabilization. The differences in those conditions reflect longstanding differences in policies and in the political developments that preceded – and followed – the breakdown of the one-party state.

Even with conservative macroeconomic policies, all socialist countries were plagued by shortages resulting from supply rigidities and forced substitution in demand at administratively fixed prices. Resolving such microeconomically induced shortages is part of the liberalization problem, and a one-time correction of the price level will be needed to accommodate large changes in relative prices, along with sufficient macroeconomic discipline to preserve stability in the liberalized environment. Countries also faced macroeconomically induced imbalances, reflected in a mix of shortages and open inflation (depending on the degree of price control) and, to the extent that overexpansive policies had been externally financed, high external debt.

Only some of the core countries faced an urgent internal stabilization problem at the start of reform. In Bulgaria, Poland and Romania the weakening of the communist regime was manifested in progressive loss of economic control and increasing macroeconomic imbalances driven by growing consumption. But Czechoslovakia, in keeping with a long tradition of macroeconomic conservatism, preserved spending discipline throughout its political transition. The stabilization problem was also less urgent in Hungary, where both the political and the economic transitions began in a more stable and liberalized environment and involved far more continuity than the transitions in the other countries. Like Bulgaria and Poland, however, Hungary had accumulated large foreign debts. In contrast, Czechoslovakia was essentially debt-free, and Romania had repaid preciously contracted foreign debts by the end of the 1980s.

The magnitude of the initial stabilization problem the core countries faced is suggested by the strength of open and repressed inflation in their economies. Open inflation was most serious in Poland, and repressed inflationary pressures were strong in Bulgaria, Poland and Romania. Czechoslovakia's economy was macroeconomically balanced yet microeconomically distorted, with key relative prices way out of line and a large foreign exchange premium on a small parallel market.

The core countries faced structural problems of varied seriousness that were reflected particularly by dependence on CMEA trade and the size of industry's share in the economy. Other conditions shaping the reform environment included the extent to which the old economic system had been reformed and the strength of the labour movement after reform: a strong labour movement tended to produce a wage push, which complicated the stabilization effort. In addition to external debt Bulgaria inherited perhaps the most difficult structural problem: its high dependence on CMEA trade implied losses of 16 per cent of GDP or more with the collapse of that trade. The trade collapse was a large external macroeconomic shock for all countries, with particularly severe effects for sectors that depended on the Soviet market. Romania's industry was unusually concentrated, with a hydrocarbon-based complex dependent on imports from the Soviet Union. Poland too had serious structural problems, as well as high foreign debt and strong trade unions; however, following reform, its private agricultural sector outperformed state-dominated systems elsewhere. Other than dependence on CMEA trade the main liability of Hungary's relatively open and reformed economy was its high level of foreign debt. At the other end of the spectrum, debt-free Czechoslovakia had a weak trade-union movement, and the Czech Republic would later be able to separate away its most serious problems of industrial structure with its split from Slovakia.

Also vital for the reform environment are political developments during economic transition. Hungary has been close to a model of political stability, with a smooth transition and the government freely elected in March 1990 still in power in 1994. Czechoslovakia's far more radical political transition involved elections in June 1990 and June 1992, both held according to a predetermined timetable. The country's split in early 1993 was a serious political shock, resulting in fiscal gains to the Czech Republic and losses to Slovakia, yet in the Czech Republic the same economic team has functioned since December 1989.

The other countries have experienced far less political stability. Poland formed its first non-communist government in September 1989 and launched its reform programme three months later. Following presidential elections in late 1990, a new government was seated in early 1991. Nevertheless, essentially the same basic team was responsible for the economy until December 1991. After the parliamentary elections in October, however, the pace of political change visibly quickened. By April 1994 Poland had gone through three governments and five ministers of finance; three of the ministers resigned. In Bulgaria, where a coalition government initiated an economic programme in early 1991, the period up to February 1994 saw two parliamentary elections and three governments. Since early 1991 Romania has had as many governments, and it held parliamentary elections in September 1992. Romania has been the only country in which the government was forced to resign (in September 1991) under the pressure of widespread industrial unrest and riots.

For a stabilization plus transition programme, perhaps even more than for stabilization in a non-transition economy, political developments form an important part of the conditions for implementation. Elections in an early stage of implementation tend to raise inflationary expectations and reduce the propensity of state enterprises to adjust because of expectations of a change of direction in economic policy. Frequent turnover of governments and ministers slows the implementation of structural and institutional reforms. Thus the political framework for stabilization has been less favourable in Bulgaria, Poland and Romania than in Hungary and the former Czechoslovakia. As discussed below, experience shows that the period of 'extraordinary politics' that follows a major political breakthrough and the discrediting of the old order can create conditions conducive to effecting a determined stabilization. A vital element of that breakthrough in Eastern Europe (as in the Baltics) was undoubtedly the sense that the long period of Soviet domination was at an end.

Economic Policy and Political Breakthrough

Given initial conditions, whether economic policy can shape outcomes in a controlled way depends on political developments. Extreme political instability may render economic policy uncontrollable, so that the outcome is a product of initial conditions, external factors, and political chaos. With that in mind, consider three important dimensions of economic policy:

- Launching speed: the interval between a political breakthrough and the launching of a coherent economic programme.
- Phasing: the timing of the launching and implementation of the main components of the programme.
- The implementation rate for each main component.

The importance of launching speed becomes clear when we analyse economic transition from the perspective of political economy. The period following a great political breakthrough, such as those experienced in Eastern Europe and the Baltics, is characterized by a special mass psychology. In the interval between the discrediting of the old political elite and the coalescing of new interest groups, conditions are especially favourable for technocrats to assume positions of political responsibility. There is also a greatly increased probability that the population will accept difficult, normally controversial economic policy measures as necessary sacrifices for the common good. But the experience of Eastern Europe suggests that this period of 'extraordinary politics' usually lasts no longer than one to two years. Then 'normal politics' re-emerges, when political groups are much less willing to accept such measures – or their distributional implications. The timing of difficult economic measures can therefore be expected to affect their acceptance.

With respect to phasing, consider the three sets of policy reform measures: macroeconomic stabilization, microeconomic liberalization, and deep institutional restructuring. Stabilization policy involves fiscal and monetary restraint, exchange rate management, and possibly wage or other controls. Liberalization policy eliminates legal or bureaucratic restrictions on economic activity, including price controls, quantitative restrictions on foreign trade, limits on foreign exchange convertibility, rationing and the command mechanism, and barriers to setting up and developing private firms.[2] Liberalization policy primarily supports a rapid shift toward a market economy and spontaneous growth of the private sector. Institutional restructuring policy, which involves, for example, privatization of state enterprises and reform of legal codes and tax administration, creates the fundamentals of a capitalist economy and makes possible well-functioning financial and labour markets. As discussed below, single policies alone do not determine economic outcomes. Stabilization outcomes, for example, are the result of liberalization and institutional restructuring as well as the stabilization policy.

The implementation rate is the rate at which reformed policies are effected relative to the maximum possible speed for that type of change. We term rapid policies as more radical and more gradual policies as less radical.[3] Gradualism may reflect initial conditions. For example, if a government had earlier undertaken substantial price liberalization or started reform from a balanced macroeconomy, only limited further decontrol or macroeconomic tightening may be needed. Or the initial economic situation may allow radical approaches, but the actual policy may be gradualist by design or because of political drift. Radical reforms, in contrast, are invariably introduced deliberately.

Clearly, stabilization and liberalization policies can be implemented much faster than most deep institutional changes. A radical strategy thus involves a two-stage transition to a market economy. In the first stage the economy is largely 'marketized', thanks to liberalization policy, and stabilized, thanks to stabilization policy, but it remains market socialist rather than capitalist. In the second stage, if stabilization and liberalization policies are successful, their gains are consolidated and deep institutional change is completed under macroeconomic stability. Alternative scenarios involve delaying or interrupting stabilization or liberalization, or both, or implementing them over a longer period during which deep institutional change might be effected.

A comparison of the economic reform policies of the core countries, focusing on the speed with which reform packages were launched and the scale of changes achieved, suggests some general observations:

---

[2] For a more detailed breakdown of policies, see Fischer & Gelb (1991).

[3] The term *radical* is preferred to the more emotive *big bang* because the second term implies a possibility of effecting all changes immediately; see Chapter 13.

- Bulgaria and Poland responded to severe macroeconomic im-balances with radical programmes introduced soon after the political breakthrough (three months afterward in Poland but a year afterward in Bulgaria). Private sector liberalization and institutional change advanced much more slowly in Bulgaria, however, and by the end of 1993 growing fiscal imbalance and rising enterprise losses and arrears threatened to derail reform. Romania, inheriting a less severe macroeconomic situation, adopted a less consistent, stop-go macroeconomic policy but launched a renewed stabilization and liberalization programme at the end of 1993.
- With a far smaller stabilization problem but distorted relative prices, Czechoslovakia implemented radical liberalization safe-guarded by tough macroeconomic policy.
- Hungary responded to a moderately difficult macroeconomic situation with more gradualist stabilization and liberalization policies. The response largely reflected initial conditions, including a more liberalized price system, but it was also a deliberate choice; the government could have opted for a more radical programme, which the main opposition parties favoured. In contrast, Romania's gradualism did not reflect favourable initial conditions but was dictated by political factors.
- The countries that adopted radical stabilization policies also adopted radical price liberalization, raised many administered prices, and largely liberalized foreign trade. In contrast, Romania implemented a much more stepwise liberalization and delayed decisive price and interest rate adjustments.
- Countries undertaking radical reforms also tended to take a radical approach toward external debt inherited from the old regime. Among the heavily indebted countries, only Hungary continued to fully service its debt.

Stabilization Outcomes

What were the outcomes of these moderately heterodox stabilization programmes for inflation, internal and external balance, and the restruc-turing of the economy? None of the countries implemented an orthodox stabilization programme that relied solely on fiscal and monetary restraint. The severity of initial distortions ruled out broad reliance on price controls (as in some of the heterodox programmes imple-mented elsewhere). But the dominance of the state sector and the absence of owners who would resist excessive wage pressures called for temporarily maintaining, or even strengthening, inherited wage controls. All countries maintained tax-based wage controls, at least through the initial phase of transition. Among the countries facing severe macro-economic problems, Poland devalued its currency and pegged the exchange rate, Bulgaria floated its currency, and Romania floated its currency but intervened heavily in foreign exchange markets and restricted convertibility. Czechoslovakia devalued and pegged its exchange rate; Hungary devalued and moved to a crawling peg. Thus there were two variants of the somewhat heterodox programmes: one with wage controls and one with both wage controls and pegged exchange rates.

DISINFLATION AND ELIMINATION OF SHORTAGES

In Bulgaria, Poland and Romania, where repressed inflation was strongest, prices and exchange rates might have been expected to overshoot longer-run equilibriums at the start of reform; in the event, initial price increases greatly exceeded projections (Bruno 1993). Czechoslovakia's price increase also exceeded projections. But perhaps because inflationary expectations had not become deeply institutionalized, except in Romania, the initial inflationary burst lasted only a few months. Nevertheless, only Czechoslovakia – where initial macroeconomic imbalances had been least serious – managed to bring inflation to below 20 per cent after a year. Hungary kept inflation moderate in 1990 and 1991 as it further decontrolled its already relatively liberalized price system and raised administered prices.

Continuing to exert upward pressure on price levels, however, were the need to finance fiscal deficits that re-emerged after the first year of reform, the introduction of new indirect taxes (notably valued added taxes), and the adjustment of key administered prices (rents, energy, public transport) (Orlowski 1993a,b). Although no country fully adjusted prices in one step, Poland effected especially large adjustments at the beginning; Czechoslovakia and Hungary adjusted prices more gradually. At the end of 1993 most countries still subsidized residential rents and household utilities, however.

Romania's inflation profile was an outlier. Despite an apparently tight macroeconomic programme and far slower price liberalization than in the other countries, inflation remained above 200 per cent after 1990 and reaccelerated after 1991. An initial phase of decontrol in 1990 stalled and partially reversed in 1991; liberalization was resumed in 1992 but became pervasive only in May 1993 with the lifting of restrictions on trade margins. Romania also maintained a number of export restrictions.

Price and trade liberalization and the elimination of restrictions on private business, combined with restrictive macroeconomic policies, were remarkably effective in eliminating shortages. Agricultural markets in Poland, for example, swung from chronic shortage to excess supply in little more than a month as households and farmers dishoarded stocks and food ceased to be used for animal fodder. Food aid and export controls added to food surpluses (Kwiecinski & Quaisser 1993). Business surveys and interviews with managers of industrial state enterprises in several countries suggest that a demand barrier rapidly replaced input shortages as the main constraint on output, at least for established firms. Surveys in Poland show that most managers saw the new environment as credible and not as a short interlude before a return to 'business as usual'. Sharp increases in nominal interest rates in January 1990 appear to have played an important signalling role, even though real rates did not immediately become positive. Many state enterprise managers began to take initiatives toward restructuring, despite high uncertainty about the macroeconomic outlook, constraints on corporate governance set by enterprise councils and trade unions, and limited information about their options (Gelb *et al.* 1992; Pinto *et al.* 1993). Whether managers in other countries took such initiatives is less clear.

FISCAL DEFICITS, EXTERNAL FINANCING AND MONETARY POLICY

Reform initially led to sharp reductions in reported fiscal deficits, particularly in Bulgaria and Poland, where deficits had been large before reform. The largest turnaround, more than 10 per cent of GDP, came in Poland, which ran a sizeable surplus in 1990. In 1992, however, large fiscal deficits re-emerged in all the countries except Czechoslovakia, which, along with Hungary, initially maintained a conservative fiscal stance. But Hungary's deficit widened sharply in 1992 and 1993, to more than 7 per cent of GDP. The increase reflected mainly an unexpectedly large decline in corporate taxes – a surprising result considering that Hungary had by far the most reformed tax system. Bulgaria saw its deficit explode to 13 per cent of GDP in 1993. The re-emergence of serious fiscal deficits reflected depressed economic activity, as well as longer-run processes of systemic change and costly social policies.

Current accounts, like fiscal balances, were at first unexpectedly strong. Bulgaria, Czechoslovakia, Hungary, and Poland all ran surpluses in the early stages of reform, although Bulgaria and Poland would not have been able to had they been fully servicing their foreign debts. By 1993, however, for all but the Czech Republic (which gained a fiscal benefit of some 4 per cent of GDP on the separation from Slovakia), current accounts had swung back into deficit. The deterioration was especially sharp for Bulgaria and for Hungary, which in 1992 had been able to finance its deficit domestically because a sharp rise in household financial savings coincided with a sharp fall in net domestic credit to enterprises.

Romania again followed a different pattern. A demand explosion combined with a contracting economy to worsen the current account by 14 per cent of GDP between 1989 and 1990. Current account deficits continued through 1993 even though the budget was in ostensible surplus until 1992; current account deficits and sharply higher inflation therefore preceded an open fiscal deficit by three years. Romania's failure to stabilize after 1990 reflected mainly a self-fulfilling monetary policy failure that helped to undermine the credibility of the reform programme and made subsequent stabilization far more difficult. At the start of reform Romania had a command, rather than a market-socialist economy, and strong ties between industrial ministries and enterprise managers continued after 1990. Far more than in the other countries, industrial lobbies, representing heavy and petrochemical industries and *regies autonomes* (strategic sectors that were not to be commercialized) exerted great political power, as did the agricultural lobby. Firms continued to have access to credit at interest rates far below inflation. Real rates on bank loans averaged about –58 per cent in 1991–3, and National Bank rediscounts were available even more cheaply until the end of 1993. National Bank losses contributed to a real consolidated government deficit of about 21 per cent of GDP in 1992, which was financed in part by monetary expansion.

In Romania, as in the other countries, deflated monetary aggregates and credit to enterprises contracted at the start of reform. The enterprise sector responded to the cut in real bank credit by increasing inter-enterprise borrowing, which soared to 190 per cent of bank credit by the end of 1991. Surveys of Romanian enterprises left little doubt about their payment priorities: wages first, suppliers last (Calvo & Coricelli 1993). That ranking of priorities suggests that weak credibility – not involuntary lending – caused the credit explosion. In contrast, inter-enterprise credit actually declined relative to bank credit in Poland in 1990, as the credibility of the hardening budget constraint and the high real cost of borrowing made enterprises less inclined to extend such credits. Interenterprise credit was contained at 20 per cent of bank credit in Czechoslovakia and Hungary. At the end of 1991 Romania eliminated the overhang of interenterprise debts, which had made evaluating creditworthiness impossible, through a global compensation scheme.

Cancelling out the net debt required the injection of heavily subsidized credits from the National Bank, which added to inflationary pressures and undermined the credibility of future stabilization policies. Further compensations have since been needed, suggesting a 'low-discipline arrears equilibrium'.[4]

In addition to continued credit subsidies from the National Bank, Romania's inflation in 1992 reflected the need to finance an open fiscal deficit of 7 per cent GDP. This deficit was caused in large part by fiscal subsidies, which increased from 8.6 per cent of GDP in 1991 to 11.4 per cent in 1992 (subsidies in the other countries had by then been cut to an average 3.6 per cent of GDP). By 1993 fiscal balance ostensibly had been restored by sharp spending cuts, but off-budget interventions were still significant, and the inflation tax was being levied on rapidly shrinking leu balances. Romanians were building up foreign exchange deposits (a third of M2 by early 1994) and fleeing the leu. Until initiation of its stabilization programme in late 1993, Romania's monetary policy, and the erosion of its financial balances, was not unlike that of Russia after 1992 (Easterly & Vieira Da Cunha 1994). Both countries formally 'deregulated' deposit rates, but their state- and enterprise-dominated banking systems have temporarily benefited from inflationary expropriation of householders' deposits.

In contrast, the radical stabilizers that raised deposit rates to positive real levels soon after the first shock of price liberalization saw sustained remonetization and conversion of foreign exchange deposits into domestic assets as their currencies reappreciated from initially very devalued levels. The cumulative dollar return on Bulgarian deposits for the two years after May 1991 was about 60 per cent.

STABILIZATION AND RESTRUCTURING

What did the financial side of stabilization imply for the restructuring of the real economy? In the three radical reformers – Bulgaria, Czechoslovakia, and Poland – real interest rates were negative during the sharp initial spike of price liberalization, so that the real burdens of domestic debt were suddenly written down (much like external debt in Bulgaria

---

[4] The countries that have needed to resort to global compensation (Romania and Russia) have also achieved less policy credibility for stabilization. Bulgaria's experience in 1993 supports the view that decreased credibility of reform (in Bulgaria's case, the stalling of institutional restructuring after initial stabilization and liberalization) leads to explosive growth of arrears of all types (ACED 1993); if sufficiently widespread, these arrears create a low-discipline equilibrium (see Rostowski 1992).

and Poland). In Hungary, where price liberalization had been under way far longer and reform involved more gradual adjustment in the price level, the writedown was more modest and was soon reversed, but external debt service was sustained, at heavy fiscal cost. Real borrowing rates subsequently averaged about 15 per cent in Poland and Hungary and 9 per cent in Czechoslovakia.

With modest growth in deflated credit volumes net of enterprise deposits and large interest rate spreads,[5] the net resource transfer from banks to enterprises (defined as the expansion of net credit less the net interest bill due from the enterprises to the banks) was negative. Enterprises therefore had to proceed with physical restructuring in a highly resource-constrained financial environment and to rely on cash flows for new investments. The main question about the banking system, then, is how it redistributes scarce resources between firms: efficiently – toward profitable, growing (private sector) firms – or perversely – rolling over loans to loss-makers and postponing adjustment? This question is taken up below.

Net transfers followed a different pattern in Romania. Negative real interest rates offset the contraction of real credit, particularly in 1991, the year of the global compensation. The net resource transfer from banks to firms was therefore positive but unsustainable because of the erosion of leu deposits.

EXCHANGE RATE OUTCOMES

Although the three radical reformers pursued different exchange rate management, their exchange rate profiles after reform showed strong parallels. The initial devaluations in Czechoslovakia and Poland set their newly unified rates at about 4 times the purchasing power parity (PPP) level; Bulgaria, with low reserves, saw the freely floating lev briefly devalued to almost 10 times PPP.[6] Nevertheless, independent of whether exchange rates were pegged or floating, real rates converged within a year toward levels of between 1.8 and 2.5 times PPP, with Czechoslovakia maintaining a more competitive rate than Poland. The lev reappreciated strongly toward a market to PPP ratio of 2 until October

[5] Large spreads in transition countries reflect four factors: limited competition, costly reserve requirements, the banking system's need to generate resources for modernization, and the need to provision against loan losses and recapitalize the banks.

[6] Because historical indicators of real exchange rates are not a useful guide to long-run equilibrium market rates, a ratio of nominal exchange rates to estimated purchasing power parity (PPP) rates is used to suggest the level of the real exchange rate.

1993, when the widening fiscal imbalance and an increasingly chronic build-up of tax, social security, and interest arrears helped to provoke a foreign exchange crisis and a series of devaluations that halved the lev's external value. The expected ratio of market to PPP rates for countries with real per capita incomes comparable to those of Eastern Europe is about 2, according to 1985 data of the United National International Comparison Programme (Ahmad 1992); in this sense the exchange rates were converging toward 'normal' levels.

Hungary's real exchange rate had slowly depreciated by 25 per cent over the period 1985–90. More so than the other countries, Hungary pursued a deliberate exchange-rate-based stabilization after 1990. It encouraged foreign borrowing and foreign direct investment to offset its heavy debt service burden and at the same time to build reserves. Hungary's policy of limiting devaluations considerably dampened inflation, particularly for industrial goods (Solimano & Yuravlivker 1993), but resulted in steady real appreciation, with the forint reaching a value of 1.6 times PPP by early 1993.

In real exchange rate movements Romania again displayed a distinctive pattern. With continued heavy intervention in goods and foreign exchange markets, the exchange rate moved erratically, and the official rate tended to depreciate relative to PPP rather than to firm at levels close to expected longer-run values. By 1993 the official rate was still more than 3 times PPP. Grey and black foreign exchange markets were active, however, with the National Bank allocating limited foreign exchange on a pro rata basis on the official auction and with premia between 25 per cent and 40 per cent. The real effective exchange rate was therefore even higher than the official rate. Strong depreciation of the leu reflected the partial and contradictory nature of Romania's reforms, particularly the subordination of monetary policy to cushion loss-making firms rather than to re-establish confidence in the currency. In late 1993 Romania initiated renewed stabilization efforts, including sharp increases in interest rates to positive real rates and exchange rate unification. These efforts led to a substantial decline in inflation, to 5 per cent a month by early 1994, and a considerable firming of the leu.

WAS RADICAL REFORM TOO RADICAL?

Monetary and fiscal policies thus have been powerful tools in containing inflation and stabilizing exchange rates, possibly because inflationary processes were not deeply institutionalized at the start. But were the radical programmes too tough? Not only were the initial price increases higher than projected, but deflated credit aggregates and measured output levels were lower, and current accounts considerably stronger, than expected (Bruno 1993). Considering data lags and the uncertainty accompanying the programmes, deviations from projections are not surprising. How should policies have responded to new information? Should they have been relaxed to take advantage of space on the external account? Or should they have been maintained (or tightened further) to reduce the likelihood that the unexpectedly strong surge in prices would translate into sustained high inflation?

Such conundrums are endemic in stabilizing programmes. Both options have risks that cannot be considered in isolation from the political situation. Policies could indeed appear too tough to be credible, particularly if there is no major political breakthrough. But relaxation poses risks of rising inflation, progressive indexation, loss of credibility, and costlier (and politically less acceptable) stabilization in the future. The transition economies generally were not highly indexed; that could argue for speedy relaxation once the initial price spike had dissipated. But maintaining macroeconomic stability in a liberalized economy requires fundamental changes in behaviour, particularly for enterprise managers long used to an accommodating budget constraint and a passive banking sector. This problem is compounded by the inevitable lag of institutional reforms, including privatization, behind radical stabilization and liberalization. Because the phase of current account improvement was short, and because all the countries (with the possible exception of Czechoslovakia) faced an external balance constraint again by 1992, the risks of relaxation far outweighed any temporary benefits.

Liberalization, Relative Prices and Competition

After price and trade liberalization, most relative price ratios appear to have approached world levels relatively rapidly in Bulgaria, Czechoslovakia, Hungary and Poland (Berg 1993a). In some cases policy slowed the transmission of international prices; in other cases, notably agricultural marketing and input supply, domestic monopolies in processing and distribution prevented a full pass-through of world prices. Although the ratio of market to PPP exchange rates is only a rough indicator, it suggests that prices for a wide range of goods should have converged to close to their long-run levels within about a year of the start of radical reforms; comparative costs would then play a more important role in determining real exchange rates. The elimination of temporary 'exchange rate protection' exposed firms to the full pressures of domestic and international competition, squeezing industrial enterprises' margins and creating pressures for selective protection (Schaffer 1993; ACED 1993).

The persistent undervaluation of the leu seems to have limited competitive pressure from abroad in Romania; although data are inadequate, the pattern of reported profitability in the *regies autonomes* and the commercialized sectors suggests that price controls were more important than foreign competition in determining mark-ups and profits.

Large formal devaluations did not simply imply a relative price shift in favour of sectors producing traded goods. Exchange rate unification reduced the relative prices of many goods (especially high-quality consumer durables and foreign travel) that had been obtainable only through parallel exchange markets with high premia. Not surprisingly, consumption of high-quality consumer durables increased sharply at the same time that the corresponding domestic industries faced a demand barrier. Thus consumers benefited from unification, while state enterprises that had purchased commodities at official prices and sold at artificially high market prices lost.

Interpreting inflation rates and exchange rate movements in transition is further complicated by the divergence between consumer and producer prices in most transition economies. In Bulgaria, Hungary and Poland consumer prices rose more rapidly than industrial producer prices, while Romania showed, if anything, the opposite tendency. In addition to indirect taxes and technical factors that can cause price indexes to diverge,[7] the relative rise in consumer prices appears to reflect two transitional processes. First, relative prices of previously heavily subsidized essential services are realigned, and second, trade and distribution margins widen from previously repressed levels as the service sector is privatized and Western marketing patterns take hold. Indeed, the service sector has often led to CPI inflation. In contrast, service prices lagged behind the CPI in Romania until May 1993, when margins were freed. Romania was also the only country in which budgetary subsidies increased as a share of GDP after reform. These important differences in pricing policies show up in household budgets, where the share of non-food essentials rose sharply in the other countries after 1989 but fell in Romania despite a possibly deeper decline in living standards (Cornia 1993; UNICEF 1993).

A widening wedge between industrial producer prices and the CPI

---

[7] The consumer price index (CPI) is a Laspeyres index, and weighting may be inaccurate; the producer price index (PPI) is a Paasche index, and coverage of industrial products may be limited. The continued divergence between CPI and PPI, especially in Bulgaria, suggests that measurement anomalies are serious.

has several implications. Part of the CPI inflation in the period following an initial stabilization comes from a relative price adjustment in favour of previously suppressed or heavily subsidized non-traded sectors. This price adjustment increases financial pressures on industry and agriculture – the traditional tradables sectors – which must contend with wage demands boosted by rising consumer prices. Increases in the prices of non-tradables offset, in part, the impact of an initial devaluation on competitiveness. To the extent that price increases reflect cuts in consumer subsidies, higher wages represent a progressive monetization of the overall consumption bundle; to the extent that they reflect growing trade and distribution margins, they are part of the process of shifting resources away from state-dominated industry to build private wealth in the service sectors. For these reasons, as well as the fiscal consequences of systemic changes, it is unrealistic to expect inflation rates to fall to levels typical in OECD countries immediately after initial stabilizations. They need to be sufficiently high for a period to accommodate relative price shifts.

Is Stabilization Sustainable? Feedbacks from Systemic Change

The larger process of transition involves many interrelated transitions: from public ownership toward private, from industry toward services, from an economy dominated by large enterprises to one with many small firms, from seller's markets to buyer's markets (including the labour market, where open unemployment replaces hidden unemployment), and from CMEA product standards toward world market standards (Kornai 1993). Another fundamental change is to transform the financial sector from a passive player to an active one and to desocialize risk-bearing.

Eastern Europe already has seen huge changes along these lines. The private sector's recorded shares in the economy have increased especially rapidly in the Czech Republic and Poland, at first in trade and services but later in other sectors (Rostowski 1993). Little of this private sector growth is directly attributable to the privatization of state enterprises. Although private sector development has lagged in Bulgaria and Romania, thriving private economies have nevertheless arisen in these countries too. The share of industry in output and employment has fallen sharply in all the countries in favour of services and, in Romania, agriculture. Layoffs and breakups are transforming the structure of industrial employment; for example, employment in Hungary's largest industrial firms fell by half between 1989 and 1991 while small firms multiplied.

What do such structural and institutional transitions imply for the sustainability of macroeconomic stabilization? We consider three areas important for the credibility and sustainability of stabilization programmes: the supply response, fiscal sustainability and banking reform.

SUPPLY RESPONSE

The asymmetric response of private and public sectors to reform argues for a dual-sector framework for explaining the supply response (Aghion & Blanchard 1993; Berg 1993c; Chadha & Coricelli 1993).[8] Because of the composition of its output the state sector became demand constrained after markets were liberalized, competition emerged, and CMEA trade collapsed. But the private sector has benefited both from demand substitution effects and from the recognition and guarantee of private property rights, which is equivalent to a growth-enhancing supply shock.

Cross-country comparisons suggest two possibly surprising conclusions. First, radical stabilization is not associated with lower measured output over a period of two to three years. Indeed, the association is positive in our sample, where the largest cumulative contraction is in Romania, the least successful stabilizer, and the smallest in Poland, the most successful stabilizer. Secondly stabilization does not seem to slow the transition to a private economy. Indeed, some supply-side stimuli to the private sector have been directly related to the severe financial squeeze on the state sector. In addition to freeing up labour for the private sector, cash-strapping public enterprises have sold and leased assets to private firms. Where state firms have not responded to a tightened budget constraint (as in Bulgaria), the private sector has tended to be crowded out.

These two observations are related. Although Poland shows that state industry can recover under credible hard budget constraints (Pinto *et al.* 1993) one clear message of the past three years is the importance of private sector growth for the initial stage of output recovery and job creation – and hence for the sustainability of stabilization.

[8] Extensive discussion of the relative importance in explaining output of measurement errors, demand shocks, supply shocks (including those effected through credit contractions), trade disruption, decline in 'information capital,' and increased uncertainty due to the change in economic system is beyond the scope of this article (but see, for example, Blejer *et al.* 1993).

FISCAL SUSTAINABILITY

Before reform, fiscal revenues came mainly from three taxes collected through the state enterprise sector: the profits tax, the turnover tax, and the payroll tax, which funded social payments. Together these taxes accounted for almost 80 per cent of tax receipts in Czechoslovakia and Poland and about 50 per cent in Hungary. Because the enterprise sector concentrated surpluses and employment in large units, governments did not need to develop the capacity to tax large numbers of individuals and small businesses. But with competition, constrained demand, and an end to cheap credit, enterprise sectors could no longer concentrate fiscal resources for governments.[9] Meanwhile, widespread private sector underreporting is encouraged by high profit tax rates and payroll and wage taxes that can cause gross labour costs to be double net pay. As would be expected, transition has eroded tax revenues.

Fiscal sustainability is not essentially a revenue problem, however. For the core countries, excluding Romania (which followed a different fiscal profile), the average ratio of government expenditure to GDP was 61 per cent in 1989. Of this, 16 per cent represented subsidies and 13 per cent social transfers, so that redistributive current spending accounted for half of total government expenditure. Ratios of government spending to GDP normally are far lower for market economies at comparable levels of PPP income: about 21 per cent of GDP for revenue and 22 per cent of GDP for expenditure (Krumm *et al.* forthcoming). Recent research suggests that, allowing for the level of income per capita, an increase of 10 percentage points in the ratio of fiscal expenditures to GDP is associated with a 1 percentage point drop in the growth rate (Easterly & Rebelo 1993). That suggests a high premium on constraining fiscal spending – beyond simply containing the deficit – during the transition.

Between 1989 and 1992 fiscal expenditure fell relative to GDP only in Bulgaria and Czechoslovakia. The considerable increase in Romania can be attributed to rising producer and consumer subsidies. In the other countries subsidies declined sharply, so that the average ratio of non-subsidy spending to GDP rose by 5 percentage points. Social spending accounted for almost all of this increase, rising on average from 13 per cent to 17 per cent of GDP between 1989 and 1992.

---

[9] This effect has been somewhat offset in the early stages of reform by cuts in subsidies and deficient inflation accounting, which sustained taxes by decapitalizing enterprises (Schaffer 1993; Barbone & Marchetti forthcoming). For an extensive treatment of fiscal issues in transition, see Tanzi (1993).

Although the fiscal costs of registered unemployment have been limited, other social expenditure programmes are comprehensive, with pensions by far the largest component. Transition generally has led to a retirement boom; only a small part of the sharp increases in the ratios of pensioners to population after 1989 has been due to demographic factors. Some early retirement has substituted for unemployment, but much has occurred under the many special regimes offering full pensions far earlier than even the low official retirement ages. As the number of pensioners increases, the number of contributors to pay-as-you-go state pension schemes shrinks, raising dependency ratios in Bulgaria to a high of 87 per cent by 1992. Ratios of average pensions to wages also have tended to rise; in Poland they climbed from 43 per cent to 63 per cent between 1989 and 1992.

With minimum wages little above poverty lines and a need to drastically restructure employment, transition countries face a huge challenge in designing affordable social protection systems that avoid perverse incentives for workers. Moreover, because of low retirement ages and slow population growth, pensioners and aspiring pensioners weigh heavily in voting-age populations. No country except Estonia has been able to achieve radical reform of the benefit system, perhaps because reformers did not see it as an early priority.

Transition also raises the issue of intergenerational equity. The time horizons of the older generations since the onset of reform are short, and opportunities to accumulate (non-housing) wealth largely bypass them in favour of younger entrepreneurs, often well educated, skilled in foreign languages, and able to earn high incomes in the private sector. The age-specific distribution of wealth arising from transition will thus differ markedly from the long-run equilibrium distributions in market economies, where wealth tends to be concentrated among older generations. Transition thus increases the need for intergenerational income transfers through the state for several decades. This need will be greatest in countries that have failed to stabilize, because of the erosion of household savings by inflation.

BANKING REFORM AND THE ENTERPRISE SECTOR

At the start of stabilization programmes banks were typically passive and inexperienced creditors. Rollovers of loans and capitalization of unpaid interest have led to a dual financial system in which loans are heavily concentrated among a few, usually less profitable enterprises. But considerable learning-by-doing in the banking sectors of the more advanced reformers has resulted in a progressive tightening of financial constraints on loss-making firms, although loan quality probably is still deteriorating in the other countries.

In addition to improving banking services, one major objective of financial reform is to resolve the allocation of the stock of bad debt. After stabilization this stock of debt is no longer eroded by inflation but tends to expand because of positive real interest rates. A second major objective is to ensure that new credits flow to solvent, growing firms, to avoid creating another serious loan portfolio problem.

The two objectives are closely related. Incentives for prudent commercial lending cannot be established in the absence of properly capitalized banks: solving the flow problem requires addressing the stock problem. Conversely, recapitalization, if repeated as part of the process of unearthing and provisioning against bad debt, threatens to undermine the credibility of the hard budget constraint. Some argue for a third objective: to give banks an active role in corporate governance of the enterprise sector – not because they are an ideal choice but for want of other plausible outside strategic owners and because they have the most knowledge of the enterprises – and, through this arrangement, an active role in resolving the bad debt problem.

Countries are addressing this complex set of interrelated problems through various strategies, usually including a mix of debt transfers to special institutions, debt–equity swaps, and bank recapitalization and provisioning financed in part by government and in part by large spreads.[10] The ultimate fiscal costs of resolving problem loans still are not known, but they will be considerable for all countries (Dittus forthcoming; Gomulka 1993). In Hungary, for example, the costs of provisioning against bad loans accounted for 4 percentage points of the 10 percentage point spread between lending and borrowing rates in 1992, and the effect of new provisioning rules on banks' profitability cut profit tax revenues by 2 per cent of GDP.

Hardening budget constraints and moving to sound finance is not likely to be achieved quickly. The institutional change in the banking sector and other financial markets needed to fully privatize commercial risk will take time. Risk will remain high, in part because of the preponderance of new firms (including those split off from old firms) without a track record in the new economic environment. In addition, in most countries in transition legal processes still favour debtors over creditors. Necessary yet abrupt measures to fully decentralize risk could

---

[10] It is not yet clear how well the strategies have worked; for reviews of the strategies that different countries have adopted, see Pleskovic (1994); *Transition* (1994); BIS (1993); Dittus (1994).

encourage banks to hold excess liquidity and lead to the withdrawal of credit from many potentially viable clients. As a practical matter, government budgets therefore probably will have to bear some of the costs of problem loans for some time, if spreads are not to be so large as to inhibit good firms and further weaken bank portfolios.

Ten Lessons

From the perspective of stabilization, post-socialist countries now fall into two groups. Except for Romania, the core countries, together with Albania, Slovenia and two of the Baltic states, have had some success in containing inflation following price liberalization and now must consolidate macroeconomic stability while deepening institutional reforms. Most of the others, many with new currencies, have not yet succeeded in holding inflation at even moderate levels. The experience of the more advanced reformers offers lessons for both groups of countries.

A general lesson is that, in addition to economic policy, what matters in determining outcomes are initial conditions, political developments, and external factors. On balance, the core countries that faced the most serious macroeconomic problems may also have inherited the most difficult structural conditions for stabilization, as well as high foreign debt and powerful trade unions. It is not clear that countries that had earlier undergone a phase of market socialism were at an advantage. Their institutions may have been somewhat better adapted to market conditions, but decentralization of management to enterprises created difficult political problems for further reform in Poland, and an apparently less urgent need for reform may have encouraged policy drift in Hungary.

1. *Radical is less risky.* The countries of Eastern Europe and the former Soviet Union that have managed to contain inflation to low or moderate levels have all experienced major political breakthroughs combining democratization and renewed national independence. The record suggests that when there is both high initial macroeconomic imbalance and a major political breakthrough of this kind, a radical approach involving forceful stabilization measures and rapid liberalization is almost surely the least risky option. Initial stabilization has been most successful when radical programmes have been launched during an early period of extraordinary politics following the breakthrough. The reversion to normal politics after an initial hiatus complicates further stabilization by raising inflationary

expectations, slowing the implementation of structural and institutional reforms, and reducing the propensity of state enterprises to adjust – Bulgaria is an example. Normal politics is especially problematic if it involves extreme political fragmentation. Successful stabilization requires fundamental behavioural and institutional changes in an economy still dominated by state enterprises. One function of radical reform is to signal the need for such change through a fundamental shift in regime. If that change is not achieved, chronic financial indiscipline and mounting arrears can rapidly erode a reform programme and destroy the credibility of a financially disciplined equilibrium.

2. *There is no simple link between type of reform and political stability.* Contrary to popular opinion, the degree of political instability does not appear to have a simple relationship to the type of economic programme: consider, for example, the Czech Republic and Hungary (both stable but with different political transitions and very different economic programmes) or Poland and Romania (both unstable, but one sustaining a radical programme and the other not).

3. *Don't fine-tune at the start.* It is better to err on the tight side than to try to fine-tune policies in the early stages to take advantage of the temporary balance of payments relief that appears as inflation is brought under control. Failure to stabilize initially will lead to a need for further attempts, but from weakened economic and political bases and with lower credibility. In any case, the inevitable uncertainty makes successful fine-tuning impossible.

4. *Monetary and fiscal policy can stabilize in transition.* Monetary and fiscal policies can be powerful instruments for containing inflation to moderate levels (very low inflation may be difficult to reconcile with the need for continued price realignment) and for stabilizing exchange rates, possibly because inflationary processes are not deeply institutionalized at the start. Conversely, stabilization can be elusive after initial price liberalization if financial policies fail to support the holding of domestic financial assets. The main failure in Romania (and in Russia and other countries) has been monetary and interest rate policy; lack of credibility in this area may encourage arrears. Minimum interest rate targets may be needed for an extended period to protect uncompetitive, state-dominated banks from decapitalizing household balances.

5. *Wage controls are vital.* All the countries relied on wage controls, which become important as privatization inevitably lags behind stabilization and liberalization policy. The enterprise sector needs to preserve retained earnings to finance its restructuring and is likely

to have to effect a net resource transfer to the banking system as stabilization is consolidated. Some countries, such as Romania and Russia, have temporarily continued positive transfers to their enterprises, but these transfers become unsustainable as financial balances erode. And because the transfers are related to political pull rather than to performance, they also are likely to be inefficient.

6. *Liberalization reinforces stabilization.* In theory a government could achieve stabilization while retaining extensive state control of the economy. But in practice there has been a close relation between stabilization and liberalization except on the wage front. Policymakers who valued stabilization also valued liberalization. Cutting fiscal subsidies and avoiding large central bank losses due to subsidized credits (a major weakness in Romania and many countries of the former Soviet Union) have been important elements of macroeconomic adjustment. Most fundamental, stabilizing a heavily controlled economy that retains extensive price controls and strong institutional links between government and enterprises is very difficult even for a strong state because the enterprises can blame these controls for their losses. In addition, the enterprises always have better information than the government and can take advantage of their lack of autonomy to claim subsidies. Romania shows how problematic this option is.

7. *The importance of exchange rate pegs depends on the nature of inflationary expectations.* Some of the transition countries pegged their exchange rates to provide another nominal anchor. The experience of Bulgaria, as well as that of Latvia and Slovenia, suggests that the importance of fixing the exchange rate is a more open question than the need for wage controls. It may hinge on whether deeply embedded inflationary expectations concern price increases (as in Latin America) or mostly shortages.

8. *Radical stabilization and liberalization policy encourages recovery and transition to a private economy.* Country experience suggests no adverse medium-run tradeoffs between stabilization (with its accompanying liberalization) and either output or the speed of transition to a private economy. Failure to stabilize wastes valuable time and will delay recovery. Measures to promote private sector development, including privatizing small assets and providing access to commercial real estate, should be essential components of a stabilization package because of their importance for the supply response.

9. *After initial stabilization, credible, sustainable reform will require a strong growth response by the private sector; fiscal reform, especially on the*

spending side, and probably some external support; and resolution of bad debts without reducing the credibility of budget constraints. The inevitable lag of institutional reform behind stabilization and liberalization suggests that an extended phase of fiscal pressure is to be expected in a radical reform programme. In theory a fiscal balance condition can set an upper limit to the speed of transition from a public to a private economy. Although this tradeoff is appealing, in practice the aim of preserving tax receipts is a poor argument for deliberately slowing this transition because revenues are in any case not sustainable. It is counterproductive to try to maintain fiscal revenues by supporting public enterprises with quasi-fiscal subsidies through the banking system: rampant fiscal deficits will shatter the credibility of reform. However, very high (actual or anticipated) taxation will slow the private economy, which will need to finance rapid growth mostly out of retained earnings. Slow private sector growth also will undermine reform.

The main fiscal reforms must, therefore, centre on spending. Even after the elimination of subsidies, ratios of expenditure to GDP are far above those usual in middle-income countries, largely because of social transfers. Severe resource constraints will prevent economies from rapidly growing out of these ratios, particularly if the budget also has to bear the costs of previously hidden inefficiencies. Spending analyses, including detailed studies of the incidence of social benefits, are needed to show where adjustments will be less painful. But it is difficult to cut expenditures abruptly (especially after the end of 'extraordinary politics') when trying to preserve a democratic consensus in favour of reform. Unlike in non-transition stabilizing economies, fiscal deficits in transition economies must be seen in a medium-term perspective, with greater emphasis placed on reducing government spending and improving its composition. In the interim external finance will be needed to allow larger fiscal deficits than conventionally acceptable to be financed without excessive monetary expansion. For the same fiscal reasons, reductions in debt service obligations are critical to the success of radical reform in heavily indebted countries.

Especially because financial systems can transfer few resources to borrowers in the stabilization phase, measures to limit credit rollovers to loss-making state firms and to encourage lending to private firms need to be put in place relatively quickly, even if banks cannot immediately assume a leading role in initiating bankruptcies. It is also vital to 'activate' at least part of the banking system as fast as possible, to support the reorganization of the enterprise sector without, however, creating expectations of bailouts that weaken the credibility of reform. How best to resolve the bad debt problem depends on the country's conditions; the Czech Republic, Hungary, and Poland offer a range of experience suggesting that progress is possible. Across-the-board debt relief is problematic, however, and a simple one-off resolution of the bad debt problem is probably unrealistic.

10. *Failure to stabilize at first does not argue against continuing institutional restructuring and liberalization.* Consider countries still grappling with major stabilization problems in the absence of a major political breakthrough (or having failed to stabilize initially in the aftermath of a breakthrough). How should these countries proceed? Clearly, their task is difficult because of continued economic weakening and the likelihood that indexation mechanisms will be strengthened. One lesson is to exploit the credibility imparted by any major political discontinuity to implement a determined stabilization programme. Even while not yet stabilized, however, these countries should proceed with liberalization and institutional reforms as rapidly as they can. These reforms will not realize their full potential until macroeconomic stability is achieved. But they can improve the underpinnings for future stabilization and may strengthen a constituency in support of a future stabilization effort.

References

ACED (Agency for Economic Coordination and Development) 1993, *Bulgarian Economy in 1993*, Annual Report.

Aghion, P. & Blanchard, O. 1993 'On the speed of transition in Central Europe', Working Paper 6, European Bank for Reconstruction and Development, London.

Ahmad, S. 1992 'Regression Estimates of per Capita GDP Based on Purchasing Power parties', Policy Research Working Paper 956, World Bank, International Economics Department, Socioeconomic Data Division, Washington, DC.

Balcerowicz, L. 1994 'Poland' in John Williamson (ed.), *The Political Economy of Policy Reform*, Washington, DC, Institute of International Economics.

Barbone, L. & Marchetti Jr., D. Forthcoming. 'Transition and the fiscal crisis: crisis in Central Europe', *Economics of Transition*.

Berg, A. 1993a 'Does macroeconomic reform cause structural adjustment? Lessons from Poland', International Monetary Fund, Washington, DC.

—— 1993b 'Measurement and mismeasurement of economic activity during transition to the market', in Mario I. Blejer, Guillermo A. Calvo, Fabrizio Coricelli, & Alan H. Gelb (eds), *Eastern Europe in Transition: From Recession to Growth?* World Bank Discussion Paper 196, Washington, DC.

—— 1993c 'Supply and demand factors in the output decline in East and Central Europe', paper presented at the International Conference on Output Decline in Eastern Europe, November, Austria.

Berg, A. & Sachs, J. 1992 'Structural adjustment and international trade in Eastern Europe: the case of Poland', *Economic Policy* (April): 117–73.

BIS (Bank for International Settlements) 1993 *Sixty-Third Annual Report*, Basel.

Blejer, M. I., Calvo, G. A., Coricelli, F. & Gelb, A. (eds) 1993 *Eastern Europe in Transition: From Recession to Growth? Proceedings of a Conference on the Macroeconomic Aspects of Adjustment, Cosponsored by the International Monetary Fund and The World Bank*, World Bank Discussion Paper 196, Washington, DC.

Bratkowski, A. 1993 'The shock of transformation or the transformation of the shock? The Big Bang in Poland and official statistics', *Communist Economies and Economic Transformation* 5, No. 1.

Bruno, M. 1993 'Stabilization and reform in Eastern Europe: preliminary evaluation', in Mario I. Blejer, Guillermo A. Calvo, Fabrizio Coricelli, & Alan H. Gelb (eds), *Eastern Europe in Transition: From Recession to Growth?* World Bank Discussion Paper 196, Washington, DC.

Calvo, G. A. & Coricelli, F. 1993 'Inter-enterprise arrears in economies in transition', paper presented at the International Conference on Output Decline in Eastern Europe, November, Austria.

Chadha, B. & Coricelli, F. 1993 'Fiscal constraints and the speed of transition', International Monetary Fund and World Bank, Washington, DC.

Cornia, G. A. 1993 'Poverty, food consumption and nutrition during the transition to the market economy.'

Dittus, P. 1994 *Corporate Governance in Central Europe: The Role of Banks*, BIS, Basle.

Easterly, W. & Rebelo, S. 1993 'Fiscal policy and economic growth: an empirical investigation', World Bank, Transition and Macro-Adjustment Division, Washington, DC.

Easterly, W. & Vieira Da Cunha, P. 1994 'Financing the storm: macroeconomic crisis in Russia, 1992–93', Policy Research Working Paper 1240, World Bank, Macroeconomics and Growth Division and Europe and Central Asia Country Operations Division II, Washington, DC.

Fischer, S. & Gelb, A. 1991 'The process of economic transformation', *Journal of Economic Perspectives* 5, No. 1.

Gelb, A., Jorgenson, E. & Singh, I. 1992 'Life after the Polish "Big Bang": episodes of pre-privatization enterprise behavior', in Arye Hillman & Branko Milanovic (eds), *The Transition from Socialism in Eastern Europe: Domestic Restructuring and Foreign Trade*, Washington, DC, World Bank.

Gomulka, S. 1993 'The financial situation of Polish enterprises (1992–3) and its impact on monetary and fiscal policies', Eastern Europe Research Paper Series 28, World Bank, Transition and Macro-Adjustment Division, Washington, DC.

Kornai, J. 1992 *The Socialist System: The Political Economy of Communism*, Princeton, NJ, Princeton University Press.

—— 1993 'Transformational recession: a general phenomenon examined through the example of Hungary's development', paper presented at the François Perroux Lecture, Collège de France, Paris.

Krumm, K., Milanovic, B. & Walton, M. Forthcoming. 'Transfer and the

Transition from socialism: is a radical alternative necessary?' World Bank, Europe and Central Asia Regional Office and Transition Economics Division, Washington, DC.

Kwiecinski, A. & Quaisser, W. 1993 'Agricultural prices and subsidies in the transformation process of the Polish economy', *Economic Systems* 17, No. 2, 125–54.

Lipton, D. & Sachs, J. 1990 'Creating a market economy in Eastern Europe: The case of Poland', *Brookings Papers on Economic Activity*, 1, Washington, DC, The Brookings Institution.

Orlowski, L. T. 1993a 'Destabilizing factors in the economic transition in Central Europe', paper presented at the Conference of the European Association for Evolutionary Political Economy: The Economy of the Future Ecology, University of Barcelona.

—— 1993b 'Problems of corrective inflation in the transformation from central planning to a market economy: the experience of Poland', Sacred Heart University and Kiel Institute of World Economics, Kiel, Germany.

Pinto, B., Belka, M. & Krajewski, S. 1993 'Transforming state enterprises in Poland: evidence on adjustment by manufacturing firms', *Brookings Papers on Economic Activity*, Washington, DC, The Brookings Institution.

Pleskovic, B. 1994 'Financial policies in socialist countries in transition', Policy Research Working Paper 1242, World Bank, Research Advisory Staff, Washington, DC.

Roberts, B. 1993 'What happened to Soviet product quality? Evidence from the Finnish auto market', University of Miami, Miami, Fla.

Rostowski, J. 1992 'The inter-enterprise debt explosion in the former Soviet Union: causes, consequences, cures', *Communist Economies and Economic Transformation* 5, No. 2: 131–59.

—— 1993 'The implications of rapid private sector growth in Poland', Paper No. 159, Centre for Economic Performance, London School of Economics, July.

Schaffer, M. 1993 'The enterprise sector and emergence of the Polish fiscal crisis, 1990–91', Policy Research Working Paper 1195. World Bank, Transition and Macro-Adjustment Division, Washington, DC.

Solimano, A. and Yuravlivker, David E. 1993 'Price formation, nominal anchors, and stabilization policies in Hungary: an empirical analysis', World Bank, Policy Research Department and Europe and Central Asia Country Department II, Washington, DC.

Tanzi, V. 1993. *Transition to Market: Studies in Fiscal Reform*. Washington, DC, International Monetary Fund.

Transition 1994 World Bank, Policy Research Department, Washington, DC, January.

UNICEF (United Nations Childrens Fund) 1993 *Public Policy and Social Conditions*, Regional Monitory Report 1, New York.

13

Common Fallacies in the Debate on the Economic Transition in Central and Eastern Europe

This chapter describes some of what I consider to be the common fallacies presented in analysing and assessing the experiences and issues involved in the transition from a non-market economy in Central and Eastern Europe. Since many of these fallacies are put forward in these countries in political debate on economic policy in the region, they are political realities of interest to anybody following developments there. But at least some of these fallacies are also expounded by people who regard themselves as professional economists, and who are regarded as such by others; such economists are by no means only found in post-socialist countries where formerly economic education was poor. They are also found, though in lesser numbers perhaps, in Western countries. Few people commit all the fallacies that I shall discuss, and there are certainly plenty who commit none of them. However, there are enough who do subscribe to at least some of these fallacies to make the whole undertaking worthwhile.

In the sections that follow I shall present a selection of common fallacies and alternative views which I consider to be correct. I shall

This chapter was written while I was a Visiting Scholar in the Chief Economist's Office at the European Bank for Reconstruction and Development in July–August 1993. I thank Antonia Lloyd-Jones for editing and typing the text, and for translating the early sections from Polish. I was given useful comments on the first draft by Joshua Charap, John Flemming, David Hexter, Henryk Kierzkowski, Hans Peter Lankes and Nicholas Stern. The usual caveats apply. An abbreviated version of this chapter was published in *Economic Policy*, December 1994, and another version appeared under the same title as a European Bank for Reconstruction and Development Working Paper (no. 11, October 1993).

divide the chosen fallacies into six – somewhat arbitrary – groups. The first section deals with general conceptual or logical mistakes, i.e. those used in debate on the economic transition as well as in other popular economic discussions. The second section discusses fallacies which relate more specifically to the economic transformation. The third section focuses on the misuse of some empirical models (e.g. the 'Chinese model') to argue general points (e.g. gradualism versus the Big Bang). The fourth section covers fallacies about inflation and reflation within the context of the whole stabilization and transformation process. The fifth section discusses uncritical use of statistical data in analysis of the economic transition in the central and east European countries, and the final section is devoted to what I perceive to be some important fallacies regarding the social and political aspects of the economic transition.

General Conceptual or Logical Mistakes

EMOTIONALLY LOADED TERMINOLOGY AND EMOTIONAL ASSOCIATIONS

A common problem is emotionally loaded terminology, used particularly often in popular discussion, but also in some academic circles. The prime example is 'shock therapy', an expression borrowed from psychiatry, which – on purely emotional grounds – is likely to bias popular judgement against radical measures (see Islam (1993) for criticism of this expression.

The word 'social' also has great power to release emotion, but this time positive. That is probably why the term 'social market economy' has made such a fine career for itself in Poland in recent debates on the desired economic model. Few people know exactly what it means, but just about everyone is blissfully convinced that it means some sort of better market economy. The term was coined in Germany in the 1940s by a group of liberal economists to describe a freely competitive capitalist economy with a certain admixture of social protection, but to a lesser degree than in Sweden, for example. From the start of the 1970s Germany's 'social market economy' appears to have been distinctly 'oversocialized', which affected the rate of its development, and more recently contributed to the crisis in its public finances. Therefore, the *soziale Marktwirtschaft* does not seem to be the most appropriate model for the latecomers who want fast growth in order to catch up.

One area where emotionally loaded terminology and emotional associations are especially pronounced is in the debate on agriculture and agricultural policy. This might partly explain why even the urban population is susceptible to arguments about the necessity of protecting agriculture with plainly irrational anti-market policies of the CAP type, and why these policies are so prevalent in the West. Indeed, one has to look to New Zealand for a rational model. Of course, negative Western examples are used as positive models in internal debate within the post-socialist countries.[1] The emotional appeal of agriculture is based upon a mistaken association. Agriculture is often said to merit special treatment because it generates a unique product: food, which is special because it serves to sustain life. This argument sets up an equation between agriculture, food and life. This association is, of course, misleading – agriculture turns out a wide range of products, not all equally beneficial to human life, and thus the argument is a false one.

Emotionally loaded terminology is not a mistake in itself, but a potential source of mistaken judgements. One of the advantages of mathematics is that its language is entirely emotionally neutral. In discussing social phenomena, such an advantage would probably be as great as that offered by the precision of mathematical relationships.

DEFECTIVE EVALUATIONS

Every evaluation relies, whether consciously or unconsciously, on comparing the state of affairs being evaluated with some norm. Depending on the choice of that normative point of reference, a judgement may be either methodologically correct, or else a non-reflective or tendentious pseudo-evaluation. A common error is to evaluate a defined economic policy by comparing (often tendentiously selected) phenomena which can be ascribed to the period since the policy began to be implemented with the situation which preceded it; yet economic phenomena always have more causes than just a particular policy. For example, the notable fall in production in 1991 in all the countries connected with the former Soviet Union was caused to a large extent by the collapse of trade with that country, not by a particular policy.

---

[1] This is how one leader of Poland's most aggressive peasant organization (which specializes, among other things, in obstructing the highways) views Western economic policies: 'the free market is what they have in Bangladesh. The market economy is what they have in the EC countries or the USA. They have a planned market economy there. Nothing happens without the government's knowledge. The government knows where each factory stands and what is going on at the family farms. It is all recorded on computers. Every last cow. In exchange the state guarantees them prices which pay and a sales outlet for everything. There is 100 per cent intervention in farming'. ('Nie chcemy duzo . . .' 1993.)

The main error lies, however, in the basic fact that evaluations of any policy made on the basis of comparing the present situation and the past are always methodologically wrong. A particular policy should always be evaluated by comparing the phenomena which can be ascribed to it with the phenomena which would have arisen as an effect of a realistic alternative policy, conducted under similar initial conditions and in similar circumstances. Then it will become clear that one should not reject a particular policy solely by pointing out that it was accompanied by deterioration in a particular sector. This mistake is like rejecting some medical treatment just because it is accompanied by certain unpleasant sensations. Such mistakes are particularly widespread in economic debate in the countries in transition, as the extent of such sensations is inevitably much greater than in the stable market economies.

BIASED GENERALIZATIONS

This is another kind of fallacy which turns up in public debate on the economy everywhere. It is probably especially widespread in countries undergoing radical and difficult changes, as the gap between every-changing reality and the average capacity to understand it is bound to be larger than in established market economies.

One widespread example of an erroneous generalization is to assert that form of ownership has no significance, by citing examples of certain state enterprises in the West which are just as good as private ones (the list is usually rather short). This procedure is just as absurd as pointing to a female shot-putter as proof that women are not physically weaker than men. Comparing whole groups of private enterprises with state enterprises which operate in similar conditions shows that the private ones are on average more efficient than the state ones (for an overview of the evidence, see Jasiński 1992).

The reason for erroneous generalizations within wide public circles is that in a free society negative events as a rule get more attention from the mass media than positive ones. The political opposition also usually focuses its attention on negative developments, particularly if it has few scruples and a great desire to take power. All this can lead to a distortion of the public perception of phenomena which are of quite fundamental significance to the country. An important example is privatization: those who gain their knowledge of it from Polish television, for instance, are like people who have only ever been shown an old nag, so they think all horses are broken-down and lame.

A 'negative bias' in the mass media's presentation of reality is probably an inescapable effect of their freedom, just as a 'positive bias' (i.e. the propaganda of success) inevitably goes with dictatorship. I do not have to add how important political freedom is – and its inseparable partner, freedom of the mass media. However, recognizing these values does not mean automatically accepting any kind of behaviour from those who take advantage of them.

The power of a negative bias in the mass media depends on the calibre of the journalists, first of all on their intellectual class. It takes knowledge and intellect to understand the complexity of great processes and to appreciate that certain negative phenomena are the side-effects of vital positive developments, not the result of conspiracies. Secondly, it depends on the journalists' character, on their ability to resist the temptation to lead the public up the garden path, or to pander to the masses. This is a kind of opportunism typical of a free country. Under a dictatorship it is the authorities who are pandered to. A strong 'negative bias' in one's presentation of the reality of one's own country is not dangerous if the country already has a good, democratic political set-up and a capitalist economic system in place. However, it may be a serious danger in a country which is in the process of striving towards that sort of system. It can have an influence on people's electoral decisions which may put an obstacle in the way of further movement in that direction. In December 1992, in a referendum in Uruguay privatization was rejected.

All this belongs to the fascinating topic of the transition to capitalism under a newly established, and thus inexperienced democracy. I shall return to this problem at the end of this chapter. Here I would merely like to point out the fairly common, related fallacy of failing to distinguish between an increase in the *visibility* of certain negative phenomena in the countries of transition – e.g. crime, poverty, inequalities – and the actual growth of these phenomena. Political liberalization and the related freedom of expression have brought things into the open which already existed to some extent, but which were hidden from public view. The inability to control for this shift leads some observers to the conclusion that all kinds of social ills came into being only after the old regime broke down.

CRIPPLING TRUISMS

It is hard to avoid truisms. Mathematics, for example, is built upon truisms, which in that context are known as axioms. However, mathematical axioms are just a basis for reasoning, out of which not-so-obvious conclusions arise. Crippling truisms, on the other hand, are not the starting point for any kind of reasoning, but quite the opposite – they lead one into error. In debate on economic reform there are many such truisms.

The first example of this sort of truism is the statement 'there is more than one way (method)', or 'there are various alternatives' – these were often used in Poland in political debate about the economic programme of recent years. These statements are true in an obvious way, and thus they are truisms. The problem is that generally they are used to round off the entire argumentation, and often leave the recipient convinced that there are better ways. Yet the fact that there are various ways does not mean that the ones which were not tried would necessarily have been better.

Another crippling truism is, for example, the thesis that 'privatization should not be an aim in itself'. This truism, often spoken within debate on privatization, puts forward the erroneous suggestion that privatization is in fact an aim in itself. Thus this truism is also an insinuation.

Opponents of privatization and of the capitalist market economy also often use the truism 'all systems are mixed', i.e. they are not completely private. This truism carries the erroneous suggestion that it does not matter what the proportions of the private and non-private sectors are.

Another crippling truism is to call all possible strategies of economic transition 'gradualistic', because of the obvious fact that all of them take some time. This truism serves to invalidate the important issue of the choice of timing and speed of the various processes of change (see pp. 239–43).

DEFECTIVE PRINCIPLES FOR INTERPRETATION

Many specific erroneous views, often expressed in public debate on the economic transition in the post-socialist countries, but also to be found in discussions in the West, are based on a few defective principles or doctrines for interpretation. One is the assumption that if certain, usually statist, solutions are applied in some capitalist countries, then it means that they are good solutions, and thus that they should also be introduced in the post-socialist countries – if the state intervenes in a particular area in the West, then it should do so all the more in the East.

But the fact that a given solution has come into play in the West is not an adequate test of its quality and can to no extent substitute for analysing it properly. In Western countries, under the influence of mistaken theories or pressure groups, a lot of mistakes have been made which are hard to get out of later on. This is particularly true of agricultural policies or trade protectionism. Meanwhile, one of the best opportunities for the latecomers should be to learn from the mistakes of others, and there are some strong arguments why the extent of many forms of state intervention in the countries of transition should be more limited than in the West.

Another popular but mistaken doctrine is the (usually silent) conviction that any more recent solution in economic life, or in civilization in general, is better than an earlier one simply because it was applied later on. This is reflected in disdainful comparisons of 'nineteenth-century capitalism' with the 'modern' capitalism of the twentieth century. Some people appear to believe that qualifying something as typical of nineteenth-century capitalism is a sufficient argument for rejecting it. I am not really convinced that the people who make these rhetorical comparisons know the basic institutional differences between these two versions of capitalism or understand their effects. I imagine, however, that many of them make the elementary mistake of ascribing the low (compared with nowadays) average standard of living in nineteenth-century capitalist society to its institutions, rather than to the simple fact that in those days the countries of the West were only just at the start – thanks, in fact, to capitalism – of rapid economic growth of a historically unprecedented speed.[2] The most important point, however, is that the opinion that all later solutions are unconditionally superior to earlier ones is an expression of a theory taken from the philosophy of history which was especially popular (what irony!) in the nineteenth century, most of all in Marxism. It is a concept of history which holds that each successive period brings progress in relation to the preceding one. Yet this assumption is only true in relation to part of reality, namely in the sphere of the exact sciences and the associated technology. That is where the process of accumulation is truly relevant. By contrast, the theory of linear historical progress is not so true with regard to the social sciences and the institutional arrangements related to them. Twentieth-century socialism as a replacement for private market capitalism was, after all, a major historical aberration.

---

[2] The average GDP per capita for 1820–89 in the present OECD countries was 1.6 per cent a year – about eight times as fast as in the proto-capitalist epoch (Maddison 1991).

Fallacies Specific to the Debate on Economic Transformation

OVERGENERALIZING THE CONCEPT OF TRANSITION

Some analysts work with the concept of 'transition' or 'transformation', which is too general to be analytically useful, and should therefore be broken down into subsidiary concepts to describe the subordinate processes of transition. There are, of course, many possible sub-divisions, the usefulness of which depends on the particular purpose. A division which I find especially useful breaks the whole process of transition down into:

- Macroeconomic stabilization (S), mainly by means of macro-economic policy;
- Microeconomic liberalization (L), i.e. enlarging the scope of economic freedom by removing restrictions on setting up and developing private firms, eliminating price controls, bureaucratic and qualitative restrictions on foreign trade, introducing currency convertibility, etc. Liberalization includes changing the general legal framework (e.g. liberalizing the regime of property rights) and more specific regulations (e.g. removing controls on interest rates); in the West the latter is usually called 'deregulation'.
- Fundamental institutional restructuring (I), which consists of making changes to existing institutions, e.g. privatizing state enterprises, reorganizing the state administration or reforming the tax system, and also creating new ones, e.g. the stock exchange.

Microeconomic liberalization and institutional restructuring taken together can be called 'systemic transformation'. This term corresponds to the German *Ordnungspolitik*, while macroeconomic stabilization falls into the realm of *Prozesspolitik*.

UNRECOGNIZED LIMITATIONS ON THE SPEED OF ECONOMIC AND INSTITUTIONAL CHANGE

A point frequently neglected is that each process of economic or institutional change has a certain maximum speed, as measured by the minimum time which must elapse between starting the process and reaching a particular form or level of its outcome. These maximum speeds are not as easily defined as the laws of nature (e.g. the gestation period of an animal), but they are no less real.

In my view, disregard for the issue of maximum speed leads some observers to make unfounded criticisms and incorrect judgements about certain aspects of the economic transition in the East European countries. This is a special case of a defective evaluation (see pp. 234–5). As already noted, every assessment involves measuring an actual process or state of affairs against a particular yardstick. Choosing an unrealistic yardstick leads to an incorrect judgement, sometimes in the guise of a sort of academic '*besserwisserism*'. When the alleged slowness of the process is at issue, the appropriate yardstick should be its maximum possible speed, i.e. anyone criticizing an actual process for being too slow should clearly indicate what maximum speed he or she is using as the norm.[3] Assessment of the maximum speed of a process depends, of course, on the definition of its outcome. However, the basic (yet often disregarded) fact that such a speed limit does exist is true of any assumed outcome.

An interesting question which deserves separate treatment is to ask what determines – for any assumed outcome – the maximum speed of a process of institutional or economic change. All I can point out here is that at the core are ultimately the inherent human limitations of information processing and learning. They establish what one may call the ultimate *reform possibility frontier* – by analogy with the production possibility frontier. The maximum possible speed for the respective countries (i.e. the country-specific reform possibility frontier) may – to a varying extent – deviate from this ultimate frontier because of differences in the relevant knowledge possessed by individuals in key positions or because of differing legislative constraints. The actual speed in any country may in turn be slower than this country-specific maximum speed because of its chosen transformation strategy, or because of political complications.

An area where many ill-founded (for lack of indication of an assumed maximum speed) judgements are concentrated is the banking sector in the Central and East European countries, which has become a favourite whipping boy for both domestic populist politicians and some economists, in the East and in the West. This to some extent reflects the basic fact that banks everywhere are subject to conflicting pressures. If they are soft about lending and incur a lot of bad loans, then switch to much tighter policies, they lose their initial popularity.[4] If they are

---

[3] One should of course, also remember that the maximum is not always the optimum one. For example, hasty privatization of state banks may lead to their subsequent renationalization, as in Chile in 1982.

[4] It would be worth investigating what determines the proportion of bad (or non-performing) loans. My guess is that this proportion is a growing function of the rate of expansion of real credit, and the slope of this function rises with, among other things, the degree of politicization of credit allocation.

careful and selective, and maintain high real interest rates, they are unpopular all the time. The critics claim the universal lack of or insufficient pace of reform throughout this sector. For such sweeping claims to have validity, a clear indication of the assumed maximum possible speed would be necessary. One should remember that banking and financial services in general, as distinct, for example, from simple agriculture, are a knowledge-intensive industry. This means that merely changing formal rules and the structure of incentive is not enough to bring about a radical change in behaviour. In addition, much learning (or changes in the banking personnel) are required, and this takes time. Generally speaking, the required amount of learning is one of the determinants of the maximum possible speed of a given process of change.

In speaking of the reform of the banking sector in the post-socialist countries one should always remember its typical initial, i.e., pre-reform, state. There was neither a true central bank nor any genuine commercial banks – instead there was one huge structure, a monobank, sub-ordinated to the agencies of central planning. Credit was granted not on the basis of commercial criteria, but on the basis of whether or not it was in line with central planning. Each enterprise was assigned to one single branch of the monobank. There was a ban on inter-enterprise trade credit. There were no private domestic banks nor any foreign ones. The banking sector as a whole was technologically very backward. After three years of reform there have been substantial changes on all these fronts, at least in the most highly reformed countries of central Europe. There is a two-tier banking system within which the newly created central bank is being made independent and the commercial banks are learning new skills. The number of new private banks has been growing fast. Much investment in computerization and telecommunications is under way. Much still remains to be done, such as solving the problem of bad loans, but there has been plenty of positive change and learning, often by trial and error.

Generally, modern institutional economics and the related 'economics of transformation' should pay more attention to establishing (with as much accuracy as the nature of these processes permits) what the maximum possible speed of the crucial processes is, and what are the factors which determine it.[5] Otherwise, those who claim that a change is

---

[5] Another requirement, this time with respect to general theoretical economics, would be to devote more attention to formulating and proving the 'impossibility theorems' of the Arrow type instead of trying to show that anything is possible with the appropriate assumptions.

too slow may sometimes unwittingly engage in an activity which is akin to criticizing the laws of nature.

The issue of the maximum possible speed also highlights the vital problem of *differences in the speed* of the important processes of economic change. For example, the maximum speed of S and L is much higher than that of I. S consists of changes in macroeconomic policy, such as raising the interest rate or eliminating subsidies. These changes do not require massive learning and can be made by a small group of people. L is defined as removing various kinds of restriction, which is also a technically simple process not requiring a mass effort.[6] By contrast, I generally involves the more time-consuming process of changing the structure of existing organizations or of building new ones, and if it is undertaken on a country-wide scale, it requires much learning (and unlearning) by people.

Given the difference in their maximum speeds, if S, L and I are undertaken at about the same time in a largely socialist economy and at a speed close to the maximum, S and L would have to be performed before I could be advanced, i.e. in a still largely socialist economy.[7] This strategy leads to a two-stage transformation: the first stage is dominated by the effects of S and L (and those of 'small' privatization), and brings about a sort of 'socialist market economy' (incomplete markets still with a non-capitalist ownership structure), and the second stage will – one hopes – be dominated by the effects of I and should end up with a capitalistic market economy. One may also demonstrate that performing S-L in a predominantly socialist economy is risky, but that these risks are less than the dangers involved in any alternative strategies, particularly if there is dramatic macroeconomic instability at the outset (for more on this, see Balcerowicz 1993).

A more specific example of the practical relevance of the difference in maximum speeds concerns, on the one hand, liberalizing private business and foreign trade (L), and, on the other, building an efficient tax and customs administration (which is part of I). The former processes can be realized much more quickly than the latter. As a result, if all the changes in question are undertaken at about the same time, given the underdeveloped tax administration typical of the former socialist countries, an *unavoidable gap* emerges between the rapidly

---

[6] However, L does set enormous processes in motion, e.g. the removal of legal, fiscal or bureaucratic discrimination against the private sector leads to the mass creation and development of private firms, and the abolition of price controls can quickly eliminate widespread shortages.

[7] This is, of course, even more true of situations where the process of I is slower than its maximum speed.

growing number of potential private taxpayers, on average more inclined to avoid paying taxes out of their private profits than the state enterprises, and on the other hand, the only slowly increasing power of the tax administration.[8] This gap leads to the growth of a second economy in the form of tax evasion. However, I think it would be a mistake to reject the option of comprehensive and radical liberalization just because of this negative phenomenon, and to choose a gradual or delayed liberalization instead. The former strategy, as distinct from the others, ensures swift elimination of another form of second economy – caused by massive shortages, and perhaps most importantly of all, sets the powerful forces of private development in motion. Therefore, it is better to complement radical liberalization with modernizing and strengthening the tax administration, and above all with simplifying the taxation system.

The concept of the maximum possible speed should be used to classify the various alternative strategies as more or less radical, by comparing the speeds of the transformation processes analysed with the maximum ones possible. Correspondingly, by definition one can speak of a radical approach when the actual speeds are close to the maximum. I shall use this term in this sense.

Finally, one should avoid using the mere fact that all these processes take some time to describe all of them as gradualistic. This truism should not serve to invalidate the vital issue of the choice of timing and pace of the various processes of economic change.

THE LACK OF 'APPROPRIATE' CONDITIONS

Some economists are critical of reforms which have been made in the East European countries because, as they put it, certain measures were introduced without the necessary or appropriate accompanying conditions, such as, for example, a high enough level of competition for free price-setting, or enough private property for the introduction of market mechanisms. These textbook requirements are not incorrect, but they entirely miss the point, because they refer to the first-best solutions, whereas the countries concerned were faced, at least at the beginning of the reform process, with a choice between various second- or third-best arrangements. For example, the actual choice in the region was between maintaining widespread price controls with the corresponding shortages

---

[8] This is even more true of a situation where the liberalization preceded the strengthening of the tax administration. This was to some extent the case in Poland, where some important elements of liberalization were introduced by the last pre-Solidarity government of Mieczyslaw Rakowski in late 1989.

and distortions, or liberalizing prices within initially very imperfect market structures. The assertion that free prices function best under conditions of perfect competition by no means implies that the first alternative is the better. Rather, it is an argument that a comprehensive price liberalization should be complemented by a comprehensive foreign trade liberalization, i.e. the removal of quantitative restrictions, granting all firms the right to engage in foreign trade (i.e. abolishing the state's foreign trade monopoly), introducing currency convertibility, that is, eliminating foreign exchange restrictions. Therefore, there are some important forces which make for a certain *indivisibility of liberalization* in the process of transition to a market economy.

Similarly, the assertion that the market is at its best under private ownership does not necessarily justify the proposal that one should maintain central planning until the bulk of the economy is privatized – that would be absurd. But if one 'marketizes' the economy before it has become mostly private (given the differences in speed mentioned earlier), an immature, 'socialist' market economy is the intermediate result. It is hard to understand how one could use this – as some critics do – as an argument against a radical transformation strategy.

LACK OF BANKRUPTCIES AS A LACK OF EXIT

Many observers criticize the lack of spectacular bankruptcies of large state enterprises in the Central and East European countries, and on the basis of this observation some of them conclude that there has been no restructuring or 'exit' in the state sector. This is a fallacy of *pars pro toto*, as bankruptcy is only part, although a very important one, of the much broader process of 'digressive' restructuring of the larger state firms. For example, in Poland, where instances of one-off bankruptcies of large firms have indeed been rare, many of them have made radical divestitures by selling off or leasing out substantial parts of their assets. This has given an important impetus to the privatization process.

The same logical error is involved in the assertion, for example, that the pace of overall privatization in Poland has been slow simply because larger state enterprises have only been privatized slowly. This fact is true, but the privatization of the Polish economy has been rather fast in comparison with other countries, mostly thanks to the rapid growth of the private sector and the related privatization of assets of state enterprises. The private sector, excluding cooperatives and agriculture, increased its share of total employment from 13.2 per cent in 1989 to 34.4 per cent in 1992, and that does not include the 'second economy'.

Generally speaking, analysts of the transition to a market economy should pay more attention to the possibility that certain specific developments may belong to a broader class of processes which are at least partial substitutes from the point of view of a particular function or objective. There would then be fewer examples of the fallacy of *pars pro toto*. In addition, it is worth bearing in mind that there may be some trade-offs within those broader categories, i.e. the slower pace of a particular process (e.g. the privatization of whole state enterprises) may be related to the faster pace of another process (e.g. privatization of their assets).

FALLACIES AND OMISSIONS IN THE DEBATE ON PRIVATIZATION

The above remarks indicate that one should clearly distinguish privatization in the broad sense, i.e. privatization of the economy resulting in an increase in the share of the private sector, from the narrower processes of privatization, including the privatization of state enterprises. Another point is that one should avoid judging the pace of the latter process simply by counting the number of firms which are still state-owned. An impressive number of these enterprises may disguise a good deal of privatization in the form of the transfer of assets to the private sector. The extent of this transfer is greater under a radical stabilization–liberalization programme which forces or induces state enterprises to get rid of excess assets than under a lax macroeconomic policy and limited liberalization, which would allow them to keep many unused assets. Radical stabilization and liberalization is, therefore, an important factor in the privatization of a post-socialist economy (see Rostowski 1993).

A recurrent assertion, especially among analysts of statist or socialist inclination, is to claim that privatization is not in fact needed, because it can be substituted with a suitable change in the environment of the state enterprises (or in their organizational or management structures). This claim has surfaced recently in connection with the World Bank study of the Polish state enterprises, which shows that many of them have been adjusting quite successfully (see Pinto *et al* 1992; Hume & Pinto 1993). Nevertheless, I still regard this assertion to be a fallacy. It disregards the basic fact that an enterprise's efficiency depends, on the one hand, on the enterprises' environment as determined, among other things, by the price – and foreign trade regime – and on the other hand, on their internal structures, including their ownership form. (Certainly, a change in the structure of one group of enterprises changes their behaviour, and in this way affects the environment of other enterprises.) The environment of enterprises and their structure are in *an additive relationship*: 'hardening' and liberalizing the enterprises' environment can bring about some growth in their productivity, even if their basic ownership structure remains intact. However, this is not an argument against privatization, as a much higher increase in efficiency can be expected if these changes in environment are accompanied by a growing share of the private sector, because private firms in the same environment are on average more efficient than public ones.

But it is true that some important problems related to property rights and ownership structures are not adequately explained by the existing theories. One of them is the fact that the size of the private–non-private efficiency differential clearly depends which sector of the economy is involved. For example, it is much larger in agriculture or manufacturing than in the transmission of electric energy. Therefore, not only the size and share of the given sector are relevant, but also its distribution across the economy. A related theoretical gap exists in the banking sector, where the importance of private ownership is not, in my view, adequately explained. Most theories about property rights focus implicitly on manufacturing. Even more importantly, the established theories cannot come to grips with the effects of non-classical, i.e. manager-managed private enterprise (see Mueller 1992), which is so different from the classical, owner-managed type. The missing link, among other things, is the importance of the form of 'corporate governance' (see Frydman *et al.* 1993), which is the name for the various combinations of supervisors in charge of an enterprise's management, an owner-supervisor being only one of the possible types. But the basic question of whether a shift from (usually small) owner-managed, or self-supervised enterprises to (usually larger) manager-managed and outsider-supervised enterprises brings about an improvement in the overall economic efficiency remains, in my view, unanswered. There are some indications that economies which have had a high proportion of small or medium-sized classical, capitalist firms (e.g. Italy, West Germany, Taiwan) have been rather successful. This is why in the countries of transition it may be advisable to focus on developing such firms through a comprehensive liberalization and stabilization program. Finally, the effects of the rapid increase of the share of institutional investors in the Western countries after the Second World War, especially that of the pension funds, have not been adequately analysed in the established theories. This is surprising, as the fund managers may have distinct supervising characteristics, which is of importance for the operation and performance of those enterprises whose shares are held by the funds.

Returning to privatization, let me note that one of the beliefs which is taken for granted by many analysts is that faster privatization leads to *more open unemployment* – at least in the short run – than slower privatization. This may indeed be the case, but it is a fallacy to take it for granted, because there are two opposing forces at play here, both related to the pace of privatization. Firstly, private firms are more likely – being profit-motivated – to be interested in shedding what they perceive as permanently unnecessary labour than non-private ones. But secondly, private firms are also on average keener – again in the interest of profits – to use their existing labour force more efficiently than non-private ones, and on average they are more capable of providing the extra investment necessary to maintain and enlarge the labour force, thanks to their greater – on average – capacity to generate profits. The balance of these two effects cannot be determined *a priori*. Therefore, one should refrain from making a general statement that faster privatization necessarily leads to more unemployment than slower privatization. It is worth remembering that in some cases a state enterprise which resists restructuring and privatization in the face of external shocks accumulates *hidden unemployment* which may then be turned into open unemployment, if privatization eventually comes into being. To attribute the entire increase in open unemployment to privatization is then equal to committing the particular fallacy of failing to control estimates of the growth of a certain phenomenon for an increase in its visibility (see p. 236).

COUNTRY SPECIFICITY VERSUS THERAPY SPECIFICITY

A common fallacy is to use country specificity as a sufficient reason to argue that the same basic economic disease can and should be treated with radically different, country-specific therapies. This idea is especially prevalent in discussions about hyperinflation, e.g. in demanding that because Russia is a specific case the standard macroeconomic stabilization cannot and should not be used, but that some radically different strategy should be applied. The same has often been said, for example, in Brazil.[9]

Every country is specific in some respects, and the mere fact that a country is specific does not imply that there is any good specific strategy available to cure its basic economic ills. A Chinese and a Russian are different in some respects, but if they have tuberculosis, say, the best

---

[9] 'Brazilian policy makers are living monuments to the frivolous naiveté of arguing "you do not understand. Our country is different, inflation is stable, there is a plateau".' (Dornbush 1991, p. 175.)

therapy available would be the same. Country specificity may be reflected not in the form of the best available therapy for certain economic problems, but in the fact that the side effects of the same best treatment may be more serious in one country than in another. For instance, the side effects of stabilizing a socialist economy are probably bound to be greater than those of stabilizing a capitalist one. A comparison of the West German miracle after 1948 with the collapse of the East German economy after 1989 is very instructive in this respect. Of course, there were other factors at play in East Germany besides just a socialist ownership structure. I shall return to these factors on p. 251.

All these comments have dealt with the fallacy of jumping from country specificity to a demand for therapy specificity in relation to some *basic* problem. This is not to deny that some countries may have *specific* economic problems which require some special measures to be incorporated into the overall economic programme. For example, the huge military-industrial sector in Russia and Ukraine cannot be left completely unattended.

The widespread confusion of country specificity with therapy specificity implies that one of the important tasks of economic theory is to elaborate a list of economic problems and the best related economic policy measures (therapies) which are invariant from country to country. In my view, this list comprises, among other things, radical macro-economic stabilization as a response to hyperinflation, comprehensive price liberalization and the liberalization of supply (both domestic and foreign trade) as a therapy for massive shortages, a fundamental simplification of the tax system and the elimination of detailed bureau-cratic regulations as a response to corruption.

THE ROLE OF THE STATE IN TRANSITION

I have already discussed fallacies connected with the role of the state in transition in Chapter 10. Let me only recall here that the erroneous beliefs include: the conviction that to identify a market failure is enough to justify state intervention; that a genuine preoccupation with human problems gives rise to an emotional tendency to look for solutions for all sorts of problems to the most visible institution – the state; and finally, the mistaken explanation of the success of Japan and the other East-Asian 'Tigers' in terms of some special forms of state intervention, instead of looking to an unusual accumulation of fundamental economic factors. On top of these genuinely held but deeply mistaken beliefs about the economic role of the state, there are, of course, the interest groups which push the state towards various interventions.

The proper view of the state should consider these fundamental premises: (1) the state has only limited resources in terms of time, administrative capacity and money; (2) the capacity of the state to deal with different problems varies, mainly because of varying informational requirements. Together these two arguments largely suffice to establish a rational basis for a limited state.

These are some of the important reasons why a well-focused state is even more necessary in transition economies than in established market economies. The state resources in transition economies are much more limited, while the fundamental tasks of systemic transformation and monetary stabilization are far greater than in any developed market economy.

The Misuse of Empirical Models in General Discussion of Economic Transition

THE 'CHINESE WAY' AS AN ARGUMENT FOR 'GRADUALISM'

There is a fairly common tendency to claim that the 'Chinese Way' is for some reasons superior to the approaches to economic transformation applied in the Central and East European countries, and superior in particular to the Big Bang. One of the problems with this assertion is that the 'Chinese Way' is rarely defined precisely enough to allow one to make an analytically well-founded comparative assessment. Some people see the superiority of the 'Chinese Way' in the fact that market-oriented reform preceded political democratization. They assert that repeating the classic sequence: 'capitalism first, democracy later', creates better chances of achieving both than the reverse order, as in the Central and East European countries. This relates, of course, to the vast discussion of the role within economic development of democracy versus authoritarianism. The empirical results show that political democracy is not in itself a factor in economic development (for an overview of empirical research, see Sirowy & Inkeles 1990). But authoritarian rules are no guarantee of economic success for the simple reason that there are various kinds of autocracy. Apart from the *pro-capitalist autocracies* of the Taiwanese or South Korean type there are *populist autocracies*, as exemplified by Argentina under Peron. A populist autocracy is no better for the economy than a weak democracy, and if a weak democracy were to be replaced by authoritarian rule it would most likely be of the populist type. So clearly it is better to try to strengthen democracy by means, among other things, of a good Constitution and good electoral law which reduces the fragmentation of the party system. All the more so since democracy, in the contemporary world at least, is important for the dignity of man in his relations with the state and nowadays represents the most efficient way of legitimizing state control, at least in the societies which belong to Western culture. This European invention has spread as a model – in an important example of cultural diffusion – to other societies as well.

However, even if it were true that *on average* authoritarian regimes have a better chance of realizing a successful economic transformation, and if this chance were better in China than in the East European countries, one cannot derive any practical conclusions about these countries from these premises, even with the benefit of hindsight. The democratic evolution in Eastern Europe was largely a spontaneous (i.e. unplanned) historical development. Once it had started, the sequence of 'democracy first, capitalism – it is hoped – later' was inevitable, as it takes less time to organize elections and political parties than to privatize the bulk of the economy. This is another example of the important consequences ensuing from differences in the potential speed of vital processes of change.

The 'Chinese Way' is also used as an argument in favour of gradualism and against the Big Bang. To my mind this is a patent misuse of the facts. First, the issue of the 'cold turkey' approach is especially relevant to the macroeconomic situation one has inherited. At the beginning of its reforms in the late 1970s China was facing only a relatively mild macroeconomic imbalance, whereas, for example, Poland in mid-1989 was confronted by a macroeconomic catastrophe, as most of the post-socialist countries were later. Radical stabilization was a necessity in Poland, as was later in those countries, but it might not have been quite so necessary in China. Second, what happened in China was a massive *de facto* privatization of agriculture, in which 80 per cent of the population was employed. This gave a powerful impetus for the development of a non-agricultural private or mixed sector. Such a massive revolution in property rights and ownership structure is at odds with any meaningful concept of gradualism. Third and most importantly, the Chinese economic success was largely related to the peculiar feature of China's initial conditions – the aforementioned fact that 80 per cent of the population was employed in agriculture and that this agriculture was technologically divisible, and thus easy to privatize.

Privatization of agriculture, although necessary, could not bring about such spectacular results in Russia, for example, where agriculture takes up less of the economy and is technologically much less divisible (though it might work very well in Vietnam). Finally, the large influx of foreign capital into Southern China (predominantly of overseas Chinese origin) also seems to be a largely specific factor, i.e. difficult to reproduce on such a large scale in most of the Central and East Europe countries.

To sum up, to take the success of the Chinese economic reform as an argument in general discussion about gradualism versus the Big Bang is an expression of some serious methodological errors and in particular shows an inability to understand the role played by specific initial conditions and the specific factors which accompanied this transition.

THE EAST GERMAN COLLAPSE AS AN ARGUMENT AGAINST A RADICAL APPROACH

Some commentators engaged in general discussion of gradualism versus the Big Bang use the collapse of the East German economy as evidence of the bankruptcy of the latter approach. This too is a fallacy, because the exceptional collapse of output – the main problem in the former GDR – cannot be attributed to the general features which define this approach, but should be largely related to factors specific to the German economic reunification: the conversion ratio of 1:1 of the East German mark against the Deutschmark, and even more so to the subsequent wage explosion. Indeed, what happened in East Germany was the peaceful bombardment of enterprises with explosive wage increases far ahead of productivity growth. This destroyed the economic value of the enterprises, i.e. their stream of future profits. An economic effect of this kind is almost as devastating as the physical destruction of machinery and buildings. To compensate for either requires huge amounts of investment.

In Poland, which is another example criticized by the same opponents of the radical approach to economic transformation, these particular factors were not present. (One of the elements of the stabilization programme was strong wage control, only to be removed when an enterprise was privatized.) The decline in Poland's GDP in 1990–92 was the smallest of all the post-socialist countries, and its overall GDP was the first to start growing again (see Chapter 16).

Fallacies in the Debate on Inflation and Stabilization

In this section I shall deal with some of the fallacies prevalent in economic discussions on inflation and macroeconomic stabilization within the Central and East European countries, which have many proponents among local economists and some politicians. One also comes across economists in the West who hold similar views. Interestingly, practically all of these mistaken beliefs are essentially based upon repeating, unwittingly, perhaps – about twenty years on – the once fashionable theories propagated in Latin America by various schools of 'structuralism' or dependency, and in some older textbooks of development economics.

NEGLECTING THE CONSEQUENCES OF HIGH INFLATION

One of the most hotly debated issues in the Central and East European countries is the impact of very high inflation (over 100 per cent per annum) and ways of dealing with it. A number of economists regard this inflation as a relatively minor issue compared with the 'real' factors, output and GDP. This is probably because high open inflation is a relatively new phenomenon in the post-socialist countries, as massive suppressed inflation or shortages were typical features there. It also reflects the fact that output was by far the most important indicator of success in the socialist economies and was hailed as such in socialist economics. These economists usually neglect the negative impact of high inflation upon longer-term growth or even claim that one can 'buy' more growth with higher inflation, ignoring the fact that it is already very high (see pp. 256–7).

A related argument concerns ways of dealing with the inheritance of very high inflation, or in other words the methods and pace of disinflation. There has been widespread criticism of the Big Bang among the economists of the region. Clearly, economists who have neglected the seriousness of inflation have also tended to criticize this approach for destroying the 'real' economy. There have been other economists, who sometimes refer to themselves as Keynesians, who have also criticized the Big Bang, favouring much more gradualist, milder approaches. The belief that a gradualist approach is milder in terms of its social consequences is a fallacy, if one is dealing with near hyperinflation, as it was in Poland in mid-1989, or at times in most of the countries of the former Soviet Union. What is crucial in such circumstances is to change the basic monetary conditions and to eliminate or at least reduce inflationary expectations. In such a situation a consistent and credible radical stabilization is much more likely to succeed and could be far less costly than a gradualist approach. Interestingly, the opponents of the radical approach criticize it as 'monetarist', when it is really more in line with the school of rational expectations. A standard monetarist prescription would be to recommend a gradualist approach on the assumption that people's expectations are adaptive and not 'rational'.[10]

ECONOMIC STRUCTURE AND INFLATION

One particular variant of the 'anti-monetarist' critique of radical approaches to stabilization claims that high inflation is brought about by a poor economic structure, and thus tough stabilization centred on the demand side is at best ineffective and most probably harmful. This can easily be proved a fallacy. The economic structure of the former Czechoslovakia was probably no better than that of Poland or Hungary, but the post-stabilization rate of inflation there is much lower than in those two countries. Generally, the inflation rate in any short term (three to four years, say) depends mainly on the initial inflation rate and on the sort of macroeconomic policies pursued during this period. The latter explains why the present rate of inflation in the Czech Republic, Slovakia, Hungary and Poland is lower than in most other post-socialist countries; the former largely explains the difference between the still relatively high rate of inflation in Poland and the comparatively low rate in the Czech Republic.

There is certainly a connection between economic structure and inflation, as the former determines the political difficulty of introducing and sustaining a disciplined macroeconomic policy. At this point it is worth introducing the notion of *'pure socialist output'*, i.e. that part of output which can be maintained at an unchanged level only under socialism, if at all, e.g. a vast military industrial complex, overgrown heavy industry, etc. A high proportion of this kind of industry clearly makes the job of stabilizing the economy *en route* to the market politically complicated, as the decision-makers face the dilemma of either effecting the required tough stabilization and the corresponding growth of open unemployment in politically important sectors, or of financing rising hidden unemployment and the high inflation which

---

[10] The general nature of people's expectations probably depends on past experience, and therefore may differ across countries and historical periods. Persistent application of a macroeconomic policy which could only be effective if the expectations are adaptive, eventually makes them 'rational', and in this way destroys its own foundations. In the case of hyperinflation, clearly the role of expectations is crucial, and the most important task of government policy is to convince the rational economic agents that it pays to assume that inflation will be brought down very quickly. This can be vest achieved by a sharp reversal of macroeconomic policy.

comes with it. But understanding this dilemma does not mean the same as accepting the latter option; it could only make the economic, and thus the social situation increasingly difficult. Paradoxically, a preoccupation with structural factors and the corresponding neglect of macroeconomic ones freezes the poor economic structure which is seen as the principal engine of high inflation in the first place. Under this sort of policy there are no incentives for people (and other resources) to move to other sectors – they are being paid simply for coming to work. Tough stabilization and comprehensive liberalization seem to be the necessary conditions for any meaningful structural change, and in this role they are probably more important than microeconomic reforms in the state sector. Such an environment encourages many state enterprises to restructure, transferring their resources by selling them off or leasing them to the private sector, and/or to change their sphere of operations. This at least has been the Polish experience (Pinto *et al.* 1992).

Of course, the required tough stabilization may stretch limited political resources, especially if it is put into effect with a delay, after the period of 'extraordinary politics' (see pp. 247–8), but the alternative strategy of tolerating high and rising inflation is politically even more risky, only in the slightly longer run.

MONOPOLIZATION AND INFLATION

Another variant of the 'structural' theories of persistently high inflation attributes it to the high degree of inherited monopolization. However, monopolization can contribute to the price jump following the price liberalization, but it cannot explain a sustained high inflation. On empirical grounds we can see enormous differences in the inflation rate among the post-socialist countries, and these differences can in no way be explained by the differences in monopolization. One should look instead to the differences in the subsequent macroeconomic policies.

In any case, the monopolistic position of enterprises in the post-socialist countries is often exaggerated, because it is defined in relation to the domestic market only. This probably reflects the previous situation of the largely closed socialist economy. But the comprehensive foreign trade liberalization introduced in such countries as Poland, Hungary and the former Czechoslovakia has opened up these economies. It is this liberalization which we should point out as the necessary complement to price liberalization to those who rightly fear that the autonomous enterprises may misuse their position – not by producing persistently high inflation, but by pursuing inefficient policies.

FIXED-COST THEORY OF INFLATION

A related argument against tough stabilization is a special variant of *cost-push inflation*: tough stabilization is accused of causing a deep decline in output, which in turn brings about increases in the *unit fixed costs*, and these increases push up inflation. Therefore, tough stabilization is a self-defeating exercise. This argument can once again be refuted on empirical grounds. The stabilization programme in Czechoslovakia in 1991 was much tougher than in Hungary, and the Czechoslovak decline in output was much deeper than the Hungarian. Nevertheless, Czechoslovakia (and later the Czech Republic) turned out to have the lowest inflation, thanks to its low initial level and the tough stabilization.

On theoretical grounds it can be pointed out that an alleged increase in unit fixed costs is a one-off event. Therefore, it can, if at all, bring about a one-off increase in the price level, but not persistently high inflation.

PRICE LIBERALIZATION AND INFLATION

Some economists, especially in Russia and Ukraine, blame radical price liberalization for the ensuing hyperinflation. This is again a fallacy, of attributing persistent inflation to a one-off factor. On the theoretical level it is obvious that the cause of lasting high inflation cannot be the initial price jump resulting from the comprehensive price liberalization, but that it is fuelled by a persistently inflationary monetary policy. On the empirical level we know of countries (e.g. Czechoslovakia, Poland, Estonia, Albania) where thanks to a disciplined macroeconomic policy the radical price liberalization did not erupt into hyperinflation.

A more sophisticated variant of an alleged link between price liberalization and consequent high inflation asserts that there are certain *thresholds* to the initial price jump, above which near hyperinflation is very likely or inevitable. This is much harder to refute on both theoretical and empirical grounds, on the latter because even those countries which effected the most radical price liberalization did not adjust all prices in one go. Usually, energy prices were adjusted in several steps. This sequencing was motivated not so much by the fear of triggering hyperinflation as by concern that one huge price jump could outstretch the adaptive capacity of the economy.

The issue of an optimum size for the initial price jump or, in other words, the idea of sequencing the price liberalization, is (as often happens in economics) an empirical question, i.e. one where general considerations cannot determine exact magnitudes. However, there are several arguments in favour of concentrating most price liberalization measures, and hence price increases, in one big move early in the process of transition. The first argument concerns *political capital*, which is gradually depleted with time (see the final section of this chapter). This calls for a concentration of politically sensitive price increases in the first period. Second, radical price liberalization is necessary (and largely sufficient) to remove widespread shortages quickly, which is in turn necessary not only for the consumers' well-being, but also to enable enterprises to operate more efficiently and to be more attracted by socially useful innovations. Third, slow price liberalization would prolong the existence of distorted prices, and under such prices indicators of the enterprises' financial success cannot reliably reflect their true economic performance. In such a situation a soft budget constraint on state enterprises is likely to persist as loss-making firms subject to liquidation could claim that their financial problems are due to these distorted prices and not to their own inefficiency. Without hardening this constraint one cannot expect much of an increase in their overall efficiency.

REFLATION AND PSEUDO RESERVES

Those economists who regard high inflation only as a minor issue and who criticize the radical approach to disinflation, not surprisingly call for strong reflationary measures in order to revive what they call the 'depressed' economy. They claim that such measures would bring large increases in output, with only a small increase in inflation, if any. (Some even assert that inflation might fall as a result of the strong supply response activated by demand!) This *fallacy of primitive Keynesianism* disregards the dangers of still-high inflation and takes an extreme position on the division of the effects of the monetary impulse between output and prices. There are two mistakes involved here; each is enough to render this view fundamentally wrong. First, these economists justify the expected strong real effect of the proposed stimulus of demand by pointing to what they call 'enormous reserves' of production capacities, resulting from the fall in output related to the Big Bang of which they are so sharply critical.

This fallacy is very widespread among the politicians and many economists in the post-socialist countries. It was also at the core of the catastrophic policies pursued under Alan Garcia in Peru.[11] The point is, however, that these 'reserves' in the post-socialist countries are largely a myth; they consist of capacities which are mostly able to produce 'pure socialist output', i.e. they can only be activated *en masse* by returning to the old regime of distorted prices, shortages and the corresponding forced substitution. Hence this belief in massive reserves is an example of confusing physical and economic phenomena to an extreme degree.

Second, even if sizeable spare capacities were available, it is a mistake to assume that their existence is a sufficient condition for the stimulus of demand to have strong real effects. They are just a *necessary* condition; a lot depends, among other things, on the enterprises' pricing behaviour. It may well be the case that enterprises which are far from profit maximization, i.e. which are not privately owned and are influenced by the workers' interests, may be more willing to take the easier option of price increases, enabling the wages of workers who are already employed to grow, rather than the more troublesome route of increasing output. This is one of the predictions of the neo-classical theory of labour managed firms. If this is true, the economy's ownership structure will partly determine its response to the stimulus of demand, and privatization would be important, among other things, because it could increase the proportion of consequent output and limit the increase in price levels.

Uncritical Use of Statistical Data

GENERAL PROBLEMS IN THE COUNTRIES IN TRANSITION

Even in the established market economies statistical indicators do not provide a fully adequate description of the economic reality, because, for example, of well-known problems of statistical representation of changes in produce quality, or the inadequacy of comparing data on unemployment in various countries. Even in these countries there are many

---

[11] As Ricardo Lago (1991) points out, in Peru 'the widespread existence of industrial capacity was interpreted as indicating that excess demand was not a problem . . . . Furthermore, a reactivation of aggregate demand would lead to higher firm activity levels and thus to lower per-unit costs, thereby contributing to deflation rather than inflation'.

instances of the poor interpretation of statistics. Professional economists tend to put too much emphasis on the aggregate time series as the only hard economic information, which sometimes borders on the fallacy of misplaced concreteness and leads to disregard for other kinds of information (for the latter view, see, e.g., Solow 1988). The broader public mistakenly thinks changes in the GDP are strictly related to changes in welfare, and even marginal changes in official statistical indicators can acquire great political significance, especially during an election campaign. Modern democratic politics encourages the misuse of statistics. Dictatorships often abuse statistics outright.

These problems of the inadequacy of statistical descriptions of the economic reality are bound to be far more serious in the countries of Central and Eastern Europe as they undertook a dramatic trans- formation and were subjected to powerful external shocks; it is safe to assume that the adequacy of such statistical description decreases as the extent of structural changes grows. Yet there are many instances of uncritical or downright incorrect use of statistical indicators in discussions on the economic transformation in these countries. This poor use of statistics lies at the root of various theories, e.g. those which proclaim the superiority of the gradualist approach over the Big Bang. Selected statistical indicators pertaining to the fall of output or the GDP have also been used extensively in political debate.[12]

Therefore, it is all the more important to realize:

- that the official statistical indicators are – probably inevitably – subject to a *large systematic negative bias*;
- that the extent of this bias is likely to be larger in countries which are undertaking a radical and comprehensive programme than in countries guided by the strategy of 'muddling through'.

This negative bias concerns first of all the officially reported growth of output and GDP, and is caused by the following main factors:[13]

- A radical change of economic system means, among other things, a transition from a regime where there are strong incentives to

[12] For example, in Poland the official figure of a 30 per cent decline in output in 1990 and an alleged 30 per cent decline in real wages were cited extensively by opponents of the radical economic programme. One of the critics who heavily cited these and other figures of this sort published a book in 1992 subtitled *Who is the Culprit?'*.

[13] I am drawing largely on an excellent article by Bratkowski (1993).

inflate output and value-added statistics to one which has strong incentives for under-reporting the true magnitudes for tax considerations. For example, a radical transition to a market economy eliminates the old incentive to increase the reported 'output sold' by artificially subcontracting.

- Market-oriented reform reduces the scope of the public sector and increases that of the private one. But the inherited statistical system focuses on the former, and is unable to reflect fully the growth of the latter. Therefore, the data for global output and GDP are biased downwards. This effect is magnified by the fact that the growing private sector has on average a stronger tendency to under-report output, sales and profit data than the public one.

- Market-oriented reform involves positive changes in the quality and range of goods and in the composition of output, which are under-represented in conventional statistics. Neither the elimination of shortages nor of the related 'forced substitution', i.e. frequently buying goods with high profit margins for lack of a better choice, is reflected in these statistics. All this means that the newly emerging output is more closely geared to the consumers' welfare than the old output, but this is ignored by the continuing traditional statistical methods, which give the same 'welfare weights' to the pre-reform statistics as to those gathered during and after the reforms.

The extent of all these distortions increases with the speed of economic change. This is why the negative statistical bias is likely to be greater in the countries which introduced radical reforms than in other countries.

THE POLISH EXAMPLE

All these general comments call for a systematic comparative study of statistical descriptions of the economies in transition. For lack of any such study I shall illustrate my general point about the pitfalls of official statistics in these countries and the need to use them with caution with examples of mistakes made in statistical reporting and their interpretation with respect to the economic transition in Poland. The Polish case includes the aforementioned general problems of the inadequacy of the statistical description as well as other problems tending in the same direction, which may be specific to Poland (see Bratkowski 1993).

Here are the main findings:

- The official figure of an 18–20 per cent decline in GDP in 1990–91 massively overstated the true dynamics. A more recent assessment, from the Research Institute of the Main Statistical Office and the Polish Academy of Sciences, put the decline at 5–10 per cent, merely by estimating the growth of the private sector which had not been fully recorded (Rajewski 1992). But there were other reasons why the official data largely misrepresent the true dynamics of GDP figure for 1990–91: the GDP in 1989 was inflated through some methodological errors, including using an improper GDP deflator, and the fall in non-market GDP in 1991 was put at a larger figure than the decline in employment financed out of the state budget; the effects of improvements in the quality of goods and of the removal of shortages were not included, etc. (for more on this, see Bratkowski 1993; Rajewski 1992).
- The official figure for the decline in aggregate consumption in 1990–91 is 9 per cent, which is *by far the smallest decline in all the post-socialist countries*. But it is still a wide exaggeration, partly because of the above mentioned problems with estimating GDP. Another reason was an assumed unrealistic increase in the value of stocks in 1990 which artificially lowered the statistical indicator of the rate of growth of aggregate consumption. The official data of a 9 per cent decline in the consumption are also at odds with the more detailed official statistics based on household surveys (see Chapter 16).
- These figures also undermine the widely used statistical indicator of sharply falling *real wages* in 1990–91. This is based on the primitive error of mechanically comparing the statistics for real wages in 1990 with those in 1989, without asking what happened with nominal wages and prices in 1988–89. The point is that nominal wages increased in 1988–89 much faster than prices, which were still largely controlled; in the fourth quarter of 1989 the resulting 'real' wages were 41 per cent higher than those in 1987! Needless to say, this was mainly reflected in the growth of queues and shortages and not in any improvement in the standard of living.
- Finally, one should question the widespread use of the terms 'recession' or 'depression' to describe the economic processes in Poland post-1989. This is at odds with the statistics on aggregate dynamics quoted above, and with much other evidence of fundamental structural changes: in ownership, in the composition of output, in organizational structures, in the role of foreign trade and its geographical orientation (for more on this subject, see Chapter 16).

Misunderstandings Related to Social and Political Aspects of Economic Transition

The overall transition in the Central and East European countries is a complex interplay of economic, social and political developments. It is a largely unprecedented historical change, which is already giving rise to many theories and *ad hoc* explanations. In this section I shall deal with some of the beliefs, which I perceive to be mistaken, about the relationship between, on the one hand, economic, and, on the other, social and political developments.

EXCESSIVE SOCIAL COSTS AND RISKS OF RADICAL ECONOMIC STRATEGIES

Many fallacies have at their root a misrepresentation of the set of choices initially facing the decision-makers in the post-socialist East European countries. The same basic methodological mistake is involved in this fallacy, which consists in focusing on the social costs of the radical approach to transformation and in arguing on this basis for the rejection of this strategy in favour of a 'milder' approach. 'Social costs' are here understood as the negative phenomena which accompany a radical transition (and not as opportunity costs). But even taking this first, popular concept of social costs it is obvious that merely registering some negative phenomena which one associates with a certain strategy can never be enough of a reason for rejecting that strategy, because one should always *compare* the costs, the risks (and the benefits) of the various alternative options presented by the initial situation and the expected conditions which will influence the transformation process without being affected by it. The reason why some people tend to reject a radical strategy because of its social costs may be that under such a strategy some of these costs (e.g. open unemployment) emerge more quickly and in a more dramatic manner than under alternative strategies, but so do some of the benefits. The range of sensible options depends very much on the initial situation, and especially on macro-economic conditions. If the macroeconomic situation is catastrophic (near hyperinflation and massive shortages, as in Poland in mid-1989) the 'cold turkey' approach to stabilization is the *safest* one. Its relative merits may change under a more moderate initial macroeconomic imbalance, although the school of rational expectations would argue that even in this situation the radical approach to stabilization is the least costly, as it could reduce inflationary expectations very quickly.

The same comparative approach should be applied with regard to the ex ante assessment of the risk of *social protest* related to introducing an alternative economic strategy. It is not enough to say that a radical approach to stabilization involves high social risks, and to reject it for that reason alone. One's response to that should be to imagine what social risks would eventually emerge if one were to delay stabilization in the face of inherited hyperinflation. In other words, it is the *relative* and not the absolute level of risk which really counts in rational decision-making. It may well be that the least risky option in one situation would be far riskier than the most risky option in another situation. This also applies to a country's economic programme.

Successful Economic Reform and Social Discontent[14]

If one starts under very difficult economic conditions, then – after a possible short period of 'extraordinary' politics (see the final section of this chapter) – there is bound to be discontent, regardless of the economic strategy.

A strategy of accepting the status quo or muddling through is bound to generate growing discontent, since under such a programme the economic situation can only progressively worsen. But a successful radical transformation also inevitably generates widespread dissatisfaction. Therefore, to reject a reform strategy only because it produced dissatisfaction is similar to making the mistake of expecting to move on Earth without producing any friction. This sort of fallacy is committed by some observers of radical economic reform. Instead, one should understand how to identify the sources of discontent related to a *successful* economic reform and try, if possible, to reduce or diffuse them.

First, given the very difficult initial situation, some people's standard of living declines, as compared with the past. It might have declined even more under the strategy of accepting the status quo, but usually people do not realize this. The problem is that most people tend to compare their present situation with the past, and on this basis they form judgements about the government's policies. As already noted, this is a methodological error, because one should compare one's actual situation with the hypothetical situation that would exist under the best alternative policy, given the same initial and other conditions. But few people act like trained economists, and there is not much one can do to change that.

---

[14] This section is largely based on Balcerowicz (1993). See also Chapter 9.

But a decline in some people's standard of living is not the only reason, and perhaps not the main reason for social discontent. In East Germany most people's standard of living rose noticeably, thanks to massive financial transfers from the West, but most East Germans are still dissatisfied. In Poland the standard of living of many members of the 'intelligentsia' declined, but this is the group which gives the strongest support to radical economic reform so far. So there must be other forces at work to generate dissatisfaction.

A second force arises from the fact that under the old system general economic freedom, that is, the opportunity for major economic advancement, was strongly restricted for everybody. The new system radically enhances general economic freedom, but people's potential to take direct advantage of it is uneven, depending on their age, education, the region in which they live, etc. Thus, the opening up of economic freedom produces, at least in the first stage, a new sort of social stratification consisting of those who can easily take direct advantage of the new opportunities and those who cannot do it as well. A normal phenomenon arising from this experience among people in the second group is a kind of psychological cost: envy. This is particularly pronounced if people think – whether rightly or wrongly – that the economic winners do not deserve their economic success because they are regarded as members of the elite of the old system, or gained their money through activities which under this system were branded as 'speculation'.

A third, related source of discontent stems from the fact that every economic system has a specific hierarchy of pay and prestige, and the hierarchy typical of a non-market, state-dominated economy is very different from that typical of a competitive market economy. Therefore, as a country moves successfully from the former system to the latter, many changes occur in *relative social positions*. Some groups move up and others go down. The latter include, for example, workers in heavy industry and mining, sectors which were once the backbone of wasteful centrally planned economies. Those who lose in relative terms cannot, on the whole, be very supportive of radical market-oriented reform.

And finally, such reform is bound to generate some open unemployment and deprive people of the main advantage guaranteed by the old economic system: complete job security.

But successful economic reform, as distinct from a failure or accepting the status quo, also produces some important sources of support for itself. On this point I am basing my observations on the Polish experience. Radical elimination of shortages and queues and a broader range of goods and services are appreciated by the general public, especially by women, who had more than their fair share of the burden of shopping. Those who can tap straight into the opportunities offered by an increase in economic freedom are usually supportive of market-oriented reform, and thanks to the rapid growth of the private sector their number is rising. But the workers employed at private firms are also on average more supportive of the economic reform than those at state firms. Thus privatization may generate support for the capitalist market economy. Finally, better educated people are more inclined to support the radical economic reform than the less educated, perhaps because on average they are more capable of understanding the challenges and chances offered by such reform.

RADICAL ECONOMIC TRANSITION AND POLITICAL CAPITAL

Some observers blame radical economic transformation for the political complications which emerge in its course. This is a typical fallacy of *post hoc ergo propter hoc*. It is true that economic problems do affect political behaviour, and the greatest challenge facing the post-socialist countries is how to maintain and strengthen democracy and to complete the transition towards a capitalist market economy. But political developments also have their own dynamic determined by non-economic factors, and in some cases these are more important than the economic ones. This was certainly the case in Poland where, for instance, the rather unfortunate timing of elections (the presidential elections of 1990, i.e. in the first year of the economic transformation, and the parliamentary elections of 1991) had nothing to do with economic factors. These political developments were generally the objective constraints of economic reform, and one could argue that positive economic results were achieved *in spite of* these developments (for more on this see Chapter 15).

Rather than blaming radical economic reform for political complications, one should see it as a factor which makes it possible to make use of the specific *political capital* (*PC*) in the interests of advancing the economic transformation. For a discussion of the upper part of Figure 13.1 see Chapter 9.

The lower part of Figure 13.1 illustrates a radical economic strategy, as symbolized by the length of lines *S, L* and *I*, which symbolizes their duration corresponding to their maximum possible speed. Alternative strategies would have longer lines, or would be shifted to the right, e.g. *S* shifted to the right would symbolize a delayed stabilization, as in Ukraine or in Russia. The upper part of the diagram illustrates the political scene, as characterized by the function $r=r$ (*t*), which expresses

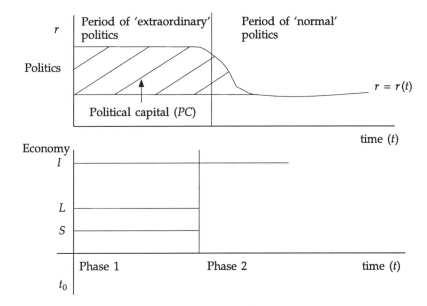

Fig. 13.1 *The interaction of economics and politics*

the level of readiness to have radical economic measures accepted, starting at moment t_0, which is close to a great change in a country's history.[15] It is based on the assumption that major discontinuities, i.e., liberation from external dependence and a political liberalization, produce a special state of mass psychology and a corresponding state of political system which are reflected in an abnormally high level of r; this can only be maintained for a relatively short time.[16] This period of 'extraordinary politics' gives way to 'normal' politics, as described by the public choice theory of James Buchanan and others, when r is much lower. The 'surplus' of r over this 'normal' level is the PC. It can be regarded as a precious resource which is gradually depleted by time. It is probably a non-renewable resource, granted by history.

Concentrating radical and drastic measures in the period shortly after a great change in a country's history enables one to tap a precious

[15] r may be interpreted as the probability of acceptance of tough economic measures.

[16] This short-lived state of mass psychology is similar to the one produced by a revolution. The initial revolutionary euphoria inevitably leads to the frustration of many expectations.

reserve of political capital. In contrast, delaying these measures by applying milder economic strategies involves a much lower probability of eventually getting them accepted, or conversely a much higher risk of social protest, as the level of r is lower in periods of 'normal' politics.

It is important to realize that the $r=r(t)$ function is here depicted in its most general, invariant form, illustrating the basic fact that major positive discontinuities in a country's history produce an exceptionally high level of r which can only be maintained for a relatively short time. Beyond that basic fact there is great variability of actual or possible experiences, reflected in the initial level of r, the duration of 'extra-ordinary' politics, the downward slope of $r=r(t)$ after this period, the subsequent level of r under 'normal' politics, etc. All these aspects should be addressed by the political economy of the reform. Its most important task is to investigate what determines the level of r over time. At this point I would venture only a few conjectures. One of the major factors is the development of the economic situation, although it is wrong to assume that there is a simple correlation here. It is interesting to wonder whether a tough economic programme shortens the period when r is exceptionally high because of its unpopular consequences, i.e. a sharp increase in the prices of formerly subsidized goods. However, a successful tough economic programme also produces rapid widespread benefits, e.g. the quick elimination of massive shortages and a substantial increase in the range of goods available in the shops. It is difficult to say theoretically what the net effect of these opposing changes is. The economic situation also depends on external factors, such as the collapse of exports and a shock in trade or terms of trade (such as those experienced by the smaller East European countries in their commercial relations with the former Soviet Union), or access to Western markets. Western protectionism reduces r not only by worsening the economic situation in the post-socialist countries, but also by setting a bad example, which undermines the legitimacy of liberal economic reforms and strengthens the position of their political opponents. That is when the following fallacy comes into play: 'if the West is doing this, then we should be doing it all the more' (see pp. 237–8). The reformers are then easily accused of being naive or doctrinaire liberals who do not know the real world.

In the West in turn among some politicians and a broader public there appears to be a mistaken belief that the Western countries *as a whole* are somehow making an economic sacrifice if they open up their markets to poorer countries, including those in Central and Eastern Europe. The basic truth that both sides can gain from freer trade, a truth which in my view has not been undermined by any newer theories of international trade, is strangely missing from popular perception in the West. In fact, what is required from the West is not economic sacrifice, but rather some courage and imagination on the part of the politicians which would measure up to the unprecedented changes that have happened in the East, and which have been so conspicuously and sadly missing in dealing with the Yugoslav crisis. The principle of assessing the relative risks should also apply to Western policies towards the countries of central and Eastern Europe.

Returning to the determinants of r, one should include the important influence of the newly liberated mass media, especially the television. I have already noted the phenomenon of an inevitable negative bias in presenting the realities of a free country (see pp. 235–6). But the extent of this bias is likely to vary across the countries in transition, which may in turn have an influence on the level of r.

The type of political opposition to the economic programme is also relevant. There is no shortage of political demagogues in any country but there is no reason to assume that they are equally represented and equally vocal in all countries. Differences in the degree of their presence, especially if in conjunction with the differences in size of a 'negative bias' on television, may have a major impact on r.

The question of opposition to a radical economic programme is related to the important issue of its *credibility*, which is especially important in combating very high inflation. If the government says that it will eliminate hyperinflation, but the opposition announces that it will soon throw out the government just because of its anti-inflationary actions, the programme cannot be very credible, and hence it cannot be very effective either. Unfortunately, this sort of political stalemate seems characteristic of some countries of the former Soviet Union, including Russia and Ukraine. This is another argument for introducing the tough stabilization programme in the period of 'extraordinary' politics, i.e. before this sort of opposition has a chance to develop. Taking a normative viewpoint, one could say that liberating the country from the catastrophe of hyperinflation is – because of the importance of mass expectations – the *joint responsibility* of the government and the opposition.

The timing of elections is also an important determinant of r. Elections are usually an occasion to bombard the public with negative messages about current policies and sometimes with unrealistic promises. It is clearly better for them to be organized in the fourth year of the implementation of the economic programme (as in Hungary) rather than in its first year (as in Poland).

Finally, it is interesting to wonder whether there are any measures which would make economic sense, or at least would not be economically harmful, and would at the same time have a special power to raise or sustain *r*. One possibility is privatization through a voucher scheme, which is a feature of a kind of 'popular capitalism'. Another one could be the 'solidarity fund' used by President Salinas in Mexico, although one might wonder whether such a device would be effective in a truly democratic system.

References

Balcerowicz, L. 1993a 'Eastern Europe: economic, social and political dynamics', University of London, School of Slavonic and East European Studies.
—— 1993b 'Political economy of economic reform: Poland, 1989–92', in *Political Economy of Economic Reform*, Institute for International Economics, Washington.
Bratkowski, A. 1993 'The shock of transformation or the transformation of the shock? The Big Bang in Poland and official statistics', *Communist Economics and Economic Transformation*, no. 1.
Dornbush, R. 1991 'Experiences with extreme monetary instability', in Simon Commoner (ed.), *Managing Inflation in Socialist Economies in Transition*, The World Bank, Washington, DC, pp. 175–96.
Frydman, R., Phelps, E.S., Rapaczynski, A., & Schleifer, A. 1993 'Needed mechanisms of corporate governance and finance in Eastern Europe', *Economics of Transition* 1, April, pp. 171–208. See also Frydman, R., & Rapaczynski, A. 1993 *Privatization in Eastern Europe: Is the State Withering Away?* Budapest Central European University Press, Ch. 4.
Jasiński, P. 1992 'The transfer and redefinition of property rights: Theoretical analysis of transferring property rights and transformational privatisation in the post-STEs', *Communist Economies and Economic Transformation* 4, pp. 163–89.
Lago, R. 1991 'The illusion of pursuing redistribution through macropolicy: Peru's heterodox experience, 1985–1990', in R. Dornbush & J. Edwards (eds), *The Macroeconomics of Populism in Latin America*, Chicago University Press, Chicago.
Maddison, A. 1991 *Dynamic Forces in Capitalist Development: A Long-Run Comparative View*, Oxford University Press, Oxford.
Mueller, C.D. 1992 'The corporation and the economist', *International Journal of Industrial Organisation*, Vol. 102, reprinted in *Economics Alert*, no. 3, 1993, pp. 1–3.
'Nie chcemy dużo: jakies 60 bilionów' 1993, z Andrzejem Lepperem rozmawia Jacek Żakowski, *Gazeta Wyborcza*, 19 August, pp. 10–11.
Pinto, B., Belka, M., & Krajewski, S. 1992 'Transforming state enterprises in Poland: Macroeconomic evidence on adjustment', Policy Research Working Paper 1101, The World Bank, Washington, DC, March.
Rajewski, Z. 1992 'Produkt krajowy brutto', in L. Zienkowski (ed.), *Gospodarka polska w latach 1990–1992*, Warsaw.

Rostowski, J.C. 1993 'The implications of very rapid private sector growth in Poland', mimeo.

Sirowy, L. & Inkeles, A. 1990 'The effects of democracy on economic growth: a review', *Studies in Comparative International Development*, 25, no. 1, pp. 126–57.

Solow, R. 1988 'Growth theory and after', *American Economic Review*, June.

Part III

Polish Economic Reform: 1989–93

14

Polish Economic Reform, 1981–88: An Overview

August 1980 produced, among other things, a demand for economic reform in Poland. An official reform proposal appeared and was approved by the Party Congress and the Parliament in 1981 (*Kierunki* . . . 1981).

The document laid down the two basic *objectives* of the reform: increased economic efficiency and restoration and maintenance of the market balance, i.e., elimination of chronic shortages. It outlined a new economic system which aimed at achieving these objectives. The crucial proposal was to abolish the directive nature of central planning. Enterprises were to be freed from both compulsory targets and the administrative allocations of inputs. They were to acquire broad financial autonomy but be required to cover their expenses from their sales revenues (possibly supplemented by genuine bank credits) or face bankruptcy. Within the enterprises, workers' councils were to obtain broad powers. The proposed abolition of command planning did not, however, entail a clear endorsement of the market. Instead the economy was to 'operate on the principle of central planning with the utilization of the market mechanism' (*Kierunki* . . ., p. 23). The reform proposal envisaged a transitional period of two to three years to reach the proposed system.

The imposition of martial law on 13 December 1981 profoundly

This chapter was written in 1988 and originally published in *Economic Reforms in the European Centrally Planned Economies*, United Nations Economic Commission for Europe, Economic Studies, No. 1, United Nations, New York, 1989, pp. 42–50.

changed the social and political situation in Poland[1] but the economic reform was initiated as planned on 1 January 1982. Massive legislative developments affected the position of enterprises and the state administration. But the economic system did not evolve according to the reform project. This was admitted by the authorities when they put forward, in 1987, the programme for the 'second stage' of economic reform.

In this chapter, the original reform proposal and the system in practice will be briefly discussed with regard to some selected functional areas. The final section offers some general comments on the reform.

The Ownership Structure

As in any other centrally planned economy (CPE), the *state sector* in Poland enjoyed a dominant position in the whole economy, with a monopoly or near-monopoly in mining, heavy industry, most manufacturing, foreign trade, banking, insurance, etc. Its share in total employment (including self-employment) declined slightly during the reform, from 56.5 per cent in 1980 to 55.2 per cent in 1987.[2]

The *cooperative sector* played a particularly important role in domestic trade and in housing. The problem is, however, that the units formally called 'cooperatives' were subjected to similar rules to the state enterprises: compulsory grouping in the heavily bureaucratized unions, very limited autonomy, arbitrary shifting of assets, appointment of management by the party bodies etc. (Balcerowicz 1981, p. 9; Wisniewski 1988).

The reform proposal called for full autonomy to be restored to the cooperatives. The 1982 Law on Cooperatives had, however, preserved the compulsory grouping of cooperatives in the unions and the administrative restrictions on their founding. On the other hand the cooperative sector partly regained the ground lost by administrative fiat in 1975, by slowly moving into trade in industrial consumer goods. The share of cooperatives in total employment fell slightly from 11.9 per cent in 1980 to 11.7 per cent in 1987.

The share of the *domestic private sector* in employment rose during

---

[1] Trade unions, including Solidarnosc, were first suspended and then dissolved. Self-management bodies in enterprises were also suspended, to be gradually reactivated on a case-by-case basis. Many directors of state enterprises were dismissed.
[2] These and other figures quoted in this section are computed on the basis of *Rocznik statystyczny 1987* and *Maly rocznik statystyczny 1988*.

the same time from 26.6 to 28.7 per cent.[3] One must distinguish here between agriculture and the rest of the economy.

Private farms increased their share of ownership of the total arable land from 74.5 per cent in 1980 to 76.6 per cent in 1987. Yet the share in 1970 had been 81 per cent but then fell as a result of increased discrimination in favour of the less efficient socialized sector. In reaction to this, a demand was put forward in 1980–81 to give the system of private agriculture a permanent role in the Polish economy. Such a clause was in fact inserted in the Constitution in 1983.

The non-agricultural private sector, traditionally relegated to a marginal role, gained most in terms of employment, by increasing its share from 4.9 per cent in 1980 to 8.2 per cent in 1987. This development was mainly due to the increased number of entrepreneurs, caused by growing disillusionment with employment in the socialized sector, rather than any radical change in official policies – which remained restrictive (Wisniewski 1988; 'Czapka . . .' 1988; Kowalska 1988). Local authorities frequently imposed constraints on the founding of private enterprises. Taxes and strict limits on employment did not allow firms to grow.[4] Private firms continued to face discrimination when they tried to buy from or sell to state enterprises.[5]

There were also some small firms owned by foreign nationals, called *Polonia firms* because most of the entrepreneurs involved were Polish expatriates. The share of these firms in total employment was 0.3 per cent in 1987. A separate Law on Joint Ventures with Foreign Capital was enacted in 1986.[6] Its provisions were regarded as being less attractive to foreign partners than the terms offered in Hungary and China (Gruszecki 1988).

Organizational Structures in the State Sector

In July 1981, nine industrial ministries were merged into four. But the new ministries replicated the internal structures of their predecessors (*Raport o reformie* . . . 1984, p. 6). These structures suited the task with

[3] The figures for the shares of the sectors discussed do not add up to 100 per cent, mainly because of the existence of enterprises belonging to various social organizations.

[4] Average employment per enterprise (including owners and their family members) was 1.8 persons in 1981 and 2 in 1987.

[5] One experienced observer considered these restrictions more severe under the reform than in the 1970s (Wojciechowski 1987).

[6] The previous Law of 1976 did not succeed in attracting a single foreign partner.

which the ministries were entrusted under the reform (enterprise-specific interventions, personnel policy, etc.). However those tasks did not suit the objectives of the reform.

Below the ministries, the traditional branch amalgamations of enterprises were dissolved in 1981. In their place there appeared in 1982 associations – voluntary or obligatory (a minority). Most associations were composed of the same enterprises as the previous amalgamations, and 93 per cent of all enterprises entered the associations. Highly monopolistic organizational structures were thus recreated, and the situation has changed little since then. An important factor in the creation and survival of these associations has been the widespread administrative allocation of inputs, as it generated the need for inter-mediate bodies between the allocators and the users. The industrial ministries were thus putting pressure on enterprises to join the associations;[7] this did not meet much resistance on the part of enterprises (Fornalczyk 1984, p. 9).

After 1982, and especially in 1985, the central bodies continued to initiate pressure for enterprise mergers. One reason for this was that the obligatory associations had to be dissolved by the end of 1986.[8] As it turned out, they were either converted into voluntary associations or other enterprise groupings were created in their place (*Ocena* . . . 1988, p. 150). Some of these groupings were formally limited liability companies, where enterprises were stockholders and some state administrative body had a major share. This transformation affected some voluntary associations, too. However, it provoked strong criticism. One objection was that the new structures might lead to recentralization, as the enterprise workers councils – the strongest single source of resistance to this tendency – were losing much of their decision-making powers in the process. Another point was that the new organizations were usually built on the traditional 'branch principle', thus preserving the highly monopolistic structure of Polish industry.

The Position of the State Enterprises

The 1981 Law on State Enterprises maintained the principle that each enterprise must be 'ascribed' to one (usually sectoral) ministry or to a

---

[7] This applies to voluntary associations; the obligatory ones were created by fiat.

[8] This was because the 1981 Law on State Enterprises allowed the creation of an obligatory association for five years only. This provision was dropped in 1987.

local authority,[9] besides being subject to specialized regulations from the other organs, e.g., the Ministry of Finance. (The organs to which the enterprises were 'ascribed' were renamed 'founders'.) But the previous right of the state administration to intervene in any affairs of the enterprises has been replaced by the principle that the enterprise's autonomy might be overruled only in some legally specified cases. These were: defence, emergencies, fulfilment of external obligations.[10] Moreover, a major change in the enterprise's activity required the permission of the founder.[11]

Producing enterprises also needed a permit from the Ministry of Foreign Trade if they wanted to market their products or buy inputs abroad.

The founder was given broad powers with respect to the enterprise's director. In the 'enterprises of national interest',[12] the founder appoints and dismisses him, subject to the veto right of the workers' council. In other enterprises, the opposite is true. In addition, during the period of martial law it was the founder who determined the salary and other terms of employment of the director, regardless of the category of the enterprise. This provision was included in 1987 in the modified Law on State Enterprises.

The founder was also permitted to merge, divide and liquidate an enterprise – the first two with the consent of the workers' council. In 'exceptional cases' the Council of Ministers could group enterprises in an (obligatory) association. The founder was empowered to monitor the performance of an enterprise and of its director. All enterprises had the duty to prepare annual plans and development programmes, and to disclose their basic elements at the request of the state organs.[13] There were some other restrictions on enterprise autonomy, especially with respect to pricing (see below).

The actual autonomy of enterprises was much more limited than that envisaged in the reform proposal and the basic laws. For the legal

---

[9] The state enterprises may be divided into those which are subject to general legislation, and those whose autonomy is reduced by some special regulations (e.g., defence industries, railways, airports, public utilities). This and the following sections deal with the enterprises of the first group. It might be added that the restrictions on autonomy present in this case also apply to the second group, while the reverse is not true.

[10] Government contracts and operational programmes were later added to this list.

[11] In October 1987 this was replaced by the provision that the founder may order the enterprise to discontinue the new activity.

[12] Beginning in 1982 this group, arbitrarily formed, included almost 1,400 of the biggest enterprises. In March 1988 this number was reduced to 329.

[13] In addition, the Council of Ministers can order selected firms to draw up five-year and perspective (long-term) plans.

provisions that might have acted to limit this autonomy in fact did so, while some other limitations appeared or were maintained. The first group includes, above all, the regulations which made the salary and the career of the enterprise director dependent on the founder. On account of this the director was understandably susceptible to pressure from the founder. The directors also depended on the party organs which maintained their extra-legal powers to influence the choice and the dismissal of the managers. It seems, however, that the party organs were moving from the pre-reform policy of promoting their own candidates to one of opposing the persons they considered undesirable (Kawalec 1988, pp. 25–7).

Other limiting factors include the vast scope of administrative allocation of inputs and the massive redistribution of enterprises' financial resources (both dealt with in the following sections). All these limitations notwithstanding, the autonomy of enterprises seemed to be – on the whole – considerably greater than before the reform, although it certainly fell short of the original conception.

Central Planning and the Allocation Mechanism

Traditional central planning has the following main features: (a) it tries to determine in great detail the structure of domestic production, of foreign trade, and of investment; (b) it prescribes the allocation of basic inputs among various uses and users via the material balances and administrative rationing; (c) the central plan and the plans of lower-level organizations are products of a hierarchical exchange of information (involving a great deal of manipulative bargaining), whereby the enterprises are finally given the planning targets – i.e., they do not plan autonomously. At the same time the central planners rely heavily on the plan proposals which the enterprises have to send upwards.

The reform project called for the abandonment of this type of planning. In practice, however, there has been massive central intervention in the structure of production. Two instruments were introduced to this end: *operational programmes* and *government contracts*. The former aim at stimulating the growth of broadly defined areas, the latter are more sharply targeted. The government contracts, which became the main instrument, should not be confused with those in Western countries; in Polish practice they are not for government consumption and the main inducement for the suppliers is not financial gain but privileged access to scarce inputs. In addition, if this fails, administrative coercion may be legally used. Outside the fields covered by operational programmes and government contracts there are some other areas which enjoy supply priorities (i.e., exports, defence industries, investment projects supported by Soviet credits ('Zasady . . .' 1988)).

It is evident that the broad use of this instrument had to be combined with widespread administrative intervention in the allocation process. Indeed, this type of intervention was estimated to affect 80 per cent of the sales of producer goods in 1986 (Wojciechowski 1986). The reform brought about only some changes in its form. The scope of traditional direct central rationing shrank while that of the indirect type increased. The main form of the latter is 'obligatory intermediation', whereby the centrally designated wholesale trade organizations became the sole sellers of specified products, subject to priorities and guidelines laid down in the central plan.[14] Another new form was connected with government contracts: the organizations which administered them also allocated the resulting output, again subject to the instructions of the central bodies.[15] Under these conditions the central material balances, the core of traditional planning, were bound to play a prominent role.[16]

There was yet more change with respect to the third feature of central planning. Enterprises did not have to submit their plans for approval to superior bodies, and consequently they were not assessed on the basis of plan-fulfilment.[17] A corresponding change took place in the central planning information system. The Planning Commission operated a questionnaire system which covered the plans of the 2,000 biggest enterprises. The sectoral ministries, which assisted the Commission in the planning process, operated similar systems in their domains (Cwiertnia 1987).

The change was, however, far from complete, for the government contracts tended to recreate some features of directive central planning. One of them was the important role of the sectoral ministries in proposing the list of contracts and in overseeing their realization. The former entailed familiar inter-level bargaining as the enterprises, and

---

[14] Their producers were forbidden to sell directly to users or to other trade organizations.

[15] These were largely the same organizations which operated the 'obligatory intermediation'.

[16] There were 88 such balances in 1982, 180 in 1984 and 173 in 1988 ('Zasady . . .' 1988, p. II; Skowronek 1985, p. 10).

[17] This extends to investment – the enterprises do not have to seek the permission of the superior bodies for projects they want to undertake out of their own financial resources.

ministries on their behalf, tried to get as many supply privileges as possible (Smuga 1987, p. 4).

The Pricing System

The reform project called for prices to be set at the market-clearing level. But it did not pay much attention to the crucial issue of who was to fix what prices. The declared government objective was, however, to decentralize price-setting, except for the prices of basic consumer and producer goods. The 1982 Law on Prices distinguished *administrative*, *regulated* and *contractual* prices. The level of *administrative* prices was determined by the appropriate organs of state administration. *Regulated* prices were fixed by the sellers themselves who, however, had to comply with the price formulae (mostly cost-plus) determined by those organs. *Contractual* prices were not defined by the law but by presumption – they were to be fixed by free negotiations between the supplier and customer.

The share of administrative prices increased from 1982 to 1983 while that of contractual prices fell. From then on the share of administrative prices was almost constant while contractual prices gaining ground lost by the regulated ones.[18] But this does not mean that a movement towards market-determined prices took place, for the contractual prices came under increasingly severe administrative controls (Ćwiertnia 1987; Smuga 1987, p. 4). Since 1984 they have to be based on officially-defined 'justified costs; which in 1983 were made the basis for determining regulated prices. Thus there is no difference between the two. Besides, there have been long periods of price freezes, restrictions on passing on the increases in cost to prices, and limits to their growth. All this had led to contractual prices being mostly below the market-clearing level. The second effect is that traditional cost-based pricing predominates. (It also extends to many administrative prices.) This means, given the lack of competition and the inherent inefficiency of administrative controls over producers' costs, that there are strong disincentives to reduce them.

---

[18] The value of goods sold under administrative prices (in per cent of total sales) was in the case of consumer goods 35 per cent in 1982, 45 per cent in 1984 and 45 per cent in 1987. The respective shares for regulated prices were: 15, 15 and 2 per cent and for contractual prices: 50, 40 and 53 per cent. For the producer prices of procurement goods (basic and raw materials), the respective shares were: 20, 32 and 29 per cent (administrative prices), 5, 13 and 3 per cent (regulated prices), 75, 55 and 68 per cent (contractual prices (*Raport o reformie* . . . 1984; *Ocena* . . . 1988).

The Budgetary and Fiscal Instruments

The reform replaced the traditional system of highly individualized enterprise payments to the budget with a system of taxes having pre-fixed and – in principle – uniform rates.[19] There are seven main taxes:

(a) *turnover tax* – a one-stage tax paid by producers or importers on sales to wholesale trade and levied on consumer goods – and, since 1987, on selected investment goods (*Ocena* 1988). The 1982 Law on Taxes introduced two basic rates but there has been a growing difference between the rates since then;

(b) *profits tax* – progressive in 1982–83 and linear since 1984. The rate was raised from 60 to 65 per cent in 1985. The revenue from this tax accounted for 42 per cent of the revenues of the central budget in 1987; the turnover tax had a similar share;

(c) *tax on wage-bill increases* – paid out of net profit (i.e., after the deduction of the profit tax) and progressively increasing as the wage bill surpassed a certain threshold defined by another formula. The purpose of this tax was to restrain the growth of wages and not to raise revenue;

(d) *tax on wages* – flat rate of 20 per cent of the wage bill;

(e) *social security tax* – amounting first to 25 and since 1983 to 43 per cent of the wage bill;

(f) *tax on real estate holdings* – set at 2 per cent of the value of buildings and land, and earmarked for the local budgets. Taxes (d), (e) and (f) are accounted as elements of costs;

(g) payment of a *share of amortization*.

Taxes have been accompanied by extensive and growing *exemptions and rebates*. The amount of relief from profit tax was equivalent to 10 per cent of nominal tax revenues in 1983 and to 31 per cent in 1987. By far the biggest single category are rebates related to exports. They accounted for 35–40 per cent in 1983–86 and for 52 per cent in 1987 (*Raport o reformie* 1984).[20] In addition to rebates granted at pre-fixed and – in principle – uniform rates, relief is frequently given on an individual basis, often to bail out enterprises in financial difficulties.

---

[19] There was, however, a separate tax system for the socialized and private sector. The present section deals only with the former.

[20] There are also rebates for defence industries, for selected types of investment, for the production of high-quality goods, etc.

There has also been widespread relief from the tax on wage-bill increases. Most enterprises did get some, usually case-by-case and often *post hoc*. There are also many exemptions and rebates from the payment of amortization, so that the average effective share of the budget has been 15 per cent, as against the 50 per cent nominal rate (Dziewulski & Lipiński 1987, p. 71).

Besides tax relief, which is an implicit subsidy, there are *formal subsidies* paid out to socialized enterprises (although in part benefiting consumers). They amounted to 31.1 per cent of state expenditures in 1980 and, despite massive price increases after 1981, they were still 28.4 per cent in 1985 and 28.7 per cent in 1986.[21] A considerable part of subsidies is individually tailored for loss-making enterprises. These subsidies are a counterpart to enterprise-specific tax relief.

Despite the reform some characteristic features of a traditional centrally planned economy are, therefore, still present. One of them is that the superior authorities heavily tax enterprises' gross profits but then channel them – to a large extent and in an arbitrary way – back to enterprises.[22] That the enterprises are the main beneficiaries of fiscal redistribution distinguishes the centrally planned from the market economies.[23] The second feature has to do with *which* enterprises are the beneficiaries. The problem is that a great deal of fiscal assistance flows to enterprises in financial difficulties, and that practically all such enterprises are bailed out (Mujżel 1985). As a result, government financial aid levels out differences among enterprises (World Bank 1987).

Money and Banking

One of the main limitations of the role of money in a traditional centrally planned economy is that – because of administrative allocations and shortages – possessing it does not guarantee access to scarce goods. The reform project called for the elimination of both these

[21] Estimated on the basis of *Rocznik statystyczny 1987*, pp. 107 and 110. Subsidies included in state investment expenditures are disregarded and so are export subsidies paid out of the separate foreign trade equalization account.

[22] Besides the state budget there are some other channels of cross-subsidization, i.e., the foreign trade equalization account and the funds operated at the level of the branch organization. Both are present in the Polish case, although the latter only in some branches (e.g., coal, cement).

[23] In 1980 the socialized enterprises contributed 76.5 per cent of state budget revenues and received 66.3 per cent of current expenditure. In 1987 the respective figures were 79.4 per cent and 50.2 per cent (estimated on the basis of *Mały rocznik statystyczny 1988*, pp. 76–7).

constraints, i.e., for the enhancement of the role of money, but this objective has not been achieved. In addition, the reform has been accompanied by rapid inflation, which has weakened the position of domestic currency.[24]

The banking system of the traditional centrally planned economies is a monobank one (i.e., no commercial banking; the entire system is dominated by one state bank which combines central banking functions with credit activity, each enterprise being tied to one bank, etc.). The reform proposal did not call for a radical overhaul of this model. The 1982 Banking Law allowed for the creation of new banks, but this provision remained a dead letter.[25]

The biggest change has been the introduction of the formal criterion of 'creditworthiness': plan fulfilment as the basis for granting credits to socialized enterprises was to give way to considerations of financial viability. The banks have been required to grant credits only when enterprises' financial situations promised their repayment. Enterprises declared 'non-creditworthy' were to present a recovery plan acceptable to the bank. If they failed to do so or the plan did not work, the bank should stop further financing and demand repayment of the previous loans. The liquidation of the enterprise by its founder or a separate bankruptcy procedure might then follow.

As one can see, this was an attempt to commercialize the credit system without commercializing the banks. The problem is, of course, whether the two can be separated. Non-commercial banks lack the basic incentive for a careful scrutiny of credit applications: fear of bankruptcy. In addition, they are susceptible to pressures from central or local bodies acting on behalf of the enterprise.[26] Still, some firms were declared 'non-creditworthy',[27] but most were bailed out by subsidies or tax relief. A small group of enterprises was liquidated, but mainly by merging them with financially stronger ones. Bankruptcy has been practically absent.

All this provoked complaints that budgetary policy was undoing the tough credit policy. But the irony is that fiscal paternalism has partially been made possible by the policy of printing money to cover the continuous deficit in the state budget. Besides, the allocation of

---

[24] One sign of it is a tendency among the population to carry out major transactions in hard currencies.

[25] Except for the founding in 1987 of the state-owned Export Development Bank.

[26] It is here that party nomenklatura comes into play. The director of the local branch, who is subject to it, is not very likely to resist urgings from the local party committee interested in maintaining social peace in the enterprise.

[27] There were 112 such enterprises in 1982, 332 in 1986 and 114 in 1987. But in Poland there are almost 7,000 state enterprises and 15,000 cooperatives.

credits to massive central investment was in fact automatic, regardless of cost overruns and the prospects for repayment. Also the enterprises involved in operational programmes and government contracts (and the execution of other centrally determined priorities) were given preferential treatment by the banks. The criterion of creditworthiness was bound to suffer in the process.

All in all monetary policy was rather passive, both with respect to the supply of money and the distribution of credits. This recalls the traditional centrally planned economy. The expansion of the money supply created powerful inflationary impulses, which were countered with price controls. These in turn aggravated shortages, and that strengthened the traditional penchant for administrative allocation. Allocations brought their own inefficiencies, e.g., they reduced the price elasticity of supply, which in turn provided an argument against price liberalization, etc.

The Foreign Trade Regime

Here a distinction must be made between Poland's trade with the other CMEA countries and her trade with the hard-currency countries. In the first case, accounting for over 50 per cent of the total, there was little room for major changes, as intra-CMEA trade procedures remained highly centralized. Accordingly, the domestic foreign trade plan continued to be highly detailed and formally binding on the foreign trade organizations. In drawing up this plan, the material balances, the core of traditional planning, were instrumental. The producing enterprises can also be legally ordered to undertake tasks related to 'external obligations'.

There was more room for changes in the trade regime with respect to the hard-currency area. Here are the main ones:

(a) The producing and consuming enterprises (including private ones) could be issued permits to engage directly in foreign trade related to their main activity. The number of permit holders rose from 245 in 1982 to 597 in 1987 (*Maly rocznik statystyczny* 1988, p. 258) and they reportedly accounted for 10 per cent of exports in 1986 (Dziewulski & Lipiński 1987, p. 27). That this was such a small share was partly due to bureaucratic restrictions in granting the permits and partly to the cautious attitude and the lack of the necessary skills on the part of the producing enterprises ('*Bank . . .*' 1988, pp. 1 & 4).

(b) The exchange rate was to be set, as before, by the authorities (i.e., no comprehensive foreign exchange market was envisaged), but at a level ensuring that the value in 'transaction prices' (i.e., foreign market prices converted through the official exchange rate) of the most profitable 75–85 per cent of exports would exceed their costs.[28] The rest was to be subsidized. The exchange rate was also to link domestic with external prices: the administrative prices of imported producer goods, especially basic materials, were to be based on their transaction prices, and the administrative prices of domestic producer goods were to be based, if possible, on the transaction prices of comparable goods in exports or imports.[29] The change in the exchange rate (or in external prices) was therefore to affect – via an administrative rule – the level of domestic prices. In practice, however, there were major departures from these rules. The rate of inflation outpaced the rate of devaluation. As a result the share of exports requiring subsidies paid out of the traditional equalization account was much greater than planned,[30] and the account itself recorded continuous deficits, contributing to the overall deficit of the state budget. The fear of stimulating inflation delayed the adjustment of the domestic prices of producer goods to the transaction prices. Besides, the administrative prices of goods produced at home were usually cost-based (Ćwiertnia 1987).

(c) After 1982 exporters had the option of buying back at the official rate part of their export earnings, determined on a case-by-case basis and depending on the import-intensity of the export production. The foreign exchange obtained this way could be used to finance imports of inputs and investment goods. The enterprises could also transfer their entitlements to their own suppliers to cover their import requirements. The proportion of imports financed out of enterprises' retention rose from 2.8 per cent in 1982 to 14.9 per cent in 1985, but declined to 13.9 per cent in 1986 (Rymarczyk 1985, p. 12, 27, p. 11). This was due to the overall shortage of foreign exchange, which led to delays in granting permission to enterprises to use the entitlement. In 1987 the right to repurchase a part of export earnings was replaced by actual ownership of hard currency, which could be held in accounts at Polish foreign exchange banks. But the share of export earnings which could be kept by the enterprises was reduced by about 20 per cent and the accumulated entitlements were frozen, to be gradually released in 1988–95. The official objective was, however, to increase the share of imports

[28] This rule was to apply to trade with both currency areas.

[29] No such rules were, however, proposed for the administrative prices of consumer goods. The prices of imported goods were to be set 'in appropriate relation' to the prices of domestic goods, and the latter's prices were to be based on 'justified costs' (Crane 1987).

[30] It fell in 1985–87, however, due to increased devaluation of the Polish zloty (*Raport o reformie* . . . 1984, p. 82).

financed from enterprises' own resources and thus decrease the share of centrally financed imports (dominant in 1989), and of the related rationing of imported goods.

(d) After May 1987 foreign exchange held by enterprises in bank accounts could be traded through the Export Development Bank. It was hoped that in this way a foreign exchange market would gradually develop (*Raport o realizacji* 1985). But the procedure of sales had little to do with market-type allocation and the amount of hard currency traded in 1987 was only $8.5 million (*Ocena* 1988), p. 87). Similar sales of foreign exchange to socialized enterprises, but involving the banks' own resources, were conducted after 1983. However, the amounts traded were minimal.

Comments on the Reform, 1982–87

After reviewing developments in the respective areas of the economic system, a few general comments on the 1982–87 reform are in order:

- Although it is impossible to give a precise assessment of the impact of the systemic changes on economic performance (for we do not know exactly what would have happened without these changes), it is clear that the system which evolved during the period 1982–87 did not achieve the basic objectives stated in the reform proposal: a considerable increase in economic efficiency[31] and the elimination of chronic shortages.
- The basic reason for this failure is to be seen in the fact that the reform has not been sufficiently comprehensive and radical. There have been many partial changes, e.g., enlarged planning autonomy of enterprises, the appearance of active self-management bodies in some state firms, less rigid financial system of enterprises, the possibility of producers engaging directly in foreign trade and retaining part of their export earnings. But the problem is that the basic features responsible for the poor performance of the transitional centrally planned economy with respect to efficiency and market balance have remained, although sometimes in a weakened, modified or disguised form. These remaining features include: widespread central intervention in the structure of production and in the allocation of inputs: pervasive price controls, extreme

---

[31] For more on this see World Bank 1987; and *Raport o przebiegu*, 1987.

organizational concentration and the related monopolization; dependence of enterprise directors on party and state bodies; massive fiscal redistribution from and to socialized enterprises by bureaucratic financial institutions; the related soft budget constraint of these enterprises; and severe constraints on the private sector. Because of these basic invariants, the indicated partial changes could only have had – at most – a small positive impact.

- Due to the survival of these basic features, the system which evolved during the reform gave rise to two phenomena typical of the traditional centrally planned economy as well: a complete lack of competition among suppliers (a pervasive producers' market) and massive bargaining by enterprises with superior bodies about the most convenient terms of activity.[32] It is evident that no economic system with these two characteristics can display high economic efficiency.

- There was no attempt on the part of the authorities to create the organizational preconditions for competition; rather the reverse was true as they pressed for the creation of branch-based monopolies. At the same time they tried to substitute the discipline of competition with various administrative controls and manipulation of fiscal instruments; this was not only largely ineffective but also made the system more and more complicated.

- Regarding the bargaining phenomenon, it may be pointed out that while it still covered the administrative allocations of inputs, it spread to fiscal instruments as well, which to a large extent became enterprise-specific (Bobek 1987). A process well-known from the Hungarian experience has thus taken place, except that in Hungary bargaining about the 'regulators' seems to have largely replaced bargaining about allocations.

- The Polish case shows (as does the Hungarian) that one can move from comprehensive directive planning without introducing a market mechanism. The experience with such intermediate systems is not very encouraging. But this should not be interpreted as meaning that the efficiency-enhancing economic reform is to be sought in perfecting a system based on such planning. Attempts of this type are, in the author's view, futile. What the Polish experience shows is, rather, that a move from such a system must be much more radical.[33]

---

[32] This phenomenon could be analysed in terms of 'rent-seeking' (Parkoła & Rapacki 1987), but its scope is much greater than in any developed market economy.
[33] See the next two chapters for discussion of reforms in Poland after 1989.

References

Balcerowicz, L. 1981 'Jak przebudować strukture organizacyjną', *Życie Gospodarcze*, No. 48.

'Bank w przebudowie i w dzialaniu – wywiad z W. Baką', *Trybuna Ludu*, 1988.

Babek, J. 1987 *Reforma a stan i perspektywy rozwoju gospodarki krajowej*, Warsaw, Zaklad Badan Statystyczno-Ekonomicznych GUS i PAN.

Crane, K. 1987 'An Assessment of the Economic Reform in Poland's State-Owned Industry', manuscript.

Ćwiertnia, R. 1987 'Koncentracja organizacyjna a centralna regulacja planistyczna', mimeo.

'Czapka na miare – rozmowa z Maciejem Krogulcem, dyrektorem Towarzystwa Handlowega "Pelko"', *Życie Warszawy*, 1988, No. 103, p. 3.

Dąbrowski, M. 1988 'Watpliwa metoda reanimacji', manuscript.

Dziewulski P. & Lipiński, J. 1987 'Ceny i narzędzia ich kształtowania', in J. Lipiński & U. Wojciechowska (eds), *Proces wdrażania reformy gospodarczej*, Warsaw, PWE, pp. 101–29.

Fornalczyk, A. 1984 'Zrzeszenia przedsiebiorstw', *Życie Gospodarcze*, No. 33.

Gruszecki, T. 1988 'Spótki z udzialem zagranicznym – po roku', *Przeglad Organizacji*, No. 1, pp. 27–33.

Józefiak, C. 1988 *Proba oceny i przebiegu reformy gospodarczej*, Warsaw, PTE.

Kawalec, S. 1988 'Kontakty przedsiebiorstw z wladzami', manuscript.

Kierunki reformy gospodarczej, Warsaw, 1981.

Kowalska, M. 1988 'Prywaciarze', *Życie Gospodarcze*, No. 10, pp. 1 and 4.

Mały rocznik statystyczny 1988, Warsaw, 1988.

Mujżel, J. 1985 *Problemy cenotwórstwa w II etapie reformy gospodarczej*, Warsaw, PTE.

Ocena przebiegu i wyników wdrażania reformy gospodarczej w 1987 r., Komisja Planowania przy Radzie Ministrów, 1988.

Parkoła, A. & Rapacki, R. 1987 *II etap reformy w handlu zagranicznym – propozycie rozwiązań*, Instytut Gospodarki Swiatowej, Warsaw.

'Program realizacyjny II etapu reformy gospodarczej przyjety przez Sejm II Iutego 1988 r.', *Reforma Gospodarcza*, 1988, No. 127–34.

'Raport o przebiegu i wynikach wdrażania reformy gospodarczej w 1986 r.', *Reforma Gospodarcza*, 1987, No. 13.

Raport o realizacji reformy gospodarczej w 1984 r., Warsaw, 1985.

Raport o reformie gospodarczej – ocena i wnioski kierunkowe, Warsaw, 1984.

'Raport o wdrażaniu i skutkach reformy gospodarczej w 1982 r.', *Reforma gospodarcza* (supplement to *Rzeczypolita*, 1983, No. 12–13.

Rocznik statystyczny 1987, Warsaw, 1987.

Rymarczyk, J. 1985 'Proba diagnozy', *Życie Gospodarcze*, No. 33.

Skowronek, Cz. 1983 'Ewolucja systemu zaopatrzenia', *Zycie Gospodarcze*, 1983, No. 45.

Smuga, T. 1987 'Niezłe ale zle używane narzedzie', *Życie Gospodarcze*, No. 13.

Tollison, R.D. 1982 'Rent Seeking: A Survey', *Kyklos*, pp. 575–602.

'Ustawa z dnia 26.02.1982 o cenach', *Dziennik Ustaw, z 1982*, No. 7, pos. 52.

Wiśniewski, E. 1988 'Spółdzielczosc w reformie', *Nowe Drogi*, No. 1, pp. 103–111.

Wojciechowski, T. 1986 'Reglamentacja materialów: przyczyny, skutki i możliwosci ograniczenia', *Gospodarka Planowa*, No. 10, pp. 390–4.

—— 1987 'Możlowości osiagania równowagi na rynku środkow produkcji w polskich warunkach gospodarczych', mimeo.

World Bank 1987 *Poland: Reform, Adjustment and Growth*, 'Annex I: The Economic System', Washington, DC.

'Zasady i organizacja zaopatrzenia materialowo-technicznego w latach 1988– 1990', *Reforma Gospodarcza*, 1988, No. 120.

'Zysk to nie wyzysk – rozmowa z Kazimierzem Modzelewskim, przewodniczacym Krajowej Rady Rzemiosla', *Życie Gospodarcze*, 1984, No. 33, p. 3.

15

The Political Economy of Economic Reform: Poland, 1989–92

The Historical Background

After the Second World War Poland fell under Soviet domination, with two resulting fundamental changes in its institutional system: first, the establishment of an authoritarian political system of a party–state type centred around the Polish United Workers Party (PUWP), and second, the replacement of private property and the market by central planning and state ownership. One major exception to state ownership was agriculture, which after the attempt at forced collectivization in the first half of the 1950s remained largely private.

The centralized economy of Poland, similar to that of other socialist countries, initially grew fast, thanks to the very low point from which it started and very high rates of investment. However, as time went on, the efficiency of investment and of the economy as a whole continuously declined because of the decreasing ability of the centralized economic system to cope with progressively more complex economic problems. As the efficiency of investment declined, there was a tendency to try to compensate for it by increasing the rate of investment. This in turn increased the complexity of the economy, and so on. The overall result of this vicious circle was declining rates of growth of national income

I am indebted to Ewa Balcerowicz, Marek Dąbrowski, Marek Jaśkiewicz, Jerzy Koźminski, Peggy Simpson, and Edward Wnuk-Lipiński for comments on the first draft. The usual caveats apply. I also thank Robert Konski and Malgorata Sedek for their help in editing this paper. This chapter was first published under the title 'Poland' in John Williamson (ed.), *The Political Economy of Policy Reform* (Washington DC, Institute for International Economics, 1994), pp. 163–77. All rights reserved.

and almost stagnant consumption, already witnessed as early as the late 1960s.

Against this background, there was a forced change of political leadership in 1970 after the brutally suppressed protests in Gdańsk. The new leadership under Edward Gierek promised an improvement in the standard of living. The key to it, as it turned out, was massive foreign borrowing, which partly financed increased consumption and partly new investments in Western technology. The underlying assumption was that these investments would increase Poland's export potential to such an extent that the country would be able to service the debt and still achieve a higher level of GDP and consumption. However, this did not happen. The foreign borrowing proved excessive, and the related investments on the whole proved misdirected and inefficient, largely because they were undertaken within the framework of a basically unchanged centralized economic system. After rapid growth of the national income and consumption in 1971–78, Poland entered a long period of economic crisis with a huge and growing foreign debt. The drastic cuts in imports, due to the balance of payments difficulties, had brought about a decline in net material product of 27 per cent between 1978 and 1982.

An extraordinary change in Poland's sociopolitical system then occurred: after a wave of massive strikes in August 1980, the authorities agreed to the creation of an independent trade union, Solidarity. This ran against the basic rule of the communist system, that there are no organizations independent from the party–state. Trade unions in this system served as 'transmission belts' from the party to the masses. The form of a trade union was chosen largely because the leaders of the opposition rightly considered the proper organization – that of an opposition political party – totally unacceptable in the then-existing geopolitical situation. But Solidarity was a trade union only in name; in fact, it was a massive political movement for reform, which at its peak had 10 million members out of an adult population of 21 million. Despite this size, the presence of a common opponent – the authorities – and the common danger – Soviet invasion – produced a remarkable degree of unity and explained the self-limiting nature of Solidarity's demands, which may appear modest from today's perspective. In the area of economics, the principal demand was to replace central planning with market mechanisms without, however, privatizing the state enterprises.

The period of uneasy coexistence between Solidarity and the Communists ended with the introduction of martial law in December 1981 by General Wojciech Jaruzelski. The role of Soviet pressure is undoubted, although historians might quarrel about how large the risk of Soviet invasion was in the absence of the repressive measures the Polish authorities themselves took.

Solidarity was first suspended and then declared illegal. It continued, however, to work underground. The authorities launched an economic reform in 1982. It was even more modest than the one officially envisaged in 1980–81, and it preserved, among other things, a large measure of central allocation of inputs and the bureaucratic organizational structures necessary to operate such a mechanism. The authorities heavily relied on the increased output of coal, achieved by a radical strengthening of incentives for miners to work on Saturdays. This raised the relative wages of miners, the single most powerful industrial group, with about 450,000 people in 1985.

The autonomy of the state enterprises was, however, increased, and the workers councils, introduced in the second half of 1981, were gradually restored. Limited in scope and heir to many economic burdens, the reform failed to improve the performance of the economy.[1] In this respect, it was not much different from the slightly more radical Hungarian economic reform.

Amongst the growing economic and social tensions, 1988 emerged as the initial year of accelerated change, as it turned out, in the final period of Communist rule in Poland. The last Party-dominated government of Mieczyslaw Rakowski, formed in October 1988, introduced substantial economic liberalization with respect to the private sector and foreign trade. This was, however, accompanied by very lax macroeconomic policy, accommodating the growing wage pressures. As a result, both inflation and shortages caused by price controls increased rapidly. In February and March 1989 the 'Round Table' negotiations between Solidarity, led by Lech Wałęsa, and the authorities took place and culminated in an agreement signed on 5 April and approved by the Party-dominated Parliament a few days later. The agreement provided for political liberalization, including the legalization of Solidarity and other independent associations and quasi-free elections.[2] The results for the economy were rather mixed. The private sector was to be given equal rights to develop, but there was no mention of privatizing the state enterprises. Besides, the opposition managed to get approval for indexation of wages[3] and many wage and social benefits for the largest social

---

[1] This reform is discussed in the previous chapter.

[2] The elections were totally free for the newly created Senate, but crucial for the Sejm; that is, Solidarity was permitted to contend for only 35 per cent of the seats.

[3] The wages had to be increased by 80 per cent of the price increases in the preceding quarter in excess of normal, spontaneous wage increases.

groups.[4] This was partially due to the 'trade-unionist' nature of the opposition's economic negotiators and advisers, to the still-perceived political constraints, and probably to the conviction that it would be up to the government to implement these concessions. Another reason was the lack of overall coordination of the negotiations.

The results of the June elections surprised both sides. The Party suffered a crushing defeat, and Solidarity scored an unexpected victory. As a part of the political compromise, General Wojciech Jaruzelski was elected by the new Parliament to a newly formed post of president of Poland. His designated prime minister and closest ally, the former Minister of Interior Czeslaw Kiszczak, failed, however, in forming a government. After two months of hesitation, Solidarity decided to take the responsibility for the government by creating a coalition with two parties that used to be the junior parties of the PUWP. This government, led by Tadeusz Mazowiecki, was formed between 24 August and 12 September 1989. The author, after short but strong hesitation, accepted the dual job of deputy prime minister, responsible for the economy, and of finance minister.

Initial Conditions in 1989

The inherited economic conditions are described at greater length in the next chapter. Let us only note here that they included: the state-dominated and heavily distorted economic system; an economic structure burdened by a heavy dependence on the Soviet market for exports in such sectors as machinery, textiles, electronics, and pharmaceuticals and shaped during many years of import substitution; a large foreign debt.

However, the most important specific feature of the initial Polish economic situation was the dramatic state of the macroeconomy. Wages in the first quarter of 1989 were 120 per cent higher than a year earlier. However, the real explosion happened in the following months. The growth of wages quickened, followed by the increase in prices. Sharp increases in the state purchase prices of agricultural products and the

---

[4] The largest groups – miners, railways workers, farmers – had their own negotiation groups, which acted only in weak coordination. The representatives of these groups usually pressured for commitments that wages in their respective sectors be, for example, 200 per cent of the average wage in the economy. (Farmers demanded equivalently high guaranteed prices.) All these concessions were scrapped when the radical economic programme was launched, but they were a source of conflict with the respective groups.

continued controls of the consumer prices of foodstuffs produced an explosive budget deficit, increasingly financed by the creation of money. In this situation, after the freeing of food prices in August 1989, consumer prices jumped in that month by 40 per cent and wages by 90 per cent. The free market rate of exchange in early September 1989 was eight times the official one. Poland was entering hyper-inflation, accompanied by massive shortages. There was also a heavy burden of foreign debt.

The sociopolitical conditions prevailing in Poland at the start of economic reform were rather peculiar. There was a sense of a newly gained freedom, but there was no euphoria because the economy was in bad shape and there was still some uncertainty with respect to the Soviet Union. Solidarity achieved an unexpectedly great victory, and the Communist Party was, on the whole, ready to cooperate. But there were some more radical opposition groups, which did not participate in the Round Table discussions. Some of them later became more and more active, accusing the participants of a conspiratory deal with the Communists and propagating an extremely populist economic programme.

Solidarity, with its idealistic ethos of a movement for the general good, was again legal and expanding, and was strongly represented in the Parliament. It was widely expected that Solidarity would provide an umbrella for the economic reforms. However, helped by hindsight, one remembers that Solidarity was united mainly by the presence of the common opponent: the Soviet Union and the Communist Party. There was no elaborated, shared positive programme of how to organize the political and economic life after communism, and once these unifying elements disappeared, splits were inevitable.

There was also a peculiar social structure from the point of view of the transition to a capitalist market economy. The numerically largest group – the industrial workers – was the product of socialist indus-trialization; paradoxically, it was they who organized the strikes, supported and co-organized by intellectuals from the opposition, and undermined socialism. This gave the workers (and this was probably partly their own perception) a kind of romantic aura, superimposed upon the Marxist propaganda of the proletariat as the avant-garde. The Solidarity period also enshrined and popularized various forms of workers' protests, even hunger strikes, usually accompanied by a display of the national flag. These were the workers who had to face the negative consequences of the transition to a market economy, the first being actual or potential unemployment.

Another large social group, the farmers, were generally considered, and likewise considered themselves, as the preservers of private property. The average size of the 2.7 million private farms was only 7.2 hectares, and 30 per cent of the farmers had less than 2 hectares (they usually had the status of farmer-workers). They had functioned for many years in a nonmarket environment characterized by a mixture of discrimination and tutelage from the state. The former consisted mainly of much lower administrative allocations of inputs compared with those obtained by the state farms and restrictions on enlarging the size of private farms. The latter took the form of subsidized credits and guaranteed purchases of agricultural products by the parastatal organizations. Moreover, in 1989 the farmers achieved large windfall gains, thanks to the freeing of the prices of foodstuffs by the last Communist government. Also, the hyperinflation in 1989 practically eliminated the real burden of taxation of the farmers, which was low in any case. The complementary liberalization of the prices of inputs to agriculture to be introduced in 1990 and the adjustment of tax rates took these windfall gains away from them. This sequence was politically unfortunate, but it was unavoidable because of the initial conditions in the country.

The existing interest groups were relatively strong on the labour side, which included the trade union Solidarity and its main rival, the Polish Confederation of the Trade Unions (OPZZ), which was organized after the introduction of martial law and the proscription of Solidarity. By contrast, the employers' organizations were very weak, and the same was true of the consumers' movement. There were several organizations fighting for influence among the farmers, both former allies of the PUWP and linked to Solidarity.

The Economic Strategy: Concept and Launching

This strategy was elaborated during late 1989 and it was launched, as a comprehensive package, in early 1990. While we were working on the comprehensive economic programme, we also took measures aimed at coping with the current situation in such a way as to prepare the ground for the decisive operation in 1990. For example, there had been a series of devaluations preceding the unification of the exchange rate in 1990, interest rates were increased, and the wasteful system of subsidizing coal mining was replaced by a more rational one. Also, the excessive indexation of wages was abolished, and a much more modest system was introduced, to be replaced by a tough wage restraint in early 1990. Two successive budgets for the remaining part of 1989 were prepared. All this was done while negotiating with the International Monetary

Fund (IMF) and lobbying the Western governments for a $1 billion stabilization fund.

The development of the economic strategy is described at greater length in the next chapter. Here I would note that the peculiar feature of the Polish economic programme (and later that of other programmes in the post-socialist countries) was that, in view of the initial economic system, the systemic transformation had to be far more comprehensive and radical than in any previous cases of market-oriented reform. Another characteristic of the Polish programme was that the systemic change had to be combined with radical economic stabilization because of inherited hyperinflation and massive shortages. This distinguished the Polish situation from that of Czechoslovakia and Hungary, which were macroeconomically much more stable, and made it similar to the situation in some Latin American countries and to the initial conditions in the former Soviet Union as well as Bulgaria, Romania and Albania two years later.

The Polish economic programme had, since its earliest incarnation, devoted special attention to dealing with the foreign debt.[5] The goal here was to achieve a radical debt reduction, in the first place from the official creditors (who hold about two-thirds of the total debt). We assumed that the pioneering role of Poland in the political trans-formation of Eastern Europe and the radical nature of its economic programme made such a goal realistic. The debt reduction was viewed in turn as a factor that increased the chances for success of economic stabilization and transformation.

Political acceptance of the radical economic programme required special mobilization on the part of the government's economic team. In the second half of November 1989, the team set up a special task force to coordinate the preparation of the final version of the basic eleven laws and related regulations. After a series of consultations in parliament, I obtained approval of the idea by a special all-party parliamentary commission to work on the government's draft laws. This enabled a radical acceleration of the legislative process to take place, as compared with the normal procedure of sequential discussion of draft laws by several parliamentary commissions. A similar special commission was set up in the Senate, which normally would discuss the draft laws only after they had been accepted by the Lower House (the Sejm). But this time the Senate's commission agreed to work in parallel with the Sejm.

The draft laws prepared by the special working groups were first

---

[5] Jeffrey Sachs was especially helpful in working out this part and in presenting the Polish case to the Western public.

discussed by the Economic Committee of the Council of Ministers, of which I was chairman. These discussions went quite smoothly.[6] Then, the laws were submitted to the entire Council of Ministers. All this happened in the first half of December 1989. Given the amount of the proposed legislation and the time pressure, these debates had some dramatic moments.[7] But all of the draft laws and the budget for 1989 were accepted before the agreed deadline for the opening of the parliamentary debate, 17 December, which happened to be a Sunday. This speed underscored the extraordinary nature of the whole undertaking and gave some additional drama to my introductory speech on behalf of the government.

The special commissions of the Sejm and the Senate worked extremely intensively and in close collaboration with the government's experts. Any attempted major deviation from the government's proposals was quickly reported, and the economic team intervened. The legislative package was adopted by the Sejm on 27 December and two days later by the Senate, in both cases by a very wide margin. Just before the end of 1989, the package was signed by President Wojciech Jaruzelski, and it became law. The major legislative phase was over.

The Developments of 1990–92

In early 1990 a radical, comprehensive stabilization–liberalization programme was launched. Initial inflation turned out to be higher than expected and the fall in output deeper. Open unemployment started to emerge. But the inflation rate quickly started to go down,[8] and shortages and queues rapidly disappeared. The supply of goods improved dramatically. The newly convertible zloty held stronger than expected. Exports to the West surged.

---

[6] Some of the sessions of the Economic Committee in December 1989 were chaired (while I was negotiating with the IMF mission or conducting political consultations) by Deputy Prime Minister Jan Janowski, who came from the party that used to be a junior partner of the PUWP and represented artisans and small entrepreneurs. Janowski turned out to be a close ally of the economic team during his service in the Mazowiecki government.

[7] An important role in these crucial moments was played by Waldemar Kuczynski, an economist who acted as the chief adviser to Prime Minister Tadeusz Mazowiecki and supported the radical economic program.

[8] It was almost 80 per cent in January, 23.8 per cent in February, 4.3 per cent in March, 1.8 per cent in August, but then it increased to 4.6 per cent in September.

On the institutional front, in May 1990 there were elections to new, genuine local governments, and in July 1990 the parliament passed, after five months of deliberations, a comprehensive law on the privatization of state enterprises. Meanwhile, privatization of shops and restaurants (so-called 'small privatization') was proceeding very quickly. Other important laws were passed, too, such as a law disbanding the compulsory 'quasi-statist' associations of cooperatives, a law on insurance, an anti-monopoly law, a telecommunications law, a bankruptcy law, a law abolishing some 50 extrabudgetary funds, and a social safety law.

On the social and political front, after the initial calm between January and April 1990, the situation started to get more complicated. At the congress of Solidarity in April, many delegates were very critical of the economic programme. In June, farmers blocked important roads demanding measures that would enable the dairies (formally farmer cooperatives) to pay higher milk prices. The government ordered the police to unblock the roads, provoking furious attacks in Parliament from the deputies of the peasant parties.

But most importantly, deeper and deeper splits appeared in the Solidarity movement itself. They were largely related to the growing conflict between its leader, Lech Wałęsa, and then-Prime Minister Tadeusz Mazowiecki. Wałęsa accused his opponent of being too slow in effecting political change but, on the whole, he refrained from criticizing the economic reform. In May 1990 Lech Wałęsa declared his intention to become the president of Poland, a post still occupied by Wojciech Jazuzelski. The conflict culminated in the open split in the Solidarity movement into two camps: one supporting Lech Wałęsa and the other Tadeusz Mazowiecki. In the election campaign, which dominated the mass media in the autumn of 1990, the economic programme came under attack from the three non-Solidarity candidates. The most demagogic critic, Stanislaw Tymiński, a Polish émigré not quite faithfully representing himself to the Polish public as a successful Western businessman who knew how to turn the Polish economy into a thriving business quickly, unexpectedly won second place. Wałęsa was first, and Mazowiecki, who was third, resigned together with his government.

The year of 1990 ended, therefore, in a complicated political situation. In the economy, after the rapid decline from 80 per cent in January to below 2 per cent in August, the inflation rate increased to between 4 and 5 per cent monthly in the second half of the year. This was due to increased wage pressure, stimulated by the overall political climate, and to the monetary policy, prematurely relaxed during the summer. (It was tightened in the autumn of 1990.) But the budgetary situation during the year as a whole was better than expected: foreign reserves more than doubled, exports to the West increased by 43 per cent, the shops changed beyond recognition, and privatization of the smaller units, especially in trade and services, rapidly advanced. Unemployment stood at over 6.1 per cent, and the official statistics registered a substantial decline in GDP.

In early 1991 a new government led by Jan Krzysztof Bielecki was formed; the author continued as a deputy prime minister and minister of finance with overall responsibility for the economy. The year started with massive attacks by the trade unions on the wage controls. But after tough negotiations, the government did not give any significant concessions. Private enterprises, including the privatized ones, were released from wage controls altogether by the revised law of December 1990 on the assumption that the self-interest of private owners would prevent excessive wage increases. But this fuelled accusations from the state enterprises that they were discriminated against by a 'doctrinaire' liberal government keen on 'destroying the state sector'.

However, by far the largest source of problems in 1991 turned out to be the collapse of trade with the Soviet Union and the terms of trade losses due to the move to world prices and hard currency payments. This was mostly responsible for the higher-than-expected inflation in the first months of the year, the decline in output and falling profitability of state enterprises. The two latter factors, together with forecasting errors, made the budget for 1991 obsolete after a couple of months. In the revised budget, 80 per cent of the shortfall of the nominal revenues was made up by expenditure cuts and 20 per cent by an increased deficit. This drastic revision had to be formally confirmed by the Parliament just before parliamentary elections in October 1991.

The institutional reform in 1991 included, among other things, a new securities law and establishment of the stock exchange, a new liberal foreign investment law, a law on a comprehensive personal income tax, and a law on fiscal policy. The new import tariff was introduced in August 1991 with a higher average rate, but it was more uniform and in line with the EEC classifications.

Privatization of larger state enterprises was slow, but the autonomous growth of the private sector was extremely fast and the privatization of smaller units and of assets of state enterprises rather rapid. As a result the value added generated in the private sector increased in 1991 by 33.3 per cent, and this growth occurred across the economy: in manufacturing by 42.2 per cent, in construction 64.0 per cent, in domestic trade 61.7 per cent, agriculture 10.2 per cent. In contrast, the GDP produced in the public sectors declined by 26.3 per cent (*Rzeczpospolita*, 2 December 1992, III).

In May 1991 the zloty was devalued by 14 per cent after sixteen months of a fixed exchange rate and pegged to a basket of currencies, instead of the previous peg to the dollar. In October a crawling peg was introduced with a monthly devaluation of 1.8 per cent.

In April 1991 Poland signed an unprecedented agreement with the Paris Club, whereby 50 per cent of the official debt (two-thirds of the total Polish debt) would be reduced in two stages.

The parliamentary elections in October were preceded by two months of campaigning in which sixty-five political parties took part. Most of them were very critical of the government's economic programme and presented radically different proposals. To the extent their economic programmes were defined at all, they usually included relaxation of monetary and fiscal policy, increased protectionism, and more active involvement of the state bureaucracy in the affairs of specific industries and enterprises. The elections produced a very fragmented parliament, composed of almost thirty political groups. As a result, a coalition of five to seven parties was required to form the government. The new government of Jan Olszewski was formed at the end of December 1991, after over two months of intensive negotiations. (The author ended his public service in December 1991.)

The new government started claiming a sharp break with the past but gradually toned down its revisionist declarations and basically continued the disciplined fiscal policy. But privatization of larger state enterprises was practically brought to a halt, and political debate on privatization got more and more demagogic. The Polish zloty was devalued in February 1992 by 11.6 per cent.

In June 1992 the government collapsed after a clumsy attempt at disclosing the former regime's 'secret agents' in the state institutions, and, after more than a month, the new government of Hanna Suchocka was formed. The new government, based on a coalition of two clearly pro-reformist parties with a fundamentalist Catholic party and two small peasant parties, basically continued the programme started three years before: i.e., it tried to strengthen macroeconomic stabilization, to maintain the liberal character of the economic system, and to speed up privatization. The major changes were concessions to the farmers (promises of increased protectionism, one-time subsidies on fuel for the farmers following a severe draught) and a 'social pact' with the trade unions centred on modifying wage controls and on privatization. The government had to deal with a wave of strikes in December 1992, mainly in the coal mines. The strikes ended with an agreement, but its financial implications were not completely clear.

After three years, the Polish economy was macroeconomically much more stable and substantially transformed. The inflation rate, as measured by the consumer price index, had fallen from the annual rate of 2,000 per cent in the second half of 1989 to 44.3 per cent in 1992. Producer prices in manufacturing increased by 31.3 per cent in 1992. Prices were freed, and therefore the price structure was fundamentally improved; shortages and queues disappeared, and the supply of goods was incomparably better than three years before. The private sector employed 60 per cent of the labour force and generated 50 per cent of the GDP, by far the highest ratios in the post-socialist countries. Thanks to the continuous rapid growth of the private sector across the economy and to the improved performance of some state firms during 1992, Poland was the first post-socialist country where GDP stopped falling. As a matter of fact, it is estimated to grow at a rate of between 0.5 and 2 per cent. The official GDP figures showed a cumulative drop in 1990–91 of 18 per cent, but unofficial estimates put it in the range of 5 to 10 per cent.[9] Both exports and imports increased rapidly, which sharply raised their share in the GDP. This happened despite the collapse of trade with the Council of Mutual Economic Assistance (CMEA). Foreign reserves almost doubled.

But some serious problems remained. Unemployment increased from practically zero in early 1990 to 13.6 per cent at the end of 1992. Heavy industry and coal mining required unpopular restructuring. The budget deficit had to be contained, which demanded, first of all, measures aimed at reducing the growth of subsidies to the pension system. The liberal foreign trade regime was under attack from the farmers' lobby, and rapid, unconventional privatization of state enterprises, based on free distribution of shares, was delayed for a year and half because of the elections and the political conflicts in the Parliament. All in all, maintaining macroeconomic stability and completing the transition to capitalism largely depended on a rather fragmented political system. But the economy was much more independent of the political scene, and despite the fragmentation of Parliament, a tough budget for 1993 was passed in February 1993.

[9] These estimates were made at the Research Institute of the Main Statistical Office and the Polish Academy of Sciences (Rajewski 1992, pp. 133–40).

Lessons from the Polish Experience

CIRCUMSTANCES LEADING TO THE LAUNCH OF THE ECONOMIC
PROGRAMME

The Polish programme was prepared and launched under a double
crisis: a long-term structural problem of low and falling efficiency and a
macroeconomic catastrophe. It was the latter that gave the Polish
situation a dramatic dimension. This crisis both required radical
measures, especially with respect to stabilization, and increased the
people's readiness to accept such measures. But there was an important
complement: the newly gained external freedom due to the collapse
of the Soviet bloc. Otherwise, the radical institutional programme,
especially privatization, would not have been possible. Liberalization
and a massive Solidarity victory probably motivated people to accept
the radical reforms. In the special situation of 'extraordinary politics',
there was a stronger-than-usual tendency among the political actors to
act in terms of the common good. This and the government's speed of
action explain the overwhelming acceptance of the economic
programme.

The special motivation of the people at large would not have lasted
very long and was probably cut short by the growing conflict within
Solidarity and the rather unpleasant way in which it split in 1990.
Indeed, people for whom Solidarity represented an idealistic movement
for the common good might have felt cheated and thus were willing to
look elsewhere to invest their political sympathies. This and the related
presidential elections in the autumn of 1990 certainly shortened the
honeymoon period.

Poland in 1989 cannot be regarded as a testing ground for a rival
hypothesis that 'the scope for reforms would be greater where an
incoming government won a mandate for change by the substance of its
preceding election campaign, rather than where it surprised its
supporters after winning power' (Williamson 1992). For Solidarity at the
Round Table represented, rather, 'trade unionist' demands, and it did
not expect then nor during the election campaign that it would be
forming the government in 1989. Certainly, Solidarity did not present
anything that resembled the radical stabilization–transformation
programme launched half a year later. This shift might be explained
by the changed macroeconomic situation (price eruption in August
1989) and by the fact that the government's economic team was composed of people not present at the Round Table who had a critical view
of the economic part of the agreement reached there. A different

composition would probably have meant a different – most likely less radical – economic programme.

Given these circumstances, notably the 'third-way' elements in the Solidarity tradition and the speed with which the programme was launched, the Polish public could not have been psychologically well-prepared for the radical economic measures. It is however, highly doubtful whether the delay would have brought about much more understanding, and it definitely would have worsened the macro-economic situation.

As to the opposition in Parliament, it formally consisted of the PUWP. But because it partly comprised disguised (or open) liberals and because there was a general atmosphere of national unity in late 1989 and the PUWP had suffered a crushing defeat in June 1989, it did not seriously challenge the programme. There was much more opposition from the United Peasant Party, formally a coalition partner. In general, the distinction between the ruling parties and the opposition was not very pronounced, as far as the attitude towards the economic pro-gramme was concerned. And although the parliamentary debates on the economy got more and more critical over time, until August 1991 (just before parliamentary elections) it was possible to persuade Parliament to adopt all the major economic legislation proposed by the government and to block any initiatives that would constitute a major deviation from the government's economic programme.

THE ECONOMIC TEAM

An economic team with coherent views was an important factor in the Polish case. Here, I think I have to say a few words about myself. In August 1989 I still did not imagine for a second that I might be responsible for free Poland's stabilization–transformation economic programme. But I had worked for almost fifteen years on economic reform and institutional issues,[10] and in a paper written in April 1989 for a conference in Poland, I sketched out what I thought were the necessary elements of a radical and comprehensive economic package for Poland: price liberalization, convertibility of the Polish zloty, tough macroeconomic policy, privatization. In 1978 I formed a group of ten young economists to work on economic reform. After August 1980, our work was given much publicity, and the group was often called the

---

[10] This included the study of the South Korean economy I made as a visiting fellow at the Institute of Development Studies at the University of Sussex in 1985 and the research of Ludwig Erhard's reform, which I made in Germany in 1988.

'Balcerowicz group'. (It was probably because of this that I was offered the position in the government nine years later.) After the introduction of martial law in December 1981, the group's members and some sympathizers continued to meet at my institute for seminars to discuss various problems of the economic system, including the importance of property rights and privatization. When I accepted the job in Mazowiecki's government, it was agreed that I would be responsible for the makeup of the economic team (with Mazowiecki's final approval, of course). This applied without caveats to my deputies in the Ministry of Finance and also to the main economic ministries. This was also true of the formation of the second government in early 1991.

In 1989 some of the members of the 'Balcerowicz group' or other participants of the seminar became my closest associates.[11] Besides, I happened to know personally from my student days at the Central School of Planning and Statistics (now once again the Warsaw School of Economics) some of the people who were already in high positions in the Ministry of Finance and remembered them as capable and energetic individuals.[12]

The shared background, commonality of purpose, similar age (around 40), and the common pressures created what quickly became known as the 'Balcerowicz team'. This applied, first of all, to the deputies in the Ministry of Finance who had to defend the tough economic measures within the government structures, in Parliament, and against the public. An important intellectual support was offered by some advisers.[13]

Throughout my service in the government, there had been good cooperation with the central bank, headed in 1989–90 by Władysław Baka and in 1991 by Grzegorz Wojtowicz. This seems to be a sharp contrast with the situation in Russia in 1992. More generally, issues

[11] For example, Marek Dąbrowski, who was my deputy in the Ministry of Finance until the summer of 1990, and Stefan Kawalec, who was first my chief adviser and then my deputy in the same ministry, responsible for financial institutions.

[12] This applied to Janusz Sawicki, my deputy at the Ministry of Finance, responsible for foreign debt negotiation, and Andrzej Podsiadło, who was overseeing the state enterprises in the Ministry. Grzegorz Wójtowicz, first deputy chairman of the Polish National Bank and its Chairman in 1991, graduated the same student year in my faculty of Foreign Trade of the Central School of Planning and Statistics. Wojciech Misiąg and Ryszard Pazura, my other two deputies in the Ministry of Finance, also graduated from the Central School of Planning and Statistics.

[13] This group included both foreign advisers – Jeffrey Sachs and David Lipton, Władysław Brzeski, Stanislaw Gomułka, Jacek Rostowski and Stanisław Welisz – and Polish ones: Karol Lutkowski, Andrzej Stanisław Bratkowski, Antoni Kantecki, Adam Lipowski, Andrzej Parkoła and Andrzej Ochocki. Most of the foreign advisers were of Polish origin.

related to the central bank and its relationships to the government's economic team are important in the context of radical stabilization–transformation programmes.

It was also of importance that as a deputy prime minister I was chairing the sessions of the Economic Committee of the Council of Ministers, which comprised economic ministers and chiefs of other economic agencies (including the governor of the central bank). The committee acted as a vehicle for coordination and the preparations of decisions to be taken by the Council of Ministers.[14]

As deputy prime minister I had created a special section of overall coordination that focused on political aspects of the economic programme – that is, contacts with the respective political parties, with the Parliament and with the mass media. This section was directed by Jerzy Koźminski, who used to be one of my best students of international economics. He played an important role in devising and sustaining political support for the economic programme, as well as its overall coordination, especially in the crucial moments of December 1989.

Political Leadership and Economic Reform

The relationship of political leadership to economic reform was not clear because the issue of political leadership itself was not completely clear. In late 1989 and the first months of 1990, Lech Wałęsa, leader of the victorious Solidarity, stayed in the background in Gdansk, and the prime minister, Tadeusz Mazowiecki, became the most popular Polish politician (he reached popularity ratings of over 80 per cent). Mazowiecki, a man of deep principles, certainly had a vision of history. (Elections at that time were in any case not in sight.) But for a number of reasons, the programme was not identified with him but was known already in October 1989 as the 'Balcerowicz programme'. One of the reasons was the tacit agreement that I would take overall responsibility for the economy.[15] Another reason might have been the speed with which the economic programme was launched and the visible role the economic team played in it. The economic team thus assumed an important political role.

Since May 1990, there had been a growing conflict within Solidarity, mostly on noneconomic and personal grounds. I tried and largely managed to keep the economic programme outside this dispute. Wałęsa himself declared in his short presidential address in December 1990 that

[14] The secretary of this committee was Alfred Bieć, one of my closest associates.

[15] During my first meeting with Mazowiecki, he said he was looking 'for his Ludwig Erhard'.

he would 'support the Balcerowicz programme', and he largely kept his word.

The new government formed in January 1991 displayed similar composition and orientation with respect to Poland's economic problems, and new Prime Minister Jan Krzysztof Bielecki, an economist by profession and one of the leaders of the Liberal Party, was courageously defending the tough economic programme. But the political situation grew more and more complicated, especially after August 1991, when the coming parliamentary elections dominated the political scene. The election campaign was dominated by ever more virulent attacks on the economic programme, and in the new, fragmented Parliament, formed in November 1991, groups opposing the programme had a stronger representation than in the previous one.

The issue of the political leadership's attitude towards the previous economic programme became almost schizophrenic under the third government, headed by Jan Olszewski. He and some of his ministers were very critical of this programme and came to power under the heading of 'breakthrough' – that is, a radically different strategy. But with respect to fiscal policy, they largely continued the previous line.[16]

The situation became much clearer under the government of Hanna Suchocka, since both she and some of her ministers are representing the reform parties that participated in the first or in the second government. The fact that the new forces of development turned out in 1992 to be stronger than declining tendencies also made it easier to identify in public with the economic programme started three years before.

Dynamics of Political and Economic Reform

The economic strategy in Poland was based mostly on economic principles but was supplemented by some psychological and political constraints. The economic rationale behind the radical economic programme has already been discussed: hyperinflation and massive shortages called for

---

[16] This government started operation at the end of December 1991, when a tough provisional budget for the first quarter of 1992 and some other accompanying laws, prepared by the previous government under my direction, were already in Parliament. The Olszewski government upheld these laws and the budget, claiming that they did not like them but that they had inherited them. Later, probably better understanding the constraints and thanks to Minister of Finance Andrzej Olechowski, the Olszewski government prepared a tough budget for the entire year. Another reason for this continuity was also that the budget department in the Ministry of Finance had been directed since September 1989 by the same person, Deputy Minister Wojciech Misiąg.

tough stabilization measures, the previous unsuccessful attempts at partial reform spoke in favour of launching a comprehensive and radical transformation programme, and so on. But I also remembered from Leon Festinger's (1957) psychological theory of cognitive dissonance that people are more likely to adapt internally to quick, radical changes in their situations if they consider them irreversible than they are to adapt to gradual changes. Finally, I also sensed that the period of 'extraordinary' politics was short-lived and that one should use it to introduce tough economic measures. The full significance of that became obvious only in the second half of 1990 when the political situation deteriorated considerably.

The timing of political events, including the elections, was not planned in advance by any strategic centre because of the conflicts and lack of efficient communication among Solidarity elites. For economic policy-making, the elections were a given – not fully known in advance and, clearly, not with a fortunate outcome. The two successive election campaigns in the first and the second year of implementation of a tough economic programme probably magnified public discontent and certainly contributed to wage pressure and to a slowing in state enterprises' adjustment to the realities of the market economy. In this respect, a contrast can be drawn between Poland and Hungary where, after free elections in early 1990, the next elections were held in 1994. The change of Parliament and even more frequent changes in the ministerial positions have slowed down some important reforms, especially the mass privatization of larger enterprises.

But given the unplanned and uncontrollable sequence of political events and the equally uncontrollable external shocks, it is highly doubtful whether there could have been a radically different economic strategy that would have made more economic sense and would have been politically more acceptable. The main reason for the success of the Polish economic reform seems to be the great speed of its early phase, when fundamentals of a liberal economic system and macroeconomic stability were established. It was easier for the supporters of the market-oriented reforms to defend them as *fait accompli* than it would have been to build reforms gradually in the face of strong populist opposition in Parliament after the elections of October 1991.

Besides this general explanation, there are related, more specific reasons for the sustainability of Polish economic reforms. One of them is the independence of the central bank, introduced as an element of the comprehensive reform package in December 1989 and strengthened in 1991. This independence has allowed the bank to act as a constraint upon an irresponsible budgetary policy. Another reason has been the convertibility of the currency for current account operations, another element of the first reform package. In the absence of convertibility, it would have been easier to engage in populist macroeconomic policies. In this respect, convertibility plays a similar role as a check upon government policies, as does export-oriented growth. Third, the rapid elimination of shortages in a country plagued by them for over forty years provided a strong, popular justification for free prices and, to some extent, for the overall economic programme. The disappearance of queues and the significantly wider range of goods available in the shops contributed the most important forms of popular compensation for the radical economic reform in its early phase.

The fourth reason for the sustainability of economic reform has been the growth of the private sector. True, the privatization of larger enterprises has been delayed for political reasons. But other processes of the overall privatization of the economy – the spontaneous growth of the private sector, small-scale privatization, and privatization of the assets of state enterprises – have been fast. As a result, the share of people employed in the private sector, outside the already largely private agricultural sector, increased from 13.2 per cent in 1989 to 34.4 per cent in 1992.[17] Surveys show that those employed in the private sector are typically much more in favour of the market-oriented reform than employees in the public sector. Privatization has, therefore, an important political dimension.

The failure to introduce mass, unconventional privatization in 1991 and in 1992 based on the free distribution of shares probably thus entailed some foregone gain in political support for market-oriented reform. But the introduction of this privatization could not have positively influenced the economic situation in these years because of the lags between privatization and the change in the economic performance of affected enterprises.

Communicating with the Public

There have been constant and justified complaints that the 'information policy' of the government – that is, the explanation and prediction of the consequences of economic change – was inadequate. There were a

[17] These figures refer to a narrow definition of the private sector that excludes cooperatives. On a broader definition, including the cooperatives, the share of the private sector outside agriculture increased from 31.2 per cent in 1989 to 44.4 in 1992 ('Informacja o sytuacji społeczno-gospodarczej kraju. Rok 1992.' *Główny Urząd Statystyczny*, 1993, p. 51). This shows that a part of the growth of the narrowly defined private sector came from the privatization of parastatal cooperatives.

number of reasons this was so. As far as policy-makers – including myself – were concerned, there was a perennial problem of how to divide the limited time between making economic policy and explaining it. Since the number of problems to be tackled was rather unusual, the time spent on the latter was clearly insufficient. I also found it psychologically and intellectually difficult to make firm predictions. I was reasonably sure of the direction of general developments but could not predict their exact timing and magnitude. But there was the constant demand to commit 'the fallacy of misplaced concreteness': to say when exactly things were going to get better, when the standard of living would rise. The economic reform was helped by the support of practically all the major national newspapers, which published articles and commentaries by a small group of very good economic journalists.

On the other hand, a number of factors served to counter attempts at explaining radical, market-oriented reform to the Polish public. Most of these factors could be regarded as by-products of the transition to democracy. First, in the newly freed mass media and especially in television, which was subjected to especially stringent political control under communism, there emerged a strong tendency to focus on the negative and the sensational. The same was true of most local newspapers. Part of the opposition press constantly presented various conspiracy theories as explanations for the economic difficulties.

Second, the decisive majority of Polish economists were very critical of the programme. This might have conveyed to the public the impression that Polish 'experts' were, on the whole, against the reforms. To some extent, this impression was probably counterbalanced, particularly in 1990, by the echoes of favourable Western opinion.

Third, and by far most important, there were two election campaigns in the first and second years of economic reform. Election campaigns nowadays always have elements of propaganda or psychological 'warfare', given the power of television and radio. This raises the interesting empirical question of how the election campaigns influence the economic views of the public. In Poland, especially in 1991, the media bombarded the Polish public with messages that the Polish economy had been struck by economic catastrophe and that there should be a radically new programme to improve the situation quickly. This proposed programme had three familiar elements: relaxation of monetary and fiscal policies, protectionism and state intervention at the industry level.

Fourth, under the previous regime there was a large apparatus for propaganda and information. The democratic revolution involved the abolition of this structure, and it took time to build a new government information structure to deal with the independent mass media and with the public at large.

External Influences

One should distinguish between external influences with respect to the content of the economic programme and those factors that affected internal support for the programme. In the Polish case, the latter was much more important than the former. In negotiations with the IMF, multilateral banks and Western governments, there was very little pressure with respect to economic strategy and its crucial details because the Polish programme was basically in line with the goals of these organizations.

Within the government and in parliamentary debates, I used conditionality only as additional argument in favour of the economic programme. In other words, I stressed that the programme was motivated by our internal considerations, but in addition, its implementation meant the support of the IMF (and of other international organizations), and this support was needed to make the programme internationally credible and to obtain sizeable debt reduction. This was not only truthful but also probably politically more effective than trying to push through tough measures on the pretext that the IMF had imposed them. This view of conditionality also helped recently to push through the tough budget for 1993. Of importance in increasing the support for the radical stabilization–liberalization package discussed in December 1989 was the prospect of obtaining the $1 billion stabilization fund. This was interpreted as a sign of the positive assessment of the programme by Western governments, and the fund increased the confidence of the reformers in the feasibility of convertibility of the Polish zloty. Without the stabilization fund, convertibility would not have been launched.

General Remarks

CHARACTERISTICS OF THE REFORMERS

Based on introspection and on observations, I cannot help but agree with John Williamson's assertion that there are policy-makers whose characteristics and actions are at sharp variance with the stylized, self-interested politicians of public-choice theory. There are, in my view, two basic differences between 'technopols' and the stereotypical politician. First, his or her economic knowledge may give a 'technopol' – an economic technocrat in a position of political responsibility – a better picture of the available options and their economic and social consequences than is typically the case with career politicians. Second, there are motivational differences. One does not need to speak of altruism in the case of technopols (although it cannot be ruled out), but one may simply state that they attach different 'motivational weights' to economic options than do typical professional politicians. These differences may be partly caused by differences in perception: for example, technopols may more clearly see the danger of populist strategies than other politicians do. Another motivational characteristic is differences in the need for self-esteem. The self-esteem of a technopol suffers if his economic reform is implemented and then fails from an economic standpoint. His self-esteem would probably suffer less if reforms that could have been successful if implemented were socially or politically rejected, costing him a job. The self-esteem of a career politician suffers the most if he loses in the political game. It is also probably of importance that technopols have alternative careers (in the field of academia, business, international financial organizations), and their reputation in those fields depends on how they conducted economic reforms. A professional politician usually has to stick to politics, and abandoning politics may mean a life failure.

'EXTRAORDINARY' VERSUS 'NORMAL' POLITICS

I have used the concept of 'extraordinary politics' to describe the Polish situation in the second half of 1989 and early 1990. But this concept can be generalized to some other historical contexts. 'Extraordinary politics' by definition is a period of very clear discontinuity in a country's history. It could be a period of very deep economic crisis, of a breakdown of the previous institutional system, or of a liberation from external domination (or end of war). In Poland, all these three phenomena converged in 1989.

The new political structures, including political parties and interest groups, are fluid, and in a sense, there are usually no professional politicians during such a period. The older political elite is discredited, and the politicians representing the new order have not yet emerged or have not had enough time to become professional. Among the political elites and the population at large, there is a stronger-than-normal tendency to think and to act in terms of the common good.

In such a case, the period of extraordinary politics both calls for and creates especially favourable conditions for the emergence of technopols. There is no guarantee, though, that they will appear, for there is a large element of chance. Also, the countries that are in greatest need of domestic technopols, because of the past devastation (foreign technopols not usually being admitted to high government positions), are the least likely, because of this devastation, to find them. Depending largely upon whether technopols appear on the scene or not, the increased chances for extraordinary actions inherent in extraordinary politics are used or wasted.

Extraordinary politics is a short period and gives way to 'normal' politics: politics of political parties and of interest groups, a sharply reduced willingness to think and act for the common good, and stronger institutional constraints with respect to the individual political actors. In the period of extraordinary politics, these constraints are fluid or loosely defined.

During the time of normal politics, the appearance and the continued operation of technopols is much less likely than during extraordinary politics.

Public-choice theory, as positioned by James Buchanan and Gordon Tullock (1962) and others, is much more applicable to normal than to extraordinary politics. The main reasons for the latter's inapplicability are the high frequency of technopols reaching positions of power and the fluidity of institutional constraints.

References

Buchanan, James M., & Tullock, Gordon 1962 *The Calculus of Consent*, Ann Arbor: University of Michigan Press.

Festinger, Leon 1957 *A Theory of Cognitive Dissonance*, Stanford, Calif., Stanford University Press.

Rajewski, Zbigniew 1992 'Produkt krajowy brutto', in L. Zienkowski (ed.), *Gospodarka polska w latach 1990–1992*, Warsaw.

Williamson, John (ed.) 1992 *The Political Economy of Policy Reform*, Washington, DC, Institute of Political Economics.

16

Transition to the Market Economy: The Polish Case, 1989–93

The process and outcome of any economic transition depend on (1) the initial conditions, (2) the transition strategy, and (3) the conditions prevailing during the process, which have an effect on it while being largely or entirely independent of the actual transition.

The next section discusses the initial condition, the following section the choice of economic strategy and the conditions for its implementation. Then we deal with the economic outcomes, and the final section deals with the main lessons learned. I concentrate on the economic aspects of Polish reform as I have discussed the political economy in the previous chapter.

Initial Conditions

There are at least five main categories of initial conditions which are especially relevant for the transition to a market economy: (1) the macroeconomic situation, (2) the economic system, (3) the structure of the real economy, (4) the net foreign debt, and (5) the level of human

I obtained useful comments on the first draft of this chapter from Herbert L. Baer Jr., Alfred Bieć, Andrzej Bratkowski, Christopher Giessing, Wojciech Kostrzewa, Anthony Levitas and Andrzej Ochocki. The next version was prepared while I was a Visiting Scholar at the Institute for Human Sciences in 1994, and Vera Budway assisted me in editing it. The present version originally appeared in *Economic Policy*, December 1994, and I obtained useful comments from the editors of the journal, Georges de Menil and John Black. The usual caveats apply.

capital. We can characterize Poland's initial conditions in the middle of 1989 by identifying the state of affairs in each of these five categories and comparing them with the situation found in the other countries of Central and Eastern Europe in their pre-reform stage. This will allow us to determine what conditions were specific to Poland and what conditions were shared by other countries of the region.

Along with other socialist countries Poland had a special type of non-market economic system. This system was dominated by the state sector, characterized by heavy industrial concentration, accompanied by distorted prices due to massive price subsidies and controls, geared to import substitution and deprived of both internal and external competition. There was a regime of multiple exchange rates and the currency was not convertible. Institutions necessary for a market economy were absent, as capitalism had been destroyed and not merely suspended as in West Germany before 1948 or distorted as in Latin America. There was no genuine central bank, nor any true commercial banks, no stock exchange, no governments bonds to finance the budget deficit and no genuine local government.

This system of 'destroyed capitalism' was burdened by an extensive and increasingly inefficient *'socialist welfare state'* which included easily obtainable disability pensions, long maternity leave, relatively long holidays, heavily subsidized sanatoria, cheap holiday facilities for the employees of large state enterprises, etc.

The second typical feature was the *economic structure*, shaped by many years of forced industrialization under import substitution. The industry was 'overgrown' and the service sector underdeveloped. There was a heavy dependence on the Soviet market for exports in such sectors as machinery, textiles, electronics and pharmaceuticals, and for imports of oil and gas at below world market prices. Forty-four per cent of Polish exports in the last pre-reform year (1989) went to the CMEA compared with 45 per cent from Hungary, 51 per cent from Czechoslovakia, 63 per cent from Bulgaria, and 25 per cent from Romania (see Chapter 12). The inefficient economic system and socialist industrial structure left a legacy of serious environmental pollution, especially in regions with a high concentration of mining and heavy industry.

Like the other former socialist countries, Poland suffered from a profound shortage of specialists in marketing, finance, modern accounting and the professional civil service, i.e. in all the fields that are vital for a market economy to function properly. However, one of the few positive legacies of socialism was a fairly high level of *general education*, which allowed specific skills to be rapidly acquired.

Let us now turn to those aspects of the initial conditions in Poland

Table 16.1 *Poland's initial macroeconomic conditions in a comparative perspective**

	Poland	Czechoslovakia	Hungary	Bulgaria	Romania
(1) Broad money (end-year, %)					
1988	63.0	–	–	–	–
1989	526.50	3.5	13.8	10.6	5.3
1990	–	0.5	29.2	16.6	22.0
(2) CPI inflation (end-year, %)					
1988	73.9	–	–	–	–
1989	640.0	1.5	18.9	10.0	0.6
1990	–	18.4	33.4	72.5	37.7
(3) Fiscal balance (GDP %, last pre-reform year	–7.4	0.1	0.5	–12.7	1.2
(4) Repressed wage pressure 1987 until reform (%): change in deflated wage less change in deflated GDP	20.4	–9.1	0.6	20.3	21.6

Source: (1), (2), (3): *Transition Report* (1994), EBRD; (4): see Chapter 12, based on Bruno (1993), World Bank, national sources, and *Planecon*.

* The last pre-reform year for Poland is 1989 and for the other countries 1990.

which clearly departed from those typical for all socialist economies. The most important feature was the *dramatic state of the macroeconomy*. Table 16.1 shows that the macroeconomic imbalance in Poland during the last two pre-reform years was more serious than in Bulgaria and Romania, not to mention Hungary and Czechoslovakia. Poland was the only post-socialist economy (except for the former Yugoslavia) which started its economic transition from a position of near-hyperinflation and massive shortages. The latter are measured by the difference between the 1987-reform change in deflated wages and the same change in deflated GDP. On this measure, repressed inflation in Poland was far more dramatic than in Hungary and Czechoslovakia and similar to that in Bulgaria and Romania.

Another non-typical feature of Poland's initial situation was *the high level of foreign debt*, incurred mostly in the 1970s. Net foreign debt in the last pre-reform year stood at 44 per cent of GDP as compared to 16 per cent in Czechoslovakia, 61 per cent in Hungary, 63 per cent in Bulgaria and 2 per cent in Romania.

Poland's economic system contained fewer elements of the command mechanism and of input rationing than those of most other socialist economies, but it was less reformed than the Hungarian economy. However, the last pre-Solidarity government removed restrictions on the creation and development of private firms and considerably liberalized foreign trade.

Finally, there were two other features which were *strictly specific to Poland*. One of them was the *especially strong position of the workforce*, both within the socio-political system in general and within state enterprises in particular. This was caused by the peculiar nature of Poland's opposition, which originated in 1980 in the form of the trade union 'Solidarity'. After the 'Round Table' negotiations in the spring of 1989, 'Solidarity' was legalized, and it was strongly represented in Parliament. The agreement reached at the 'Round Table' included massive concessions to the more powerful groups of employees (for example, miners and railworkers) and an extreme form of wage indexation. All this had to be eliminated a couple of months later. The strong position of labour was likely to produce irresistible wage pressure and to reduce the scope for the central control of some important processes of change, such as privatization.

Another specific feature was the nominally *private ownership* of 78 per cent of arable land. However, the average size of the 2.7 million private farms was only 7.2 hectares and 30 per cent of farms had less than 2 hectares (their owners were usually farmer-workers). The farmers had functioned for many years in a non-market environment, characterized by a mixture of discrimination and state tutelage. In 1989 they received large *windfall gains*, thanks to large increases in the purchase prices of foodstuffs by the last Communist government. Also, hyperinflation in 1989 practically eliminated the real burden of taxation on farmers, which was low in any case.

Considering all the initial conditions in Poland, we notice that the nominally private agriculture may be regarded as on the positive side. However, given the extreme fragmentation of private agriculture, the windfall gains which had to be eliminated and the potential for numerous private farmers to be mobilized into conservative interest groups within the newly emerging democratic political system, even this feature appears to be a mixed blessing. The same may be said of the more decentralized nature of the Polish economic system. All the other non-typical characteristics of Poland's initial situation: the macro-economic disaster, the especially strong position of labour and the large foreign debt, are clearly on the negative side. We may, therefore, conclude that the starting conditions in Poland were much more difficult than in Czechoslovakia (not to mention the Czech Republic), which had a much more favourable situation on all three counts. The conditions were also less favourable than in Hungary, which shared with Poland a large foreign debt burden, but had inherited a much better macroeconomic situation and much less labour militancy. The degree of the overall difficulties existing in Poland's initial economic conditions appears not to be lower than that of Romania, which had a much more rigid economic system but less dramatic (although serious) macroeconomic imbalance, was much less dependent on the Soviet market for exports and had no foreign debt. Only Bulgaria with its serious macroeconomic instability, large foreign debt, rigid economic system and especially high dependence on the Soviet market appears to have had more difficult initial conditions than Poland.

The Economic Strategy and the Conditions for Its Implementation

Economic strategy developed in three steps: (1) identifying the main problems arising from Poland's initial situation; (2) determining what kind of economy should be reached at the end of the transition process; (3) specifying the types of economic policy measures, their timing and the speed of their implementation.

Poland suffered from two main 'disorders': an extreme macroeconomic imbalance and a faulty economic system, which was responsible for a low and declining overall economic efficiency. There were two additional problems: the distorted economic structure and the huge foreign debt. They were, however, considered to be logically secondary to the macroeconomic and systemic 'disorders': one could not solve the structural and foreign debt problems without eliminating these deficiencies.

The vision of the target system played an important role in guiding the policy measures. They key assumption was that Poland had become free to choose, among other things, its economic order and that it should choose the system which would create the best chances for rapid, long-run economic development. Using this criterion it was easy to determine the main general features of the target economy: macroeconomically stable, competitive, capitalist, outward-looking, equipped with flexible labour markets, etc.

The third step consisted of linking the inherited problems to the perceived solutions. The macroeconomic imbalance called for macro-economic stabilization (the *S* policy), i.e. reducing the budget deficit, controlling the money supply so as to move towards positive real interest rates. In addition, I believed that the institutional imbalance in wage-determination, due to the dominance of the public sector, required wage controls. The case for them was strengthened by the inherited wage–price spiral developed in 1988–89. Such controls were introduced within the comprehensive package of measures launched on 1 January 1990.

The fixed rate of exchange was another 'nominal' anchor. Specifying the level at which it had to be fixed constituted one of the most difficult decisions, preceded by a wide range of alternative proposals.[1]

Poland's macroeconomic imbalance was reflected not only in near-hyperinflation but also in *massive shortages* (repressed inflation). Short-ages in Poland were due to both expansive macroeconomic policies and to the microeconomic distortions and rigidities of prices and supply. This was in contrast to Czechoslovakia, where, given conservative macroeconomic policies, shortages were mostly microeconomically induced. In the Polish case, the *S* policy was to take care of the open inflation and of the macroeconomic component of repressed inflation. The remaining microeconomic determinants of shortages called for microeconomic liberalization, or *L* policy; i.e. enlarging the scope of economic freedom by eliminating a massive and detailed state intervention so as to increase the flexibility of supply and prices.

The second main problem, the *faulty economic system*, required a *fundamental institutional transformation*. This policy, in turn, can be broken down into: (1) the already mentioned microeconomic liberalization and (2) fundamental institutional restructuring (*I* policy) which consists of transforming many organizations and whole institutional subsystems.

The *L* policy, therefore, constituted a common solution to both macroeconomic and the systemic problems. The programme of the *L* policy in Poland was very broad. It included the removal of the remaining restrictions on private activity, liquidation of the remnants of the central allocation of inputs, price liberalization, removal of the bulk of the quantitative restrictions on exports and imports, unification of the exchange rate and the introduction of the convertibility of the Polish zloty for current account operations.

The programme of *deep institutional restructuring* was also very

---

[1] The same was true of Czechoslovakia, where the setting of the rate of exchange at CSK 28 per US$ was preceeded by proposals ranging from CSK 16 to 35–40 per US$ (see Klacek & Hrncir, 1994).

pervasive due to the legacy of 'destroyed capitalism'. The most important steps were: privatization of the bulk of the state sector, breaking up domestic monopolies and introducing tough anti-monopoly legislation, strengthening the institutional independence of the central bank, reform of the financial sector, the reform of insurance, tax reform, the creation of genuine local government, and the establishment of a social safety net.

The S, L and I policies were assumed to be key elements of the solutions to two additional inherited problems: the distorted structure of the 'real' economy and the huge foreign debt. The economic structure is the product of past investment and production decisions, and these are strongly influenced by the systemic and macroeconomic framework. This is why a change in these two areas is crucial. But some parts of the industrial structure, where the need for quick downsizing was especially great and the informational requirements for the central decision-makers were relatively simple, called for and allowed a *strictly selective restructuring policy*. Such a policy, limited basically to mining, energy and metallurgy, was included in the overall economic programme. It had, however, nothing to do with the typical 'industrial policy' of picking winners or bailing out losers.

The future burden of the inherited foreign debt and the capacity to service it depended on Poland's development which in turn was strongly influenced by the policy of systemic transformation and that of macroeconomic stabilization. But given the huge size of the debt and the wretched state of the Polish economy, economic development would have been impossible without radical *debt reduction and restructuring*. The chances for obtaining such a reduction from the Western creditors, especially from the Western governments who owned two-thirds of the Polish debt, depended on Poland's adoption of a comprehensive and radical economic programme, which was in any case required on domestic grounds.

The economic strategy dealt not only with the type of measures to be taken, but also with their phasing and speed of implementation. Phasing determines how various measures are combined in time. For example, one could have delayed stabilization and price liberalization until enterprises were privatized. This was the essence of the 500 Days Plan in Russia proposed in 1990 but not implemented (Fisher 1994). This option was never seriously considered by the economic team in Poland, as it would have implied among other things tolerating inflation for a longer time, thus increasing the costs and difficulty of its eventual elimination. The alternative strategy of a largely simultaneous launching of S, L and I was thus selected.

Each policy measure has its maximum possible speed of implementation; it is much higher for S and L than for most of I policy. One can term 'radical' those policy options the speed of which is close to the maximum possible one. 'Gradualist' options by definition, clearly depart from this speed. Poland opted for radical stabilization. Trying to stop inflation slowly was perceived as a hopeless task. We also chose radical L and I policies to be launched together, and simultaneously with S policy. The case for such a strategy was based on the perceived failures of previous gradualist reforms and on the assumed existence of strong synergistic links between various policies. For example, radical price liberalization was required for a rapid improvement in relative prices without which, in turn, the autonomous decisions of enterprises could have socially undesirable consequences, and the bankruptcy mechanisms would have eliminated some efficient enterprises. Radical price liberalization was also needed for a rapid elimination of shortages, which was necessary both for consumers' welfare and for the more efficient operation of the enterprises. But such a liberalization had to be accompanied by swift elimination of quantitative and other restrictions in foreign trade in order to introduce competitive pressure on domestic enterprises, freed from the command mechanism; to increase the flexibility of supply which was along with price liberalization a precondition for eliminating shortages; and to link domestic prices to world market prices. All these links make for *indivisibility of liberalization*. Radical price liberalization and dismantling of the command mechanism (either in the form of traditional central planning or in the guise of 'government orders') were necessary for avoiding a situation whereby the controlled enterprises would lobby successfully for open or hidden subsidies, thus undermining required radical liberalization. Successful stabilization, therefore, required radical liberalization. Rapid price liberalization, however, had to be safeguarded by a tough S policy, if one were to avoid the initial price jump leading to sustained high inflation. Finally, it was assumed that privatization and other institutional reforms can bring full results only under increased macroeconomic stability, but also that some of these reforms (e.g. the tax reform) were needed to sustain and strengthen macroeconomic improvements. These were the mutual links between L and I.[2]

These economic considerations were sufficient for choosing a comprehensive and radical S, L and I programme. But there were also some important considerations regarding the political environment for

[2] These were some of the conclusions I reached in the 1980s in my work on comparative economic systems, on the inefficiency of the socialist economy and on its transformation (Balcerowicz 1989a and b).

the economic reform which strengthened the case for such a programme and for launching it quickly after the great political breakthrough that occurred in the middle of 1989. A gradual or delayed reform would mean wasting the political capital presented by public readiness to accept difficult radical economic steps. This sort of political capital is a typical benefit of any large-scale political breakthrough, but it quickly vanishes, giving way instead to 'normal' politics conducted by political parties, a game of special interests. Finally, social psychology tells us that people are more prone to adjust their attitudes to the surrounding environment when this environment has just undergone profound change than when it is going through gradual change.

This strategy was developed into a detailed programme in 1989 in cooperation with an IMF team and the assistance of a group of Polish and foreign advisers. A comprehensive and radical economic programme was launched early in January 1990. It focused on stabilization, liberalization, changes in the tax system and the social safety net. A comprehensive privatization law was accepted in February by the government and passed by parliament in July. Some other laws on the strengthening of the central bank and on institutional restructuring were passed in the first half of 1990, such as a law on insurance, an anti-monopoly law, a bankruptcy law, and a law disbanding the compulsory association of cooperatives.

The institutional reforms in 1991 included a new securities law and the establishment of a stock exchange, a new liberal foreign investment law, a law on a comprehensive income tax, and a new budgetary law. The growth of the private sector and the related privatization of state enterprises assets continued to be very rapid, but the privatization of larger state enterprises was rather slow, due mostly to political complications. On the macroeconomic front, in May 1991 the zloty was devalued and pegged to a basket of currencies instead of a previous peg to the US dollar. In October a crawling peg was introduced. Other changes included modification in the wage control mechanism, which was attacked by the trade unions but maintained.

The turn of 1991 and 1992 marked a visible political change. After the two reformist governments of Tadeusz Mazowiecki and Jan Krysztof Bielecki, the parliamentary elections in October 1991 gave rise to a coalition government of Jan Olszewski which started out claiming it would make a sharp break with the past. (The author ended his public service in December 1991.) But this government gradually toned down its revisionist declarations and, basically, continued a disciplined fiscal policy, constrained by a rather strict monetary policy of the largely independent central bank. However, privatization of larger state enterprises was practically brought to a halt. The Olszewski government collapsed in June 1992 and was replaced by the coalition government of Hanna Suchocka. It largely continued the economic strategy launched in 1990, although it made some concessions to various interest groups, especially farmers. This government was brought down by a non-confidence vote in parliament, which was then dissolved by the president; the elections in September 1993 gave rise to a coalition government of the two post-communist parties. It slowed down some institutional reforms, especially enlarging the competences of local government and banks' privatization. At least until 1994, it continued a disciplined fiscal policy.

As one can see, the Polish economic programme was implemented under complicated political conditions, especially after late 1990, and increasingly since the second half of 1991.[3] Frequent election campaigns gave occasions for displays of populism, which must have unfavourably affected the expectations and consequently the actions of economic agents; this resulted in renewed wage pressure and in the reduced inclination of state enterprises to take difficult restructuring decisions. With strong and rather aggressive trade unions, frequent elections and a fragmented party system, Poland had a much more difficult political environment for economic reform than Hungary or the Czech Republic.

Another group of conditions which could influence the economic transition were the external economic developments. In the case of Poland there was much difficulty, because of the collapse of Polish exports to the former Soviet Union and a sharp deterioration in terms of trade. The CMEA shock is estimated to have cost Poland between 3.5 and 5 per cent of its GDP in 1991. The relative shock was even larger for the smaller Central European economies; its impact on Hungary was put at 8 to 10 per cent, on Czechoslovakia at 6 to 9 per cent, on Romania at 10 per cent, and on Bulgaria at 16 to 21 per cent (Bruno 1993; Rodrik 1993; Rossati 1993).

Economic Outcomes

Before discussing economic outcomes it must be emphasized that the standard statistical data are bound to display a negative bias: on the one

---

[3] It is wrong to attribute these complications mainly to the radical nature of the economic programme (Balcerowicz 1993b). This is why political developments in Poland can be regarded as conditions which were largely independent from this programme but which influenced its outcomes.

hand, they are incapable of measuring the positive developments properly (for example, the rapid growth of the private sector on the elimination of shortages); on the other hand, they present as new social costs certain negative phenomena which were not shown before, because they used to exist in a disguised form (such as repressed inflation or hidden unemployment). The magnitude of this bias is likely to be especially pronounced in the case of radical economic programmes such as Poland's, as these reforms generate particularly rapid growth of positive processes which are underreported (like the growth of the private sector) and quickly turn the hidden costs into open ones, which are fully reported (see Chapter 12 for further details on this point).

In addition, in the Polish case complications related to hyper-inflation before the reform had led the statistical office to serious mistakes; practically all of them have darkened the statistical picture of the subsequent transition.[4] Finally, some observers use the standard data in a way which does not make much economic sense and distorts the comparison of various post-socialist economies.[5]

Economic outcomes can be defined as changes in the magnitude of the four inherited problems: extreme macroeconomic instability, faulty economic system, distorted structure of the 'real economy' and the huge foreign debt.

MACROECONOMIC OUTCOMES[6]

The key macroeconomic outcome is the reduction of the magnitude of open and repressed inflation. The annualized consumer price index

---

[4] One example was to hugely overestimate the increase in stocks in 1990 which, *ceteris paribus*, led to an equal overestimation of the decline in consumption. For more on this and other mistakes see Bratkowski (1993), Rajewski (1993), and Berg (1993b)

[5] A popular fallacy consists in using 1989 as a base year for calculating subsequent declines in 'real' wages, which are regarded (explicitly or implicitly) as measures of changes in the standard of living. This procedure disregards the fact that in some countries (Poland in 1988–89, Russia in 1990–91) nominal wages by far outpaced prices in the pre-reform year, which inflated 'real' wages and contributed to their sharp decline during the reform. Needless to say, the rapid increases in 'real' wages resulted mainly in increased shortages (see Table 16.2). Such increases did not occur in Czechoslovakia or Hungary. Therefore, to take 1989 as a base year gives a false impression of declines in living standards. This mistake lies behind the claim that in 1990 'real' wages in Poland declined by 25 per cent as compared to, e.g. 4 per cent in Hungary in 1991. A more correct procedure is to take a pre-inflation year as base year, e.g. 1987. Relative to that base, deflated wages have declined by 9.4 per cent in Poland and by 10 per cent in Hungary (see Chapter 12).

[6] For the sake of brevity this section omits more detailed issues such as fluctuations in the budget deficit, the real rate of exchange or the stringency of the wage controls. These issues are discussed in Berg (1993a,b), Gomulka (1994); IMF (1994); Sachs (1993); and Wellisz *et al.* (1993).

during the last five months of 1989 stood at about 3,000 per cent (Herer and Sadowski, 1994). CPI inflation (end-year) in 1990 was 249 per cent, in 1991 60.4 per cent, in 1992 44.3 per cent and in 1993 37.6 per cent. While the level of inflation is clearly still too high, one should compare Poland's *disinflation* with those in high-inflation Latin American countries. In Chile and Mexico it took roughly seven years to reduce three-digit inflation to 15–20 per cent (Solimano, 1993). It should be stressed that disinflation in Poland happened while relative prices were radically altered and that this required huge rises in some key prices, especially those of energy.

Shortages and queues were quickly eradicated. Simultaneously, there was an improvement in the range and quality of goods. To begin with, this improvement was mainly due to imports, but in time it was increasingly due to the improved availability of domestic products.

Rapid disinflation and elimination of shortages resulted, as expected, from the combination of S and L policies. Radical stabilization took care of the demand component of both open and repressed inflation. The rate of growth of broad money declined from 515 per cent in 1989 to 166 per cent in 1990 and 58 per cent in 1992. The fixed rate of exchange until May 1991 and wage controls throughout 1990–93 helped to break inflationary inertia and inflationary expectations.[7] These S policies were necessary and sufficient to end hyperinflation. However, shortages are caused by price and supply rigidities, and – given these rigidities – magnified by expansionary monetary policy. Therefore in the Polish case the rapid elimination of shortages resulted both from radical macroeconomic stabilization and comprehensive microeconomic liberalization, i.e. price decontrol, removal of restrictions with respect to the private sector and foreign trade liberalization. These measures significantly increased the flexibility of supply and prices.

Table 16.2 shows that Poland achieved by far the most radical disinflation.[8] At the other extreme is Romania, where the inflation rate (end-year) was 7.5 times higher in 1993 than in 1990. Hungary achieved modest disinflation while the Czech Republic returned to its relatively low pre-reform level of inflation, followed by Slovakia. The most radical disinflation was accompanied in Poland with the lowest cumulative

---

[7] Pinto and van Wijnbergen (1994) have shown that wage controls in Poland played an important role in limiting wage increases.

[8] This is true even if we take the year 1992 for Poland to allow for the fact that the economic programme in Poland started a year earlier than elsewhere. The disinflation indicator is then still 0.07 (for end-year CPI).

Table 16.2 *Poland's macroeconomic developments in a comparative perspective, 1990–93*

	Poland		Czech Republic		Slovakia		Hungary		Bulgaria		Romania	
	End-year	Av.	End-year	Av.	End-year	Av.	End-year	Av.	End-year	Av.	End-year	Av.
(1) CPI inflation (%)												
1989	640.0	251.0	1.5	2.3	1.5	2.3	18.9	17.0	10.0	6.4	0.6	1.1
1990	249.0	585.6	18.4	10.8	18.4	10.8	33.4	28.9	72.5	23.9	37.6	5.1
1991	60.4	70.3	52.0	56.7	58.3	61.2	32.2	35.0	339.0	334.0	222.8	174.5
1992	44.3	43.0	12.7	11.1	9.2	10.1	21.6	23.0	79.0‡	82.0	199.2	10.9
1993	37.6	35.3	18.2	20.8	24.8	23.0	21.1	22.5	64.0‡	73.0	295.5	256.1
Disinflation†	0.06	0.14	1.0	2.0	1.3	2.1	0.64	0.74	0.9	3.0	7.5	50.0
(2) GDP (%)												
1990	-11.6		-1.2		-2.5		-3.3		-9.1		-8.2	
1991	-7.6		-14.2		-14.5		-11.9		-11.7		-13.7	
1992	1.5		-7.1		-7.0		-5.0		-7.7		-15.4	
1993	4.0		-0.5		-4.7		-2.0		-6.0		1.0	
Cumulative†	-13.8		-21.6		-26.1		-20.7		-30.4		-32.3	
(3) Consumption *%)												
1990	-11.7		2.4		–		-3.5		-0.6		9.0	
1991	3.3		-7.2		–		-5.3		-8.3		-11.6	
1992	5.0		-7.1§		–		-2.0		-7.7		-8.5	
1993	5.3‡		2.2		–		0–2		–		1.1	
Cumulative†	0.8		-8.8		-8.9		-8.7 to -10.4		–		-10.8	
(4) Fixed capital formation (%)												
1990	-10.6		6.5		5.2		-7.1		-18.5		-35.6	
1991	-4.5		-26.8		-28.1		-11.6		-19.9		-26.0	
1992	-2.8		3.8		1.0		-6.4		-1.5		-2.1	
1993	-1.0		-10.5		-21.0		0–5		-8.0		-0.8	
Cumulative†	-11.4		-28.6		-39.7		-19.2 to -23.0		-39.9		-53.2	

Source: CPI inflation: *The Transition Report 1994*; EBRD (forthcoming); other data: *Economic Survey of Europe in 1993–1994.*

Notes: * Measured by the ratio of 1993 inflation to the rate of inflation in the last pre-reform year (1989 for Poland, 1990 for other countries). † Calculated by linking the annual indices of GDP (with previous year = 100) from 1990 to 1993. ‡ Estimate, *Transition Report*, EBRD. § There are no official data for 1992; I have assumed a decline in consumption equal to that of GDP; i.e. 7.1 per cent. This assumption is on the optimistic side as, according to official data, gross fixed investment increased by 3.8 per cent.

declines in GDP, consumption and fixed capital formation.[9] The differences in the rates of this decline were a joint product of the differences in initial conditions, external conditions and economic policies. An extensive analysis is needed to assess the weights of these factors. We can only say here that the differences in the rates of decline in GDP cannot be fully explained by differences in the magnitude of the CMEA shock, suffered by the respective countries. Even after using the estimates above to eliminate the CMEA shock effects, notable differences remain in cumulative GDP decline: GDP in Poland is estimated to have declined by 8.8 to 10.3 per cent for non-CMEA reasons; the estimate for Hungary is 10.7 to 12.7 per cent, for the Czech Republic 12.6 is 15.6 per cent,[10] for Bulgaria 9.4 to 14.4 per cent[11] and for Romania 22 per cent. One should also remember that Hungary and the Czech Republic did not need to experience a contraction due to the macroeconomic stabilization shock, which was necessary in the Polish case because of its specific initial conditions. The other countries also suffered this stabilization shock to a lesser extent than Poland. Much remains, therefore, to be explained by the differences in economic policy. To my mind, one of the features which distinguished Poland's economic programme was radical and comprehensive liberalization (partly started as early as 1989), combined with a decisive increase in fiscal and monetary discipline. This combination of measures sharply reduced inflation and produced a very rapid growth of the private sector which was fuelled by the transfer of assets from the – financially constrained – SOEs. In time, increased autonomy, competition, hardened budget constraints and the anticipation of privatization induced a substantial number of state companies to adjust (Pinto *et al.*, 1993).

Among the other countries under comparison, Romania until late 1993 conducted an economic policy which was diametrically different from that pursued by Poland; it was a policy of stop-go gradualism in liberalization, and of maintaining a soft budget constraint with respect to the SOEs (see Chapter 12). It should not, therefore, be surprising that compared to Poland, Romania achieved the worst results both with

[9] This conclusion remains true if, for the sake of complete comparability, we take for Poland the period 1990–92, and for other countries 1991–93.

[10] The decline in the Czech GDP corrected for the estimated reduction in GDP due to the CMEA-shock is even larger because this estimate of 6–9 per cent referred to the former Czechoslovakia, and the Czech Republic was less affected than Slovakia.

[11] The relatively low figures may to some extent be due to the fact that in 1992 Bulgaria reduced the official estimate of the decline in real value added between 1989 and 1991 by about 12 percentage points (see Bartholdy, 1994).

regard to inflation and to GDP. Romania's initial economic conditions do not appear to be more complicated than Poland's. Romania's performance suggests, therefore, what would have happened to the Polish economy during 1990–93, had Poland rejected a comprehensive and radical economic programme and opted instead for a much 'softer' approach.

The above remarks on Poland's disinflation-GDP performance *relative* to other post-socialist economies were based on official statistics – not only out of necessity but also on the assumption that the 'negative bias' in these statistics is not *less pronounced* for Poland than for other countries (see previous section). This assumption is not justified, however, if one wants to compare with Polish economic performance (or that of other post-socialist economies) with the performance of non-postsocialist countries; in the latter the transition-specific statistical biases are not present. For such comparisons one should use, for Eastern European economies, data which are freed from such distortions. This is especially necessary with respect to the GDP declines, which conventional wisdom holds to be 'unprecedented', and comparable only with the contraction experienced by the Western countries during the Great Depression. This view, however, does not hold water, at least in the case of Poland. An investigation conducted by the Research Centre of the Polish Statistical Office ('Rachunki narodowe . . .', 1993) puts the corrected cumulative decline in Poland's GDP at about 14 per cent for 1990–91, at 12 per cent for 1990–92 and at 8 per cent for 1990–93. These corrections did not include the effects of the unrecorded growth of the private sector. Another investigation estimated the impact of this factor but disregarded other biases and ended with an estimate of a 5–10 per cent decline in Poland's GNP in 1990–91 (Rajewski 1993). These estimates, for a country which started its radical economic transition under hyperinflation and experienced powerful shocks, should be compared with the contradictions suffered by some non-postsocialist economies. During the Great Depression GDP declined in the USA by 30 per cent, in Germany by 23.5 per cent, and in France by 16.7 per cent. In Great Britain, during the transition from a war to a peace economy after 1945, aggregate output declined by more than 10 per cent below the peak of the 'war economy'. And 'out of 129 countries for which data are available over the approximate period 1960–89/90, more than half have experienced at least one period of cumulative losses . . . of 10 per cent or more.' Among them was Chile with a contraction of 18 per cent, Argentina with 12 per cent, Peru with 18 per cent and Uruguay with 16 per cent (Fozouni *et al.*, 1992).

SYSTEMIC OUTCOMES

Systemic outcomes are changes in the relative prices and in the institutional framework of the economy. The main changes are outlined in this section.

On account of the radical liberalization carried out in early 1990 and supplemented by the decontrol of the price of coal in 1991, about 90 per cent of the total volume of transactions was conducted at *free prices*. Price liberalization and radical increases in the controlled prices of energy produced a *much improved structure of relative prices*. A synthetic measure of this improvement is that the ratio of the official rate of exchange to the purchasing power parity rate fell from almost 5 in late 1989 to 1.9 at the end 1993, compared with 3 to 2.5 for the Czech Republic; and to 2.4 to 1.7 for Hungary (*Polish Economic Monitor*, 1994).

The role of money as a medium of exchange increased significantly, as the Polish zloty became freely convertible into goods (thanks to the elimination of shortages). The unification of the exchange rate made a huge contribution to the improvement in relative prices and led to the convertibility of the Polish zloty for current account transactions. The Polish zloty, therefore, became convertible not only into goods but also into other currencies. The reduction in inflation and a sharp rise in real interest rates also greatly enhanced the role of the Polish zloty as a medium for savings.

The liberalization of the general regime of property rights and foreign trade liberalization, carried out in 1988–89, allowed *free entry* into the Polish economy. As a result, in 1990–93 more than one million new private firms were created (Gomulka & Jasinski 1994).

The *exit mechanisms* have been strengthened at a much slower pace. They hardly existed at the start of the reforms, and it takes much longer to develop them (for example, to train bankers, bankruptcy judges and liquidators), than to remove the restrictions which block free entry. Also, economically justified exit requires proper relative prices, and these take some time to appear. But the delay of exit processes was longer than planned, because the state enterprises had more reserves (stocks of raw materials bought at the low prices, foreign currency deposits, real assets to be sold or leased, etc.) than had been expected. As a result, outright liquidations and bankruptcies in 1990–91 were fewer than expected, but many large enterprises underwent a radical down-sizing by selling or leasing assets to the private sector, which contributed to the development of that private sector. This *gradual form of exit* turned out to be the dominant one. It was brought about by a visible hardening of the enterprises' budget constraints: the correlation between profits across enterprises before and after taxes and subsidies increased for a sample of 1,899 large industrial enterprises from 0.38 in 1989 to 0.71 in 1991 (Berg 1993b).

Poland's economy has been becoming increasingly more private. The share of the private sector, excluding agriculture and cooperatives, grew from 13.2 per cent of the total workforce in 1989 to 34.4 per cent in 1992. If we include agriculture and cooperatives, the share of employment in the private sector jumps to about 60 per cent of employment at the end of 1992 and to about 50 per cent of the GDP. The share of output produced by the private sector in manufacturing increased from 7.4 per cent in 1989 to 36.6 in 1993, the corresponding figures for construction output are 33.4 and 85 per cent.

The rapid privatization of the Polish economy was mainly due to the fast development in the private sector, which was supported, as noted, by the transfer of assets from the state enterprises through leasing or sales (Berg 1993b; Rostowski 1993; Gomulka & Jasiński 1994). The privatization of small and medium state-owned enterprises has been rapid, but privatization of large enterprises was rather slow, because of political factors such as frequent changes of governments and privatiz-ation ministers. Proposals to accelerate privatization began to become the subject of political struggles in the second half of 1991.

The rapid growth of a number of mostly small private firms, the spontaneous down-sizing of the larger state firms and the de-mon-opolization of a number of industries imposed by the government in 1990–91 (for example, in the meat industry, the sugar industry and bus transport) produced a rapid *organizational deconcentration* of the Polish economy. Employment in industrial firms with 51–100 employees increased in 1989 to 1991, by 202 per cent, while that in firms employing over 5,000 workers declined by 35.6 per cent (Góra 1992). There was a surge in employment in small firms (those with up to 50 employees). This is, however, not captured by Polish official statistics.

The organizational deconcentration, combined with the liberal-ization of foreign trade and a liberal regime of property rights has increased the flexibility of supply and the competitive pressure upon the suppliers.

In the first half of the 1989 Poland's banking sector started to depart from the typical socialist *banking sector*, characterized by a monobank structure with its non-commercial criteria for the allocation of credits, total quantitative controls of the volume of credit, no clear separation between the banking system and the state budget, a ban on trade credit, etc. (Balcerowicz 1993a). There has been an accelerated change and much 'learning by doing' in the banking sector since early 1990. The central bank has been made more independent of the government and Parliament and its policy towards the commercial banks has become increasingly market-based and indirect (Kostrzewa 1994).

The number of commercial banks increased from seven to more than eighty (disregarding the cooperatives), and they have undergone a thorough technical modernization process and transition to commercially-based lending practices under growing competition. However, the lack of experience and the unusual level of uncertainty in the economy due to the very process of its transformation under powerful external shocks, have led to the accumulation of bad debts. They were *estimated to be at the level of 20 to 30 per cent* of the banks' total portfolios by the end of 1992 (*The Banking System in Poland* 1993) and at 5.2 per cent of Poland's GDP. In early 1993 an innovative law on the financial restructuring of banks and enterprises was adopted to deal with the issue.

In May 1991 nine large commercial banks were turned into joint-stock companies and staffed with independent supervisory boards in order to shield the banks' management from political interference. Three banks had been privatized by March 1994.

Another segment of the financial sector, *the non-banking financial institutions* and the stock exchange, had to be built totally from scratch. A technologically modern stock exchange was opened in July 1991. There is a small but growing number of non-banking financial institutions, providing equity capital. They should play an increasingly important role as they are on average better suited than the banks to finance projects with high levels of risk, of the kind that is inherently linked to economic transition.

During 1990–93 Poland made the transition from the complicated and fragmented *tax system* typical of a socialist economy to a modern Western-type system. The corporation tax was stripped of its previous numerous exemptions. A modern personal income tax was introduced early in 1992, and a value added tax in July 1993. The tax offices were increasingly computerized and a fiscal police department was introduced in 1992. Despite all these developments, tax evasion has undoubtedly grown. This is largely an unavoidable consequence of successful liberalization, which has resulted in the rapidly growing number of mostly small and private firms and the inevitably slower pace at which the tax administration has been strengthened (see also Chapter 13).

On the *expenditure side of the fiscal system*, many extra-budgetary funds were eliminated in 1990 making Poland's public finances much more integrated and transparent. Budgetary procedures were clarified and streamlined thanks to a new budgetary law enacted in 1991. There were some changes in the financial framework of the health service. But a fundamental reform is still under discussion.

Along with the introduction of a radical reform programme in early 1990 and the related elimination or drastic reduction of price subsidies and the reduction of the role of state enterprises as centres of welfare services, a targeted system of *unemployment and social assistance* has been developed. However, it still leaves much to be desired.

The pension and invalidity system turned out to be a special problem in Poland's transition to a market economy. Because of demographic trends, the overgenerous indexation of pensions introduced in 1990, and the regulations which allowed employees to obtain a pension while continuing to work, the share of social security subsidies in total budgetary expenditure increased from 13 per cent in 1989 to about 28 per cent in 1993 and pension expenditure jumped from 7 per cent of GDP in 1988 to 15 per cent in 1993 ('Emerytury i renty . . .' 1993). The number of pensioners in Poland increased by 4.1 per cent in 1990 and by 11.8 per cent in 1991, compared with 1.1 and 2.1 per cent in Czechoslovakia. This difference explains much of the difference in the fiscal developments in 1991–92 between the two countries (Barbone & Marchetti 1993). The future of the pension system became a political issue in 1990, so only a partial correction to the regulations has been possible, and this problem has contributed to a fiscal crisis.

Conclusions: *on the systemic outcomes* Poland has made large strides towards a competitive, private-enterprise market economy. There has been a huge improvement in the structure of relative prices and in incentives for exports, input saving and quality-enhancing innovations. The ownership structure has been changing rapidly, mainly due to the radical S–L programme and less so to the privatization of the state-owned enterprises. Due to the unavoidably slower pace of thorough institutional restructuring, product markets have been improving much faster than the labour and capital markets. The developments in the pension system have probably been the weakest part in Poland's economic transition. Another weak spot has been the slow pace of privatization of the larger state-owned enterprises, due to political complications. The remaining agenda includes privatization of most of the remaining state-owned enterprises and of the banks, the development of the financial sector, carrying out major reforms in the health service, education and the social security system. These reforms are necessary to increase efficiency and the macro-economic stability of the Polish economy and thus to sustain rapid economic development.

CHANGES IN THE 'REAL' ECONOMY

The macroeconomic stabilization and the market-oriented reform produced many important changes in the real economy.

Output restructuring at an aggregate level is reflected in the declining share of industry (including construction) from 52.3 per cent of the GDP in 1989 to 46.6 per cent in 1991. In contrast, the share of the service sector has increased from 34.8 to 46 per cent (*Rocznik Statystyczny* 1993).

Telecommunications have been growing rapidly: the number of telephones installed between 1985 and 1989 increased by 38,000 and between 1989 and 1993 by 310,000 (*Biuletyn Statystyczny* 1994). Thus the fastest growing sectors have been the ones which were the most neglected under socialism. But the most important changes in the composition of output have been reflected in the introduction of many new or improved products in practically every industry. This is largely due to the adaptation and imitation of goods from the more advanced countries – a rational procedure for a latecomer.[12]

Output restructuring is part of a broader process of *technical change and improved efficiency*. There are so far no studies which would show the changes in total factor productivity, country-wide or with respect to the large sectors,[13] but all the available partial information indicates that the typical symptoms of socialist inefficiency are rapidly disappearing:

- The tonnage of goods transported has declined by 43 per cent between 1989 and 1992 (*Biuletyn Statystyczny* 1994), much more than the decline in GDP. This reflects both the reduction in the relative importance of mining and heavy industry and the rationalization of the network of supplier–buyer relationships.
- The value-added produced in private agriculture increased by 4.8 per cent in 1990 and by a further 24.7 per cent in 1991 as a result of economizing on the use of inputs of chemical fertilizers and pesticides in response to their sharply increased prices.

[12] Polish hardware and software computer firms numbered 800 in late 1993, with total sales of about 1 billion US dollars. Warsaw Computer Expo fairs are the largest and most prestigious event of this kind in Central and Eastern Europe (*Gazeta Bankowa*, Komputer Expo 1994). Another indicator is the surge in the number of new product types exported to Germany: 3,500 in 1993 against 1,500 in 1992, consisting mostly of high quality products (Mylonas, 1994)

[13] Such studies should operate with measures of aggregate output, corrected for improvements in the quality and availability of goods, which are not captured by the conventional statistics.

- The traditionally low share of expenditure on machines and equipment has been rising; it was higher in 1993 than in 1989. In contrast, expenditure on construction has been declining. This is mainly due to the shift from the large state-financed investment projects to numerous small and increasingly privately financed projects, with the focus on renovation and modernization.
- Investment in machinery and equipment has been growing rapidly. Especially rapid growth occurred in imports of investment goods from the OECD countries, which in 1990–92 rose by over 150 per cent (Bratkowski 1993). This may be interpreted as an indicator of the growth of the technical quality of the installed machines and equipment.

Since 1990 there has been a *rapid decline in the volume of all types of pollutants*. The amount of waste water fed into rivers in 1992 was 40 per cent lower than in 1989; that of liquid pollutants declined by 50 per cent, and the emission of gaseous pollutants decreased by 40 per cent. This decline in the production of environmental 'bads' has been achieved by the aforementioned changes in the structure and efficiency of production. At the same time outlays for environmental conservation and to save water increased from 3.7 per cent of total national investment in 1990 to 6.5 per cent in 1992 (*Rocznik Statystyczny*, 1993).

Profound changes occurred in the role of *foreign trade*. Exports to the West increased by 60.8 per cent in 1990–91 and by 13 per cent in 1992–93; imports by 53 and 40 per cent.[14] This appears to represent trade expansion and not just the effect of the reorientation of exports from East to West (Mylonas 1994). Poland became a much more open economy, much more strongly linked to the advanced economies of the OECD countries, especially Western Europe. The annual inflow of *foreign direct investment* increased from about US$ 60 million in 1989 and US$ 105 million in 1990 to over US$ 1.5 billion in 1993 (Kubielas, 1994).

Radical changes in relative prices and the removal of shortages brought about rapidly increased *purchases of consumer durables* which became relatively cheaper and much more available on the market. As a result there has been a fast rise in the share of households possessing them – see Table 16.3. Interestingly enough, this jump in the possession of consumer durables was not accompanied by a decrease in the average consumption of meat or fruit. At the same time the share of total

---

[14] In 1992 to 1993 there has been a large increase in Polish–German cross-border trade, consisting mostly of Polish exports which were not recorded in the official trade statistics.

Table 16.3 *Percentage of various kinds of households possessing particular consumer durables (end of year)*

	Employee households (%)		Farm households (%)		Pensioner households (%)	
	1989	1992	1989	1992	1989	1992
Radio (stereo)	22.6	40.8	6.0	14.8	5.4	13.4
Colour TV	50.7	91.4	19.8	48.9	21.0	52.7
Video player	4.7	53.4	0.9	15.5	0.7	13.5
Tape recorder (stereo)	24.3	49.8	8.0	24.6	4.3	13.4
Automatic washing machine	59.1	69.7	23.2	28.5	27.3	39.5
Freezer	20.3	30.3	33.7	56.6	9.1	16.3
Car	30.7	41.4	30.4	41.7	9.2	15.0

Source: GUS (Main Statistical Office).

expenditure going on energy increased sharply, due to a radical increase in energy prices from an extremely low level in 1989.

The last Polish change to be discussed refers to the labour market. The radical economic programme in Poland brought about a decline in official employment and a sharp increase in recorded unemployment.[15] From 1990 to 1992 total employment in Poland declined by 10.4 per cent, as compared to 8.8 per cent in the Czech Republic, 13.5 per cent in Slovakia, 12.1 per cent in Hungary, 28.7 per cent in Bulgaria and 4.5 per cent in Romania.[16] Official unemployment at the end of 1992 stood in Poland at 13.6 per cent, in the Czech Republic at 2.6 per cent, in Slovakia at 14.4 per cent, in Hungary at 12.9 per cent, in Bulgaria at 16.4 per cent and in Romania at 10.1 per cent. Thus, the decline in employment in Poland was (disregarding Romania) the lowest after the Czech one. The

---

[15] The reader must be warned that the official concepts of employment and unemployment, borrowed from the market economies, are highly misleading in transition economies. Formal employment includes hidden unemployment, which varies widely across the latter economies, depending on their economic programme. This, of course, bears directly on the level of official unemployment. For example, on the formal definitions, there was full employment in Ukraine in 1993 and unemployment of 15.7 per cent in Poland, while the decline in Ukrainian GDP from 1990 to 1993 was 39.3 per cent, while in Poland GDP declined by 13.8 per cent. Also, official unemployment includes an increase in the number of people employed in the second economy, and that number also varies across transition economies. It was estimated that in the region of Łódź, in Poland, one with an especially high rate of unemployment, the number of people employed in the second economy equalled that of recorded unemployment persons (Iwaszkiewicz & Zarychta 1994).
[16] Data drawn from *Economic Report* (1994) except for Poland, for which official Polish data are used (IMF 1994).

relatively high unemployment rate in Poland, especially as compared to that in the Czech Republic, cannot be attributed, therefore, to particularly unfavourable developments on the employment side, but to other factors. These include differences in the eligibility rules for unemployment; tougher rules in the Czech Republic must have led more workers to be non-participants rather than unemployed. If similar rules were applied, the excessive difference between the unemployment rates in Poland and the Czech Republic would have been much smaller (Blanchard *et al.*, 1993).[17]

The difference between the rate of decline in GDP and in that of employment may be used as a rough indicator of the change in hidden unemployment or excess employment (cf. *Economic Report* 1994). For 1990 to 1992 this indicator was: Poland 6.7 per cent, the Czech Republic 10.8 per cent, Slovakia 9.9 per cent, Hungary 7.0 per cent, and Romania 28.5 per cent. (Only Bulgaria with its extremely deep decline of employment recorded a reduction (of 2.8 per cent) but see fn. 11.) In 1993 a strong growth of GDP accompanied by a decline in employment reduced the discussed measure in Poland to 0.9 per cent; lack of growth in other countries must have meant that if there was a reduction, then it was only through a decline in employment.

As one can see, Poland has been undergoing not a traditional recession but profound institutional, economic and technical restructuring (cf. Berg 1993a) of the supply side. These supply-side transformations combined with macroeconomic stabilization have enabled Poland to achieve economic growth in the third year after launching its radical economic programme, despite powerful external shocks and rather unfavourable domestic political conditions.

FOREIGN DEBT

After tough negotiations Poland concluded in April 1991 an unprecedented agreement with the Paris Club which owned about two thirds of Polish debt. Thanks to this agreement the net present value of the debt was reduced by about 50 per cent in two tranches. Negotiations with the London Club were delayed by the change of government in Poland in 1992–93, and agreement for a similar degree of debt reduction was finally concluded with them in March 1993.

[17] For more on the reasons for the exceptionally low level of official unemployment in the Czech Republic see BIS (1994).

The Lessons Learned

Polish economic reform points out to a number of specific lessons:

- Traditional tools of macroeconomic stabilization (reducing the budget deficit, controlling the money supply and providing some nominal anchors, such as a stabilized rate of exchange) work in a largely socialist economy. But they probably have to be supplemented by an additional instrument – strong wage controls – which takes care of an important characteristic of a socialist economy: the influence of the wage-earners in the wage-setting process due to the inherited dominance of the public sector. The case for such controls is further strengthened if, as in Poland in 1988–89, the country has developed a wage–price spiral.
- A radical stabilization–liberalization programme is capable of abolishing massive shortages in a couple of weeks and of increasing substantially the range of goods available to buyers in the course of one or two years. This has shown, as expected, that shortages were caused by widespread price and supply rigidities, and – given these rigidities – were magnified by an expansionary monetary policy. This experience casts doubt on the alternative view, made popular by Janós Kornai, that relates shortages principally to the soft budget constraints of enterprises.
- The Polish example shows that it is possible to introduce internal currency convertibility in one move instead of doing it gradually over a couple of years, as was the case in Western Europe in the 1950s.
- Radical stabilization and liberalization forces many state enterprises to sell or lease part of their assets to private firms. In this way, radical stabilization and liberalization contributes to the rapid growth of the private sector and thus to the privatization of the entire economy.
- Radical stabilization and liberalization induced many state enterprises to adjust to the more demanding, but also potentially more rewarding, conditions of the market economy (Pinto *et al.* 1993). However, an even larger increase in their overall economic performance could have been achieved, on average, if they had been privatized. For this performance is determined both by the environment of enterprises, shaped mainly by S-L policies, and by their structure. These two factors are in an additive relationship. Changing both can result, therefore, in larger improvement in enterprise performance than changing just one. In addition, a large

state sector is likely to be increasingly politicized, and will tend, therefore, to undermine the initial gains in the efficiency of SOEs.

- The radical economic programme induced widespread restructuring of output and rapid reductions in the typical inefficiencies which prevailed under the socialist economic system. Output restructuring and increased efficiency have, in turn, brought about a rapid decline in the emissions of environmental pollutants.
- Poland achieved a better disinflation-GDP performance in 1990–93 than other countries of the region. The reasons for that require further examination. We can point out here, that the lesser magnitude of external shocks (however significant) and initial conditions are not sufficient to explain these differences. One must look, therefore, to features of the economic policy.

This brings us to a *general lesson*: the strategy described above has proved right in the sense that different strategies, given Poland's initial and external conditions, would have brought about much worse results. In this sense the Polish economic programme has been a success.[18]

I can see three main reasons for this. First, being radical and comprehensive, the programme was able to break down the inertia and structures of the inherited economic system, respected the links and synergies between the various processes of economic reform and could benefit from the political capital that emerged in the wake of the great political breakthrough of 1989. Second, the programme was, on the whole, implemented consistently in spite of growing criticism and pressure, especially in 1991. Third, one of the basic rules in devising and implementing the programme in 1990–91 was to avoid differentiating between sectors or – even worse – between enterprises. Introducing the new general rules was considered absolutely essential to create a transparent legal framework, to improve efficiency and to avoid pervasive rent-seeking by various interest groups. It is in these last two features in particular that the Polish economic reform of 1990–91 strongly differs, in my opinion, from that in Russia and most other post-Soviet countries. Another important difference is that in Poland the decisive stabilization effort came at the very beginning of the economic transformation process, while in Russia it came later, to be interrupted

---

[18] Some critics use a yardstick for judging this programme its original targets, and then point to deviations from these targets to condemn the programme as a failure. This approach ignores the role of uncertainty, which must be especially pronounced in a transition economy experiencing powerful shocks, and confuses forecasting errors with policy mistakes. Besides, the revised data, especially with respect to GDP, substantially reduces the gap between the original targets and the results achieved.

after only a couple of months in the middle of 1992; in Ukraine it has been delayed for longer.

References

Balcerowicz, Leszek 1989a *Systemy gospodarcze. Elementy Analizy Porownawczej* (Warsaw).
—— 1989b 'Zmiany strukturalne w krajach socialistycznych: Synteza badan', mimeo, Warsaw.
—— 1993a 'The direction of change in the financial system in Central and Eastern European countries', paper presented at a Conference on Banking and Finance: The Experience of Central Europe, mimeo.
—— 1993b 'Why the Leftists have won the election in Poland', *Wall Street Journal*, 26 September.
Bank for International Settlements (BIS) 1994 *64th Annual Report*, Basle.
Barbone, Luca, & Marchetti Jr., Domenico 1993 'Economic transformation and the fiscal crisis: a critical look at the Central European experience of the 1990s' World Bank, mimeo.
Bartholdy, Kaspar 1994 'Statistical Review', *The Economics of Transition*.
Berg, Andrew 1993a 'Supply and demand factors in the output decline in East and Central Europe', mimeo, IMF.
—— 1993b 'Does macroeconomic reform cause structural adjustment? Lessons from Poland', IMF, mimeo.
Biuletyn Statystyczny 1994, GUS.
Blanchard, Olivier, Commander, Simon & Coricelli, Fabrizio 1993 'Unemployment and Restructuring in Eastern Europe', mimeo, The World Bank.
Bratkowski, Andrzej 1993 'The shock of transformation or the transformation of the shock? The Big Bang in Poland and official statistics' in *Communist Economies and Economic Transformation*.
Bruno, Michael 1993, in Mario I. Blejer, Guillermo Calvo, Fabrizio Coricelli, & Alan H. Gelb (eds), 'Eastern Europe in transition: from recession to growth?', Proceedings of a Conference on the Macroeconomic Aspects of Adjustment, co-sponsored by the International Monetary Fund and the World Bank, World Bank Discussion Paper No. 196, World Bank, Washington, DC.
'Emerytury i renty pracownicze' 1993 Ministerstwo Pracy i Polityki Socjalnej, May.
Gaspard, Michael 1993 'Incomes and living standards in Central and Eastern Europe and the former Soviet Republics: recent developments, current situation and outlook', in Reiner Weichhardt (ed.), *Economic Developments in Cooperation Partner Countries from a Sectoral Perspective*, NATO, Brussels.
Gomulka, Stanislaw 1994 'Budget deficit and inflation in transition economies', in V. Bart & M. Schneider (eds), *Stabilization Policies at the Crossroads?*, Laxenburg, IIAS.
Gomulka, Stanislaw, & Jasiński, Piotr 1994 'Privatisation in Poland 1989–1993: policies, methods and results', Polish Academy of Science, Institute of Economics.

Góra, Marek 1992 'Industrial adjustment during transition: the case of Polish industry', Research Paper No. 7, Enterprise Behavior and Economic Reforms, PRDTE, World Bank.

Hume, Ian 1994 'Financing Poland's growth', mimeo, Warsaw.

'Informacja o sytuacji spoleczno-gospodarczej kraju. Rok 1993' 1994, Warsaw, GUS.

International Monetary Fund (IMF) 1994 'Republic of Poland: background papers', Washington, DC.

Iwaszkiewicz, Jerzy & Zarychta, Henryk 1994 'Na czarno' in *Życie Gospodarcze*, No. 10, March.

Klacek, Jan, & Hrncir, Miroslw 1994 'Macroeconomic policies: stabilization and transition in former Czechoslovakia and the Czech Republic', Centre for Social and Economic Research, Studies and Analyses, Warsaw, No. 15.

Kostrzewa, Wojciech J. 1994 'Bank Centralny a sektor bankow komercyjnych', mimeo, Warsaw.

Kubielas, Stanislaw 1994 'The attractiveness of Poland to foreign direct investors – trends and factors, 1989–1993', Polish Policy Research Group, Warsaw University Discussion Paper, No. 28.

Mylonas, Paul 1994 *Republic of Poland, Background Papers*, International Monetary Fund, March 16.

Pinto, Brian, Belka, Marek, & Krajewski, Stefan 1993 'Transforming state enterprises in Poland: evidence on adjustment by manufacturing firms', *Brookings Papers on Economic Activity*, No. 1.

Polish Economic Monitor 1994, *PlanEcon Report*, February.

Rajewski, Zdzislaw 1993 'Podukt krajowy brutto', in Leszek Zienkowski (ed.), *Gospodarka polska w latach 1990–1992*, Warsaw.

Rodrik, Dani 1993 'Making sense of the Soviet trade shock in Eastern Europe: a framework for some estimates', mimeo, Harvard University.

Rosati, Dariusz K. 1993 'The Impact of the Soviet trade shock on output levels in Central and East European economies', paper presented to International Conference on Output Decline in Eastern Europe, Austria, November.

Rostowski, Jacek 1993 'The implications of very rapid private sector growth in Poland', University of London, mimeo.

Sachs, Jeffrey 1993 'Poland's jump to the market economy', Cambridge, Mass., MIT Press.

Wellisz, Stanislaw, Kierzkowski, Henryk, & Okolski, Marek, 1993 'The Polish economy, 1989–91', in Henryk Kierzkowski, Marek Okólski, & Stanislaw Wellisz (eds), *Stabilisation and Structural Adjustment in Poland*, London, Routledge.

17

Conclusion: Personal Reflections on Poland

I would like to end this book with some personal recollections of my experience of having extraordinary responsibilities during extraordinary times. I hope that these remarks will both provide readers with an understanding of the Polish transition, and some broader insights as well.

How I Became a Reformer

I was helped in this respect by my education and, later, my research. I graduated in 1970 from the Faculty of Foreign Trade of the Warsaw School of Planning and Statistics (now the Warsaw School of Economics), which was probably the most Western-oriented faculty of economics in the Comecon countries in the late 1960s.

Between September 1972 and January 1974, I studied business administration, specializing in economics, at St John's University in New York, which gave me an opportunity to get better acquainted with Western macro- and microeconomics. While working on my doctoral dissertation, I read widely on the economics of technological change .

In 1974, I returned to the Central School of Planning and Statistics

I am drawing on selected fragments of my book *800 dni. Szok Kontrolowany*, Warsaw, 1992. I am grateful to Amanda Klekowski and Marek Michalski for translating them into English. I have also used some parts of my contributions to the book edited by Mario Blejer and Sylvio Corricelli, *The Making of Economic Reform in Eastern Europe: Conversation with Leading Reformers in Poland, Hungary and the Czech Republic*, Studies of Communism in Transition (Edward Elgar, 1995).

in Warsaw, where I taught international economics while working on my doctorate, which dealt with the social costs of speeding up product innovations. I defended it in 1975.

Since the early days of my academic career, I've had a feeling that 'institutions matter', that is, that behind differences in economic performance there are differences in institutional arrangements or, in other words, in economic systems. This led to my interest in the economic reform of the socialist system.

In 1978 I formed and directed an informal group of young economists working on a project for economic reform in Poland. This group became widely known as 'the Balcerowicz group'. The result of our intensive work (we met almost every week for more than two years) was a thorough discussion of many important issues, including how to prevent workers in cooperative enterprises from consuming profits, what instruments of indirect control the state should have in the economy, how to build a two-tier banking system and what powers a local government body should have.

When in August 1980 Solidarity came into being, there was a great demand for 'social' – that is, unofficial – proposals for economic reform, and 'the Balcerowicz group' project was recognized by many as the most radical and complete. It generated wide interest among members of Solidarity, which for myself, as for many other Poles, was important as a broad-based movement for reform rather than as a trade union. In March 1981 I was elected vice-chairman of the Polish Economic Association with responsibility for economic reform (from which I resigned in December 1982 because I believed that, in the situation created by martial law, radical economic reform had little chance of being pursued). From 1982 onwards, the task force on economic reform became something of a seminar on the basic problems of economic systems (that is, property rights, the proper role of the state in the economy, shortages and inflation) and continued at a lesser pace until democratization in 1989.

I entered the government in September 1989 with some members of the original group and others who had joined it later. There was no doubt among the members of the economic team that a radical economic change was imperative. The views about the general directions of the reform were shared partly because they had been discussed beforehand, during the seminars in my institute.

One of the basic questions I was interested in as a student of economic reforms was, first, why the economic reforms in the socialist countries had been partially or wholly reversed, and secondly, why they had failed to bring about any significant increase in overall efficiency.

My general response to these questions was that the economic reforms failed because they were not radical enough, that is, they did not reach a certain threshold of necessary changes rapidly; in other words, a 'critical mass' of such changes was not achieved. So I entered the government with a strong 'anti-gradualist' attitude towards economic reform. This belief was based not only on the experience of the previous reforms, but also on the conclusions I drew from social psychology, especially from Leon Festinger's theory of cognitive dissonance. One of the findings of this theory is that people are more likely to change their attitudes and their behaviour if they are faced with radical changes in their environment, which they consider irreversible, than if those changes are only gradual.

With respect to the content of the 'critical mass', my view was that a centrally managed economy had a certain 'constructional logic': being a non-market economy it relied on targets, rationing and administrative prices, which in turn require monopolistic and heavily concentrated organizational structures. Such structures could be maintained only if organizational rights, that is rights to set up, reorganize and liquidate enterprises, were largely in state hands. According to this view, the critical mass should break up the 'constructional logic' of the system by liberalizing prices and foreign trade, removing all the remnants of central allocation of goods and services, breaking up the domestic monopolies and decentralizing the organizational rights – in other words by introducing the freedom of entrepreneurship (liberal rights).

I was also familiar with the main examples of reforms in the non-socialist countries. Indeed, one of my main interests in the 1980s concerned economic transformations that brought about unexpectedly good results. I spent five months in 1985 as a visiting fellow at the Institute of Development Studies at the University of Sussex in England, investigating the South Korean case, and to some extent the Taiwanese economy. In the autumn of 1988 I spent three months in Marburg in West Germany studying the effects of Ludwig Erhard's reforms in 1948. I was also interested in the stabilization programmes in Latin America.

With respect to stabilization, I knew that, irrespective of the institutional differences, a radical approach was needed to put the brakes on the momentum of hyperinflation. The institutional differences had, I felt, two consequences. First, given the asymmetry of the labour market, because of the absence of private owners in what was still a socialist economy, there was a need for extraordinarily tough wage controls to rein in the tendency towards runaway inflation. Second, because the tough programme of stabilization had to be introduced into a basically non-private economy, its supply response was more uncertain and could be even worse than that seen in Latin American economies. But the alternative strategies had, I believed, much less chance of success.

With respect to the elimination of shortages, I believed the problem was price controls and the rigidity of supply, and not the 'soft budget constraint' of enterprises. The latter, in my opinion, was one of the main factors responsible for their low efficiency, as it implied the absence of competition.

Another important lesson was that the absence of competition, import substitution and the heavy regulation of the economy are sufficient to cause low efficiency and widespread rent-seeking; formally, private property cannot remedy this situation. These were the negative conclusions I drew from the experiences of many Latin American countries and India, and from the economic literature, especially from the writings of Bella Balassa and Anne Krueger.

In the spring of 1989 I wrote a paper on the conclusions to be drawn from the experience of various economies, and from economic theory, regarding the changes desirable in the Polish economy. I had no idea that a few months later I would be in charge of the Polish economic stabilization and transformation. But the conclusions were rather similar to the main points of the economic programme adopted in the autumn of 1989: rapid liberalization of prices, tough macroeconomic policy, convertibility of the Polish zloty, the liberalization of the foreign trade regime, the fastest possible privatization, and so on.

The Diagnosis and the Therapy

When I entered into government in September 1989, I perceived that the key objective was to put the Polish economy on the path towards efficiency and to improve the average standard of living. To do so required dealing with the macroeconomic disaster and solving the structural problem of low and declining efficiency. I had a clear perception from the very beginning that because of the inherited hyperinflation, we had to choose between an almost hopeless strategy and a risky strategy. There was no option without risk. An almost hopeless strategy would have consisted in neglecting the stabilization part of the programme, and in focusing instead on the transformation part.

It was my view that the strategy of tolerating hyperinflation would make stabilization more and more difficult with the passage of time, and the related chaos of hyperinflation would make rapid transformation, including privatization, scarcely possible. So this strategy, 'privatization first, stabilization later', would probably have resulted in neither privatization nor stabilization.

It was thus reasonable to choose a strategy that was merely risky but not hopeless: that of starting stabilization and transformation at about the same time. Stabilization measures and the liberalization part of the programme of transformation could be implemented more rapidly than privatization and other drastic institutional reforms. The radical strategy consisted, therefore, in the rapid introduction of a linked stabilization and liberalization package while at the same time undertaking more time-consuming institutional reform. This implied, given the differences in the possible speed, that radical stabilization and liberalization had to be introduced in the economy before it was fundamentally transformed. The risk in this strategy was that the supply response of such an economy was weaker and could be more uncertain than in a free-market economy. But I always compared these risks with those of delaying stabilization or liberalization (or implementing them gradually). It was obvious to me that the latter strategies are almost hopeless.

I perceived some uncertainty about the possibility of implementing and sustaining the chosen strategy. But my task on accepting appointments as both deputy prime minister and minister of finance was to push through the radical strategy, as the positions did not in themselves hold much attraction for me. So my attitude was that if it turned out to be impossible, I would resign, and I certainly would have done so. The worst possible scenario for me was to preside over an economic programme that was politically acceptable but failed, because it was not sufficiently radical and consistent.

What I had in mind as a warning was the fate of Raul Alfonsin in Argentina who started a radical stabilization programme as a very popular politician and who lost both the popularity and the stabilization. This is why I tended to prefer those policy options which were associated with the higher risk of being rejected by society but which, if implemented, promised to bring better economic results than those that were socially less risky but economically also less promising.

There were some specific concerns about the working of the respective mechanisms. Perhaps the single most important source of perceived uncertainty was the convertibility of the Polish zloty, which we decided to introduce at a low level of foreign exchange reserves. This is why it was so important to obtain the US$1 billion for the stabilization fund.

Practically all the important economic variables were subject to great uncertainty. For example, there were conflicting hypotheses about how fast the initial large price increases would spread across the economy; in other words what the inflation path would look like. I did not know how long we would be able to keep the exchange at its initial level. We were uncertain when and on what scale the bankruptcies of enterprises would occur. In fact, they started later and on a smaller scale than we had expected. We forecast a moderate growth of exports in 1990. In fact, they exploded, growing by 43 per cent.

However, I was reasonably certain about the general directions of change, that is, the general relationships between the policy measures and the changes in the economic variables, the time lags between the two, and the magnitude of the reaction. Therefore, I was sure that the stabilization and liberalization package, if maintained, would stop hyperinflation and eliminate shortages. I was also sure that sooner or later, privatization of the economy, competition, and export-oriented growth would bring about greatly enhanced efficiency; in other words, it would solve the perennial problem that plagued the former socialist economy.

There was, in my view, no alternative to standard macroeconomic policies, that is, to disciplined fiscal and monetary policies, as a means of stopping hyperinflation and of stabilizing the economy. But there were two additional points related to them. First, they had to be supplemented, as already mentioned, by tough wage controls, not only to brake the inflationary momentum, but also because of institutional bias in the labour market in favour of the employees. Second, our enlarged and heterogeneous programme of stabilization had to be linked to the radical liberalization of prices and foreign trade. This was because the task was not only to stop hyperinflation but also to abolish the shortage economy; otherwise no change in the efficiency of operation of the respective enterprises would have been possible.

The structural problem of low efficiency required a fundamental change in the economic system. With Poland's newly gained freedom to shape her institutions, we were no longer condemned to search for a kind of 'third way' solution. Instead, we could now put into place the least imperfect of the real world economic systems, namely, the competitive capitalist market economy. The institutional transformation also included radical changes in the social safety net (for example, introducing mechanisms to deal with open unemployment and strengthening targeted social assistance).

The reasoning was simple:

(i) first, a market economy is to be preferred to a centrally planned economy;

(ii) second, a private enterprise market economy is to be preferred to 'market socialism', since the latter has all the main economic weaknesses of the private enterprise market economy (for instance, a stronger tendency for unemployment), but less innovativeness and dynamism. Hence I firmly believed that we should rely on 'proven models', which we know of from real market economies.

Not everything in these economies had proved itself, and I hoped to avoid the introduction of certain mechanisms which would be difficult to reverse, if not actually irreversible. My major concern was to avoid adopting a Western type of protectionist and overregulated policy with respect to agriculture, especially of the European Community's CAP type, or the sort of industrial policy whereby the state bureaucracy would pick winners by manipulating the tax system or credit policy. State policy with respect to the economy should be as uniform as possible, avoiding detailed intervention. Otherwise a weak public administration would get involved, as in the case of central planning, in widespread bargaining with enterprises about the terms on which they functioned, which would culminate in massive rent-seeking and the same type of soft budget constraint for enterprises as in the socialist system.

I viewed the economic reforms in terms of a radical and comprehensive package, the elements of which complement one another. Within the overall process of economic transformation, I distinguished between liberalization and institutional reform. I knew that the former can be implemented more rapidly than the latter. At the same time, slowing down liberalization and stabilization, in order to enable them to keep pace with the fundamental institutional reform, was for me a more hazardous option than trying to implement all the changes with maximum speed, knowing, however, that stabilization and liberalization had to be largely completed before the institutional framework of the economy could be radically changed.

Within liberalization, the freeing of prices was a crucial measure, necessary for the rapid elimination of shortages and for obtaining better price information. Radical price liberalization required, in my view, a decisive liberalization of foreign trade, which in turn included the unification of exchange rates and currency convertibility. They were also indispensable for obtaining better relative prices. In addition, the fixing of the newly unified exchange rate played an important role in the programme of stabilization, and the introduction of convertibility signalled a decisive break with the past partial and unsuccessful reforms.

Liberalization also included the elimination of the restrictions on the creation and growth of private firms. This was a very important part of a legal framework for economic activity, as it introduced the mechanism of free entry and enabled the spontaneous growth of the private sector. Privatization of enterprises was for me the key part of the institutional restructuring. I viewed privatization as the most important type of enterprise reform, and as the most important condition for enterprise restructuring. The extension of private enterprise was, to my mind, crucial for solving the main structural problem (and of all the post-socialist economies, for that matter): that of low and falling efficiency. But I remembered that the potential inherent in the private sector can be fully released only if there is competition and an outward orientation of the economy. That is why a *liberal foreign trade regime* was for me an important complement to privatization and an important condition for increasing the overall efficiency of the economy. I also believed that some increase in that efficiency might be achieved through foreign trade liberalization, free prices and hardening of the enterprises' budget constraint, preceding the full privatization of state enterprises. However, in order to obtain the maximum possible increase in efficiency, privatiz-ation and other changes must be combined.

I viewed *wage determination* as connected to the ownership structure of the economy, that is, to its privatization. The absence of private owners gives rise to an institutional imbalance within the labour market, and hence to wage-push. The intensity of this tendency depended, in my view, on the inherited macroeconomic situation, and on the role and militancy of the trade unions. Both of these factors made wage-push in Poland stronger than in Czechoslovakia and Hungary, and in my view it called for stronger wage controls. An additional reason for these controls was, of course, the inherited hyperinflation. But I was fully aware that any wage controls are imperfect mechanisms for slowing down wage pressure generated by strong socio-institutional forces, and that these controls bring about some microeconomic distortions; besides, the efficiency of wage controls declines over time.

All this strengthened, I believed, the case for rapid privatization, as the only way to remove the institutional imbalance that was generating the excessive wage pressure. But I also knew that the mechanisms of wage determination differed even in capitalistic economies, depending on the structure and the role of the trade unions and on the related properties of the collective bargaining process. This was one of the points I saw as crucial in the Polish situation. Given the 'trade-unionist' tradition of the opposition movement Solidarity, which brought down socialism in Poland, this was a very sensitive point, and I delayed its resolution until the latter part of the economic programme, when it was hoped that there would be many more private employers. But I supported the development of employers' organizations and that of the consumers' movement as countervailing forces to the trade unions.

I considered *strengthening the independence of the central bank* to be a key to stable monetary policy. A law to this effect was enacted as early as the autumn of 1989. The reform of the commercial banks played a crucial role in the general economic reform, and it included setting up new, largely private banks and strengthening the capabilities of the existing state commercial banks.

The tax reform also figured largely in the transformation programme. One of the main directions here was the elimination of the widespread tax breaks and concessions, which were often granted on an *ad hoc* basis. I considered this a necessary condition for the hardening of enterprise 'budget constraints', and the emergence of the market. In addition, tax reform comprised the introduction of value-added tax and of a comprehensive system of personal income tax.

Choosing People and Setting the Rules of the Game

I was aware of the administrative difficulties. I knew that the state's economic administration was rather weak both in terms of numbers and competence, but I also realized that it was not possible to change it quickly for the better because of the shortage of people with adequate knowledge of a market economy and because of the great number of urgent problems. In this situation, I did two things. First, within two or three weeks of taking office, I formed a group of my closest associates, consisting partly of newcomers and partly of insiders, some of whom I already knew. This required me to dismiss some people from their functions in order to make room for the newcomers. With respect to the members of the newly formed economic team, I tried to create a relationship of trust and a sense of common mission. An *esprit de corps* had emerged and was an important factor in keeping the group and the programme together.

Second, I made structural changes to the institutions of which I was in charge. In the Ministry of Finance, we abolished the bloated Department of Prices (responsible mainly for price control) and we created, practically from scratch, the department dealing with financial institutions (banks and insurance companies), headed by a colleague of mine, Stefan Kawalec. We also strengthened the departments responsible for the budget. In my Deputy Prime Minister's office, I created a number of coordinating committees and a group of strategic advisers distinct from those who were dealing with current problems. An important role was played by the section responsible for overall coordination and dealing with the political aspects of the economic programme, that is, with political parties, parliament, office of the president, the trade unions, the mass media, and so on. This section was ably managed by my former student, Jerzy Koźminski.

From my studies of psychology, I recognized the danger of information overload. Therefore, I tried to define the information to be recorded, in order to avoid the overload produced by offices, documents and notes. Many times, unfortunately, I had to ask specific questions and demand certain information, because bureaucrats were only prepared to register the data passively in accordance with the old ways, though the situation at that time demanded a new perspective.

By September I had encountered a technique known as 'muddling through' in bureaucratic jargon. In KERM (Economic Committee of the Council of Ministers), various departments were trying to produce as much paper as possible so as to demonstrate their activity, although, in this new situation, the danger of being completely overburdened was imminent. So I proposed a new principle, whereby KERM would only deal with interdepartmental projects prepared well in advance.

Another, equally important, issue was determining how to treat telephone calls. In all the various offices, there was a tendency to arrange things by phone. 'The clients' thought that by using the phone they would be able to get concessions, because whoever received the call would not be prepared and would agree. I was aware of this danger – particularly in the case of the Ministry of Finance, where many decisions were made – and, because of this, I introduced the rule that there would be practically no *ad hoc* phone conversations with me. My secretaries knew that they were not able to contact me immediately, unless the telephone calls were especially important, for example, from the president or prime minister. Similar rules were created concerning visits and personal contacts – only my closest associates had access to me at any time, if they requested the meeting by phone. However, in the Ministry of Finance, where there were no special permits for visitors issued, people sometimes arrived and demanded to see me immediately. Usually, my secretaries found a way to calm the situation, but sometimes the conversation also involved a security officer. Perhaps it was a coincidence, but both gentlemen from the office of government security had degrees in education and counselling.

Meetings with international visitors formed a special category, in which selection was also necessary. Otherwise, I would have had to spend all my time receiving foreign delegations. In general, I followed the rule that a meeting ought not to be purely ceremonial. I also avoided meetings with particular foreign investors, knowing that one could quite easily become entangled, not being adequately prepared for a particular case. Such matters – and also meetings with domestic investors and entrepreneurs – should be delegated to specialized administrators.

Carrying out one or more meetings or sessions every day, I had to follow strict rules for discipline of meetings. First of all, I announced in advance how much time we had. Secondly, I presented an agenda. Thirdly, on each item on the agenda, I followed a specific procedure: defining the issue to be decided; determining various options; comparing and contrasting the options and, on this basis, arriving at a decision. Comparison was sometimes easy, when one of the variants seemed to be decidedly better than others. It was more difficult when two alternatives were very similar. And frequently, it was not as simple as in decision theory, where one can identify all the variants and put them down to one simple denominator. Usually, there was an element of weighing the criteria, often by intuition. At the beginning, I worked out certain ways to weigh the criteria, being aware that whatever I did was likely to be risky.

In spite of the attempts to rationalize organization of my work, I usually spent about thirteen hours in the office each day. One of my rules was that I did not bring work home. I considered that after a certain point my marginal productivity became negative, which meant that, at a certain level of tiredness, continued reading was a pure waste of effort. It is better, in such instances, to read the next morning when you have a clear mind and can appreciate the argument more sharply, than to tire yourself out by reading into the small hours, only having three hours to sleep. Saturday was usually a working day for me, even though I finished work earlier than on the other days. However, I tried to keep Sundays free, using it to catch up with the newspapers.

In all of my government activities, the techniques which I learned as a researcher were a great help to me: speed reading, directing a research team, and the technique of taking notes.

Preparing the Breakthrough

We set the date for launching the economic programme for 1 January 1990, the first day of the fiscal year. This reason, however significant, was not the most important. We were aware of the fact that, in the face of dramatic changes in other countries of Eastern Europe, after a few months Western countries' interest in Poland would wane. But more important were internal conditions: inflation was soaring and every month of delay deepened the economic chaos. Waiting would increase costs. Precious 'political capital' would be depleted without any economic benefits. I knew the period of 'extraordinary politics' would be short – but it turned out to be shorter than I thought.

The deadline of 1 January 1990 meant that we did not have much time to prepare the necessary laws and get them accepted by the Parliament (Sejm) and Senate, to agree upon a programme with the International Monetary Fund, to prepare executive orders, or to deal with 'ongoing' issues. It was a really trying time.

Some of the people in government circles maintained that it was impossible to do this in such a short period of time. However, in the economic team we did not even contemplate the thought of cancelling the 'zero hour'. In October, the Council of Ministers approved the 'economic programme of government'. However, debates continued and time was running out mercilessly. In the second half of November, I established a special operations group, whose tasks and activities were scheduled daily or even hourly. The last date in this schedule was 31 December, when the president was to sign the accepted statutes.

The work was done on three levels. First, a task force – each run by a deputy minister of the finance or another department – prepared one proposal of a statute. Some members went from one task force to another because they were simultaneously working on several statutes.

The draft laws prepared by these groups were then sent for discussion to KERM. However, before they arrived there, they were generally subject to initial critical review by a small group of key people. The idea was that KERM should receive the final product and not need to spend precious time on long discussions.

The third level was the Council of Ministers which discussed the laws sent by KERM. There were several long meetings. We had to finish before 17 December 1989 – this date was set by the Sejm. The 17 December actually fell on a Sunday, but we calculated that delaying the debate in the Sejm even by one day could endanger the entire programme. We prepared eleven proposals for statutes, essentially changing the legal framework of the economy. They included a new tax law, banking law and foreign exchange law, a law regarding foreign investors in Poland, law on customs, the legal foundations governing credit, and a law on taxing excessive wage increases. From then on, everything depended on the efficiency of the Sejm. To discuss these laws in the normal way would have taken at least several months. Therefore, a special legislative procedure was required.

At the beginning of December, I held a series of meetings with the leadership of the Sejm and the Senate who agreed to support the proposal establishing an extraordinary commission. I also met with the leaders of all the political parties represented in the Sejm and received a favourable reaction to my proposals.

We asked the military to help us print the statutes, and also, eventually, to distribute them to the members of the Sejm, as the capacity of the government printing office might not be sufficient. We were also afraid that members of the Sejm would be scattered all over the country and would not receive the statutes in time – that is, at least a few days prior to 17 December.

'The great unveiling' took place in the Sejm on 17 December 1989. In a speech broadcast on television, I said that the task of transforming the economic system – difficult in itself – had come when circumstances were unfavourable: huge inflation, lack of foreign exchange reserves and the strenuous burden of foreign debt. The tasks which Poland faced were overwhelming and without precedent, and it was necessary to take quick and decisive steps. . .

After the speech, an economic debate ensued and many questions were asked. I grouped them according to themes and distributed them among the ministers and deputy ministers, sometimes writing my own suggestions on where to put emphasis in the answers. Every minister with an economic portfolio had an opportunity to speak. It was an important moment, drawing the economic team together. At the end, I also spoke, giving additional explanation and providing some comments. I had the impression that all of us felt that this was the beginning of something great and important.

The parliamentary session ended that day by creating the 'extraordinary commission'. It comprised dozens of members of parliament from diverse political parties and from various parliamentary commissions. The work of this commission was probably one of the most important and marked one of the better periods of that parliament. Its members later recollected that it was 'a romantic endeavour' when political divisions disappeared. And they worked a dozen or more hours a day, even during the holidays, to get everything ready before the 'zero hour'.

The commission was immediately divided into various task forces working on specific laws. Members of the economic team participated all the time in this work. These task forces worked practically non-stop; the prepared proposals were subsequently sent to the extraordinary commission, where they were analysed and approved.

In addition to direct participation in the work of the commissions, my colleagues watched what was happening in the Sejm. We tried to discover how quickly and in what direction the work was going, so that when problems appeared, we would have enough time to intervene by presenting additional explanations or persuasion. When difficulties or serious deviations from the proposed solution appeared, we intervened immediately.

Parallel with the Sejm, the Senate also worked closely with us. According to the normal procedure, the Senate debates various legal acts only after they are approved by the Sejm. This time, the draft laws approved by the extraordinary commission of the Sejm were sent immediately to the special commission of the Senate which worked on them.

While the Senate and the Sejm were practically in 'constant assembly' we were still engaged in one difficult task: collecting contributions to the stabilization fund from the Western governments. These contributions, of US$1 billion each, were to support the convertibility of the Polish zloty.

The last declarations were still arriving on 29 December. A large number of Western countries promised to provide us with credits or grants, but we had to get them on time. The US Department of the Treasury and, particularly, the Deputy Secretary of the Treasury, David Mulford, turned out to be a great help in mobilizing these contributions. However, delays in making payments occurred nevertheless. I held dramatic telephone conversations, first with the managing director of the International Monetary Fund, Michel Candessus, to whom I said that we were doing everything that we had declared in our programme but that the West was delaying its support for the stabilization fund. Just before Christmas, I was forced to ask David Mulford for help. I phoned all over the United States looking for him. Finally I found him, suffering from 'flu in a Brussels hotel. He received my phone call, and promised to intervene. As a result, a significant amount of the stabilization fund was collected: before the end of December, some $400 million were confirmed and we were assured that the remainder would be available before 7 January 1990.

On 27 December, the Sejm passed the legislative package. The last step required was the president's signature on the statutes. Prior to sending the proposal to the Sejm, I paid a visit to President Jaruzelski. I informed him of the main direction of the economic plan and about the extraordinary legislative procedure. President Jaruzelski told me he supported our approach. We checked the schedule for 30 and 31 December in order to be sure that he would have time to sign all these statutes before the New Year. Knowing that he planned to leave Warsaw for the New Year, we found out what time he would depart. . .

It Works

The first weeks of 1990 were very nervous. We were diving into the unknown. With growing tension, I followed the inflow of information. The first signals were alarming. At the beginning of January, the minister of domestic trade informed us that the reserves of grain, meat and food were low. The minister of agriculture confirmed it. Great pressure was put on me to ask the West for additional food support. I made a number of calls to Brussels, as well as to the United States requesting an immediate supply of food. I had no way of verifying the departmental information because the statistical data were always significantly delayed. I had people observe, see what happened in the shops, and how prices changed. In the first two weeks, we recorded significant jumps in prices, particularly of food products. Unfortunately, it was not followed by a clear improvement in the supply of food. The increase in the price level in January, i.e. corrective inflation, was in fact an element of the programme. We did not know, however, precisely when these price increases would stop. The second goal was to eliminate shortages. Both of these goals appeared to be in danger. On the basis of partial data, we could only surmise. In February we learned – it was an unpleasant surprise – that price levels had not increased by 45 per cent, as we assumed, but by 78 per cent. However, an important positive signal in January was the emergence of street trade. Many farmers decided to sell their produce independently on the streets. Trucks full of goods of industrial products also appeared on the streets. This street trade, even though criticized for its primitivism, played an important role at that time. First of all, it ensured better supply and lower prices than in state-owned stores and, secondly, it created competition for them. Thanks to street sales, shortages quickly disappeared and by February there was already a significant improvement in the situation on the market. At the end of January, the first signs of price reductions were seen; price increases in February were radically lower than in January. I remember how in the second half of January my advisers tried to cheer me up. At least twice they put information on my desk showing that the price of eggs had fallen. I had this checked, but it turned out that the information was patchy. Only one thing was certain about eggs: at the end of January, prices not only levelled, but in certain parts of the country they in fact dropped.

Knowing that after the New Year the economy would be undergoing a difficult transformation, I began to build a more effective system of information-gathering. In late December 1989, I set up several specialized teams. One of the first and the most important was the intervention team. Beginning early in January 1990, this team gathered information weekly and, whenever necessary, even more frequently, and they dealt with almost every possible issue, both current issues and the problems related to systemic reforms. The second group comprised the team monitoring the economy. This team was charged with making a sort of photographic snapshot of the economic situation.

The third group comprised a team analysing public opinion regarding the economy. It was managed by Jurek Koźminski, who in addition was in charge of my staff in the deputy prime minister's office. This team was truly an innovation in our post-socialist administrative system. The representatives of existing and emerging institutes of public opinion and invited journalists as well as managers of departments of the Sejm and Council of Ministers participated in their work. Sociologists and political scientists were also invited.

The Battles to Sustain the Programme

Radical changes in the economy during the first months did not cause serious social reactions. The trade unions were not preparing any dramatic protests. Everybody waited to see what would happen, what would be the real results of the programme of stabilization and liberalization. The situation began to change after a few months. At the end of March 1990, I had my first open confrontation with the unions. The union members came from the Mazovia region. The meeting was stormy. A key topic of this debate was a question I had often been asked before: 'Will society have to bear it all?' Many of those who asked this question emphasized that people were reaching the limits of their endurance.

The main issue, however, focused around the new situation in which the state enterprises found themselves. Moreoever, questions were asked about 'nomenklatura' privatization. It was pointed out that the people who seemed to get rich most quickly were those who had taken advantage of the former system. Another question raised was the likelihood that Poland would become a 'colony' of the West, exporting our raw materials.

A meeting with activists of the Mazovia region turned out to be an invaluable lesson for me in a subsequent serious public test to which I was exposed during an April Solidarity General Assembly in Gdansk.

In the aeroplane I prepared an outline of my speech. On my arrival at the hall, I found already several hundred people gathered and waiting. I was immediately asked to speak. I began by describing the key changes in our economy in the past several months. 'We're at the point,' I said, 'where the continuation of successful economic performance depends primarily on the behaviour of the state enterprises. We have to break away from old habits and attitudes. In particular, we have to stop looking to "the top", to the state, because it is a relic of the old way of thinking. Solidarity has played an important role in removing the old and ineffective economic system, and I am convinced that it will play an equally significant role in the difficult process of creating a new system.' I also said that the role of trade unions should not be taken for granted. There are many different types of trade union. One such type is purely confrontational; but other types also existed: witness the harmonious cooperation between trade unions, employers and governments, for example in Finland, Austria and Sweden. This type of trade union focuses on alleviating the unavoidable costs of modernizing the economy. I wanted Solidarity to be this latter type of trade union.

A flood of questions followed, which I did my best to answer. I was asked whether energy prices would increase. Members of the audience demanded that a debate be held on alternative economic programmes. They complained that the mines could not export their products independently. There were also questions about state aid for families, support for privatizing enterprises and the process for replacing higher level management. One man asked whether I was aware of the hostility towards me among such groups as the retired, teachers, and health-care workers. I replied that I was aware of the unavoidable price that all members of society had to bear in the transition to a market economy. Many people expressed concern about unemployment. I explained that hidden unemployment, which had existed before 1989, was becoming open unemployment.

The year 1991 started with conflict over wage controls. This was one of the side-effects of the presidential campaign of autumn 1990, during which taxation of excessive wage increases was sharply criticized. The trade unions wanted to use the change of government to extract concessions on this matter. Negotiations with these unions were difficult, because I did not see any possibility for concessions. Normally, in every negotiation, one has to have some position from which one can pull back if the pressure is too high. Here, however, movement was limited. Simultaneously, it was clear that the trade unions had to 'get something' in order not to return home empty-handed. In such situations, one usually forms a task force to maintain the negotiations hoping that a compromise will be found. We created such a task force, but devising the agenda was harder.

On the first Monday of February 1991, President Lech Wałęsa, who had succeeded General Jaruzelski in 1990, was due to speak live in a Polish radio phone-in broadcast. I decided to visit him in his presidential office at Belweder, just in case the wage tax was brought up. It was clear that radio listeners would be asking him about this; the tension among employees was very high. The issue, as it turned out, was the starting point for our conversation. We also talked about types of leadership. I mentioned the example of a former president of Argentina, Raul Alfonsin, who was elected as a popular chief of state. He followed a short-sighted economic policy which caused rapid deterioration of the economic situation. As a result, he had to leave his own government in disgrace.

I think that to some degree as a result of my visit to Belweder, during the next meeting with radio listeners, President Wałęsa not only did not support eliminating the wage tax, but also formulated the famous sentence that it was necessary to lower costs and prices – by 'fifty or even by a hundred per cent'.

When the battle over '*popiwek*' (the tax on wages) slowly began to subside, another conflict emerged. More and more frequently there were signals that protest was about to begin in rural areas. I think that to some degree this resulted from the presidential campaign in 1990, which had increased farmers' expectations. For a whole year farmers had met increasing difficulties in the world of new economic reality. They demanded guaranteed minimum prices for agricultural products, low interest rates on credits, and more and more protection at the borders. In addition, there were increasing strikes of workers on state agricultural farms.

From the very beginning, I was of the view that agriculture should not be excluded from the reform process, even though farming is special. However, from the beginning, there was strong pressure from the farmers for high customs barriers and duties on agricultural products.

Another frequently repeated demand from the farmers, which I resisted, concerned preferential credits which farmers had been used to in the past. In general, I considered that the radical approach of pro-agricultural activists resulted not only from the great difficulty being experienced in the rural areas, but also because of the competition between various political parties for the farmers' votes. Experience in other countries has shown that farmers have a bias towards radical movements, maybe because, in contrast to workers in industry, they do not risk losing their jobs. From observing the European Community, I also recognized the harmful effects of artificially increased agricultural prices and the difficulty of moving away from such a policy. It was very important for me not to commit the same mistake. With respect to production, private agriculture adjusted rather well to the economic programme. However, taking income level into consideration, farmers really did experience deterioration, particularly in 1990, because in 1989 they had obtained large windfall gains. In 1989, prices of agricultural products after liberalization increased significantly more quickly than prices of industrial products purchased by farmers, which had not been decontrolled. Thus, what farmers gained in 1989, they lost in 1990, when price movements were reversed. In addition, in earlier years, farmers had been provided with ample cheap credit. This changed in 1990.

Thinking about agriculture, I realized that we were facing both a great problem and a great opportunity: a higher percentage of the population was employed in agriculture in Poland than in other countries, for instance, in Greece or in Spain. This was a factor which could accelerate growth if we could move significant numbers of the less productive labour force in agriculture to more productive sectors of the economy.

With hindsight, one can see that the Polish political calendar was not very opportune. The political construction of the 'Round Table', a pioneer development in 1989, unexpectedly quickly turned out to be a liability. In Hungary and Czechoslovakia, by the first stage of the process of departure from the previous system, new elections were called. This gave both countries the higher political stability necessary for economic reforms. In Poland we had the reverse sequence: first there was a radical economic programme for the economy and only then the successive dismantling of the 'contractual political system'. In addition, dismantling was taking place in the reverse order: we began with presidential elections, while parliamentary elections were moved to the end of 1991. In the years 1990 and 1991, we had two electoral campaigns and we changed government twice. Even in countries which have a stable economy, political tension caused by election campaigns may have a negative influence on the economic situation. All the more reason to be concerned for a country which was undergoing a massive process of social and economic transition. In addition, the more the economy is state-owned, the more susceptible it is to politicization. Even during the presidential campaign of 1990, the economic programme caught the attention of most of the participants. I was concerned that during the forthcoming parliamentary campaign in 1991, even more tension would be caused by populist slogans.

However, until mid-1991 cooperation with the Sejm worked quite well. By giving enough explanation and persuasion, I was able to obtain the support of a majority of the Sejm for the proposed economic legislation. The best period from this point of view was December 1989 when, with immense concentration and mobilization in parliament, it was possible to pass the package of statutes which formed the new economic programme on 1 January. In spite of tension between the government and the Sejm, we were usually able to find satisfactory solutions.

The Foreign Debt Reduction Campaign

Foreign debt was one of the largest burdens on the Polish economy inherited from the socialist era. In September 1989 I was certain that Poland would not be able to eliminate galloping inflation, change its economic system and simultaneously service the large inherited debt. It was clear that the problem of our debt had to be solved by a triangle: Poland, the International Monetary Fund, and the creditors officially represented by the Paris Club and more that 500 Western banks, known as the 'London Club'.

Poland's debt had grown during the 1970s and particularly in the second half of that decade. In 1975 it was already more than $8 billion and in 1980, $25 billion and, by the end of 1989, approximately $41 billion dollars. From the credits obtained in the 1970s, only 20 per cent had been utilized for investment purchases, while 65 per cent had been devoted to importing equipment and materials, and the remaining 15 per cent had been spent on consumption imports. Poland was at that time a huge net importer of food products (the situation turned around in 1990, when we became a net exporter).

Almost two-thirds of Polish debt was in the form of credits guaranteed by Western governments. The second largest group of creditors was formed by the 'London Club'.

As early as 1981 a very sharp balance of payment crisis had emerged in Poland which prevented the service of debt. For the first time Poland had requested restructuring of debt or a moratorium on payment of debts. In April 1981, an agreement was signed with the Paris Club that postponed 90 per cent of repayment for the four years 1986–89 on the capital, but simultaneously obliged Poland to repay the interest. The imposition of martial law led to the Western representatives severing ties with the Polish government. As a result, Poland did not service any debts for several years. However, commercial banks represented in the London Club did not break off relations and as a result they came to an agreement regarding debt restructuring. In this way Poland shifted the burden of debt to later years. It eased the situation in the short run. However, during 1988–89, it turned out that even this significantly reduced payment obligation was far too high in relation to the payment abilities of Poland. On 15 September, or three days after I took office, I became aware of discussions and negotiations with commercial banks regarding our debts to them. We were not able to service the debt by the date agreed earlier. We had dramatic debates with representatives of some Polish banks. We were forced to mobilize our modest financial resources to pay foreign banks. Simultaneously, we agreed that we would produce only 15 per cent of the interest due and that 85 per cent of the interest would be repaid at a later date.

In September 1989 we estimated that Poland was short of some US$500 million necessary to cover essential imports. Therefore, during my first meetings with finance ministers from Western countries at the end of September 1989, I presented them with a request for emergency credit of almost US$500 million in order to avoid serious economic upheaval. I was able to obtain credit by December 1989 – US$215 million as a so-called 'bridging loan' from the Bank for International Settlement in Basle. The rest were short-term credit guarantees from the West. It was not until 1990 that we achieved a high surplus in the trade balance and the balance of payments crisis disappeared.

We were aware that without agreement with the IMF on the economic programme it would not be possible to obtain any satisfactory solution to Poland's debt problem. Therefore, for the whole of that autumn there were intense negotiations which ended in December with a mutual agreement, the so-called 'letter of intent'. This document stated that Poland would strive to obtain full relief from payments of both capital and interest in 1990. In addition, the document stated that Poland intended to conclude an agreement with creditors on the permanent reduction of the debt burden. Then many months followed in which we worked strenuously to obtain support for this unconventional solution. The main problem was that the essential debt reduction, mainly debt owed to the Paris Club, had no good precedents.

The agreement with the IMF paved the way to an agreement with the Paris Club in February 1990. In it we obtained full debt relief from all payments until March 1991. This gave us time to pursue our efforts to reduce the debt burden. An agreement with the Paris Club opened a way for foreign credit guarantees.

In January 1990, Prime Minister Tadeusz Mazowiecki sent a letter to creditor heads of state requesting a debt reduction. It did not bring any direct results, but it certainly was an important element in the whole scheme of things. We waited several months and in May 1990 I decided to take the next step. It was at the time of the interim committee meeting at the IMF in Washington, DC. All the ministers of finance from the West took part in this meeting. I proposed the plan for debt reduction whereby Poland would have to pay no more than 2 per cent of its total debt per annum, and the growth of the debt would be arrested. This would correspond to debt reduction by some 80 per cent. Today, I do not have to hide the fact that the extent of the proposed debt reduction was dictated by negotiation tactics. The first step in negotiation had to be proportionally bold.

Our proposals were obviously received without enthusiasm. Immediately after my speech we began an explanatory campaign. Soon afterwards, I held a series of meetings with the ministers of finance from the United States, the United Kingdom, France, Japan, Germany and Canada, as well as representatives from the Senate and Congress of the United States. The ministers were rather reserved in negotiation and they avoided specific commitments. The degree of their restraint, however, varied. The Japanese delegation was the most reserved during the meetings. By contrast, the representatives of the United States were the most favourable during the period of subsequent meetings and discussions. The conversation had a specific structure. In the beginning, I briefly presented the internal programme of Poland's reconstruction, what we had done, what we planned to do, and against this background, the external conditions necessary for the success of the Polish reforms. Here we presented a proposal to reduce the debt. I always spoke without an interpreter in these discussions, which made the conversation more natural and allowed direct contact with my counterparts. I said that we not only had to reduce financial obligations which were associated with servicing the debt, but also we had to reduce the debt burden itself. The second was necessary, I argued, to reduce uncertainty, which was detrimental to the investment and political climate in Poland. No one directly questioned my arguments. If there were any questions, they usually related to reform issues: what had we done? what were we planning to do? They let us know clearly that some exceptional conditions had to exist in order to obtain exceptional debt relief.

I used all of my foreign trips after May 1990 to lobby for debt relief from the creditors. In June 1990 I went to Germany where I met with Chancellor Helmut Kohl and with the minister of finance, Theo Waigel. Chancellor Kohl attentively listened to my arguments regarding reducing Poland's debt. Visits to Washington followed in September 1990. The United States was suffering from a budget crisis and some state employees had not received their salaries on time. I appreciated all the more the fact that leading politicians found time to meet me. I met President Bush, telling him what we were doing in Poland and how important the debt reduction was for us. Then I spent 18 and 19 October in Rome. I met the prime minister, the minister of finance and the minister of foreign affairs. Prime Minister Andreotti clearly stated that he would support Poland's desire to obtain debt reduction. I was very pleased to hear that. Minister of Finance Guido Carli was more restrained and began the conversation by painting a dramatic picture of the Italian finances. As a matter of fact, they had a deficit totalling 10 per cent of GDP and an unstable political situation. I told him that I knew what it meant to limit public expenditure and that Italians certainly ought to understand why we tried so hard to reduce our burden of debt. However, the conversation was very difficult. The next day I was received by the Pope John Paul II. The conversation with John Paul II lasted almost forty minutes. The Pope was cordial and direct. He asked whether it was possible to create a just market economy in Poland. He also asked me about the economic situation in the country. Of course, I presented the problem of Poland's debt and our efforts to reduce it.

In Warsaw, I received ambassadors from creditor nations and various foreign delegations which had arrived in Poland. No matter what topic we discussed during the conversation I always repeated my theme that debt reduction had to go forward. At the beginning of 1991, as part of our 'debt release offensive' President Wałęsa sent a letter to leaders of most of the industrialized countries in the world, the G-7. After meeting in the United States in January 1991, the G-7 issued a communiqué in which they stated that the problem of debt would be dealt with. To me, that was a great step forward.

The beginning of 1991 was a real race with time: in March, the agreement with the Paris Club, signed in February of 1990, on the basis of which we were not required to service our debt, was going to expire. We knew we needed to find a new solution and a new agreement – again we wanted to have a clause about debt reduction. However, in order to get to this point we needed to sign a standby agreement with the IMF, which was a precondition for passing the budget in the Sejm. The debate on the budget in the beginning of 1991 was delayed. We were in a hurry, however, and therefore the tone of my speech during the parliamentary debate on the budget seemed 'dramatic', as was later commented. I felt that Poland's political honeymoon was rapidly fading. It was the last opportunity to play on the exceptional nature of the Polish situation in order to obtain foreign debt reduction.

In this context, there was a very important visit to Poland on

6 March 1991, by the deputy secretary of the US treasury, David Mulford, who was considered the chief 'operator' on world debt issues. Mulford was unequivocal: 'Your request for 80 per cent of debt reduction is unrealistic. If you stick to it, your efforts may fail entirely. It may be realistic to get a maximum reduction of 50 per cent. You might be able to count on slightly more if you obtain acceptance by creditors. But here, we would have to persuade Japan to agree to the debt reduction. I may try to persuade them of a 50 per cent reduction; however, I am not able to fight for more,' said Mulford. We had to take a position. Our group concluded that Mr Mulford was right. We agreed that 50 per cent was quite a lot.

Mulford's visit was an important stage of preparation for President Wałesa's trip to the United States. Americans were concerned that the president might again discuss the issue of the lack of positive response from the West. We wanted to have our agreement before his visit to Washington. Before Mulford left Warsaw, he met the president and prime minister and repeated the US position on the 50 per cent debt reduction. In Paris on 14 March 1991, there was a meeting of a working group of creditors during which there was a public announcement regarding debt reduction rules for Poland. That was a watershed. The press communiqué announced that the creditor countries were aware of the exceptional situation in which Poland found itself while engaging in an unprecedented transformation towards a market economy. These countries expressed their willingness to reduce debt – utilizing various mechanisms, 50 per cent of the net present value of Poland's debt towards the Paris Club in two phases, 30 per cent in the first phase and 20 per cent in the second phase, provided that the IMF agreement were successfully completed.

Some discussions and debates dealing with technical issues were very important, and we had some nervous moments before the agreement was signed, on 20 April. The Polish delegation with Janusz Sawicki was in Paris to negotiate with representatives of the Paris Club. The delegation was in touch with the task force organized by me at the National Bank of Poland (NBP). We received faxed pages of the proposed agreement and after discussion we made corrections which we faxed back to Paris.

Trips to Moscow

During the summer of 1991, there were negotiations on a meeting with Mikhail Gorbachev who had expressed interest in discussing the Polish economic reforms. The visit was scheduled for the early part of August and a few days later the Polish ambassador to Russia, Ambassador Ciosek, informed us that at that time there would be an important plenary central committee meeting in Moscow which might be decisive for the future of the Soviet Union. We decided therefore to postpone our meeting until the end of August when Mr Gorbachev would have returned from vacation. In Warsaw we were haveing a heated debate in the Sejm when suddenly the news came from Moscow of the 'coup' which had removed Gorbachev from power. It seemed that any visit to the Soviet Union, would not be in the near future. But later the leaders of the coup were placed under arrest and information arrived from Moscow confirming the government's interest in my visit there. On 2 September, I found myself on the plane to Moscow. The official host was the Russian government, and an individual meeting with Gorbachev was scheduled. When we landed, it turned out to be much more complicated. It was not always clear who was represented by whom and many people in the Russian cabinet were simultaneously performing various functions in the Soviet apparatus. This was the case with Ivan Silajev, the Russian prime minister, who was simultaneously performing the function of chairman of the committee for current management of the Soviet economy. Conversations were held in an atmosphere of high uncertainty. Literally in front of our eyes, in place of the Soviet Union, a new, but not yet very well-defined state was emerging.

There was an unpleasant incident. Just before the press conference in the Polish embassy, I was told that a moment earlier Prime Minister Silajev had given a live television speech in which he said that Poland wanted to participate in the newly formed Economic Commonwealth – an economic successor to the Soviet Union. Furthermore, he said that he had personally received this information from Mr Balcerowicz, currently in Moscow. I felt myself go cold and then broke out in a sweat. During the meeting with the press, there was of course a question about my reaction to Silajev's statement. I responded that I did not know anything about this statement and that I had certainly never endorsed Poland's participation in the community.

After the conference, embassy employees ran to me with notes sent by major press agencies which were already citing Silajev's statement that 'author of Polish reform L. Balcerowicz expressed an interest in having Poland becoming a member of the [Russian] community'. I could imagine such a communiqué being received in my country: Balcerowicz wants to annex Poland to the Soviet Union . . . The mayor of St Petersburg, Mr Anatoly Sobchak, came to my aid. He went to Silajev and persuaded him that he should issue a retraction, and so Silajev called a late evening press conference where he publicly expressed contrition.

Then, as had been planned, I met with Boris Yeltsin. The next day I talked with Mikhail Gorbachev during a lunch break. Gorbachev appeared to be relaxed, but acted very vigorously. He said it would be a historical paradox if problems emerged in Polish–Russian relations just as the Soviet Union was interested in discovering the Polish path to economic reform. As we said goodbye, he said he would like to meet me in the near future for a longer time and discuss economic reform.

However, on my next visit to Moscow, in December, I only talked with Yeltsin. This second visit had its own history. At the beginning of November 1991, Sergei Stankievich, Yeltsin's personal representative, arrived in Warsaw to convey the invitation of the Russian president to Moscow for a 'meeting of leading world economists'. I decided to go, as long as I could also negotiate a trade agreement with Russia. This was eventually accepted by the Russian side.

My trip was scheduled for 9–11 December. But at that time the prime minister resigned and I took over the function of running the government. On 7 December, in Białowieża, there had been a meeting of the presidents of Russia, Byelorussia and the Ukraine which laid the groundwork for the dissolution of the Soviet Union. Tremendous changes were taking place in Moscow. We did not know whether to go to Moscow or not, whether the announced meeting of economists would take place or whether we would be discussing the specifics of Polish–Russian trade agreements. We decided to postpone the visit, and eventually departed on 18 December.

At the airport, I was greeted by Konstantin Kagalovski, an adviser to Prime Minister Gaidar. I had met Kagalovski along with another radical economist, Yavlinsky, in the fall of 1990 in Warsaw, when they had come to study the Poland's experience of economic reform.

With Gaidar, we spoke first of all about the initial economic situation in Russia and the planned Russian 'shock therapy' and compared it to the Polish situation. The Russian deputy prime minister remarked that Russia might have some advantages over Poland because there was more discipline and stronger management in Russian enterprises than in Poland. Then he described the main premises of the Russian reform programme. I agreed with Gaidar that galloping inflation and vast shortages cannot be abolished gradually. There has to be an anti-inflationary shock and severe repression of demand by limiting the supply of money from various sources. And of course there has to be price liberalization.

The Russian stabilization plan differed significantly from the Polish one in at least two aspects: it did not include wage controls of any sort, and it introduced a flexible rate of exchange for the rouble (instead of a fixed one). One could say – indeed Gaidar confirmed this himself – that their stabilization programme was much more orthodox than ours was. The monetary restraint was to be the only anti-inflationary barrier. Enterprises granting excessive wage increases would basically face bankruptcy, and their workers, unemployment. In our programme, there were two additional lines of defence – brakes on wages, and the fixed rate of exchange which should have calmed inflationary expectations. By January 1992, it turned out that there was another significant difference in the programmes: the liberalization of prices in Russia was much more limited.

The culmination of my visit to Moscow was the meeting with Boris Yeltsin. The conversation with him was held in the Kremlin in the former office of the secretary of the Communist Party of the Soviet Union and lasted approximately an hour. Yeltsin spoke quite a lot. He said that he had made up his mind to create a community of independent states and that in the new construction there would be no room for Mr Gorbachev. Speaking of the approaching date for price liberalization, he asked me whether I thought that prices would double or treble, as the economists argued, or increase tenfold, as he himself feared. He asked me when one could expect improvement in the form of more commodities on the shelves.

I told him that, based on our experience, it was better to err on the side of pessimism. We had also had some very nervous moments in January 1990 when it became evident that the jump in prices was much larger than we had expected and when it turned out that the decline in production was deeper than expected. There are two stages in the process of departing from a high-inflation shortage economy, I said. The first is 'market revolution'; it requires a rigorous macroeconomic policy and massive liberalization of the economy. The second stage consists of changing enterprises and other institutions – this takes much longer. The key political question is how to maintain support for reform in the second phase when most of the good things (full shelves, stabilization of prices) have been achieved, but there is still a need to continue the painful restructuring operations. Such natural dynamics of economic reform create problems because people take the gains from stabilization and liberalization for granted and resist the pains of the second stage of reform. It is difficult to explain that increasing real purchasing power may be only gradual and, moreover, conditional on restructuring the economy. Serious problems tend to emerge, particularly in large state enterprises, which require massive change but are used to the old ways and retain political power.

At the end of the conversation Yeltsin said (I reconstruct from my notes):

> We are concerned about how society may react to the price liberalization. We are determined to do it in spite of the very meagre reserves of commodities in the market. Though there is credit and humanitarian aid from the West, it is small compared with the great needs of Russia . . . We have been criticized because this critical operation is led by an inexperienced, young team but their youth and dynamism is an asset, in our view. To support those young ministers' reform, I am ready to risk my own position. Gorbachev did not have the chance to implement such bold and unpopular reforms. With his low public support that move would have been political suicide. We will part with Mr Gorbachev in a civilized European way, as you did with Mr Jaruzelski. Each of us has to face a departure from the political scene. We are following the Polish reforms with great interest and are open to your advice and propositions. We are very much interested in cooperation with you. This is for us the most difficult moment since the end of the Second World War. Whichever way our reform goes, whether in victory or defeat, will be relevant for the entire world . . .

I left proposals of cooperation without giving a specific answer. The function of a regular adviser could not really be considered, although I was very interested in the Russian reform and I was willing to maintain contacts.

After meeting Yeltsin, there was a press conference for Mr Gaidar and me. Quite aggressive journalists' questions addressed to Mr Gaidar reminded me of my experience in Poland. For example, what will happen to cultural institutions, which, it was implied, might collapse? I was asked about similarities and differences between Polish and Russian economic programmes.

The Final Days

On 6 December, 1991, during the swearing-in of Jan Olszewski as new prime minister, I was at the Sejm. I congratulated the new prime minister and we agreed to meet at the Council of Ministers later that day. Olszewski asked me to run the cabinet until the new government had been formed. I, for my part, presented him with the major issues and general problems which the new government would be facing. We held several other meetings later on. Subsequent cabinet meetings were devoted to resolving the discussion of the preliminary budget proposal for the first quarter of 1992. The discussion regarding the draft budget began at the end of November but did not end in any agreement. As usual, when discussing budgetary issues, ministers spoke about the 'absolute minimum' for their departments, painting catastrophic pictures of what would happen if they were to receive less than that. I stressed the need to maintain the budget deficit within the specific limit; we returned to the budgetary debate in December. The discussion went according to the usual schedule: that means, it commenced with an appeal to increase expenditure. During the intermission I invited members of the Council of Ministers to my office and I offered them some small increases in allocations which were within the modest reserve framework that we had at our disposal. I knew that this provisional budget had to be accepted and there was no possibility of constructing a better one. I also knew that there was little time for further discussion. My proposals were accepted when we returned to the official room and the budget proposal was quickly approved.

From my first meeting with Prime Minister Olszewski, it was clear on both sides that I would not be participating in a new government, even though that was never mentioned directly during our conversations. Some potential candidates for the position of minister of finance asked me for advice. Thanks to my experience, I had a clear picture of what characterized a good finance minister. It was not enough to know basic macroeconomic truths such as that the deficit must be limited, that money should not be too easy and and that it is impossible to lower interest rates when inflation is too high. What really counts is the ability to organize a good team capable of resisting pressure. Every minister of finance is the subject of incessant pressure for increasing expenditure – and sometimes a dramatic one. Moreover, a finance minister must be alert because at any moment there may be a proposal from any side directly or indirectly leading to higher expenditure. In my opinion, the selection of an inappropriate candidate for the position of finance minister would threaten the stability of the economy. However, in no way did I intend to interfere in the process of forming the new Cabinet. I wanted the new government formed as soon as possible. I could not imagine that the provisional situation would continue for long.

On Monday 23 December, the Sejm approved the new cabinet. That evening, I met with the prime minister and presented him with information regarding the most essential economic issues and decisions which needed to be taken by the new government. The next morning, Christmas Eve, I visited the Council of Ministers' building for the last time. I collected my notes, in which I had registered various strategies and decisions and memoranda from my advisers . . . After more than two years, quite a lot had accumulated. I said good-bye to my colleagues and I wished them a merry Christmas. Later I went to the Ministry of Finance and met with the people with whom I had worked for more than two years, thanked them for their help and asked them to stay at least for a while to keep the continuity of work in this important department. I was ready for that day to come and everything was moving efficiently and followed naturally. What did I feel on leaving the Cabinet? Uncertainty regarding the future of the economy, the fate of my colleagues and in some sense a sort of relief . . . Essentially, I am not a sentimental man.

Index

Page references followed by 'n' indicate the note(s) on that page, those in italics indicate that the reference occurs in a figure or a table.

aggregate consumption 60
agriculture 90, 172, 173, 183, 189, 207, 213, 220, 233–4, 246, 316
  and CAP-type policies 346
  Chinese 'responsibility system' 47
  conflict over reform 357–8
  Poland 275, 290, 294–5
Alfonsin, Raul 344, 357
Andreotti, Giulio 362
asset privatization 192–3, 196

bad debts 224, 229
Baka, Władysław 304
Balcerowicz, Leszek
  curriculum vitae 303–4, 340–1, 342
  economic reform, views on 341–3
  enters office (1989) 293, 341
  in office
    appointments and organizational changes made by 348–50
    conflict with farmers 357–8
    confrontation with trade unions 355–6
    economic programme, preparation of 350–3
    implementation, monitoring of 354
    foreign debt reduction campaign 359–63
    foreign trips (1990) 361–2
    to Moscow 363–7
    reform strategy 343–8
  resignation (1991) 300, 367–9
Balcerowicz group 304, 341
Balcerowicz programme 305

Balcerowicz team (1989–91) 304
Bank for International Settlement, Basle 360
banking 204, 206, 214, 215, 216, 227, 228, 329–30
  defective evaluation of 240–1
  reform 223–5
Banking Law, Poland (1982) 283
bankruptcy 79, 181, 192, 228, 327
  alternatives to 52
  and rational calculation 38
  as part of reform 244–5
  effect of lack of 43
  Poland (1980s) 283
Bieć, Alfred 307n
Bielecki, Jan Krzysztof 299, 306, 321
Big Bang 168, 178–83, 249–51, 252, 256, 258
Bratkowski, Andrzej Stanislaw 304n
Brus, Włodzimierz 46
Brutzkus, Boris 37–8, 40–1, 43–4, 46
Brzeski, Władisław 307n
Buchanan, James 265
Bush, George 365

Candessus, Michel 356
capitalism
  compatibility with democracy 133–5
  competitive 114, 118, 119, 120
  destroyed 203–6
  distorted 130, 134, 203–4
  market 121, 129, 130, 132, 135, 155, 159
  suspended 203–4
Carli, Guido 362

central planning 37–42, 53, 66, 118, 162, 274
Central Planning Board 38
Central School of Planning and Statistics (*now* Warsaw School of Economics) 304
'Chinese Way' 51, 172, 249–51
Ciosek, Stanislaw 367
CMEA (Council for Mutual Economic Assistance) 33, 77, 78, 156, 204, 206, 207, 220, 221, 284, 301, 322, 326
cognitive dissonance, theory of 13
Comecon, effects on transition 172
command-rationing mechanism *see* CRM
command socialism 114, 118, 119, 120, 121
competition 115, *116*, 117, 119, 218–20
competitive capitalism 114, 118, 119, 120
constructivism 195
consumer durables, Poland (1989–93) 333–4, *334*
consumer price index (CPI) 205, 219, 220, 323–4
cooperative socialism 30
corruption 100, 160
Council for Mutual Economic Assistance *see* CMEA
Council of Ministers, Poland 277, 297
    Economic Committee (KERM) 297, 305, 349, 351, 355, 367, 368
CPE (centrally planned economy) *see* central planning
CPI (consumer price index) 205, 219, 220, 326–7
credit, interenterprise 214
CRM (command-rationing mechanism) 52–4, 55, 56, 66, 69, 72, 73, 76, 79, 80
    and economic reform 77, 80
currency convertibility 180, 310, 327, 344, 353
current accounts 213, 214, 218

Dąbrowski, Marek 304n
debts 215–16
democracy
    compatibility with capitalism 133–5
    compatibility with socialism 131–3
    concept of 125–7
    effect on economic growth 135–40
    limited 151
    mass 151
    non-tyranny 126, 127
democratization, post-communist 151–3
deposit rates 215
destroyed capitalism 203–6
devaluation 212, 216, 219, 285, 300, 321

DFI (direct foreign investment) 197
directive central planning *see* CRM
disinflation 212–15, 324
distorted capitalism 130, 134, 203–4
domestic property law, closed 53

Economic Committee, Council of Ministers *see* Council of Ministers, Economic Committee
economic efficiency 114–15, *116*, 119
economic growth, type of political regime and 135–40
economic performance 112–21
    ownership and *116*
economic reform *56*
    'Chinese Way' 51, 172, 249–51
    in Eastern Central Europe
        non-radical 159, 160, 162
        radical 158–9, 162, 164–5
    Poland
        evaluation of 336–7
    types of 55–7
economic structure, inflation and 253–4
economic systems 125, 128–30, *129*, *131*, 173–4, 183
economic transition
    analysis of 166–74
    country specificity *v.* therapy specificity 247–8
    economic outcomes 169
    exogenous determinants 167–9
    inherited conditions 167–8, 169
    policies 169, 171
    social costs, misinterpretation of 261–2
    social discontent during 262–4
    speed of, evaluation of 239–43
    state, role of in 248–9
economy
    definition of 167
    factors affecting 167, 170, 171
education, need for 61, 109
elections 164, 208, 267, 292, 300, 309
electricity 90, 246
employment *see* unemployment
enterprises, ownership types of 92–104, 105
entrepreneurial socialism 31, 46
entrepreneurship regime (*ER*) 90, 104–10, 112, 114–21, *116*, 128–9, 133, 139, 187–8, 189, 190, 194
environmental issues 60, 120
European post-social economies 190–1
exchange rates 212, 216–17, 218, 219, 227, 321
Export Development Bank (Poland) 286
external finance 213–15

Festinger, Leon 309
fiscal deficits 213–15
fiscal policy 226, 228
fiscal sustainability 222–3
Fishkin, J.S. 126, 127
foreign debt 207, 208, 213, 225, 318, 320, 338
   in Eastern Central Europe 157
   reduction campaign in Poland 357–62
foreign trade 170, 177, 180, 204, 284–6, 333
foreign trade regime 116, 117, 120, 121
fundamental institutional restructuring (*I* policy) 155, 157–60, 163, 174, 178, 209–10, 229, 239, 321–2, 323
   Poland (1989–92) 297–8
   speed of reform 242, 264, *265*

G-7 365
Gaidar, Yegor 365, 366, 367
GATT 177
GDP 187, 204, 207, 213, 214, 215, 219, 222, 224, 228, 251, 258, 260, 301, 326, 327, 329, 330, 331, 332, 334, 335, 362
   and military output 173
German reunification 146, 179, 251
Gierek, Edward 291
Glass–Steagall Act 112
Gomułka, Stanislaw 307n
Gorbachev, Mikhail 106, 150, 363, 364, 365, 366, 367
gradualism 178–83, 210, 211, 249–51, 258
Great Depression 327

hard budget constraints 224
Hayek, Friedrich A. 39–40, 41, 42, 44, 195
Hoff, T.J.B. 37, 41, 43
human capital 12–13, 61, 156, 314, 316
human nature, author's definition of 6–12
Hungarian Workers' Party 20–1
hyperinflation 157, 179, 180, 185, 247, 252, 255, 323
   Balcerowicz's views on while in government 343
hysteresis 181

Illyrian socialism 30, 31n, 33, 102
IMF (International Monetary Fund) 175, 295–6, 310, 321, 351, 359, 360, 361, 362, 363
incentives 40, 60, 64, 65, 68n, 71n, 73, 119
inflation 85, 114, *116*, 120, 156, 160, 172, 173, 180, 184, 204, 206, 207, 212, 214, 218, 219, 220, 224, 225, 226, 227, 297, 299, 301, 323–7
   debate on, fallacies in 251–7
infrastructure 198–9, 200

innovations and innovativeness 59–81, 114, 118–19, 132, 171
   barriers to 64–5, 67–70, 71–2, 75–6, 78, 80
   choice of 61–2
   'consumption' efficiency (*CE*) 60, 64, 65, 66, 68, 69, 71, 74
   cost-saving 69–71
   economic reform and 76–80
   instruments for increasing levels of 72–4
   product 71–80
   rate of (*R*) 60–2
institutions, author's definition of 4–5
inter-agent distribution of property rights (*AD*) 106, 108, 109, 112
interest rates 215, 216, 224, 226
intra-capitalism differences and developments 112, 113
intra-enterprise capitalism 30
investment 42–3, 46, 118, 170, 197
I policy *see* fundamental institutional restructuring

Janowski, Jan 297n
Japanese model 113, 175
Jaruzelski, General Wojciech 291, 293, 297, 298, 353, 367
John Paul II 362

Kagalovski, Konstantin 365
Kantecki, Antoni 304n
Kawalec, Stefan 304n, 348
KERM *see* Council of Ministers, Economic Committee
Kiszczak, Czeslaw 293
Kohl, Helmut 361
Koźminski, Jerzy (Jurek) 305, 349, 355
Kuczynski, Waldemar 297n

labour-market institutions 120, 121
Lange, Oskar 38, 39, 42, 44–5
Law on Cooperatives, Poland (1982) 274
Law on Joint Ventures with Foreign Capital 1986 (Poland) 275
Law on Prices, Poland (1982) 280
Law on State Enterprises, Poland (1981) 276
Law on State Enterprises, Poland (1987) 277
Law on Taxes, Poland (1982) 281
leasing model 31, 33
Leibenstein's X-efficiency 114–15, *116*, 119
Levi-Strauss, Claude 7
liberalization 99, 346–7
   effects of 129
   of foreign trade 157, 170, 177, 180
   Poland 47

liberalization policies (*L* policy) *see* microeconomic liberalization
Liberal Party (Poland) 306
Lipowski, Adam 304n
Lipton, David 304n
Liska, Tibor 46
local government 182
London Club 335, 359
L policy *see* microeconomic liberalization
Lutkowski, Karol 304n

M2 215
macroeconomic developments
    in Eastern Central Europe 156, 157, 162–3
    Poland 1990–93 *325*
macroeconomic stability and instability 157, 188, 189, 200
macroeconomic stabilization (*S* policy) 167, 173, 174, 178, 180, 182, 185, 192, 194, 196, 197n, 209, 210, 211, 225, 227, 229, 239, 318, 319, 320, 321, 324
    in Eastern Central Europe 155, 157, 158, 159, 160, 163
    speed of reform 242, 264, *265*
Main Statistical Office, Research Institute of 260
management buy-outs 94
market capitalism 121, 129, 130, 132, 135, 155, 159
market competition 23–5
market economy 28–33
    macroeconomic policies in transition to 202–29
market-oriented reform 145, 146, 152, 157–8, 167, 170, 171, 173, 174, 259
market socialism 46, 47, 114, 118, 120, 132
Marx, Karl 24–5, 134
Marxism 47, 238
mass media 132–3, 134
    influence on reforms 235–6, 267
    reaction to reforms 309
    role of, in transition *149*, 152–3
Mazowiecki, Tadeusz 293, 298, 304, 305, 321, 360
microeconomic liberalization (*L* policy) 178, 180, 182, 192, 194, 196, 197n, 200, 206, 209–10, 211, 212, 213, 218–20, 225, 227, 229, 239, 318, 319, 320, 321, 324
    conditions for reform 243–4
    in Eastern Central Europe 155, 156, 157, 158, 159, 160, 163
    speed of reform 242, 264, *265*
military output 173
mining industry 172, 198–9
Ministry of Finance, Poland 304, 348, 369

Mises, Ludwig von 37–8, *39*, 40–1, 44, 47, 110
Misiąg, Wojciech 304n, 306n
MITI (Ministry of International Trade and Industry, Japan) 175
monetary policy 213–15, 226, 351
monetary systems *116*, 120
monobanks 53, 66, 241, 329
monopolization 53, 55, 57
    extreme 66, 68, 77
    inflation and 254–5
Mulford, David 353, 363
Myrdal, Karl Gunner 182

National Bank of Poland (NBP) 307n, 363
National Bank of Romania 214, 215
neo-classical economics, orthodox 45
New Economic Mechanism (NEM), Hungary 77–80
NICs (newly industrializing countries) 59
nomenklatura mechanism 52, 54, 55, 57, 63, 355
non-banking financial sector, creation of, Poland (1989–93) 330
non-democracy 127–8
    dictators 136–7
    effect of on economic growth 135–40

Ochocki, Andrzej 304n
Olechowski, Andrzej 306n
Olszewski, Jan 300, 305, 306, 321, 322, 368
OPZZ (Polish Confederation of Trade Unions) 295
organizational deconcentration, Poland 329
output restructuring, Poland (1989–93) 332
ownership
    capitalist 38
    economic performance and 111–21
    private (property income) 23–4
    property rights
        distribution of 104–10
        structure of 110–11
    social (labour income) 23–5, 26
    supply and demand sides and 85–6
    systems 86–91
    types of enterprises 92–104
ownership law 86–91
ownership monitoring 97–8, 100, 101n, 113, 120
ownership structure *OS* 104–10, 112, 114–21, *116*, 128, 139, 187, 189, 274–5

Pareto-satisfactory equilibrium 38
Paris Club 300, 335, 359, 360, 362, 363
Parkoła, Andrzej 304n
Pazura, Ryszard 304n

PC (political capital), radical reforms and 264–8, *265*
pensions 223, 331
planning
central 37–42
price-guided schemes 45
pluralism 131–2, 169
Podkrepa (Bulgarian trade union) 163
Podsiadło, Andrzej 304n
Poland 207, 208, 211, 212, 213, 215, 216, 218, 220, 221, 225, 226, 229
Council of Ministers 277, 297
Economic Committee (KERM) 297, 305, 349, 351, 355, 367, 368
economic reform
1981–8 77, 80, 273–87
author's evaluation of 286–7
budgetary and fiscal instruments 281–2
central planning and allocation mechanism 278–80
demand for 273
foreign trade 170, 177, 180, 284–6, 333
money and banking 282–4
ownership structure 274–5
pricing system 280
state enterprises, position of 276–8
state sector organizational structures 275–6
1989–92
characteristics of reformers 310–1
developments (1990–92) 297–301
dynamics of reform 306–8
economic programme, launch of 302–3
economic team 303–5
economic strategy 295–7
external influences on 310
extraordinary *v.* normal politics 311–12
historical background from Second World War 290–3
information policy 308–9
initial conditions (1989) 293–5
political leadership and 305–6
market economy, transition to (1989–93) 179–80
economic outcomes 322–35
changes in 'real' economy 332–5
foreign debt 335
macroeconomic 323–7, *325*
systemic 327–31
economic strategy 317–22
initial conditions 313–17, *315*
martial law (1981) 273, 291
Ministry of Finance 277
Ministry of Foreign Trade 277

policy evaluation
defects in interpretation 234–5, 237–8
effects of generalization 236–7
Polish Academy of Sciences 260
Polish Confederation of Trade Unions (OPZZ) 295
Polish Economic Association 341
Polish parliament (*see also* Sejm; Senate) 292, 296, 298
Polish Statistical Office, Research Centre 327
Polish United Workers Party *see* PUWP
political breakthrough, psychology of 209
political capital (*PC*) 264–8, *265*
political systems
in economic growth and 135–40
types of 125–8, *131*
politico-economic systems 130–1, *131*
politics, two-stage model *161*
pollution 115, 333
Polonia firms 275
PPI (producer price index) 219n
PPP (purchasing power parity) 216, 218, 327
price distortion 53, 55, 204
price fixing 44, 47, 53, 66, 71–2
price liberalization 218–20, 255–6
privatization 85–6, 99, 101, 117, 180–2, 186–200
criticism of pace of, in Poland 244–5
debate on, fallacies and omissions in 245–7
European post-socialist countries (1990–91) 191–9
growth of, in Poland (1989–93) 329
voucher schemes 109, 182, 268
producer price index (PPI) 219n
property law, domestic 32, 33
property rights 85–6, 87–91
distribution rights of 104–10
Roman law 87–8
pseudo-private enterprises 98–9, 105
public choice theory 265
purchasing power parity (PPP) 216, 218, 327
pure socialist output 156–7, 159
PUWP (Polish United Workers Party) 290, 293, 295, 299, 303

R & D 73, 76, 78
radical reforms
political capital (*PC*) and 264–8
social discontent and 262–4
Rakowski, Mieczyslaw 243n, 292
ratchet mechanism 69, 85
reflation 256–7
reformed socialism 77–81

reform policies, implementation rate 210
reforms, speed of 158–60
reform thresholds 55–7, *56*
rent-seeking 57, 108, 109, 160, 163, 177
restructuring, stabilization and 215–16
Roberts, John 40
Roman law, property rights 87–8
Rostowski, Jacek 304n
Round Table 292, 316, 358
Russia
  500 Days Plan 319

Sachs, Jeffrey 304n
Sawicki, Janusz 304n, 363
SCD (socialist calculation debate) 35–48
Schumpeter, Joseph Alois 42, 45, 133
Sejm (Lower House, Polish parliament) 292,
  296, 297, 351, 352, 353, 355, 358, 359,
  367, 368
Senate (Upper House, Polish parliament)
  292, 296, 297, 351, 352, 353
shock therapy (Big Bang) 168, 178–83, 233,
  249–51, 252, 256, 258
shortages 43–4, 118, 180, 191, 204, 206, 207,
  227
  chronic 66, 67n, 69, 70, 74, 76, 77
  elimination of 157, 212–15, 324
Silajev, Ivan 364–5
simulated capitalism 47, 48
simulated market (*see also* planning,
  central), price-guided schemes 45
Sobchak, Anatoly 367
social discontent, during economic reform
  262–8
socialism 31
  command 114, 118, 119, 120, 121
  compatibility with democracy 131–3
  cooperative 30
  definition of 19–26
  leasing model 46–7
  market 46, 47, 114, 120, 132
socialist calculation debate *see* SCD
socialist market economy 28–33
SOEs (state owned enterprises) (*see also*
  ownership) 99–102, 108, 190, 193n,
  197n, 326
soft budget constraints 53, 55, 66, 67, 79, 85,
  100, 115
Solidarity (Polish trade union) 106, 163,
  274n, 291–5, 303, 305
  Balcerowicz group and 341
  congress (April 1990) 298
  General Assembly, Gdańsk (1990)
    355–6
  influence on reforms 347
  Round Table negotiations 292, 316, 358

Solidarnosc *see* Solidarity
Soviet-type economic system *see* STES
Spanish Socialist Party 22
S policy *see* macroeconomic stabilization
stabilization
  banking reform 223–5
  country specific factors and 206–9
  disinflation 212–13
  exchange rate outcomes 216–17
  external financing 213–15
  fallacies in debate on 251–7
  fiscal deficits 213–15
  fiscal sustainability 222–3
  liberalization policies 218–20
  monetary policy 213–15
  outcomes 211–18
  Poland (1989–92) 295–6, 310
  restructuring and 215–16
  shortages, elimination of 212–13
  supply response 221
stabilization fund, Poland 296, 310, 344,
  353
stabilization policies (*S*) *see* macroeconomic
  stabilization
Stankievich, Sergei 365
state-owned enterprises *see* SOEs
state spending 85
statistics, misinterpretation of 257–9, 260
STES (Soviet-type economic system) 25, 44,
  51–81
  centralized state ownership 101
  characteristics of 66–7
  constructional logic 52–4, 66
  innovativeness in 59–66, 67–76
    reformed economic systems and
      76–81
  reform thresholds 55–8, *56*
stock exchange, opening of (1991) 330
strikes 171, 172
Suchocka, Hanna 300, 306, 322
suspended capitalism 203–4
systemic transformation *ST* (*see also*
  fundamental institutional restructuring
  policies; liberalization policies) 155,
  156, 167, 239

taxes 212, 213, 215, 219, 222, 281
tax evasion 158, 242–3
tax reform 182
tax system *116*, 120, 121, 330
telecommunications, Poland (1989–93)
  332
trade unions (*see also* PUWP; Solidarity) 100,
  116, 125, 134, 163, 191, 207, 208, 225,
  274n
  Podkrepa 163

transformational privatization 193, 194, 195–6, 197, 200
transition (*see also* Big Bang; 'Chinese Way'; gradualism; shock therapy)
  comparison with democratic transition 151–3
  economic, analysis of 166–74
    common fallacies in 232–68
  generally *147–9*
  in Eastern Central Europe 153–65, *154*
  initial conditions, importance of 163–5
  period of 'extraordinary' politics 160–3, 165
  period of 'normal' politics 161–2
  post-communist
    special features of 155–7
    specificity of 145–51
  role of state in 174–8, 248–9
Tyminski, Stanislaw 298

unemployment 32, 33, 60, 103, 114, 120, 132, 159, 160, 163, 170, 171, 181, 205, 206, 223, 247, 301, 334–5
United Peasant Party 303

violence, role in transition *149*, 150

visibility effect 153, 161, 164
voucher systems 86, 109, 182

wages 120, 172, 211–12, 226, 251, 323n, 347, 356–7
Waigel, Theo 361
Wałęsa, Lech 292, 298, 305, 356–7, 362, 363
Walrasian economic theory, application of 38, 39n, 42n
Warsaw Computer Expo fairs 332n
Warsaw School of Economics (formerly Central School of Planning and Statistics) 304–5
Warsaw School of Planning and Statistics, Faculty of Foreign Trade 340, 341
Welisz, Stanislaw 304n
Williamson, John 310
Wójtowicz, Grzegorz 304
World Bank 175

X-efficiency, Leibenstein's 114–15, *116*, 119

Yavlinsky, Grigory A. 365
Yeltsin, Boris 365, 366, 367